The Springer Series on Demographic Methods and Population Analysis

Volume 56

Series Editor

Scott M. Lynch, Department of Sociology, Duke University, Durham, NC, USA

This series is now indexed in Scopus.

In recent decades, there has been a rapid development of demographic models and methods and an explosive growth in the range of applications of population analysis. This series seeks to provide a publication outlet both for high-quality textual and expository books on modern techniques of demographic analysis and for works that present exemplary applications of such techniques to various aspects of population analysis.

Topics appropriate for the series include:

General demographic methods, Techniques of standardization, Life table models and methods, Multistate and multiregional life tables, analyses, and projections, Demographic aspects of biostatistics and epidemiology, Stable population theory and its extensions, Methods of indirect estimation, Stochastic population models, Event history analysis, duration analysis, and hazard regression models, Demographic projection methods and population forecasts, Techniques of applied demographic analysis, regional and local population estimates and projections, Methods of estimation and projection for business and health care applications, Methods and estimates for unique populations such as schools and students.

Volumes in the series are of interest to researchers, professionals, and students in demography, sociology, economics, statistics, geography and regional science, public health and health care management, epidemiology, biostatistics, actuarial science, business, and related fields.

Robert Schoen
Editor

The Demography of Transforming Families

Springer

Editor
Robert Schoen
Pennsylvania State University
San Francisco, CA, USA

ISSN 1877-2560 ISSN 2215-1990 (electronic)
The Springer Series on Demographic Methods and Population Analysis
ISBN 978-3-031-29665-9 ISBN 978-3-031-29666-6 (eBook)
https://doi.org/10.1007/978-3-031-29666-6

This Springer imprint is published by the registered company Springer Nature Switzerland AG
The registered company address is: Gewerbestrasse 11, 6330 Cham, Switzerland

Preface

Across the world, family patterns are transforming at an unprecedented pace. In less than two generations, the traditional nuclear family of husband, wife, and children has given way to a multiplicity of other forms, as widespread cohabitation, high levels of divorce, increasing childlessness, far below replacement fertility, and frequent multipartner fertility have emerged to an extent never before seen. This volume surveys these transformations, presenting theoretical perspectives, methodological innovations, and case studies of societies in the process of re-inventing the nature of family. The primary audience is social demographers, but the volume will be of interest to many sociologists, economists, social statisticians, and others interested in the family.

As editor, let me express my appreciation to Springer and its staff, especially Evelien Bakker, for the support of substantive and methodological work in demography. I am particularly indebted to the authors whose scholarship and dedication made this volume possible.

San Francisco, CA, USA — Robert Schoen
February 2023

Contents

Part I
Theories of Family Dynamics

Chapter 1
Introduction and Theoretical Overview

Robert Schoen

The family transformations associated with the Second Demographic Transition can be seen as the consequence of three macro factors–economic, ideological, and demographic–acting through two intermediate factors–the rise of gender competition and the fall in the social capital value of marriage and children. This theoretical perspective provides the background for a dozen focused analyses that explore theoretical issues, develop methodological innovations, and provide detailed examinations of actual populations in transformation.

1.1 A Theoretical Overview

The family in the West is in an unprecedented state. Marriage is in retreat, cohabitation prevalent, family unions unstable, and fertility well below replacement level. While there is no simple explanation for how the present situation arose, a number of theories have been proposed.

1.1.1 The Proposed Explanations

The traditional economic view, such as that espoused by Becker (1981), focuses on Role Specialization. The argument is that the benefits of unions are maximized when men specialize in economic activities and women in domestic activities. Beyond ignoring the rise in cohabitation, the Role Specialization view focuses on the male/

R. Schoen (✉)
Pennsylvania State University, San Francisco, CA, USA

R. Schoen (ed.), *The Demography of Transforming Families*, The Springer Series on Demographic Methods and Population Analysis 56,
https://doi.org/10.1007/978-3-031-29666-6_1

female wage ratio, and ignores the benefits that can accrue when one examines the sum of male and female wages (Moffitt, 2000). Family transformations have largely relegated Role Specialization to a past era.

Explanations associated with the Second Demographic Transition (SDT) concept emphasize ideational changes that stress individual autonomy and material aspirations (Lesthaeghe, 1995, 2010; Van de Kaa, 1987). Although a useful overarching rubric, the SDT is only loosely descriptive, does not explain why those ideational changes arose, and offers little guidance as to future change (Carlson, 2019; Zaidi & Morgan, 2017).

Several observers have focused on the role of gender relationships. Perhaps the most fully developed is the "gender revolution" (GR) framework in Goldscheider et al. (2015). The GR approach argues that women's paid employment initially produced stresses in family life that led to the rise in cohabitation, lower fertility, and the other features of the SDT. However, the GR predicts that the changes in women's roles will lead to changes in men's roles, increasing their involvement in home and family, and eventually reversing the retreat from marriage. While the GR view accounts for past family changes, it simply assumes that couples want more children and that men's behavior will change. There is little evidence to support either assumption.

Another line of explanation emphasizes structural changes in the economy and uncertainties in the labor market (Seltzer, 2019; Mills & Blossfeld, 2013; Vignoli et al., 2012). There certainly have been great changes and uncertainties, but in the past there have also been great economic changes and times of serious labor market uncertainty that have not produced family transformations. The uncertainty perspective provides little ability to quantify effects or to foresee future developments.

A demographic explanation has also been offered, which argues that a shortage of men relative to women–a marriage squeeze–is a major factor (Lichter et al., 1991; South & Lloyd, 1992). Empirically, however, there is no basis for believing that a marriage squeeze is responsible. Analyses by Schoen (1983) and Schoen and Kluegel (1988) found that sex ratios had little or no impact on marriage. Wilson (1987) argued that a shortage of "marriageable men" was a factor, especially for African Americans, but perceived suitability is quite different from availability.

The explanation given particular emphasis here is that of Gender Competition (Schoen, 2010; Schoen & Hargens, 2020). In this view, described in more detail below, women's increased economic independence destabilized the traditional relationship between the sexes, weakened the ties between men and their children, and led to the SDT.

1.1.2 A New Explanatory Framework

The thesis here is depicted in Fig. 1.1. It sees three macro factors as primarily responsible for undermining the traditional family: Economic Change, Ideological Change, and Demographic Change. They are linked to the micro changes of the SDT

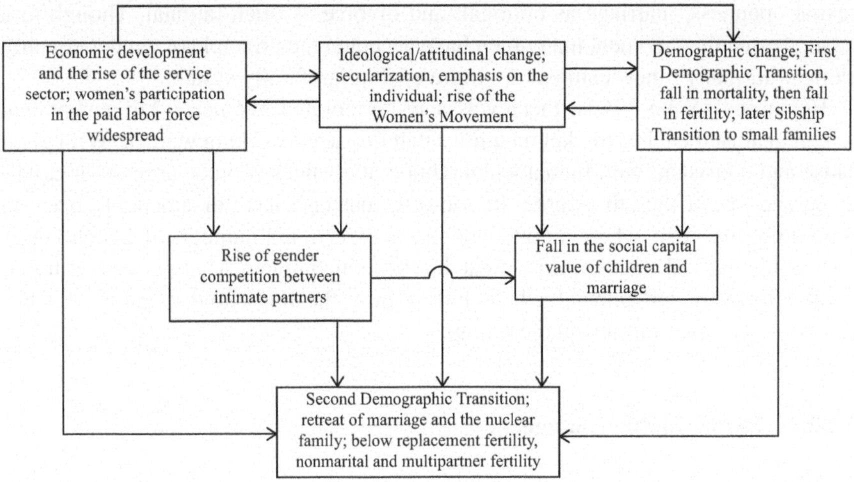

Fig. 1.1 Economic, ideological, and demographic factors in family transformation

by two key intermediate variables: the rise of gender competition and the fall in the social capital value of marriage and children. Let us look at each of those factors in turn.

1.1.2.1 Economic Change

Over the twentieth century, there was a dramatic rise in economic output and the growth of a large tertiary, or service sector. Many of the newly created jobs were open to women, who increasingly entered the labor force, and whose participation now approaches that of men (Reeves, 2022). Around 1960, full-time employed women earned about 59¢ for every dollar earned by comparable men. In 2020, the figure was 82¢. Even more telling is that, by 2019, the wage distributions of men and women had become very similar, so much so that 40% of women earned more than the average man (Reeves, 2022, p24–25). At least potentially, those earnings gave substantial economic independence to women. Such widespread gainful participation of women in the paid labor force is without precedent, and greatly undermined the traditional man-breadwinner/woman-homemaker division of family labor. The result was nothing less than a seismic shift in gender relations and family roles, whose tremors are still being felt.

1.1.2.2 Ideological/Attitudinal Change

There has been a sea change in views toward and attitudes regarding marriage, the family, and gender roles (Thornton & Young-DeMarco, 2001; Allendorf et al., 2022). Compared to 50 years ago, there is much greater belief in gender equality, sexual openness, marriage as optional, and divorce as often rational. Though to a lesser degree than women, many men have accepted the principle of gender equality along with many other features of a more egalitarian family system.

Beginning in the 1960s, there was a re-invigorated Women's Movement that fought against the labor market inequities that impacted working women. With good cause and consistent with fundamental democratic values, women argued for equality in and out of the labor force. In contrast, marriage has fundamentally been an economic enterprise, where numbers of shares owned, not numbers of shareholders, counts. Ideological change, while great, has been incomplete. Major issues central to family life were left unresolved, including how the household division of labor should reflect joint but unequal earnings.

1.1.2.3 Demographic Change

The twentieth century saw the First Demographic Transition, the shift from high to low rates of birth and death, spread to nearly every corner of the world. Advances in living standards and medicine led to great declines in mortality and increases in longevity. The number of infant deaths per 1000 births went from around 150 in 1900 to about 6 today. In 1900, life expectancy at birth in the healthiest nations was about 40–45 years. In 2020, many nations had life expectancies over 80 years.

Lower mortality and greater economic opportunities led to declines in fertility. At the micro level, lower infant mortality went well beyond allowing more children to survive. The resulting social dynamic was articulated by Kingsley Davis (1963) in his Theory of Change and Response. Couples felt pressure to have fewer children to prevent a loss of status relative to those with fewer children who could afford a higher standard of living. That pressure produced a multiphasic response that drove down fertility. In the United States in 1900, the Total Fertility Rate (TFR), the average number of children a woman would have under the prevailing birth rates, was over 3. In 2000, it was about 2. As the SDT continued, the 2020 TFR was only 1.6, a record low. The 1960s saw the near disappearance of large families in the United States, a Sibship Transition that substantially reduced the number of close kin (Schoen, 2019). To the extent that children and kin ties motivate marriage, that motivation was substantially reduced.

1.1.2.4 The Rise of Gender Competition

With the decline of the breadwinner / homemaker division of labor, couples had greater autonomy but less normative guidance. The existence of financially independent women is an unprecedented development that strikes at the heart of the very gendered traditional nuclear family. Women's enhanced economic capacity was reinforced by a major social movement and by attitudinal changes among both men and women, though more among women.

The discordance in male/female attitudes in the presence of changed economic circumstances led to a rise in gender competition, where union partners competed for power in their relationship (Schoen, 2010; Carlson, 2019). At the individual level, that gender competition provides a powerful mechanism for family change, with women struggling for more equality and men seeking to exploit their (often) still greater economic resources. As men sought to avoid the legal responsibilities of marriage, cohabitation, which lacks those constraints and gives more power to the economically stronger partner, became common. First marriage came later, with fewer ever marrying. Within unions, conflicts over leadership, competition over resources, and disputes about the division of labor fostered instability. Most cohabitations dissolve, while divorce remains high. As traditional patterns of child custody favoring mothers persist despite high levels of union dissolution, fathers are less motivated to have or to invest in children, shifting more childrearing burdens onto mothers. The male retreat from the family puts a greater childrearing burden on women, reinforcing traditional gender roles. With the lower social capital value of children, as discussed in the next section, fertility fell to historic lows and the kinship web contracted. There has been no large scale Men's Movement, but the strong pushback from men transformed family life.

1.1.2.5 The Fall in the Social Capital Value of Children and Marriage

In modern industrial societies, children are very expensive, both in terms of money (Espenshade, 1974) and parental time, though they have little economic value. The social capital that children bring, that is the social resources and social ties created by children, appear to be the major motivation for fertility (Schoen et al., 1997; Astone et al., 1999). Children represent major investments in social capital, as they create and expand the kinship network. But now kin ties are no longer the source of education or training, and have far less ability to advance careers in the labor force. Pension systems, not children, are seen as assuring support in old age. The social demands on parents are high, as children bring many responsibilities but few benefits. Children are especially burdensome to 2-career families, but in almost all families, they reinforce a traditional gender division of labor. To Reeves (2022, pages 26-28), children are the one-word explanation for the remaining male/female wage gap. As children are less valuable and more costly, including in terms of the mother's time, fertility declines and childlessness becomes more common (Schoen & Hargens, 2020).

A number of factors has brought about an accompanying fall in the social capital gained from marriage. Marriage is no longer needed in order to have "legitimate" children; indeed, that that term has virtually been discarded. Marriages are fragile, as close to half end in divorce. A spouse's kin provide less social capital. Cohabitations often produce children. With the rise of gender competition, men are less willing to support a wife's children, while women are increasingly concerned that husbands will not earn or share their earnings (Edin & Kefalas, 2005). Marriage as an institution imposes legal obligations that men, and increasingly women, want to avoid–especially the obligation to support a spouse during and after marriage.

1.1.2.6 The Second Demographic Transition

In the light of economic, ideological, and demographic change, the rise in gender competition and the fall in the social capital value of children and marriage have had dramatic consequences for the family. As summarized by the SDT, there has been a multiphasic shift in fertility, union formation, and union dissolution. Gender competition and the diminished social capital value of children have torn at the foundations of the traditional nuclear family, as there is less to be gained from marriage and relationships are harder to maintain. Marriage retreats, fertility falls below replacement, and emphasis is on the autonomous individual. Fatherhood is devalued and men retreat from supporting their children. Cohabitation becomes a customary prelude to, or substitute for, marriage. Unions, especially cohabitations, are fragile; childlessness grows. Children are increasingly born outside of marriage, and men and women frequently have children by multiple partners. The kinship web becomes smaller and more tenuous, with fewer close kin and more half siblings. In short, the SDT describes where we are now.

1.1.2.7 A Recapitulation and Some Thoughts About the Future

The system depicted in Fig. 1.1 sees the larger socio-economic context as having fundamentally shifted. The macro economy has emphasized the service sector, encouraging and enabling women to enter paid employment. Women's increased economic resources led to major attitudinal and behavioral changes, as families shrunk because of lower mortality, lower fertility, and the Sibship Transition. At the micro level, gender competition and the reduced social capital value of children have caused major changes in the behavior of couples, leading to the Second Demographic Transition and the retreat of marriage and the traditional nuclear family.

The future is uncertain, though unstable families and continued low fertility seem likely. As the incomes of men and women become more equal, couple relationships will likely stay fragile but become more egalitarian, with much housework and childcare outsourced.

Future trends in unions and fertility should be separated. Marriage, and more stable cohabitations, may not only stop retreating but rebound, as couples find more ways to successfully negotiate and compromise. Stable unions have real and substantial advantages to those in them. Still, marriage may come later in life, with many men and women never marrying.

Fertility is another matter. Childrearing remains a major problem for which society still offers couples no clear answer. Children now drive the male / female wage gap, and child care may continue to be a problem for each couple to solve. For many couples, that solution will be to have only one child or to be childless, resulting in overall fertility remaining well below replacement. Selected kin will still be important, though the social capital they bring will be modest. Western societies have yet to fully come to grips with the manifold implications of the fundamental change in the relationship between men and women that powered the SDT.

1.2 The Contributions of Future Chapters

Let me briefly introduce the 12 following chapters, each of which brings its own insights. Continuing with theoretical concerns, in Chap. 2 Frances Goldscheider considers gender dynamics in the light of the 2 × 2 array of Men/Women by Paid/Unpaid work. Recent events have rightly emphasized the third cell, women's paid work. To Goldscheider, the fourth cell, men's unpaid work, remains understudied and is of potentially great importance to the future of the family.

In Chap. 3, Andrew Cherlin reviews the development of family demography and its embrace of diversity as a preface to a focus on two current challenges. The first is the call to expand the scope of family to include unrelated individuals such as close friends, a call Cherlin endorses. The second is the challenge to "de-center" the concept of family because of its emphasis on the couple and childbearing. To Cherlin, that goes too far, and he discusses the reasons why.

In Chap. 4, Eva Beaujouan considers whether delayed fertility is a driver of fertility decline. Taking a cohort and life course perspective, Beaujouan carefully evaluates the evidence, including the issue of biological constraints on fertility in later life.

Chapter 5 begins the section on methodological analyses. In it, Robert Schoen and Lowell Hargens take on the classic Age, Period, and Cohort problem. To avoid the collinearity that exists between those elements, we consider cohort effects to be age-period interactions, and decompose arrays of age-year-specific fertility rates into age, period and age-period interaction components. Applying that "RBC" method to United States data for 1917 through 2020, we find no clear evidence for cohort effects.

In Chap. 6, Martina Lo Conte, Gianni Corsetti, Alessandra De Rose, Marco Marsili, and Eleonora Meli examine the results of projections of the Italian family from 2021 to 2041. Using a static projection method based on propensity rates, they find that the number of Italian households will likely increase substantially, while mean household size drops from 2.3 to 2.1 and the number of childless couples increases.

In Chap. 7, Robert Schoen presents a multistate life table analysis of marriage, divorce, and fertility for United States women during the years 2005–10 and 2015–20. My results show a fall in the percent ever marrying from 80% to 70%, an increase in childlessness to almost 20%, and some 40% of births to unmarried women. The retreat of marriage was not a rout, however, as the great majority of women still marry, and divorce rates appear to have stabilized.

In Chap. 8, Rhiannon Kroeger, Courtney E. Williams, Elizabeth Wildsmith, and Reanne Frank closely examine issues related to the measurement of Hispanic fertility. By carefully combining vital statistics data on births and Census population data, they estimate age-specific fertility rates for the 2006–2016 interval. Overall, Hispanic TFRs have declined substantially, but there are significant nativity, region-of-origin, and marital status differences.

Beginning the case studies section, in Chap. 9 Joeun Kim examines the nature of the "gender war" and rise in anti-family sentiments in South Korea. Taking a Gender Competition perspective, Kim shows how the rise in Korean women's participation in the paid labor force led to male hostility and then a female backlash, especially following a notorious misogynistic murder. As a result, negative attitudes toward marriage have risen sharply for both Korean men and women.

In Chap. 10, Carla Rowold and Zachary Van Winkle examine the rise in family life course complexity among twentieth century birth cohorts in the United Kingdom. Their analyses show that not only has complexity and instability increased for both men and women and for parents and nonparents, it has dramatically risen for their children.

In Chap. 11, Elizabeth Thomson and Jennifer A Holland examine union experience and the stability of parental unions in Sweden and Norway. Using a decomposition approach, they find that the increasing differentiation of parents' union histories substantially contributed to observed increases in the likelihood of parental union separation.

Chapter 12 begins the section on deviance and the family. In it, Brittany Ganser and Karen Benjamin Guzzo examine the effects on fertility of criminal offending trajectories during the transition to adulthood. Using AddHealth data, they find, perhaps counter-intuitively, that for both men and women offending is linked to fewer children.

In Chap. 13, Marissa Landeis, Karen Benjamin Guzzo, Wendy D Manning, Monica A Longmore, and Peggy C Giordano analyze the influence of intimate partner violence (IPV) on unintended parenthood. Using the Toledo Adolescent Relationships Study, they found that women and men involved in IPV were not more likely to become parents by age 25. Instead of a causal relationship, they concluded that prior IPV experience and unintended parenthood were distinct events, both of which were associated with young adulthood.

As always, the transformed family will continue to evolve. In the words of Stoetzel (1946, page 88) "demographic behavior, like all human phenomena ... [represent] the result of the general dual processes of competition and cooperation that characterize the struggle for life."

Marriage is in retreat, but not on all fronts. Men and women live more independent, autonomous lives, and increasingly establish themselves economically before marriage. Children remain more closely tied to their mothers, while couples are largely left on their own to reconcile gender equality with the differential demands of childrearing. Each chapter here offers its distinct contribution to understanding why we are where we are, and where we might go in the future.

References

Allendorf, K., Young-DeMarco, L., & Thornton, A.. (2022). *Developmental idealism and a half century of family attitude trends in the United States*. Paper presented at the April Meetings of the Population Association of America in Atlanta.

Astone, N. M., Nathanson, C. A., Schoen, R., & Kim, Y. J. (1999). Family demography, social theory, and investment in social capital. *Population and Development Review, 25*, 1–31.

Becker, G. S. (1981). *A treatise on the family*. University of Chicago Press.

Carlson, E. (2019). Reformulating second demographic transition theory. In R. Schoen (Ed.), *Analytical family demography* (pp. 7–26). Springer.

Davis, K. (1963). The theory of change and response in modern demographic history. *Population Index, 29*, 344–366.

Edin, K., & Kefalas, M. (2005). *Promises I can keep*. University of California Press.

Espenshade, T. J. (1974). Estimating the cost of children and some results from urban United States. *Social Indicators Research, 3*, 359–381.

Goldscheider, F. K., Bernhardt, E., & Lappegard, T. (2015). The gender revolution: A framework for understanding changing family and demographic behavior. *Population and Development Review, 41*, 207–239.

Lesthaeghe, R. (1995). The second demographic transition in Western countries: An interpretation. In K. O. Mason & A.-M. Jensen (Eds.), *Gender and family change in industrialized countries* (pp. 17–62). Clarendon Press.

Lesthaeghe, R. (2010). The unfolding story of the second demographic transition. *Population and Development Review, 36*, 211–251.

Lichter, D. T., LeClere, F. B., & McLaughlin, D. K. (1991). Local marriage markets and the marital behavior of black and white women. *American Journal of Sociology, 96*, 843–867.

Mills, M., & Blossfeld, H.-P. (2013). The second demographic transition meets globalization: A comprehensive theory to understand changes in family formation in an era of rising uncertainty. In A. Evans & J. Baxter (Eds.), *Negotiating the life course: Stability and change in life pathways* (pp. 9–33). Springer.

Moffitt, R. A. (2000). Female wages, male wages, and the economic model of marriage: The basic evidence. In L. J. Waite (Ed.), *The ties that bind* (pp. 302–319). Aldine de Gruyter.

Reeves, R. V. (2022). *Of boys and men*. Brookings Institution Press.

Schoen, R. (1983). Measuring the tightness of a marriage squeeze. *Demography, 20*, 61–78.

Schoen, R. (2010). Gender competition and family change. *Genus, 66*, 95–120.

Schoen, R. (2019). Parity progression and the kinship network. In R. Schoen (Ed.), *Analytical family demography* (pp. 189–199). Springer.

Schoen, R., & Hargens, L. (2020). Social capital, gender competition, and the resurgence of childlessness. In R. Schoen (Ed.), *Analyzing contemporary fertility* (pp. 9–24). Springer.

Schoen, R., & Kluegel, J. R. (1988). The widening gap in black and white marriage rates: The impact of population composition and differential marriage propensities. *American Sociological Review, 53*, 895–907.

Schoen, R., Kim, Y. J., Nathanson, C. A., Fields, J., & Astone, N. M. (1997). Why do Americans want children? *Population and Development Review, 23*, 333–358.

Seltzer, N. (2019). Beyond the great recession: Labor market polarization and ongoing fertility decline in the United States. *Demography, 56*, 1463–1493.

South, S. J., & Lloyd, K. M. (1992). Marriage markets and nonmarital fertility in the United States. *Demography, 29*, 247–264.

Stoetzel, J. (1946). Sociologie et démographie. *Population, 1*, 79–89.

Thornton, A., & Young-DeMarco, L. (2001). Four decades of trends in attitudes toward family issues in the United States: The 1960s through the 1990s. *Journal of Marriage and Family, 63*, 1009–1037.

Van de Kaa, D. (1987). *Europe's second demographic transition*. Population bulletin 42. Population Reference Bureau.
Vignoli, D., Drefahl, S., & DeSantis, G. (2012). Whose job instability affects the likelihood of becoming a parent in Italy? A tale of two partners. *Demographic Research, 26*, 41–62.
Wilson, W. J. (1987). *The truly disadvantaged*. University of Chicago Press.
Zaidi, B., & Morgan, S. P. (2017). The second demographic transition theory: A review and appraisal. *Annual Review of Sociology, 43*, 473–492.

Chapter 2
The Future of Family Demography: Filling in the Fourth Cell

Frances Goldscheider

2.1 Introduction

Gender has always been central to the study of family demography, although it often wasn't noticed. This is because demography came of age in a gender-segregated world. Most men spent their productive hours in the world of paid employment; most women spent their productive hours in the world of the family. Most demographers who studied employment only studied men; those who studied the family studied women.

Hence, the study of family demography was largely the study of women's lives until well into the 1960s, with a focus on fertility, although levels and timing of marriage and parenthood, and even divorce, were also studied. Most articles on these subjects did not even mention in their titles that their studies were of women.

In this paper, I briefly review the history of family demography in gendered terms, as it has been studied and as I have lived it. I will make suggestions about where it will be going and should go. What I conclude is that what is needed is to more fully understand the fourth cell—the work-family demography of men.

F. Goldscheider (✉)
Brown University, Providence, RI, USA

University of Maryland, College Park, MD, USA
e-mail: frances_goldscheider@brown.edu

R. Schoen (ed.), *The Demography of Transforming Families*, The Springer Series on Demographic Methods and Population Analysis 56,
https://doi.org/10.1007/978-3-031-29666-6_2

2.2 History of Family Demography: The Gender-Segregated World and Its Early Breakdown

I like to illustrate how the genders relate to family tasks vs. paid employment with a simple two-by-two table—paid work and home (unpaid) work as column headings, with men and women as the rows (Fig. 2.1). Almost all the activity in the 1950s was on the diagonal; the other cells were not conceptualized. This pattern was far from eternal, however; it formed with the early industrial revolution, when men started moving away from the insecurities of the agricultural family economy (which could be conceptualized as a single cell, with men, women (and children) sharing agricultural subsistence activities) to earn wages that could better support their families, creating the notion of the separate spheres—the 2 diagonal cells (Stanfors & Goldscheider, 2017).

This diagonal structure began to break down with the growth in female labor force participation. The diagonal structure, however, had lasted long enough to seem eternal, so married women's entry into paid employment, which followed men's by about a century, seemed revolutionary. This led to a new view of the two-by-two table, by beginning to fill in the third cell—women, work and family.

If I spent my childhood and adolescence in the diagonal world, the first three to four decades of my professional life were spent in a world, characterized both in research and family life, of *three* cells, as female labor force participation, especially among married women, exploded. When it first emerged, some even called these three cells "the three sexes"! The fourth cell was invisible. The anthropologist, Margaret Mead, used that phrase, separating women into two groups—domestic women and employed women—and, of course, men. She felt strongly that men should be totally focused on developing their careers, not on caring for children, which, in those days of early marriage and parenthood, often overlapped in graduate and professional schools. (Mead, 1965).

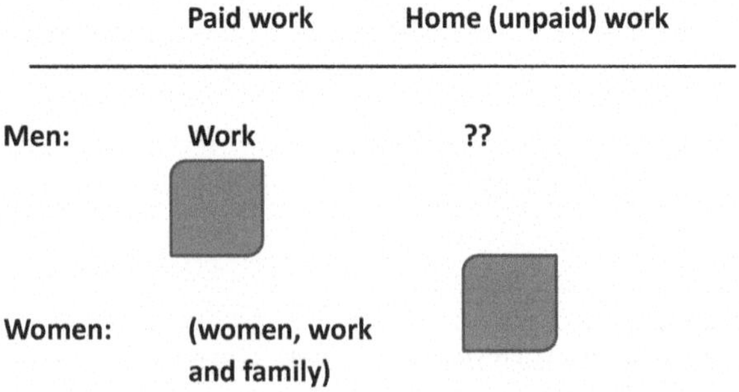

Fig. 2.1 A simple way to think about the genders, work and family

The amount of research on the determinants and consequences of women's increased labor force participation was astronomical. Vis-à-vis determinants, given the tendency to blame women for any and all problems, the early scholars of the growth in female labor force participation were unanimous that it was in response to the growth in demand for what were called female-typed jobs, as if men could not do them (e.g., Goldin, 1990; Oppenheimer, 1970). Research on the consequences of women's employment was much more complex. There was an early emphasis on its deleterious effects on children, although when the psychologists could find little signs of damage, that line of research petered out (Nye & Hoffman, 1963). For demographers, however, concern focused on the effects of women's employment on delayed union formation, lower fertility and the damage to couple relationships, for which there was considerable evidence in the 1970s and 1980s (e.g., Espenshade, 1985).

Data limitations contributed to the invisibility of the 4th cell, though few wanted to think about it anyway. The pre-IPUMS census monograph on gender (Bianchi & Spain, 1986) illustrates that those who wanted to think about gender had plenty of data to compare the work and educational characteristics of men and women. Most of the analytic chapters on family behaviors, however, compared black and white women, given how little evidence there was in the census on men's family lives, and how little interest there was in exploring such evidence as was available.

2.3 The Problem of Data

The growth in family demography took place within a context of the growth in the profession and in demographic research, beginning primarily in the 1950s. Money became available to move beyond the census data that dominated research for so long, allowing the collection of sample surveys on specialized topics. On the family side, there were fertility studies, stimulated by the semi-explosion in fertility during the baby boom in the US and the concern over the population explosion in the less developed world, as we called it then. The first survey was called the Indianapolis Study (Kiser, 1953–54). The subjects of this study were, of course, women (men's characteristics did not matter, except for their incomes). Men got their own surveys, focusing on their career characteristics.

Data collection remained sex segregated for several more decades, until the Institute for Population Research at Ohio State began a panel study that included both young men and women in 1979. (This built on their 1960s surveys of Young Men and Young Women, which had collected far more detailed information on family attitudes and behaviors for young women and far more detailed information on career attitudes and behaviors for young men (Parnes, 1975). This 1979 panel study inaugurated a new era of egalitarian data collection in family demography, which reached a pinnacle with the National Study of Families and Households (NSFH) of 1988 (Goldscheider & Waite, 1991).

I see the future of family demography as filling in the fourth cell: the work-family demography of men. In the remainder of this paper, I would like to outline a major topic within the fourth cell and then develop the many barriers to making progress on filling in the fourth cell. My main topic is the study of the male life course, together with its major subcomponents.

2.4 The Male Life Course

I got into studying the male life course because I had the opportunity to teach two courses on the subject, a senior seminar at Brown University and a graduate seminar at the University of Maryland. My memory is that I was trying to bring more male students into a family demography course (which was successful), but the real joy was getting a broader view of the subject; both courses were a lot of fun. Of course, the framework of each seminar was my existing seminar in family demography, plus a syllabus on the same subject by Suzanne Bianchi. By making men the focus, I realized how much I needed (and was able) to make more consistent gender comparisons than in my long-running family demography seminar which, reflecting the literature and my own experience, was so disproportionately focused on women.

One of the things I like to do in such seminars is to ask students to identify an age when they expected to make various work and family life course transitions. The first thing that was clear was that women had thought more about these questions than men, which is probably not very surprising, given the greater centrality of family in women's lives. And of course, both males and females were more precise re the early life course transitions, such as finishing school and beginning a career, than they were about the family transitions of forming unions and becoming parents (most felt they had already left home).

The second thing that was clear was that men's responses were often not very clear or consistent. Male students used more question marks and provided wider ranges in their answers. Most expected to marry, but to marry late. They wanted on average three to four children, considerably more than the women. But what I found most fascinating were the inconsistencies. Not only did they want to marry and have lots of children at later ages, but they were expecting to retire early, often long before their younger children would be finished with college. As we discussed the results, I pointed out to them that while women have a 'biological clock', men have a very similar economic clock if they want to help their children get a college education.

So clearly, the first thing family demographers who want to understand the male life course need to learn is whether and why men want to have families. The field understands that most women want to have a family, but I have a substantial collection of sources that assume that this is *only* the case for women. Coleman discusses parenthood only in terms of "duty", as well as "cost and inconvenience"; and "20 years of partial house arrest" (2004). Although it seems likely that he is being ironic at this point, he is far from alone among scholars discussing family changes in assuming that any benefits to parenthood, as well as costs, would accrue only to women (Fuchs, 1988; McDonald, 2010; Romaniuk, 2010). It is likely that these scholars are accurately describing the current ideal male life course, which is both focused primarily on work and idealizes the freedom to have multiple, short-term romantic relationships (McCarthy et al., 2000). But few women are likely to feel this way, nor very many men.

Next, the role of money in men's family relationships is something that needs to be better understood. Money has been extensively studied re women's family transitions. Many scholars were happy to assume that a major (if not the major) reason women wanted to marry and have children is to obtain financial support from men for themselves and their children; the structure of the separate spheres encouraged this motivation. But then women began to earn.

There is a vast literature on how partners' relative earnings affect divorce, which seems to have changed over time in the US, to vary across countries, and even within countries at different levels of education or income. However, as Sawhill has regularly pointed out (e.g., Ross & Sawhill, 1975), few studies of the effects of women's income on divorce have studied the *income effects* of her earnings, focusing only on what might be better called the 'gender competition effect.' But there are many other sources of funds, not to mention earnings trajectories, that might have effects. It reminds me of when studies of the effects of female labor force participation on children ignored women's earnings in their models, simply controlling family income, as if fathers would have earned that much more if the mothers were home with the children.

Further, there is the question of paid parental leave. Large numbers of countries and even a few US states are now offering some income replacement to parents taking leave to care for family members, most commonly for children. Many have argued when theorizing about the demographic transition that the decline in children's earning capacity, as school replaced factories and pensions replaced the need for support from children in old age, reduced the incentive to have children. But I have heard little discussion about whether paid family leave has a direct income effect; most of the discussion, like that on divorce, is on the pro-fertility effects of fathers taking family leave (again, a gender effect) rather than the direct income effect. But I know a number of Swedish couples who factored into their calculations of returning to school, or perhaps financing a move, the value of having another child and collecting more paid family leave, and have come down on having another child sooner rather than later.

Even when the focus moves beyond the cold, hard cash of women's earnings or paid family leave to a focus on modeling the various non-monetary family investments, such as joint children and other forms of joint capital (e.g., housing) and long-term relationships, we know little about how these factors affect men's life course decisions. And we could go on and on, but for now, I won't, to leave space for my final point—why women's move into employment, the third cell, seems to have gone more smoothly/rapidly than men's movement into the fourth cell of increased involvement in their homes and families. Or as so many authors who bemoan the incompleteness, or unevenness, or even the 'stall', in men's taking on more of these tasks neglect to ask: why the delay?

2.5 Why the Delay?

There are actually a large number of similarities in the working out of these two stages of the gender revolution. In both cases, the early steps were often dismissed (women were only earning 'pin money'; men were only 'playing with their children' or doing the 'easy' home tasks). This would be an interesting analysis, comparing the early years (and studies) of women's move into the public sphere with men's move into the private sphere, breaking down the separate spheres.

Nevertheless, there are important differences. Perhaps the most fundamental is the difference in the status of men's and women's activities. Anthropologists tell us that men have higher status in every society studied. As a result, it is easier for women to move into the public sphere than for men to move into the private sphere because, whatever the costs of women moving out of their sphere, they are moving 'up'; in particular, they gain earnings by going to work, for their families but also for themselves. Too many men see taking on domestic tasks, such as staying away from work to care for a sick child, as 'moving down.'

Further, men have had very little preparation for domestic roles, unlike the 100 years' increase in women's education that preceded the rise in female labor force participation (Walters, 1984) and the fact that throughout the century of the separate spheres (Stanfors & Goldscheider, 2017), many if not most women were employed prior to marriage.

2.6 Concluding Discussion

This paper addresses the future of family demography by presenting evidence linking changes in the family economy with changes in gender relationships. These changes began with the growth in non-farm occupations over the past 150–200 years, primarily for men, creating the separate spheres. As a result, most men's productive activities focused on the non-family sphere and most women's focused on the family sphere, a division that reached a peak in the 1950s.

The construct of the separate spheres can be conceptualized as a simple 2-celled table—men/work in one cell and women/family in the other; there was no need to study family demography. The move of women into the public sphere opened up a third cell, as women added employment to their family responsibilities. Not incidentally, this was linked with changes in the family: delays in family formation and increases in non-marital fertility and union dissolution, changes that created the field of family demography and made the study of sex differences, primarily in the public sphere, much more interesting.

The growth of labor force participation among married women has been called a gender revolution, which, because so little has occurred in the family sphere, is often called "stalled" or "incomplete." This paper addresses the reasons for the greater speed of gender integration in the world of work than that of the family by considering both women's greater preparation for work roles than men's preparation for family roles, and the higher status of men's roles than women's—particularly because they are paid. It challenges family demographers to expand their research to focus on the 4th cell—the interrelationships between men's work and family roles.

References

Bianchi, S., & Spain, D. (1986). *American women in transition*. Russell Sage.

Coleman, D. (2004). Why we don't have to believe without doubting in the 'Second Demographic Transition'—Some agnostic comments. *Vienna Yearbook of Population Research, 2*, 11–24.

Espenshade, T. (1985). Marriage trends in America: Estimates, implications, and underlying causes. *Population and Development Review, 11*, 193–245.

Fuchs, V. (1988). *Women's Quest for economic equality*. Harvard University Press.

Goldin, C. (1990). *Understanding the Gender Gap: An Economic history of American Women*. Oxford University Press.

Goldscheider, F., & Waite, L. (1991). *New families, no families: The transformation of the American home*. University of California Press.

Kiser, C. (1953–54). The Indianapolis fertility study-An example of planned observational research. *The Public Opinion Quarterly, 17*, No. 4 (Winter), 496–510.

McCarthy, J. R., Edwards, R., & Gillies, V. (2000). Moral tales of the child and the adult: Narratives of contemporary family lives under changing circumstances. *Sociology, 34*, 785–803.

McDonald, P. (2010, October 14–16). *Theoretical foundations for the analysis of fertility: Gender equity*. Paper presented to the bBAW/Leopoldina Conference, Lausanne.

Mead, M. (1965). *And keep your powder dry: An anthropologist looks at America*. Morrow.

Nye, F. I., & Hoffman, L. (1963). *The employed mother in America*. Rand McNally.

Oppenheimer, V. (1970). *The female labor force in the United States: Demographic and economic factors governing its growth and changing composition* (Population Monograph Series, No. 5). University of California.

Parnes, H. (1975). The National Longitudinal Surveys: New vistas for labor market research. *The American Economic Review, 65*, 244–249.

Romaniuk, A. (2010). Fertility in the age of demographic maturity: An essay. *Canadian Studies in Population, 37*, 283–295.

Ross, H. L., & Sawhill, I. V. (1975). *Time of transition: The growth of families headed by women*. The Urban Institute Press.

Stanfors, M., & Goldscheider, F. (2017). The forest and the trees: Industrialization, demographic change, and the ongoing gender revolution Sweden and in the US, 1870–2010. *Demographic Research, 36*(6), 173–226.

Walters, P. (1984). Occupational and labor market effects on secondary and postsecondary educational expansion in the United States: 1922 to 1979. *American Sociological Review, 49*, 659–671.

Chapter 3
Family Demography and Personal Life

Andrew J. Cherlin

The single word that best represents the theme of American family demography over the past half century, the main direction of its research enterprise, and the transformation it has proclaimed, is diversity. The American version of family demography began with a focus on marriage, as can be seen in a 1970 monograph, *Marriage and Divorce: A Social and Economic Study*, by two United States Bureau of the Census demographers, Hugh Carter and Paul C. Glick (Carter & Glick, 1970). The monograph reflected the dominant paradigm of the time: the functionalist view that the nuclear family was the highest and best form of family life. In 1955, Talcott Parsons and Robert F. Bales maintained that the single-earner, two-parent family was most attuned to a modern society because small groups functioned best when they separated the positions of task leader and socio-emotional leader, as did the single-earner, breadwinner (task leader) – homemaker (emotional leader) marriage (Parsons & Bales, 1955). William J. Goode, in his 1963 book, *World Revolution and Family Patterns*, argued that the single-earner nuclear family provided the best fit for industrial societies because it allowed families to move around to follow the best job offers for the husband (Goode, 1963). Neither Parsons nor Goode foresaw the changes in family patterns that would end the reign the breadwinner-homemaker family.

Carter and Glick's monograph assumed that the marriage-based nuclear family was the fundamental demographic unit of family life. There was no need to consider cohabitation, which was largely confined to the bohemian and the poor. No need to investigate fertility outside of marriage: in 1960 only 5% of children were born to unmarried women (U.S. National Center for Health Statistics, 2014). Carter and Glick treated husbands as the automatic heads of married-couple households, as did all Census Bureau publications at the time. Wives could only be classified as

A. J. Cherlin (✉)
Department of Sociology, Johns Hopkins University, Baltimore, MD, USA
e-mail: cherlin@jhu.edu

R. Schoen (ed.), *The Demography of Transforming Families*, The Springer Series on Demographic Methods and Population Analysis 56,
https://doi.org/10.1007/978-3-031-29666-6_3

household heads if they had become divorced or widowed. The authors assumed that families did not extend over more than one household. It was taken for granted that all couples would be composed of different sex individuals – no one even dreamed of asking about same-sex partnerships. In these ways, family demographers such as Carter and Glick reinforced the idea of the uniformity of family life, centered on the different-sex married couple and their children.

American family demography since 1970, in contrast, has been about moving away from the idea of uniformity to the idea of diversity. Countless studies have shown the scope of this diversity. Books and articles appeared on the significance of the rising numbers of married women in the labor force, which reduced the prevalence of the breadwinner-homemaker marriage (Oppenheimer, 1970). The increase in single-parent families, due to marital dissolution and nonmarital childbearing, became a focus (Ross & Sawhill, 1975). Family demographers reported on the sharp increase in cohabitation that began in the 1970s (Bumpass & Sweet, 1989) and pondered whether it was a precursor to marriage or an alternative to it (Rindfuss & VandenHeuvel, 1990). Others studied the extent to which the increase in single-parent families affected children's well-being (McLanahan & Sandefur, 1994). Repartnering after a divorce led to greater attention to remarriage and stepfamilies (Cherlin, 1978; Furstenburg & Spanier, 1984). Demographers studied the emergence of what was then called the gay and lesbian population (Black et al., 2000) and, more recently and more broadly, sexual and gender minority families (Reczek, 2020). In the past several years, many articles have examined the complexity and instability of family life (Raley & Sweeney, 2020; Sassler & Lichter, 2020). In all of these areas of inquiry, demographers have studied variations by class, race, and ethnicity (Duncan & Rodgers, 1988; Farley & Allen, 1987; Landale & Oropesa, 2007).

But after more than a half century of research on family diversity, challenges still remain. One such challenge, surprisingly, is whether the criteria demographers use for family boundaries have broadened sufficiently. Most demographic studies of family life do not include unrelated individuals such as close friends, intimate partners who maintain separate residences, or housemates who share cooking and home maintenance responsibilities. Nor do demographers expend much effort to study the family lives of people living alone without partners or children. Without doubt, doing so would further complicate an already complicated set of rules about what constitutes a family. Nevertheless, it is worth considering a critique has emerged that seeks to enhance, or even supplant, family life with the broader idea of personal life, in which non-kin relations are important. It has come mainly from British and other European scholars who use qualitative research methods to argue for this broader vision and from queer theorists on both sides of the Atlantic who have emphasized ties that individuals choose to make from family, friends, and current and former intimate partners. That these scholars eschew the quantitative methods and assumptions of demographers may explain why their writings have had little effect on demographic research to date. Their ideas, nevertheless, could lead to advances in the models and measures that family demographers employ.

A second, and more fundamental challenge, is whether, given all this diversity, there is still a core element to these divergent forms – a meaningful center to which we can attach the label of family. Demographers, by the substantive categories and research methods that they use, have tacitly assumed that the answer is yes. Some of the personal life / queer theory critics, however, claim that the answer is no. Rather, they argue that there is no structural or institutional basis for continuing to use the term family to describe the personal networks of individuals today. They seek to decenter the couple-based, childrearing-oriented focus of so much family demography. If they are correct, then there may no longer be a viable field called family demography.

In this chapter, I will examine these two challenges. As for the first challenge, I will argue that family demographers should indeed expand their horizons to include non-kin actors inside and outside of the household, despite the methodological challenges that such an expansion would bring. Not every study need do so, and among those that take on this methodological challenge, not every study need do so to the same degree; but all researchers need to consider this expansion. As for the second challenge, however, I will argue against decentering the family and in favor of a continuing core. I will review evidence, much of it produced by scholars sympathetic to a further expansion, that some personal relationships matter more than others – and that ties normally thought of as "family" still matter a great deal. This evidence suggests that we should retain the core concept of family life, even while extending its reach.

3.1 Expanding the Boundaries

Personal Life The literature to which I will be referring takes on the general label of "personal life." It may be more familiar to European scholars than to North American scholars, among whom it has not been prominently cited. The field of personal life first arose as a reaction to the emphasis on individualization in the theories of family life and intimacy of Anthony Giddens, and Ulrich Beck and Elizabeth Beck-Gernsheim, among others (Beck & Beck-Gernsheim, 1995, 2002; Giddens, 1992). These writers saw individualization as a central part of the late-modern, or postmodern, condition and theorized that its rise was weakening family bonds. As individuals become freer to make personal choices in their lives, it is said, their search for intimacy leads to precarious relationships that exist only so long as they are seen as personally rewarding by both partners – thus, Giddens's well-known concept of the "pure relationship" (Giddens, 1992). Intimate partnerships, Giddens argues, depend on the voluntary commitment of the partners to each other – a form of commitment that can be rescinded by either partner at any time. Moreover, individuals are increasingly freed from pre-established kinship ties (Giddens, 1991). Beck and Beck-Gernsheim argue, further, that the need for continual choice and monitoring makes assembling family ties a "do-it-yourself" project that is difficult to maintain: "The family bond thereby grows more fragile and there is a greater danger of collapse if attempts to reach agreement are not successful" (Beck & Beck-Gernsheim, 2002, p. 98). Because family ties are based on personal choices that can revised at any time, the family itself becomes a "zombie category," thought to be alive but actually dead (Beck & Beck-Gernsheim, 2002, p. 203). Individualization may lead to "atomization:" the loss of meaningful ties. "Lacking stable bridges for incoming traffic, kinship networks feel frail and threatened," wrote Zigmunt Bauman, another prominent scholar of this genre. "Kinship networks cannot be sure of their chances of survival, let alone calculate their life expectations" (Bauman, 2003, p. 31).

The personal life scholars, to be sure, accept some claims of the individualization theorists, such as the greater role of personal choice in creating one's life course and the weakening of traditional kinships bonds. But they reject the view that intimate life today is atomized and unstable. They object to the pessimistic tone of the individualization theorists with respect to personal ties. Rather, they see the potential for rich connections. They do so by emphasizing the enlargement of the field from which individuals can create meaningful ties, an expansion that can encompass not only life partners and close kin but also friends, acquaintances, sexual intimates, and relationships across households. The use of the term "personal" rather than "individualistic" signifies connections with others rather than aloneness. It also signifies broad networks not limited to conventional family ties. Carol Smart first set out this argument in detail in her 2007 book, *Personal Life: New Directions in Sociological Thinking* (Smart, 2007). She wrote:

> I have suggested that developing a field designated 'personal life' incorporates all sorts of families, all sorts of relationships and intimacies, diverse sexualities, friendships, and acquaintanceships. The term 'personal' is also significant in denoting the centrality of the individual, yet avoiding the sense in which it can convey ideas of separateness, autonomy and the conceptual slide into individualization (Smart, 2007, p. 188).

The personal life literature contains an implicit criticism of the American family diversity literature, which identifies a growing number of family forms but does not venture much beyond traditional family and kinship bonds, except for cohabiting couples, and which centers its analyses around couples, parents, and children. The criticism comes in two versions, which I will call the "radical" critique and the "liberal" critique.

The Radical Critique The scholars who present the radical critique argue not only that non-kin should be included but also that the concept of family should be decentered in favor of the broader concept of personal life. In this critique, the emphasis is on close relationships that people choose to construct from partners, family members, more distant kin, and friends. These partnerships and networks may change over time and may or may not involve cohabiting or marital partnerships. The radical critique maintains, in fact, that studies of personal networks should not necessarily focus on the couple, whether same-sex or different-sex, as the center of the network. Some of the writings arise from the queer theory critique of heteronormativity in family studies, which rejects a near-exclusive focus in the literature on the kinds of family lives that are common among heterosexuals, such as the monogamous nuclear family (Allen & Mendez, 2018; Oswald et al., 2005;

Willey, 2016). Even the legalization of same-sex marriage is seen as another manifestation of the misguided centrality of the monogamous couple. Allen and Mendez (2018) write of the inclusion of same-sex couples in civil partnerships and marriages:

> Although this inclusion undoubtedly has merits for gay and lesbian individuals and families that desire such institutional privileges, it simultaneously denigrates and subverts their queer counterparts as "other" ... (Allen & Mendez, 2018, p. 76).

The radical critique also applies to heterosexuals who do not choose to be in a couple relationship or to have children. The authors of a four-country study (United Kingdom, Bulgaria, Norway, and Portugal) criticize the "couple-norm," the idea that living as a couple is the only proper way to carry out an adult life, and what they call the "insidious grip" of the couple-norm on our sense of what it means to be a fully-recognized citizen (Roseneil et al., 2020, p. 3). The authors concede that same-sex couples, cohabiting or married, are increasingly recognized as falling within the couple-norm; and yet they argue:

> However, cohabiting, procreative coupledom remains the privileged and normative form of intimate life: the good and proper intimate citizen is no longer necessarily married or heterosexual, but they are living in a long-term, stable, sexually exclusive, co-residential partnership (Roseneil et al., 2020, p. 22).

Relatedly, two scholars criticized what they called the "reprocentric" focus in family studies on having and rearing children (Wilkinson & Bell, 2012). They maintain that the personal lives of adults, which may or may not involve long-term partners and children, should be the overarching framework:

> By seeing the 'family' as just one part of intimate life we can help to challenge the idea that family is always our most important attachment. Working within theories of personal life helps to decentre the importance of family life, seeing it as just one intimate arrangement among many (yet can still be attuned to the ways in which certain forms of 'family' are privileged over others by the state) (Wilkinson & Bell, 2012, p. 426).

In the radical critique there is no longer a central concept, a stable pattern, or an institutionalized form for which the label of family is appropriate. Family is indeed seen as a zombie category – and by extension the radical critique challenges whether family demography still coheres as a field.

The Liberal Critique Scholars who represent the liberal critique agree with more radical writers that people often have deep, meaningful relationships with friends and intimate partners that augment, and in some cases surpass, their conventional family ties. Said otherwise, they agree that the boundaries between family and friends are often blurred and that the subject matter of family studies should be enlarged. An exclusive focus on family ties, it is said, leaves out other close relationships through which individuals are attached to each other in late modern societies. Personal networks are viewed as taking many different forms that are fluid rather than fixed. These scholars sometimes use the phrases "families and relationships" (May & Dawson, 2018) or "families and intimacies" (Jamieson, 1998) in their conceptualizations of personal life.

In contrast to the radical critique, however, scholars in what I am calling the liberal critique do not argue that that family ties should be decentered. May and Nordqvist (2019) write:

> However, by saying that we wish to question the primacy of family relationships as *the* stuff of personal life, we are not claiming that these are not central in personal life – quite the contrary. We still view these 'traditional' topics as major components of personal life, but we would argue that they can only be fully understood if explored in relation to other spheres significant to everyday personal life (May & Nordqvist, 2019, p. 2)

In addition, as meaningful as friendships may be, they are seen in the liberal critique as requiring less commitment and entailing fewer obligations than kin-based ties; and they also may be more time-limited. According to Allan (2008):

> In other words, it is not that people feel no sense of obligation to offer help and support to their friends. Rather, it is that providing support to genealogically close family members is typically given priority, especially when the support needed is demanding (Allan, 2008, p. 11).

Kin-based ties, then, are still seen as a central form of personal life, although they should be set within a broader perspective. Furthermore, family ties are not viewed as in opposition to other close relationships. Davies (2019) writes:

> It is also problematic to assume that the significance of friendship is set against a decline in the importance of family relationships – the empirical evidence indicates that family relationships are still central (Davies, 2019, p. 72).

3.2 Centering Family Ties

Whether one accepts the radical or the liberal critique, then, depends on whether one thinks that family relationships are still central to personal life. Let us examine the evidence. I would argue that several recent studies are more consistent with the liberal critique that retains the family as central than with the radical argument that decenters it. Consider studies of same-sex partners and their personal networks, which are of particular interest given the prominence of queer theory in the radical critique. Same-sex relationships provide an opportunity to observe the development of personal networks outside of the context of different-gender partnerships and, until recent legal changes, largely outside of institutional support. Since the groundbreaking books *Families We Choose: Lesbians, Gays, Kinship* (Weston, 1991) and *Same Sex Intimacies: Families of Choice and Other Life Experiments* (Weeks et al., 2001), the idea of families of choice – families that are intentionally created out of friendships, current and past sexual partners, and whatever family members will accept the individual's sexuality – has been widely-cited as the basis for same-sex family life. These findings have been interpreted as undermining the conventional view of family life, which is seen as founded upon relationships that are assigned at birth and at marriage or partnership.

Steeped in the framework of families of choice, Heaphy (one of the authors of *Same Sex Intimacies*), Smart (the pioneering theorist of personal life), and Heaphy et al. (2013) studied 50 same-sex couples in civil partnerships in the United Kingdom in 2009–2010, after the Civil Partnership Act of 2004 but before same-sex marriage had been legalized. They were surprised to find that nearly all the civilly-partnered couples they interviewed considered themselves to be married, used marriage as their frame of reference, saw themselves as ordinary rather than different, and did not see much difference between their relationships and heterosexual marriages. They were also surprised to see that close friendship ties were de-emphasized relative to the couple, primarily, and to parents and other kin, secondarily. They were struck by the degree to which the people who they studied elevated their couple relationships above other relationships. What is more, 45 out of the 50 couples described their relationships as sexually monogamous or exclusive. The authors attributed these unexpected developments to the greater acceptance of same-sex relationships in the larger society today than in the recent past – a development that, they argued, allows same-sex couples to feel relatively ordinary and to form conventional relationships.

The Heaphy et al. (2013) study suggests, then, that although families of choice exist, and friendship ties may be very important, the family lives same-sex partners appear to center around their partnerships and their ties to kin. These findings led Heaphy to reformulate his understanding of same-sex relationships as evincing "reflexive convention:" intentional, chosen paths that nevertheless lead to family forms that are for the most part conventional (Heaphy et al., 2013). Here one might also mention the high take-up rate of marriage among same-sex couples in the United States after same-sex marriage became legal in all states in 2015: By 2019, more than half of all same-sex couples in the United States were married (Manning et al., 2022). This high take-up rate suggests that marriage is a meaningful marker of a successful personal life for many Americans, regardless of sexual orientation. Granted, chosen families may still be important for many LGBTQ individuals, particularly those who are unpartnered. A study of young gay and bisexual men in the Detroit area found that, when asked "Whom do you consider to be your family?", half mentioned both members of their families of origin and chosen family members such as partners, friends, and roommates (Soler et al., 2018).

The evidence for the continuing centrality of family-based ties does not only come from studies of same-sex relationships. In a three-country (Lithuania, Portugal, Switzerland) study in which people were asked who is important to them, the authors found what they called "bounded pluralism" in personal networks (Wall et al., 2018). Constraints, or bounds, exist, they maintained, on how far people deviate from normative, family-centered limits in their personal relationships. These limits, they argued, derive from factors such as class, norms, national context, and welfare regimes. The authors summarize their argument as follows:

> The main argument in this book is that despite greater freedom in the construction of personal life, largely driven by lifestyle or individual preferences as well as the questioning of blood and alliance principles, individuals' personal networks and sense of connectedness are likely to be constrained or *bounded* by life course experiences, normative orientations, and differential social positioning related to birth cohort, gender, or social class (Wall et al., 2018, p. 226).

Relationships with parents and partners, they found, were more important than were relationships with extended kin. Nuclear families, although comprising less than a majority, were the most common configurations in all three countries. And although many networks included friends, there was no trend away from incorporating family in one's network.

In the United States, Nelson (2020) embarked on a study of fictive, or voluntary, kinship among White, middle-class families and found that there is a limit to how close people feel to those who are unrelated to them. People felt more of a sense of unconditional obligation and loyalty to family members than they did to voluntary kin. The latter group were "like family." And while "like family" often meant more than just being friends, it also meant *not quite* family. According to Nelson:

> People, who have like-sibling bonds with each other, think and feel about each other differently than they think and feel about their blood/legal kin. Their like-family relationships do not weigh so heavily on their minds. Those relationships feel lighter, more buoyant, more simply based in deep-seated affection than do those they experience with their "real" kin (Nelson, 2020, p. 136).

Individuals often felt that blood or legal ties were of such emotional significance that they should try to retain them even when relationship are quite strained. Nelson writes:

> In short, when my respondents peer sideways at White middle-class family from the perspective of fictive kinship, they reveal that blood/legal ties matter intensely, that the exclusive bonds of family membership carry such great moral and emotional significance that people believe that they should make efforts to sustain and repair frayed bonds, even when that fraying is the result of abuse and neglect (Nelson, 2020, p. 138).

It is likely, to be sure, that voluntary kin play a greater role in the families lives of racial and ethnic minority groups in the United States than among middle-class Whites. A well-established literature, starting with anthropological studies such as Stack (1974), has demonstrated the importance of voluntary kinship ties among African Americans. Survey-based, nationwide studies confirm these findings. In the National Survey of Black Americans, conducted in 1979 and 1980, respondents were asked, "Is there anyone close to your family that is not really blood or marriage related, but is treated just like a relative?" Two-thirds said that there was someone who met this description (Chatters et al., 1994). Whereas these early studies suggested that voluntary kinship ties were more numerous among the African-American poor, a national survey of African Americans conducted in 2001–2003 – still the most recent – indicated that voluntary ties were more common among the non-poor (Miller-Cribbs & Farber, 2008; Taylor et al., 2022). Similarly, an older literature points to the importance of ritualized co-parenthood, known as *compadrazgo*, among Latin-American and African immigrants to the United States (Ebaugh & Curry, 2000), but more recent studies are scarce. Demographers do not have good, recent national data on voluntary kinship among racial and ethnic minority groups.

Finally, Furstenberg and his co-authors conducted a review of about 300 articles on Western kinship practices and alternative family forms (Furstenberg et al., 2020). They found considerable variation in patterns of family and kinship; and they urged researchers to expand their horizons to include a very broad range of kin and personal networks. Yet they concluded, "we see little evidence of the waning of the cultural importance of biology" (Furstenberg et al., 2020, p. 1423). Moreover, they wrote in reference to the nuclear family of married parents and children:

> Our research suggests that this model continues to have a considerable normative hold in Western societies despite significant diversification of family forms during the past half century (Furstenberg et al., 2020, p. 1404).

In sum, the findings of studies done by researchers who were open to the importance of non-kin in personal networks indicate that there still is an observable difference between ties to family and ties to friends. The former are more prevalent, more durable, and carry a greater sense of obligation and responsibility. There is still a preference for strong couple bonds that is often expressed using the language and rituals of marriage. In short, there are bounds on how pluralistic personal networks can be. The implication for family demographers is that researchers need not decenter the family from its position in their research.

Yet at the same time, these studies challenge family demographers to consider how to place families theoretically within the broader context of personal life and how to incorporate important non-kin members of personal networks, when appropriate, into their analyses. The radical critique that urges the decentering of the family is overstated, but the liberal critique, by and large, stands: Many people have meaningful relationships with friends and other non-kin that are family-like in nature. These relationships should be included in assessments of their personal lives. To simply distinguish among different, but by now standard, family forms (the stepfamily, the single-parent family, the cohabiting couple, etc.) is not always sufficient for family demographers. They may need to incorporate ties to important non-relatives. In addition, they may need to revise how they study the family ties and relationships of individuals who remain unpartnered through much of their adulthood and who do not see raising children as an important part of their lives.

3.3 From Unbounded Diversity to Bounded Pluralism

It may seem contradictory to argue for an expansion of the boundaries of family and personal life and yet to argue for retaining the biological/legal family as its core. But the case for expansion is strong, whereas the case for decentering the family is weak. As for the expansion, there is clearly more latitude for personal choice in forming and maintaining a family than in the past. This is not news to demographers. But what the personal life literature adds is the growing likelihood that family-like ties will extend to individuals who are not related by blood, marriage, or adoption. This will not be the case in everyone's personal life, but it is common enough that it can no longer be overlooked. It may be especially prevalent among certain minority groups such as African Americans or among LGBTQ individuals who choose not establish conventional partnerships or, indeed, among unpartnered individuals of any race, sexual identity, or gender. These potential ties to non-kin should not be ignored.

Yet as for decentering the family, we see empirically from recent studies that there are bounds to how far personal life diverges from conventional family relationships. There are limits, for most people, in the extent to which personal relationships with non-kin approach relationships with kin. This is how I interpret the "bounded pluralism" construct that the authors of the three-country comparative study put forward in their book (Wall et al., 2018). It is a useful way to encapsulate the tension between mainstream and innovative forms of family and personal life. Families and relationships can take on many forms that comprise biological and legal relatives as well as non-kin such as friends and partners. Granted, there are some individuals who construct deeply meaningful personal networks wholly outside of their kin. For most people, however, personal networks will include biological/legal relatives. In mixed networks – those that encompass kin and friends – obligations to kin, and expectations of support from kin, will be seen as greater than those involving non-kin, if recent studies are accurate.

3.4 Structure Versus Process

The personal life literature contains other implicit criticisms of the assumptions and methodology of family demography. One claim is that the growth of alternative paths to families and relationships is so broad and subject to so much agency during one's life course that family as a form of social structure no longer exists; rather, what exists is family as an unfolding process, with many variations, substantial fluidity, and much individual choice. For instance, where I have used the term "obligation" in describing the responsibility that family members may feel toward each other, some personal life scholars would prefer the term "negotiation" because it connotes process rather than structure (Nordqvist, 2019, p. 52). In his book on family practices, Morgan (2011), perhaps the leading scholar of this school of thought, contends that researchers should focus on how family ties are created and maintained through the active doing of family relationships, as if "family" were not a noun but a verb, in the sense of "doing family" – a phrase evocative of the "doing gender" approach to gender studies (West & Zimmerman, 1987). He prefers to define his approach as about "family practices" rather than about families. At several points in his book, he feels the need to defend using the word "family" at all, as if anticipating opprobrium from scholars on his left: Family is still important to large sections of the population, he submits, and people do distinguish between family and friends. Yet he hastens to add:

> This, of course, makes no assumption of functionality or centrality from either a societal or an individual perspective (Morgan, 2011, p. 40).

And lest he be tempted to think otherwise, he includes the following note to self:

> Beyond this, there is a reminder to myself that I should continue to use the word 'family' with some care even when it is linked to practices (Morgan, 2011, p. 65).

Morgan's rather tortured defense of retaining a limited concept of family, even though it remains important to people and even though people make distinctions between family and friends, suggests that it is difficult for personal life scholars to accept that some structure is left in family life. Without doubt, the institutionalized dimension of the family life is weaker than it was during the heyday of the nuclear family. I have written about the deinstitutionalization of marriage in the United States, particular among people who have not attained college degrees (Cherlin, 2004, 2020). Yet there still is a core of kinship that is centered around individuals and their ties to older parents, to marital and cohabiting partners, if any, and to children if they choose to have them, and secondarily to other kin. To this core are often added ties to other kin such as adult siblings (Furstenberg et al., 2020). This is structure, if less so than in the 1950s. Studies that emphasize process can be enlightening, but they do not preclude considerations of family structure.

3.5 Quantitative Versus Qualitative

In addition, both the liberal and radical critics maintain that constructivist, interpretive studies, commonly referred to as qualitative research, are better suited to studying families and relationships than are the quantitative methods that family demographers typically use. In a compendium of ten articles on families and relationships that had been previously printed in the British journal *Sociology* and were selected to be reprinted in a special issue of the same journal, only one used quantitative data. The editors of the compendium write that the imbalance reflects an emphasis on "how individuals negotiate what 'family' means, and do so in divergent and complex ways" (May & Dawson, 2018, p. 872). In other words, the emphasis on qualitative research stems from a view of family as an unfolding process. Morgan (2011) wrote:

> While, in principle, almost any tools of social enquiry might be deployed in the study of family practices, in reality it would seem that the approach more readily leads in the direction of qualitative analysis. It would seem that the key terms of the practices approach – doing, relationality, fluidity – would almost inevitably demand some form of qualitative study (Morgan, 2011, p. 168).

This claim reflects larger debates within sociology between more inductive, interpretive scholars, and more deductive, positivistic scholars, such as social demographers (Goldthorpe, 2016). It also reflects national differences in the types of sociological research that are dominant. Major sociology journals still manifest this split: A study of articles in 13 leading English-language sociology journals between 1995 and 2017 found that two prestigious British sociology journals, *Sociology* and the *British Journal of Sociology*, published the highest percentage of qualitative studies, whereas some other European and American journals were highly quantitative (e.g., *European Sociological Review*, *Social Science Research, Social Forces*), and two flagship American journals *(American Journal of Sociology, American Sociological Review*) fell in the middle (Schwemmer & Wieczorek, 2020). (Demographic journals were not included in the Schwemmer and Wieczorek study; but one would imagine that they would be at the quantitative pole.) The leading personal life scholars, many of whom are at British universities, use interpretive, qualitative methods almost entirely.

To be sure, demographic researchers are limited in the depth of understanding they can provide about the mechanisms of human behavior that underly the statistical models that they apply. But qualitative researchers are limited in the extent to which they can determine whether their findings are representative of the larger populations from which they draw their small, intensive studies. The more productive path is to combine the qualitative and the quantitative, although not necessarily in every study, in order to seek both in-depth insights on individual behavior and regularities and representativeness on a larger scale. This research agenda may be easier to carry out in the United States than in the United Kingdom. Academic demographers in the United States are typically situated in departments of sociology that include researchers who employ a broad range of methods. This heterogeneity can encourage collaboration. A movement toward combining quantitative and the qualitative research techniques in so-called "mixed-methods" research has had considerable success (Weis et al., 2019), although it requires collaborators who are willing and able to communicate across the methodological divide.

I also think that interpretive, qualitative research is attractive to critics of conventional family life because it uncovers not only what is commonly occurring, in a descriptive sense, but rather what is possible, even if only visible in a minority of cases. It can focus on case studies that are not necessarily representative but which can inform us about new ways to conduct personal life that may be viewed as liberating. It is favorable to scholars whose value positions encompass the view that conventional families are restrictive if not oppressive, and who view alternative forms of personal life as potentially freeing. It is my sense that most of the personal life scholars and nearly all queer theorists see alternative forms of personal life as positive and healthy and the older forms as constraining and inequitable. They seek to present the possibilities that these alternative forms present. Intensive, qualitative studies of particular individuals, families, and networks are conducive to this worldview. Family demographers have their own value positions, such as the importance of childrearing (see below); and they seek to discover environments that are associated with the best outcomes on a population-based scale. Thus, they are more analytic than critical (Williams et al., 2017); and survey- or administrative-record-based studies are more conducive to their aims. Neither methodological approach holds all the keys to understanding family and personal life.

3.6 Adult-Centered Versus Child-Centered

It is also notable that the personal life literature is almost entirely concerned with relationships among adults. Attention to the family lives of parents and children is lacking. To American family scholars, and especially to family demographers, the absence of attention to children is striking. Yet this absence is, at least in the radical critique, intentional. Writers fault research of the kind typically found in family demography as overly focused on the couple and on children (Roseneil et al., 2020; Wilkinson & Bell, 2012). It is certainly true that family studies should incorporate individuals who do not have, and who may not plan to have, children. And it is true that family demography has, for the most part, not done that. Even for people who will go on to have children, the adult years prior to having children – a period that has become longer because of the rising age at first birth – constitute an important life stage. Still, there is a strong rationale for paying considerable, although not total, attention to the family lives of parents and children: This is the area in which the public policy implications of family demographic research are greatest. Whereas the personal relationships of childless adults are a largely private matter, a public interest exists in raising the next generation of adults. Edwards and Gillies (2012) have criticized the personal life literature for its inability to engage in important policy debates that are focused on what policy-makers and the general public still call families. Many of those debates focus on fertility and children's well-being. American family demography has long had a strong (although not exclusive) focus the care of dependents, which probably derives from the discipline of demography's central concern with fertility. Some of the most influential presidential addresses to the Population Association of America have been about children's well-being (McLanahan, 2004; Preston, 1984). Family demographers are justified in retaining an important but non-exclusive focus on this topic.

3.7 Cross-Sectional Versus Longitudinal

As Furstenberg and his co-authors have noted in their review of kinship practices in Western societies (Furstenberg et al., 2020), we have little evidence about the durability of close relationships of friends and other voluntary kin over time. Certainly, cross-sectional studies, as well as personal experiences, inform us about the existence and importance of deep, long-term friendships. But the general question of how often voluntary-kin relationships extend over long periods of time remains unanswered. Exchanges of support between non-relatives are more reciprocal than exchanges among relatives: If someone helps a friend, that friend is more likely to return the favor than is the case in assistance among relatives, which are more likely to be one-directional (Essock-Vitale & McGuire, 1980; Hruschka et al., 2015). In other words, one must do the work of maintaining friendships by exchanging support, which many individuals try hard to do (Smart et al., 2012), whereas relations among close kin may continue to be recognized even in the absence of exchanges of interaction and support. Close relatives are more likely to feel an obligation to support their kin than to support voluntary kin, as Nelson (2020) argued. People find close friends in different settings, depending on their life course stage: at university, at work, at child care centers (Davies, 2019); and we know little about how these friendships evolve after the setting is changed. In the case of step-relationships, which can vary in nature from being close to distant, a time-diary study showed that whether older parents spend time with their adult stepchildren depended on factors such as whether there are shared biological children in the stepfamily (Schoeni et al., 2022). We need to know more about the factors that encourage or inhibit the continuation of close, long-term relationships among voluntary kin.

3.8 Measurement

Collecting information on the family-like, non-kin relations of individuals in the kinds of large-scale representative surveys used by demographers is challenging, but it can be done. It will take further methodological work, and there will be several versions, depending on the aims of the study. The decision to include this information will depend on the type of study being conducted as well as the investigator's view of what the criteria for a meaningful relationship should be. One factor will be whether to include all people the respondents regard as part of their personal networks, regardless of the degree of assistance or closeness, versus including only people who provide some type of assistance above a threshold or in a given time period. The Panel Study of Income Dynamics (2022) includes what might be viewed as a minimalist question, in that it only asks respondent to name individuals to whom they have given financial support:

> In the previous year, did you give any money toward the support of anyone who was not living there at the time, including child support, alimony, money given to parents, and things like that?

Since the PSID is a heart a study of finances, this narrow focus is reasonable. (Follow-up questions allow analysts to subtract alimony and child support payments.) But it obviously excludes ties to non-kin for all non-financial reasons. A maximalist version of the question, in contrast, can be found in studies such as the three-nation research project referred to earlier (Wall et al., 2018):

> Who are the persons who, over the past year, have been very important to you, even if you do not get along well with them?

Follow-up questions ascertained the relationships of the individuals mentioned to the respondent. This question invites the respondent to include family members they reside with, as well as important individuals who are not related to them by biology or marriage. It does not require an exchange or assistance or support.

The National Survey of Families and Households, Wave 2 (Bumpass & Sweet, 2018), conducted in 1992–1994, asked a battery of questions about support to and from kin and non-kin that was focused on assistance in specific domains. Respondents were asked if they had given or received more than $200 during the previous 12 months and, if they responded positively, the relationship of the donor/recipient to them, including non-kin. They were also asked if they had received or given emotional support (advice, encouragement) or practical support (help with transportation, child care, housework, etc.) during the previous month from individuals other than parents or children. An analysis of the responses to these questions found that Black women were less likely to have received financial and emotional support than were White women, but that Black women were more likely to have received practical support than were White women (Sarkisian & Gerstel, 2004).

As this last study suggests, another factor will be the degree to which the study is focused on the families and relationships of racial, gender, or sexual minority individuals, whose ties to non-kin may be more important than among the majority population. The National Survey of American Life (Jackson & Antonucci, 2021), which was conducted in 2001–2003 and which focused on Black Americans, asked specifically about voluntary kin:

> How many people are close to your family who are not really blood-related or marriage-related but who are treated just like a relative?

A follow up question asked, "How often do they help you out?" The questionnaire design was clearly influence by the many studies, noted earlier, of the importance of voluntary kin among African Americans. Studies of sexual and gender minority families and relationships may require non-standard ways of collecting data such as web-based surveys in order to generate sufficient sample sizes.

3.9 Toward a Demography of Kinship

In two articles on kinship, Furstenberg (Furstenberg, 2020; Furstenberg et al., 2020) argues for the establishment of a "demography of kinship" for Western industrialized societies. He argues that the study of kinship, once a major topic for sociologists and anthropologists, has waned just as new forms are arising. The demography of kinship would still include standard topics such as union formation, but it would do so with an eye for variations in marriage, cohabitation, and single parenthood that may be producing new types of kinship ties. It would also go well beyond the reach of standard studies to include the links formed by voluntary kinship and families of choice. And it would include the ways in which assisted reproduction such as surrogacy may affect one's sense of kinship. To this list one might add the families and relationships of unpartnered, childless individuals. The main point is to encourage family demographers to consider the varieties of kinship ties that are produced by the diverse ways in which individuals go about creating families and relationships. I share this view. In this chapter I have urged family demographers to accept the idea advanced by the personal life scholars of a broader conception of family – one that specifically includes the possibility of incorporating members not usually thought of as kin.

At the same time, I have rejected the position that due to these new ways of forming close relationships, scholars should no longer place the family as it is usually thought of – marriage, cohabitation, parenthood, intergenerational relations, and so forth – at the center of their analyses. The push to decenter the family is not supported by recent studies. A core set of family relationships remains important, even among individuals who have forged new types of relationships. There is no contradiction between drawing upon the insights or personal life theorists and queer theorists but nevertheless retaining a non-exclusive focus on more conventional family ties. Rather, most studies should encompass the new and old forms of family and kinship that comprise the personal networks of individuals today.

Nor should family demographers accept the criticism that quantitative methods are inferior to qualitative methods in studying contemporary family and personal life. They should not concede the related proposition that family structure has disappeared (with the implication that demographic studies are no longer useful) and that all that is left is process (with the implication that qualitative, interpretive studies are the only kind that are valuable). The investigations by the personal life scholars are indeed valuable, but they do not suffice to describe and understand family relations today. Undeniably, the models and methods of demography have limits; and demographers should maintain a degree of humility about what they can accomplish. They will need qualitative research on family and personal life in order to deepen their understandings of the day-to-day dynamics by which individuals connect to those around them. To the extent that demographers can find willing partners from the world of qualitative research, the prospects for jointly advancing the study of family, kinship, and personal life will be brighter. And to the extent that family demography can incorporate the insights of personal-life scholars without rejecting the centrality of families, it will produce more useful studies of the present and future condition of family life.

References

Allan, G. (2008). Flexibility, friendship, and family. *Personal Relationships, 15*, 1–16.

Allen, S. H., & Mendez, S. M. (2018). Hegemonic heteronormativity: Toward a New era of Queer Family Theory. *Journal of Family Theory & Review, 10*(March), 70–86.

Bauman, Z. (2003). *Liquid love: On the frailty of human bonds*. Polity Press.

Beck, U., & Beck-Gernsheim, E. (1995). *The Normal Chaos of Love*. Polity Press.

Beck, U., & Beck-Gernsheim, E. (2002). *Individualization: Institutionalized Individualism and its social and political consequences*. Sage.

Black, D., Gates, G., Sanders, S., & Taylor, L. (2000). Demographics of the Gay and Lesbian population in the United States: Evidence from available systematic data sources. *Demograhy, 37*(2), 139–154.

Bumpass, L. L., & Sweet, J. A. (1989). National Estimates of Cohabitation. *Demography, 26*, 615–625.

Bumpass, L. L., & Sweet, J. A. (2018). *National Survey of Families and Households, Wave 2: 1992–1994, [United States]. Inter-university Consortium for Political and Social Research [distributor].*

Carter, H., & Glick, P. C. (1970). *Marriage and divorce: A social and economic study.* Harvard University Press.

Chatters, L. M., Taylor, R. J., & Jayakody, R. (1994). Fictive kinship relations in black extended families. *Journal of Comparative Family Studies, 25*, 297–312.

Cherlin, A. J. (1978). Remarriage as an incomplete institution. *American Journal of Sociology, 84*(3), 634–650.

Cherlin, A. J. (2004). The deinstitutionalization of American marriage. *Journal of Marriage and Family, 66*(4), 848–861.

Cherlin, A. J. (2020). Degrees of change: An assessment of the deinstitutionalization of marriage thesis. *Journal of Marriage and Family, 82*(1), 62–80.

Davies, K. (2019). Friendship and personal life. In V. May & P. Nordqvist (Eds.), *Sociology of personal life* (2nd ed., pp. 60–73). Red Globe Press.

Duncan, G. J., & Rodgers, W. L. (1988). Longitudinal aspects of childhood poverty. *Journal of Marriage and the Family, 50*, 1007–1021.

Ebaugh, H. R., & Curry, M. (2000). Fictive Kin as social capital in new immigrant communities. *Sociological Perspectives, 43*(2), 189–209.

Edwards, R., & Gillies, V. (2012). Farewell to Family? Notes on an argument for retaining the concept. *Families, Relationships and Societies, 1*(1), 63–69.

Essock-Vitale, S. M., & McGuire, M. T. (1980). Predictions derived from the theories of kin selection and reciprocation assessed by anthropological data. *Ethology and Sociobiology, 1*(3), 233–243.

Farley, R., & Allen, W. R. (1987). The color line and the quality of life in America: .

Furstenberg, F. F. (2020). Kinship Reconsidered: Research on a neglected topic. *Journal of Marriage and Family, 82*(February), 364–382.

Furstenberg, F. F., Harris, L. E., Pesando, L. M., & Reed, M. N. (2020). Kinship practices among alternative family forms in Western industrialized societies. *Journal of Marriage and Family, 82*(5), 1403–1430.

Furstenburg, F. F., Jr., & Spanier, G. B. (1984). *Recycling the family: Remarriage after divorce.* Sage.

Giddens, A. (1991). *Modernity and self-Identity.* Stanford University Press.

Giddens, A. (1992). *The transformation of intimacy.* Stanford University Press.

Goldthorpe, J. H. (2016). *Sociology as a population science.* Cambridge University Press.

Goode, W. J. (1963). *World revolution and family patterns.* The Free Press.

Heaphy, B., Smart, C., & Einarsdottir, A. (2013). *Same sex marriages: New generations, new relationships.* Springer.

Hruschka, D., Hackman, J., & Macfarlan, S. (2015). Why do humans help their friends? Proximal and ultimate hypotheses from evolutionary theory. In *Evolutionary perspectives on social psychology* (pp. 255–266). Springer.

Jackson, J. S., & Antonucci, T. C. (2021). *National Survey of American Life: Multi-generational and caribbean cross-section studies, Guyana, Jamaica, [United States], 2004–2005.*

Jamieson, L. (1998). *Intimacy: Personal relationships in modern societies.* Polity Press.

Landale, N. S., & Oropesa, R. S. (2007). Hispanic families: Stability and change. *Annual Review of Sociology, 33*, 381–405.

Manning, W. D., Westrick-Payne, K. K., & Gates, G. J. (2022). Cohabitation and marriage among same-sex couples in the 2019 ACS and CPS: A research note. *Demography, 22*(5), 1595–1605.

May, V., & Dawson, M. (2018). 'Families and relationships' e-Special issue introduction. *Sociology, 52*(4), 865–874.

May, V., & Nordqvist, P. (2019). *Sociology of personal life* (2nd ed.). Red Globe Press.

McLanahan, S. S. (2004). Diverging destinies: How children are faring under the second demographic transition. *Demography, 41*, 607–627.

McLanahan, S. S., & Sandefur, G. (1994). *Growing up with a single parent: What hurts, what helps*. Harvard University Press.
Miller-Cribbs, J. E., & Farber, N. B. (2008). Kin networks and poverty among African Americans: Past and present. *Social Work, 53*(1), 44–51.
Morgan, D. (2011). *Rethinking family practices*. Springer.
Nelson, M. K. (2020). *Like family: Narratives of Fictive Kinship*. Rutgers University Press.
Nordqvist, P. (2019). Kinship: How being related matters in personal life. In V. May & P. Nordqvist (Eds.), *Sociology of personal life* (2nd ed., pp. 46–59). Red Globe Press.
Oppenheimer, V. K. (1970). *The Female Labor Force in the United States* (Population Monograph Series, 5). Institute of International Studies, University of California.
Oswald, R. F., Blume, L. B., & Marks, S. R. (2005). Decentering heteronormativity: A model for family studies. In V. L. Bengtson, A. C. Acock, K. R. Allen, P. Dilworth-Anderson, & D. M. Klein (Eds.), *Sourcebook of family theory and research* (pp. 143–154). Sage.
Panel Study of Income Dynamics. (2022). *Produced and distributed by the Survey Research Center*. Institute for Social Research, University of Michigan.
Parsons, T., & Bales, R. F. (1955). *Family, socialization, and the interaction process*. The Free Press.
Preston, S. H. (1984). Children and the elderly: Divergent paths for America's dependents. *Demography, 21*(4), 435–457.
Raley, R. K., & Sweeney, M. M. (2020). Divorce, repartnering, and stepfamilies: A decade in review. *Journal of Marriage and Family, 82*(1), 81–99.
Reczek, C. (2020). Sexual-and gender-minority families: A 2010 to 2020 decade in review. *Journal of Marriage and Family, 82*(1), 300–325.
Rindfuss, R. R., & VandenHeuvel, A. (1990). Cohabitation: A precursor to marriage or an alternative to being single? *Population and Development Review, 16*, 703–726.
Roseneil, S., Crowhurst, I., Hellesund, T., Santos, A. C., & Stoilova, M. (2020). *The Tenacity of the Couple-Norm: Intimate citizenship regimes in a changing Europe*. UCL Press.
Ross, H. L., & Sawhill, I. V. (1975). *Time of transition: The growth ot families headed by women*. Urban Institute.
Sarkisian, N., & Gerstel, N. (2004). Kin support among Blacks and Whites: Race and family organization. *American Sociological Review, 69*, 812–837.
Sassler, S., & Lichter, D. T. (2020). Cohabitation and marriage: Complexity and diversity in union-formation patterns. *Journal of Marriage and Family, 82*(1), 35–61.
Schoeni, R. F., Freedman, V. A., Cornman, J. C., & Seltzer, J. A. (2022). The strength of Parent–Adult Child ties in biological families and stepfamilies: Evidence from time diaries from older adults. *Demography, 59*(5), 1821–1842.
Schwemmer, C., & Wieczorek, O. (2020). The methodological divide of sociology: Evidence from two decades of journal publications. *Sociology, 54*(1), 3–21.
Smart, C. (2007). *Personal life: New directions in sociological thinking*. Polity Press.
Smart, C., Davies, K., Heaphy, B., & Mason, J. (2012). Difficult friendships and ontological insecurity. *Sociological Review, 60*(1), 91–109.
Soler, J. H., Caldwell, C. H., Córdova, D., Harper, G., & Bauermeister, J. A. (2018). Who counts as family? Family typologies, family support, and family undermining among young adult gay and bisexual men. *Sexuality Research and Social Policy, 15*(2), 123–138.
Stack, C. B. (1974). *All our Kin: Strategies for survival in a black community*. Harper and Row.
Taylor, R., Chatters, L., Cross, C. J., & Mouzon, D. (2022). Fictive Kin Networks among African Americans, Black Caribbeans, and Non-Latino Whites. *Journal of Family Issues, 43*(1), 20–46.
U.S. National Center for Health Statistics. (2014). *Recent declines in nonmarital childbearing in the United States* (Data Brief No. 162). Retrieved from https://www.cdc.gov/nchs/data/databriefs/db162.pdf
Wall, K., Widmer, E. D., Gauthier, J. A., Česnuitytė, V., & Gouveia, R. (2018). *Families and personal networks: An international comparative perspective*. Springer.

Weeks, J., Heaphy, B., & Donovan, C. (2001). *Same sex intimacies: Families of choice and other life experiments*. Routledge.
Weis, L., Eisenhart, M., Weisner, T. S., Cobb, P., Duncan, G. J., Albro, E., et al. (2019). Exemplary mixed-methods research studies compiled by the mixed methods working group. *Teachers College Record, 121*(10), 1–34.
West, C., & Zimmerman, D. H. (1987). Doing gender. *Gender and Society, 2*, 125–151.
Weston, K. (1991). *Families we choose: Lesbians, Gays, Kinship*. Columbia University Press.
Wilkinson, E., & Bell, D. (2012). Ties that blind: On not seeing (or looking) beyond 'the family'. *Families, Relationships, and Societies, 1*(3), 423–429.
Willey, A. (2016). *Undoing monogamy*. Duke University Press.
Williams, M., Sloan, L., & Brookfield, C. (2017). A tale of two sociologies: Analyzing versus critique in UK sociology. *Sociological Research Online, 22*(4), 132–151.

Chapter 4
Delayed Fertility as a Driver of Fertility Decline?

Eva Beaujouan

4.1 Introduction

A major transformation of life in the last decades has been the delay in fertility – that is, the decrease in fertility among people below age 25 to 30 (Beaujouan & Toulemon, 2021; Lesthaeghe, 2016; Sobotka et al., 2011). At the same time that fertility has been delayed, the proportion of people having children later in life has increased, but in many countries, completed fertility has declined. In this chapter I (re)consider the extent to which these three phenomena –fertility delay, increase in later fertility, and fertility decline – are related. I examine whether fertility delay causes fertility decline and review evidence that an increasing number of people are facing constraints to childbearing in later life. Finally, I discuss the relevance of changes in partnership dynamics for fertility decline, as well as some implications of fertility delay on future completed fertility.

I take a cohort and life course approach. While I acknowledge the temporality of fertility behavior and the importance of period "shocks" (e.g., recessions, pandemics), a cohort approach is the most natural way to examine the link between fertility timing (i.e., delay) and fertility quantum: the key question is, after all, whether the same people who delay fertility earlier in life wind up with fewer children at the end of their reproductive window. To explore overall trends as well as cross-country variation, I cover a range of low fertility countries at different stages of fertility delay and with different childbearing contexts over the 1940–80 birth cohorts.

E. Beaujouan (✉)
Wittgenstein Centre for Demography and Global Human Capital (IIASA, OeAW, University of Vienna), University of Vienna, Vienna, Austria
e-mail: eva.beaujouan@univie.ac.at

R. Schoen (ed.), *The Demography of Transforming Families*, The Springer Series on Demographic Methods and Population Analysis 56,
https://doi.org/10.1007/978-3-031-29666-6_4

4.2 Recent Trends in Early, Late, and Completed Fertility in Low Fertility Countries

4.2.1 The Mean Age at First Birth Has Increased

Fifty years after the first signs of delayed fertility in Western Europe, the average age at which women have their first child is now increasing in countries of most world areas (Bongaarts et al., 2017; Lima et al., 2018; Neels et al., 2017). Figure 4.1 displays the increase in women's mean age at first birth in selected low fertility countries in Europe, North America and East Asia among the cohorts born between 1940 and 1980. The mean age at first birth started increasing among women born in the 1940–50s in the countries of North America, Western and Southern Europe and East Asia (see also Frejka & Sardon, 2006). In most Eastern Europe countries, there has been a more recent but strong increase in the mean age at first birth among

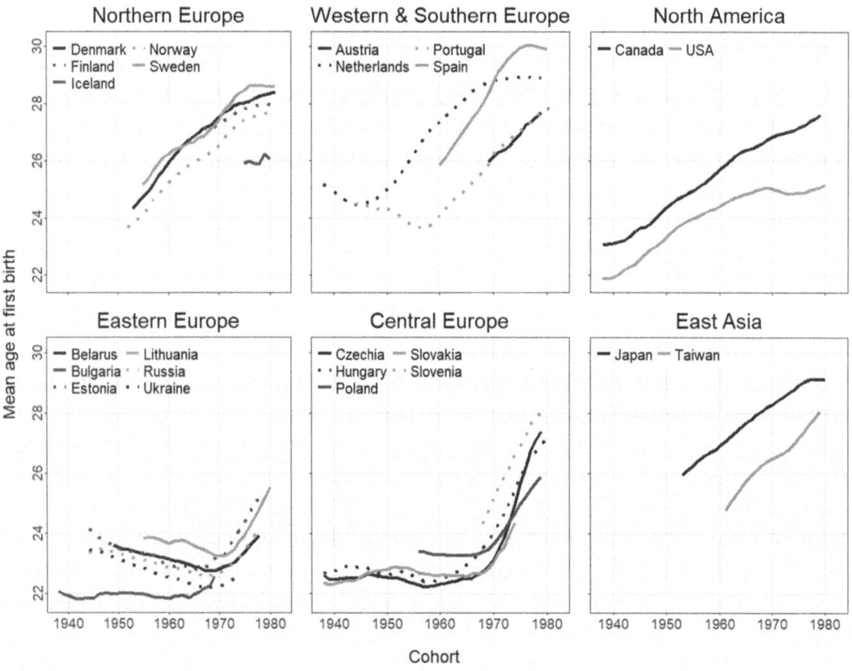

Source: Human Fertility Database (2022).

Note: Mean age at first birth is calculated as the average of cohort fertility schedules, mostly up to age 41.

Fig. 4.1 Mean age at first birth in Europe, North America and East Asia, women born between 1940 and 1980

women born in the 1960s. Compared with other low fertility countries, the Eastern European countries are at an earlier stage of their "postponement transition" (Kocourková & Šťastná, 2021). In some countries, such as the Netherlands and Spain, the mean age at first birth appears to have stabilized across birth cohorts, as well as periods (Neels et al., 2017). Variability in first birth schedule has also stabilized in these countries, which suggests that the capacity to further delay the first birth towards later ages may be limited (Kohler & Ortega, 2002; Nathan & Pardo, 2019).

4.2.2 Large Cross-Country Differences with Regard to Later Fertility

The increase in mean age at first birth can be driven by a decrease in first birth rates at younger ages, an increase at older ages, or a combination of both. To disentangle trends in earlier and later fertility in the low fertility countries, and also link them to completed fertility, Fig. 4.2 compares changes in cumulated cohort fertility rate (CCFR) up to age 30 (CCFR30) and between age 30 and 43 (CCFR30–43) as well as changes in the CFR up to age 43 (presumably close to completed fertility; CCFR43) for the cohorts born 1940–80 in selected low-fertility countries. Across all countries shown but to varying extents, fertility below age 30 has declined and fertility between age 30 and 43 has increased. Increases in later fertility can (partially) compensate for decreases in earlier fertility, so that completed fertility remains more or less stable. As seen in Fig. 4.2, with the exception of the United States, decreases in CFR30 have outweighed increases in CFR30-43, and the CFR43 has declined. Nevertheless, the degree to which increases in CFR30-43 have offset decreases in CFR30 differs quite a bit across the countries shown. For example, the drop in fertility before age 30 was similar in Austria and Sweden, but the increase in later fertility in Sweden was much larger than in Austria: completed fertility remained almost stable there, while it decreased quickly in Austria.

Many studies have confirmed that increases in later fertility have rarely completely offset decreases in earlier fertility, but also that there is substantial cross-country variation (Beaujouan & Toulemon, 2021; Frejka & Calot, 2001; Neels & De Watcher, 2010; Sobotka et al., 2011). Compared to women born in 1945–50, women born in the late 1960s in Sweden and the United States had fewer children earlier in life but more children later in life, such that their completed fertility was more or less comparable with their predecessors in earlier cohorts (Sobotka et al., 2011). In contrast, in the same birth cohorts in Austria and Spain, the increase in later fertility was much smaller in magnitude than the decrease in early fertility, resulting in a strong decrease in completed fertility (Sobotka et al., 2011). The decline in completed fertility in most countries is particularly attributable to a decline in second and higher order birth rates, but childlessness has also risen

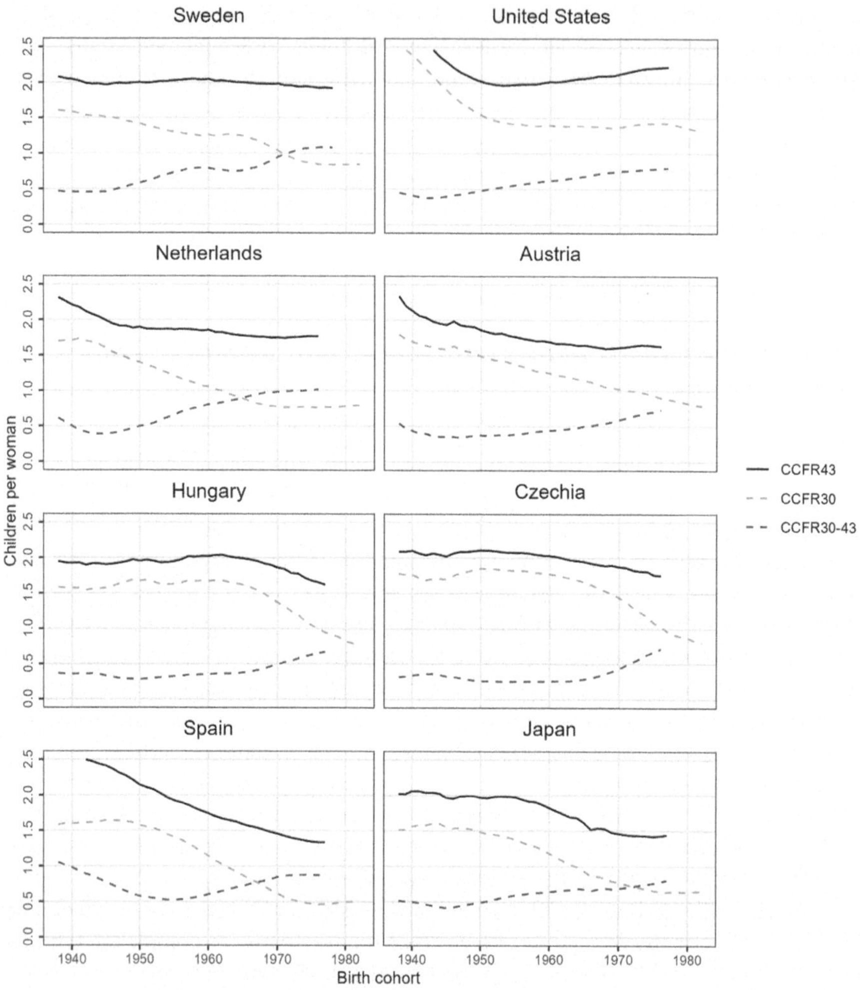

Source: Human Fertility Database (2022)

Note: I chose age 30 as the cut-off because mean age at childbearing has passed age 30 in the birth cohorts examined. In addition, from this age, biological factors slowly begin to constrain female fertility.

Fig. 4.2 Cumulated cohort fertility up to age 30, between age 30 and age 43, and by age 43 in selected low-fertility countries, women born between 1938 and 1982

quickly in Southern Europe, Western Europe and East Asia (Frejka & Sardon, 2006; Sobotka, 2017, 2021; Zeman et al., 2018).

In most countries, delay and decrease in completed fertility occurred within the same birth cohorts. Figure 4.2 shows nonetheless that decreases in earlier fertility have not always coincided with decreases in completed fertility: across several cohorts in Japan, Sweden and the Netherlands, completed fertility remained stable despite a drop in earlier fertility. In addition, in the Netherlands and Spain, a sharp decrease in completed fertility was observed in the late 1930s-early 1940s birth cohorts, even though fertility below age 30 was rather stable. This is explained by family size limitation at parity 3 and higher, prevalent in these cohorts in the Netherlands and Spain, irrespective of fertility delay (Zeman et al., 2018).

4.2.3 Fertility Delay or Postponement?

Scholars have commonly referred to the widely observed decline in fertility below age 25 or 30 as "fertility postponement", and the increase in later life fertility as "fertility recuperation" (see extensive discussion in Frejka, 2011). The terms "postponement" and "recuperation" suggest that people who do not have children at an earlier age entertain the idea of having children later, and then try to achieve a specific, pre-set fertility target later in life (Frejka, 2011). It is not obvious that this is the case, neither empirically, as we have shown previously, nor conceptually. Research suggests that most people – especially most young people – lack concrete, long-term fertility intentions (Bachrach & Morgan, 2013; Ní Bhrolcháin & Beaujouan, 2019; Trinitapoli & Yeatman, 2018). Intended family size primarily reflects a person's perceptions of the normative family (Bachrach & Morgan, 2013). Young adults in particular report wanting a number of children that is close to the number of children observed in the previous generation and their own number of siblings (Heiland et al., 2008; Régnier-Loilier, 2006). Younger peoples' fertility intentions predict their shorter-term fertility behavior fairly well, but poorly predict their fertility behavior in the longer-term (Schoen et al., 1999). Also later in the life course, fertility aspirations (intentions, desires, expectations) are rather unstable and only weakly related to future fertility (Beaujouan et al., 2019; Buhr & Huinink, 2017; Gemmill, 2018; Gray et al., 2013; Rybińska & Morgan, 2019). In sum, fertility aspirations do not appear to be a meaningful construct for many people (Ní Bhrolcháin, 1992; Schoen, 2004).

Given the nebulous nature of fertility aspirations particularly earlier in life, it seems unlikely that fertility delay has primarily been driven by a conscious decision to "postpone" and then "recuperate" fertility later in life once the structural and individual conditions for having the intended number of children were met. In the birth cohorts in which fertility delay occurred, young people probably lacked a clearly defined idea about whether they wanted to have children (and if so, how many) at the same time that they were already having comparatively fewer children than young people in the previous cohort. Instead of "postponement", fertility delay could just as well reflect that fertility has become a non-issue for young adults in more recent cohorts. Compared to their predecessors, members of more recent cohorts are more likely to be enrolled in education, unemployed or at the very beginning of their career well into their reproductive windows – all situations that are hardly compatible with childbearing (Mills et al., 2011; Ní Bhrolcháin & Beaujouan, 2012). It seems likely that such normative changes to early adult life have led young people to defer the decision to have children. It is also possible that fertility delay has been the result of lower fertility aspirations. In either case, there is no particular reason to expect that later fertility would systematically increase in response to decreases in fertility in earlier life (Ní Bhrolcháin & Toulemon, 2005). "Fertility postponement" and "fertility recuperation" would thus appear to be misnomers. I therefore prefer to use the more neutral term "fertility delay" as opposed to "fertility postponement" when referring to the decrease in fertility rates below age 30 (as compared to the previous birth cohorts) and increase in mean age at first birth. In the same vein, I prefer to use "increase in later fertility" as opposed to "fertility recuperation" to refer to increases in fertility rates above age 30 that (sometimes) follow a drop in earlier fertility.

4.3 Does Fertility Delay Cause Fertility Decline?

To what extent does fertility delay actually *cause* fertility decline? Or, in other words, to what extent does fertility delay *per se* act as a barrier to family formation and expansion? Most of the studies on the relationship between fertility delay and decline are descriptive or correlational, and hence provide little evidence of causality. It nevertheless seems probable that the fertility decline observed in cohorts born after 1940 is at least partly attributable to fertility delay for at least three reasons.

First, fertility delay implies that more people are exposed to biological constraints when they attempt to begin or expand a family. The ability to give birth to a live child decreases exponentially from age 32 among women (Broekmans et al., 2007). Other less tangible constraints related to age also seem to exist, whether cultural, normative or individual (Beaujouan et al., 2019). Consequently, women who – consciously or not – defer childbearing to a later age are much more likely to be affected by biological or normative constraints to childbearing (Leridon & Slama, 2008; te Velde et al., 2012).

Age constraints appear to be most relevant for second and higher order births (Sobotka et al., 2011). Given the overwhelming preference for two children in many countries (Sobotka & Beaujouan, 2014), one can expect that people who have had a first child will want a second one. Figure 4.3 displays the probability of having a second child by age among women who already have one child, in the same countries as in Fig. 4.2 across the cohorts born 1946–81. Figure 4.3 confirms that the probability of having a second birth in the 30s and early 40s increased massively among women who delayed having a first child (only from the 1960s for Hungary and Czechia). Sweden and Spain had the highest second birth probabilities at age

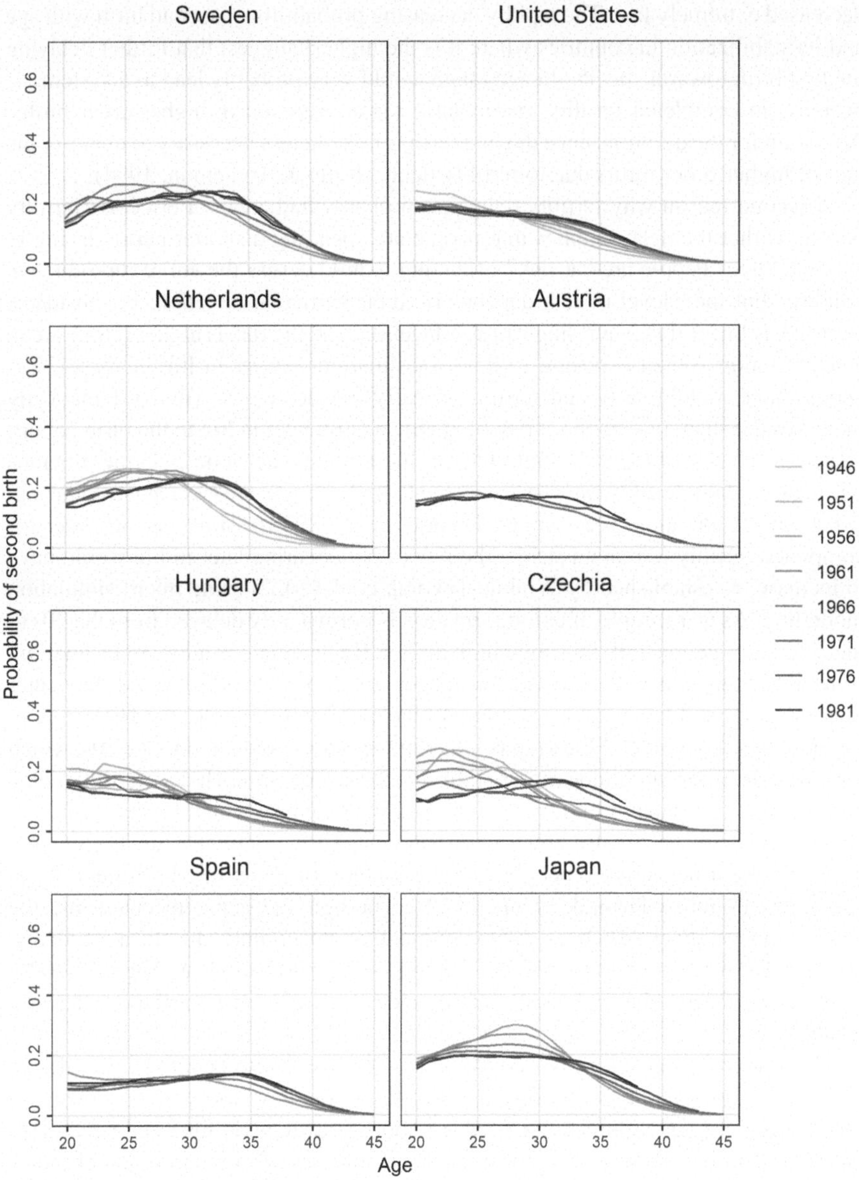

Source: Human Fertility Database

Fig. 4.3 Probability of second birth by age, conditional on having a first child

35 (around 20% of women with one child) and at age 40 (around 7%). It is however striking that from age 35, in all countries observed –even those that delayed having a first child most such as the Netherlands and Spain–, second birth probabilities

decreased extremely fast. The rapidly decreasing probability of second birth with age and its stabilization in countries where it is the highest suggest that further delaying the first birth towards the 35–45 age range would very probably lead to a systematic decrease in completed fertility, particularly via a reduction in higher order births. Adjusting for the duration since the first birth is nonetheless necessary to quantify the loss of higher order births due to fertility delay (Rallu & Toulemon, 1994).

A second reason why fertility delay has probably had a causal effect on fertility decline is that the delay implies that people are spending a shorter period trying to have children. People are "at risk" of having a child across the entire reproductive window, but their level of risk depends on their particular situation. For instance, their risk is lower if they are single or in education, and the risk is higher if they are in a stable union. When exposure to low-risk situations earlier in life increases, less people have a child early and fertility in early life decreases. This systematically increases the share of persons at risk of having a child later in life in the birth cohort. Hence, if the risk of having a child later in life remains the same as in the previous birth cohort, later fertility rates increase due to higher exposure (which we could call structural recuperation, see Winkler-Dworak et al. (2022)). However, in order for completed fertility to remain stable, the risk of childbearing later in life would have to increase, as established by Winkler-Dworak et al. (2022) using micro-simulation modelling. As an example, if union formation is normatively delayed from the 20s to the 30s, more people will be single in their 20s. Being single is a low-risk situation, so fertility in the 20s will decrease. More people will be in their 30s when they enter a partnership, and hence more people will have children in their 30s. However, so far, the overall risk of childbearing is lower in the 30s as compared to the 20s, which corresponds to lower childbearing risk for the same exposure. Hence, fertility delay does provoke systematic fertility decline, and the extent to which increases in later fertility compensate for decreases in earlier fertility is contingent upon changing behavior, for instance more people entering a union or increasing birth intensity at later ages (Winkler-Dworak et al., 2022). Through the same mechanisms, the cumulation of shocks such as unemployment or uncertainty due to a pandemic also creates periods of lower risk of having children (Comolli & Vignoli, 2021; Luppi et al., 2020; Matysiak et al., 2020), and can eventually contribute to fertility decline.

Third, there is evidence that fertility delay can also cause people to want fewer children, or none at all. As fertility is delayed, people have more time to invest in other activities (e.g., volunteering, hobbies, sports, travel, night life), and get used to the idea of living without children or in small families. The interference of childbearing with these other activities seems to frequently result in a reduced desire to have a(nother) child (Berrington & Pattaro, 2014; Morgan, 2003). Morgan (2003, p. 599) notes that "continuing delay and competing opportunities translate some delayed fertility into forgone fertility". Particularly, those who postpone fertility have smaller families than those who started having children earlier (Andersson et al., 2009; Castro, 2014; Kocourková & Šťastná, 2021; Kohler et al., 2002), and those who strongly intend to have a child after age 30 are less likely to have it than younger people (Beaujouan et al., 2019; Brzozowska & Beaujouan, 2021; Kocourková & Šťastná, 2021).

To conclude, while there are reasons to believe that fertility delay has contributed to fertility decline, it is also clear that the relationship between fertility delay and fertility decline is not entirely straightforward. Fertility delay and decline sometimes occur independently (see Fig. 4.2), and there is no evidence that increases in age at first birth between the 1952 and 1972 birth cohorts were related to decreases in completed cohort fertility across European countries (Beaujouan & Toulemon, 2021). Also, the family size of mothers starting to have children in their 30s remained strikingly low in some countries even though more people were having children at these ages (Beaujouan et al., 2023). Fertility delay is clearly not the only factor driving fertility decline, but studies that quantify the relationship between fertility delay and fertility decline are rare. So far, the direct negative impact of further fertility delay on completed fertility appears to be modest, around 0.1 to 0.2 fewer children per woman for 3–4 years of delay in the mean age of first child in France where completed fertility is around 2 children per woman (Leridon, 2017).

4.4 Evidence Suggests That an Increasing Number of People Are Experiencing Constraints to Childbearing in Later Reproductive Life

In the following, I review evidence that many people experience constraints to childbearing in later reproductive life: namely, (a) an increasing share of people would still like to have a(nother) child in the late 30s and 40s; (b) the use of medically-assisted reproduction (MAR) has increased especially among older persons; and (c) behavior becomes more conducive to childbearing as people near the end of the reproductive window.

4.4.1 Many People in Their Late 30s and 40s Would Still Like to Start or Expand Their Family

Permanent childlessness has risen dramatically across Europe (Sobotka, 2017). The extent to which childlessness is voluntary, a consequence of perpetual delay, or due to infertility is a debated topic in demography and sociology (Berrington, 2004; Fiori et al., 2017; Letherby, 2002). The instability of fertility aspirations across the life course makes it difficult to determine the extent to which childlessness is "voluntary" or "involuntary". Nevertheless, fertility intentions do tend to become more concrete as life unfolds (Ní Bhrolcháin & Beaujouan, 2019). Examining fertility intentions and fertility behavior as people near the end of their reproductive window therefore constitutes a reasonable first step in quantifying the share of persons who

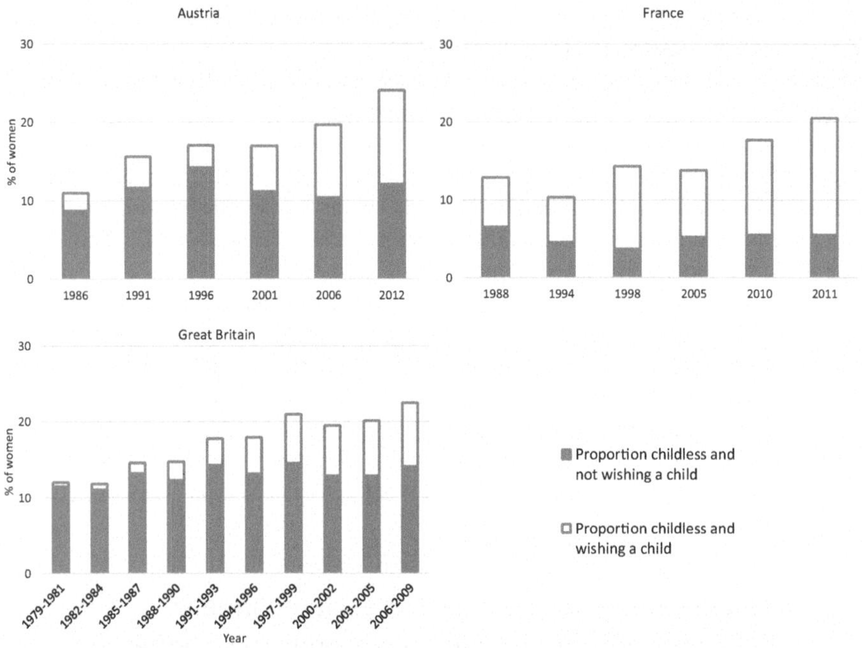

Sources: Austrian micro-censuses 1986-2012; French fertility surveys (varied sources, with small variation in formulation of the questions on intentions); Centre for Population Change British General Household Survey database (Beaujouan et al., 2011, 2015; Ní Bhrolcháin et al., 2011).

Fig. 4.4 Share of women aged 35–39 in Austria (survey years 1986–2012), France (1988–2011), and the United Kingdom (1979–2009) who are childless, decomposed between those who want a child and those who do not

unintentionally end up childless or with fewer children than they would have liked to have had because they "postponed too long" (Berrington, 2017; Tanturri & Mencarini, 2008).

Figure 4.4 shows the share of women childless at age 35–39 in Austria, France and the United Kingdom, distinguishing between those who did and did not want a child. The change in the proportion of childless women who still wanted a child at age 35–39 provides an indication of whether the share of involuntary childlessness was increasing as fertility delay was unrolling. In all the three countries, the share of women childless at age 35–39 more or less doubled from over 10 to over 20% in approximatively the same period (late 1980s to around 2010). The share of women who intended to remain childless varied greatly across countries (5% in France, 10% in Austria, 13% in the United Kingdom) but remained more or less stable over time. Most of the increase in the share of women childless at age 35–39 can thus be attributed to women who still wanted to have a child. The constancy of this feature across three very different contexts is remarkable.

Other evidence likewise suggests that involuntary childlessness and late fertility intentions are substantial and increasing. According to survey data, a non-negligeable share of childless women have tried to have a child but did not have one. In the United Kingdom, 15% of childless women born in 1970 said that they were childless due to their own or their partner's infertility (Berrington, 2017), which represents about 3% of all women and remains relatively low. In contrast, in Italy 29% of permanently childless women surveyed in 2002 reported that they had experienced difficulties while trying to have a child (Tanturri & Mencarini, 2008). In addition, more than half of childless women in Spain aged 45–49 in 2018 still wished a child (that is, around 10% of all women) (Esteve & Treviño, 2019). Among women aged 40–42 with one child, the share intending to have another child increased from almost none in 1980 to around 9% in 2003–2009 in the United Kingdom (Beaujouan & Sobotka, 2022) and from 1.5% in 1986 to 15% in 2016 in Austria (Beaujouan, 2022). At other parities however, there was little increase in the share intending to have another child, possibly because most people either stop having children once they have had the two normative children, or stop wishing for additional children if they are older and conscious of the difficulties to have them.

Together, Fig. 4.4 and evidence of a rise in late fertility intentions suggest that many people experience constraints to childbearing in later reproductive life. Moreover, it appears that fertility delay is causing a substantial share of people to fall short of their desired family size.

4.4.2 Medically-Assisted Reproduction Has Increased Particularly Among Older Age Groups

MAR has increased dramatically: across the low fertility countries, 2 to 7% of all children are currently born with the support of MAR (Gliozheni et al., 2021). Research shows that most of the increase in infertility treatments between 2008 and 2017 concerned women older than 34 years in France, and that the number of babies conceived through assisted reproductive technologies (ART) among older women has increased faster than the number of ART-babies among younger women in Australia (Ben Messaoud et al., 2020; Lazzari et al., 2021). Also, the share of treatments provided to women age 40+ has increased considerably: about 22% of in vitro fertilization (IVF) /intracytoplasmic sperm injection treatments were provided to women aged 40+ in 2018, compared with 15% in 2005 (author's calculations for 21 European countries based on Andersen et al., 2009; Wyns et al., 2022).

The marked increase in the uptake of MAR among women at the end of their reproductive window suggests that a growing share of women are trying to overcome age-related biological constraints to fertility. Most likely, this is due to the rising share of women who are trying to have children relatively late (Beaujouan, 2020). It is also possible, though unlikely (Moreau et al., 2010; Olsen et al., 1998; Sobotka et al., 2008), that access to MAR has increased more for older than for younger women who needed it. The rising number of extremely late first births (48 years and older) suggests that increasing use of MAR is fueled by increasing demand at very late ages (Beaujouan, 2020).

4.4.3 Behavior Becomes More Conducive to Childbearing as People Near the End of Their Reproductive Window

As a further indication that many people face constraints to childbearing in later life, there are hints that behavior appears to become more conductive to childbearing as people approach the end of their reproductive windows (biological or social). Few studies have examined how people react to fertility deadlines (Wagner et al., 2019), so for now this remains a working hypothesis. There is however evidence that people relax their requirements for childbearing in their late 30s and early 40s. For example, people appear more willing to have a child without a partner as they near the end of the reproductive window. Childless people aged 35–37 in Germany are more likely to intend to have a child in the short-term even when they are not in a partnership (Wagner et al., 2019). Using the Belgian census, Schnor (2022) showed that more than half of the women who have a child using MAR without a partner are over 35 years old.

Although factors such as country-level unemployment and welfare regime are related to fertility at all ages (Neels et al., 2012; Pifarré i Arolas, 2017), there is also some evidence that later fertility is less affected by negative conditions. Campisi et al. (2022) showed in the Nordic countries that variation in fertility rates of women below age 30 are more strongly related to the area's economic conditions than the fertility rates of women above age 30. Across Europe, the Great Recession had a strong effect on first birth risk among women below age 30 but no effect on first birth risk among women above age 30 (Goldstein et al., 2013; Neels et al., 2012). However, older women experienced a decrease in higher order birth rates (Goldstein et al., 2013).

Finally, there is some evidence that people try to accelerate childbearing later in life. The later people enter a first union, the faster they have their first child afterwards (Compans & Beaujouan, 2022). However, because more women have reduced fertility from age 35 onward, biological constraints may interfere with behavioral acceleration, so that looking only at birth timing is not sufficient to assess behavioral changes. Future research should investigate whether other indicators of behavioral acceleration (e.g., irregular use of contraception, less stringent criteria for a partner) increase as people near the end of their reproductive windows.

4.5 Changes in Partnership Dynamics Have Contributed to Fertility Decline

Considerable societal changes have taken place since the onset of fertility delay, including the introduction of the pill, increases in educational attainment, and increases in female labor force participation (Balbo et al., 2013; Wilkins, 2019). Recent progress in modelling demonstrates that, by reducing the time spent "at risk" of childbearing, a longer time spent in education tends to systematically reduce the total number of births by the end of reproductive life (Bijlsma & Wilson, 2020; Ciganda & Todd, 2021). Partnership dynamics have changed as well: median age at first cohabiting union has increased in a number of countries among men and women born since the 1950s, and risks of separation and divorce have skyrocketed (Sobotka & Berghammer, 2021; Sobotka & Toulemon, 2008). Consequently, the time available to have a family has declined considerably (Ciganda & Todd, 2019; Fostik et al., 2021; Winkler-Dworak et al., 2019).

Most people consider having a partner as a prerequisite for starting a family (Wagner et al., 2019). In the past, fertility was closely linked with entry into the first union. Over the past decades, the link between entering a first union and having a first child has loosened considerably, particularly in Western Europe. Most people have a partner at some point in their 20s, but many will not have a child within this relationship and many partnerships will breakup. Hence, people are more likely to be single when they start thinking of having children in their 30s (Mikolai, 2017). This has of course strong implications for fertility, as less time spent in a union contributes to lower fertility (Ciganda & Todd, 2019; Fostik et al., 2021). Nishikido et al. (2022) recently found that the reduced likelihood of having a partner before age 30 in Spain, as opposed to lower birth intensities within unions, was a crucial aspect of the difference in first birth rates in Spain and Sweden.

The decrease in union stability (more breakups, more divorce) is also highly relevant for fertility. Despite an increased risk of childbearing in a second union as compared to a stable first union, people who separate have lower fertility. This has been found in Europe, Latin America, the United States and in other contexts as well (see e.g., Fostik et al., 2021; Meggiolaro & Ongaro, 2010; Thomson et al., 2012; Van Bavel et al., 2012). Microsimulations also find a negative relationship between union separation and fertility (Winkler-Dworak et al., 2017), suggesting that the relationship is not only linked to the selection of people more apt to have children into more stable unions, but also because separation shortens the period one spends in situation conducive to childbearing. Among women born in the 1980s who ever entered a union, the microsimulations estimated a loss of 28% of completed fertility for those who separated in Italy, 18% in the United Kingdom and 20% in France. The impact was largest for higher order births. Further research confirms a strong relationship between partnership trajectories and childlessness in Norway (Hart, 2019) and Finland (Saarela & Skirbekk, 2019), where persons who lived in several short unions and those who entered the latest their first union and separated quickly were most likely to be permanently childless. Further investigations of the causal effect of delayed unions as well as of the higher frequency of "trial first unions" (short first childless unions) for fertility levels are warranted, but we can expect a clear depressing effect on fertility (Jalovaara & Fasang, 2017).

4.6 Some Implications of Fertility Delay for Future Completed Fertility

4.6.1 Access to MAR Will Increasingly Contribute to Completed Fertility

Given that more people will not start trying to have a child until later in life, access to MAR has and will become more relevant for completed fertility. The contribution of MAR to overall and particularly later fertility is already far from negligeable. It has been estimated that babies born with the support of IVF will comprise between 3.8 and 5% of children born to the 1978 birth cohort in Denmark (Sobotka et al., 2008) and around 4% for this same birth cohort in Australia (Lazzari, 2021). In Australia, it is predicted that ART will contribute to more than 25% of births after age 40 among women born in 1986 (extrapolated success and treatment rates scenario). If this is the case, ART would account for more than half of the fertility recuperation between the 1968 and 1986 birth cohorts, and the cohort fertility rate would be of 1.9 instead of 1.8 children per woman (Lazzari, 2021). Such scenarios are very likely. MAR is already relatively effective, but its effectiveness decreases with age, so it cannot be considered as a substitute to beginning attempts to have a child earlier in life (Leridon, 2004; Sobotka & Beaujouan, 2018). The success of non-donor IVF after age 40 has hardly improved over time (Sobotka & Beaujouan, 2018), but other forms of MAR such as oocyte banking, oocyte donation and surrogacy offer better chances of success to have children at older ages (CDC, 2018; Kocourkova et al., 2014; Passet-Wittig & Bujard, 2021). The increased uptake of such methods will probably improve the success of MAR, particularly at older ages, and hence become even more important for overall fertility levels. Yet, the appropriateness and efficiency of MAR as a stimulant of late fertility and fertility in general is still to be discussed in most societies (Baldwin, 2018; Rainer et al., 2011; van de Wiel, 2020).

4.6.2 Life Conditions in the 30s and Early 40s Will Become More Relevant

In a context of delayed fertility, life circumstances in the 30s and early 40s – and work and health in particular – have and will become more important determinants of completed fertility. By age 30, work has become a central component of most people's lives. Work-related factors (e.g., dedication, satisfaction, working conditions, instability) are thus likely to be much more relevant for fertility in the 30s than in the 20s. Women who work many hours may be more dedicated to their career and experience more stress, leaving less space for building a family (Bratti & Tatsiramos, 2011). On the other hand, having a good position on the labor market and job flexibility act as resources for rearing children (Rondinelli et al., 2010). At equal parity, highly-educated women, who not only tend to have the best job conditions but also better gender equality in the household, are most likely to have children in that age range (Berrington & Pattaro, 2014; Neels & De Watcher, 2010; Nicoletti & Tanturri, 2008; Rondinelli et al., 2006).

Relative to people in their 20s, people in their 30s and 40s are more likely to have a long-term illness or report worse health, which may prevent them from having children (Gray et al., 2013; Heiland et al., 2008; Mynarska & Wróblewska, 2017). Subjective well-being (e.g., stress, life satisfaction) and its relationship to fertility may also vary across adulthood (Greil, 1997; Mencarini et al., 2018). So far, little is known about how such individual characteristics (e.g., work, health, well-being) affect fertility at different points in the reproductive life span.

4.6.3 The Effect of Further Delay on Completed Fertility Will Depend on the Country

In some countries, there is probably enough leeway for most people to delay having a first child without affecting their completed fertility: they would still be fertile when trying to have a second or higher order child, despite having started later. This seemed to be the case still recently in France, and probably in many other countries. A simulation of the biological consequences of a delay of first births by 3–4 years in the French context shows a rather small drop in completed cohort fertility of 0.1–0.2 children, of which about 10–20% could be compensated by assisted reproductive technologies (Leridon, 2017). In France, Toulemon and Mazuy (2001) also projected that later childbearing in the 1980 birth cohorts (average around age 30 years) would only marginally affect their completed fertility. This suggests that, in France, cohorts have not reached yet their biological limits and most of the slight drop in completed fertility can be attributed to other elements. Further fertility delay would probably have a stronger negative impact in Southern Europe where birth schedules are already very late, and possibly weaker in Eastern Europe where the mean age of first child is still relatively young. In a study comparing France and Spain, Compans et al. (2022) show that, despite similar transition rates to second birth by age in the two countries, the very different profiles of age at first birth (much later in Spain) corresponds to a substantially lower proportion of Spanish women proceeding to a second birth than in France.

4.7 Conclusions and Outlook

Among the birth cohorts born since 1940, the proportion of women who have had a child by age 30 has steadily declined. Fertility delay probably reflects the deferral of fertility decisions until later in life due to structural and ideational changes in the conditions of early adulthood (e.g., longer time spent in education, delay in union formation). Overall, the arguments and evidence brought together in this chapter support the hypothesis that fertility delay has directly contributed to declines in cohort fertility. I have argued that fertility delay has directly contributed to fertility decline because, once they try to conceive, more people experience biological and normative age constraints to attaining the number of children they want. Another way that fertility delay affects completed fertility is by shortening the period during which one is "at risk" of childbearing, and there is also evidence that delay causes people to want fewer children. Ongoing changes in partnership dynamics also seem to contribute to fertility decline. In some countries, an increase in later fertility has at least partially compensated for the decrease in earlier life fertility. The potential to offset fertility delay by intensifying efforts to have children later in life may be more limited in countries in which childbearing already takes place very late. In light of fertility delay, conditions of life in the 30s and early 40s (work, health) and access to MAR will be more relevant predictors of completed fertility in the future.

Much more empirical work is needed to understand the relationship between fertility delay and fertility decline. Further studies would be helpful for assessing the (in)flexibility of different populations with regard to their fertility schedule and the existence of a ceiling at later ages, and for quantifying the extent to which fertility delay contributes to fertility decline. Fertility delay appears most relevant for second and higher order births (Kohler & Ortega, 2002), but estimating how many higher order births are missed as a result of fertility delay is difficult. Possibly, using parity progression ratios by age over time allows better such estimation, but again it is challenging to evaluate which children are missed due to "too much" delay, and which ones are no longer particularly expected. Comparative studies combining fertility history and fertility intention questions over time appear to have potential in that respect (Beaujouan, 2022; Guzzo & Hayford, 2023), but samples large enough to allow detailed decomposition by age are scarce.

Inequalities that might give way to and also arise from fertility delay are currently not well understood. For instance, highly-educated women have their children later and may therefore be more affected by biological and normative constraints to later fertility, but lower-educated women are less likely to use MAR at any age even in countries where it is financed by the state (Goisis et al., 2020). Also, unequal childbearing opportunities may arise from inequalities in working conditions (e.g., flexibility, income, childcare) or from health inequalities, which are more relevant at older ages. Fertility delay may thus accentuate inequalities associated with socio-economic status and education in particular. Finally, gender inequality may become increasingly pertinent as fertility is delayed, as men face less of a biological deadline than women. So far gender differences in the reproductive window have been primarily relevant for fertility in second unions or stepfamilies, but one can still wonder whether the ability of men to change partners in order to have children even when they are in their 50s and older may give them more power over women. Men delay fertility to a lesser extent than women, suggesting that if such gender inequalities develop, it will not occur until later (Beaujouan, 2020).

Acknowledgments I thank Bob Schoen and Brian Buh for stimulating discussions, Katja Köppen for feedback and Katie Bowen for language editing. This research was funded by the BIC.LATE grant from the European Research Council, European Union's Horizon 2020 research and innovation programme, grant Agreement No 101001410. The Office for National Statistics provided access to the British General Household Survey series (originally constructed by the ESRC Centre for Population Change).

References

Andersen, A. N., Goossens, V., Bhattacharya, S., Ferraretti, A. P., Kupka, M. S., De Mouzon, J., & Nygren, K. G. (2009). Assisted reproductive technology and intrauterine inseminations in Europe, 2005: Results generated from European registers by ESHRE. *Human Reproduction, 24*(6), 1267–1287. https://doi.org/10.1093/humrep/dep035

Andersson, G., Rønsen, M., Knudsen, L. B., Lappegård, T., Neyer, G., Skrede, K., Teschner, K., & Vikat, A. (2009). Cohort fertility patterns in the Nordic countries. *Demographic Research, 20*(14), 313–352. https://doi.org/10.4054/DemRes.2009.20.14

Bachrach, C. A., & Morgan, S. P. (2013). A cognitive–Social model of fertility intentions. *Population and Development Review, 39*(3), 459–485. https://onlinelibrary.wiley.com/doi/abs/10.1111/j.1728-4457.2013.00612.x

Balbo, N., Billari, F. C., & Mills, M. C. (2013). Fertility in advanced societies: A review of research. *European Journal of Population, 29*(1), 1–38. https://doi.org/10.1007/s10680-012-9277-y

Baldwin, K. (2018). Conceptualising women's motivations for social egg freezing and experience of reproductive delay. *Sociology of Health and Illness, 40*(5), 859–873. https://doi.org/10.1111/1467-9566.12728

Beaujouan, É. (2020). Latest-late fertility? Decline and resurgence of late parenthood across the low-fertility countries. *Population and Development Review, 46*(2), 219–247. https://doi.org/10.1111/padr.12334

Beaujouan, É. (2022). Late fertility intentions increase over time in Austria, but chances to have a child at later ages remain low. *Reproductive Biomedicine & Society Online, 14*, 125–139. https://doi.org/10.1016/j.rbms.2021.10.002

Beaujouan, É., & Sobotka, T. (2022). Is 40 the new 30? Increasing reproductive intentions and fertility rates beyond age 40. In D. Nikolaou & D. Seifer (Eds.), *Optimizing the management of fertility in women over 40* (pp. 3–18). Cambridge University Press. https://doi.org/10.1017/9781009025270.002

Beaujouan, É., & Toulemon, L. (2021). European countries with delayed childbearing are not those with lower fertility. *Genus, 77*(2), 1–15. https://doi.org/10.1186/s41118-020-00108-0

Beaujouan, É., Brown, J. J. J., & Ní Bhrolcháin, M. (2011). Reweighting the general household survey 1979-2007. *Population Trends, 145*, 119–145. https://doi.org/10.1057/pt.2011.21

Beaujouan, É., Ní Bhrolcháin, M., Berrington, A., & Falkingham, J. (2015). Centre for population change general household survey database, 1979–2009*: Special Licence Access [computer file]* (SN: 7666). Office for National Statistics. Social Survey Division [Original data producer]. http://discover.ukdataservice.ac.uk/catalogue?sn=7666

Beaujouan, É., Reimondos, A., Gray, E., Evans, A., & Sobotka, T. (2019). Declining realisation of reproductive intentions with age. *Human Reproduction, 34*(10), 1906–1914. https://doi.org/10.1093/humrep/dez150

Beaujouan, É., Zeman, K., & Nathan, M. (2023). Delayed first births and completed fertility across the 1940–1969 birth cohorts. *Demographic Research, 48*, 387–420. https://doi.org/10.4054/DemRes.2023.48.15

Ben Messaoud, K., Bouyer, J., & de La Rochebrochard, E. (2020). Infertility treatment in France, 2008–2017: A challenge of growing treatment needs at older ages. *American Journal of Public Health., 110*, 1418–1420. https://doi.org/10.2105/AJPH.2020.305781

Berrington, A. (2004). Perpetual postponers? Women's, men's and couple's fertility intentions and subsequent fertility behaviour. *Population Trends, 117*, 9–19.

Berrington, A. (2017). Childlessness in the UK. In M. Kreyenfeld & D. Konietzka (Eds.), *Childlessness in Europe: Contexts, causes, and consequences* (pp. 57–76). Springer Open. https://link.springer.com/book/10.1007/978-3-319-44667-7

Berrington, A., & Pattaro, S. (2014). Educational differences in fertility desires, intentions and behaviour: A life course perspective. *Advances in Life Course Research, 21*, 10–27. https://doi.org/10.1016/j.alcr.2013.12.003

Bijlsma, M. J., & Wilson, B. (2020). Modelling the socio-economic determinants of fertility: a mediation analysis using the parametric g-formula. *Journal of the Royal Statistical Society – Series A, 183*, 493–513. https://doi.org/10.1111/rssa.12520

Bongaarts, J., Mensch, B. S., & Blanc, A. K. (2017). Trends in the age at reproductive transitions in the developing world: The role of education. *Population Studies, 71*(2), 139–154. https://doi.org/10.1080/00324728.2017.1291986

Bratti, M., & Tatsiramos, K. (2011). The effect of delaying motherhood on the second childbirth in Europe. *Journal of Population Economics, 25*(1), 291–321. https://doi.org/10.1007/s00148-010-0341-9

Broekmans, F. J., Knauff, E. A. H., te Velde, E. R., Macklon, N. S., & Fauser, B. C. (2007). Female reproductive ageing: Current knowledge and future trends. *Trends in Endocrinology and Metabolism: TEM, 18*(2), 58–65. https://doi.org/10.1016/j.tem.2007.01.004

Brzozowska, Z., & Beaujouan, É. (2021). Assessing short-term fertility intentions and their realisation using the generations and gender survey: Pitfalls and challenges. *European Journal of Population, 37*, 405–416. https://doi.org/10.1007/s10680-020-09573-x

Buhr, P., & Huinink, J. (2017). Why childless men and women give up on having children. *European Journal of Population., 33*, 585–606. https://doi.org/10.1007/s10680-017-9429-1

Campisi, N., Kulu, H., Mikolai, J., Klüsener, S., & Myrskylä, M. (2022). A spatial perspective on the unexpected Nordic fertility decline: The relevance of economic and social contexts. *Applied Spatial Analysis and Policy., 16*, 1–31. https://doi.org/10.1007/s12061-022-09467-x

Castro, R. (2014). Late-entry-into-motherhood women are responsible for fertility recuperation. *Journal of Biosocial Science, 47*, 275–279. https://doi.org/10.1017/S0021932014000121

CDC. (2018). *Assisted reproductive technology.* 2016 *fertility clinic success rates report.* https://www.cdc.gov/art/reports/2016/fertility-clinic.html

Ciganda, D., & Todd, N. (2019). *The limits to fertility recuperation.* MPIDR working paper, WP 2019-02. https://www.demogr.mpg.de/papers/working/wp-2019-024.pdf

Ciganda, D., & Todd, N. (2021). Demographic models of the reproductive process: Past, interlude, and future. *Population Studies, 76*(3), 495–513. https://doi.org/10.1080/00324728.2021.1959943

Comolli, C. L., & Vignoli, D. (2021). Spreading uncertainty, shrinking birth rates: A natural experiment for Italy. *European Sociological Review, 37*(4), 555–570. https://doi.org/10.1093/esr/jcab001

Compans, M.-C., & Beaujouan, É. (2022). From union formation to first birth : The role of age at first cohabitation in the transition to motherhood and fatherhood. *Population (English Edition), 77*(3), 411–436. https://doi.org/10.3917/popu.2203.0439

Compans, M.-C., Beaujouan, É., & Suero García, C. (2022). Later fertility and birth intervals: A comparison of progressions to a second child between Spain and France [poster]. European Population Conference 2022. https://epc2022.popconf.org/abstracts/210401

Esteve, A., & Treviño, R. (2019). The main whys and wherefores of childlessness in Spain. *Perspectives Demogràfiques, 015, 1–4.*

Fiori, F., Rinesi, F., & Graham, E. (2017). Choosing to remain childless? A comparative study of fertility intentions among women and men in Italy and Britain. *European Journal of Population, 33*, 319–350. https://doi.org/10.1007/s10680-016-9404-2

Fostik, A. L., Soto, M. F., Ciganda, D., & Ruiz Vallejo, F. (2021). Union instability and fertility: An international perspective. *International population conference 2021 (IUSSP).* https://ipc2021.popconf.org/abstracts/210412

Frejka, T. (2011). The role of contemporary childbearing postponement and recuperation in shaping period fertility trends. *Comparative Population Studies, 36*(4), 927–958. https://doi.org/10.4232/10.CPoS-2011-20en

Frejka, T., & Calot, G. (2001). Cohort reproductive patterns in low-fertility countries. *Population and Development Review, 27*(1), 103–132. https://doi.org/10.1111/j.1728-4457.2001.00103.x

Frejka, T., & Sardon, J.-P. (2006). First birth trends in developed countries: Persistent parenthood postponement. *Demographic Research, 15*, 147–180. https://doi.org/10.4054/DemRes.2006.15.6

Gemmill, A. (2018). From some to none? Fertility expectation dynamics of permanently childless women. *Demography, 56*(8), 129–149. https://doi.org/10.1007/s13524-018-0739-7

Gliozheni, O., Hambartsoumian, E., Strohmer, H., Kreuz-Kinderwunschzentrum, O., SPG, Petrovskaya, E., Tishkevich, O., Bogaerts, K., I-Biostat, C. W., Balic, D., Sibincic, S., Antonova, I., Vrcic, H., Ljiljak, D., Rezabek, K., Markova, J., Lemmen, J., Sõritsa, D., Gissler, M., Pelkonen, S., et al. (2021). ART in Europe, 2017: Results generated from European registries by ESHRE. *Human Reproduction Open, 2021*(3). https://doi.org/10.1093/hropen/hoab026

Goisis, A., Håberg, S. E., Hanevik, H. I., Magnus, M. C., & Kravdal, Ø. (2020). The demographics of assisted reproductive technology births in a Nordic country. *Human Reproduction, 35*(6), 1441–1450. https://doi.org/10.1093/humrep/deaa055

Goldstein, J. R., Kreyenfeld, M., Jasilioniene, A., & Örsal, D. K. (2013). Fertility reactions to the 'great recession' in Europe: Recent evidence from order-specific data. *Demographic Research, 29*(July), 85–104. https://doi.org/10.4054/DemRes.2013.29.4

Gray, E., Evans, A., & Reimondos, A. (2013). Childbearing desires of childless men and women: When are goals adjusted? *Advances in Life Course Research, 18*(2), 141–149. https://doi.org/10.1016/j.alcr.2012.09.003

Greil, A. L. (1997). Infertility and psychological distress: A critical review of the literature. *Social Science and Medicine, 45*(11), 1679–1704. https://doi.org/10.1016/S0277-9536(97)00102-0

Guzzo, K. B., & Hayford, S. R. (2023). Evolving fertility goals and behaviors in current U.-S. Childbearing cohorts. *Population and Development Review*, online fir. doi:https://doi.org/10.1111/padr.12535.

Hart, R. K. (2019). Union histories of dissolution: What can they say about childlessness? *European Journal of Population, 35*(1), 101–131. https://doi.org/10.1007/s10680-018-9464-6

Heiland, F., Prskawetz, A., & Sanderson, W. C. (2008). Are individuals' desired family sizes stable? Evidence from west German panel data. *European Journal of Population – Revue Européenne de Démographie, 24*(2), 129–156. http://www.springerlink.com/index/10.1007/s10680-008-9162-x

Human Fertility Database. (2022). Max Planck Institute for Demographic Research (Germany) and Vienna Institute of Demography (Austria). https://www.humanfertility.org

Jalovaara, M., & Fasang, A. E. (2017). From never partnered to serial cohabitors: Union trajectories to childlessness. *Demographic Research (Descriptive Findings), 36*, 1703–1720. https://doi.org/10.4054/DemRes.2017.36.55

Kocourková, J., & Šťastná, A. (2021). The realization of fertility intentions in the context of childbearing postponement: Comparison of transitional and post-transitional populations. *Journal of Biosocial Science, 53*(1), 82–97. https://doi.org/10.1017/S002193202000005X
Kocourkova, J., Burcin, B., & Kucera, T. (2014). Demographic relevancy of increased use of assisted reproduction in European countries. *Reproductive Health, 11*. https://doi.org/10.1186/1742-4755-11-37
Kohler, H.-P., & Ortega, J. A. (2002). Tempo-adjusted period parity progression measures: Assessing the implications of delayed childbearing for cohort fertility in Sweden, The Netherlands and Spain. *Demographic Research, 6*, 145–190. https://doi.org/10.4054/DemRes.2002.6.7
Kohler, H.-P., Billari, F. C., & Ortega, J. A. (2002). The emergence of lowest-low fertility in Europe during the 1990s. *Population and Development Review, 28*(4), 641–680. https://doi.org/10.1111/j.1728-4457.2002.00641.x
Lazzari, E. (2021). Projecting the contribution of assisted reproductive technology to completed cohort fertility. *YSSP Report*. https://pure.iiasa.ac.at/id/eprint/17686/
Lazzari, E., Gray, E., & Chambers, G. M. (2021). The contribution of assisted reproductive technology to fertility rates and parity transition: An analysis of Australian data. *Demographic Research, 45*(November), 1081–1096. https://doi.org/10.4054/DEMRES.2021.45.35
Leridon, H. (2004). Can assisted reproduction technology compensate for the natural decline in fertility with age? A model assessment. *Human Reproduction, 19*(7), 1548–1553. https://doi.org/10.1093/humrep/deh304
Leridon, H. (2017). Biological effects of first birth postponement and assisted reproductive technology on completed fertility. *Population, 72*(3), 445–472. https://doi.org/10.3917/popu.1703.0463
Leridon, H., & Slama, R. (2008). The impact of a decline in fecundity and of pregnancy postponement on final number of children and demand for assisted reproduction technology. *Human Reproduction, 23*(6), 1312–1319. https://doi.org/10.1093/humrep/den106
Lesthaeghe, R. J. (2016). Following the evolution of fertility in second demographic transition settings: The life-cycle sensitive approach. In H. De Grande & H. Vandenheede (Eds.), *Back to the roots of demography* (pp. 105–114). ZenonPlus.
Letherby, G. (2002). Childless and bereft? Stereotypes and realities in relation to 'voluntary' and 'involuntary' childlessness and womanhood. *Sociological Inquiry, 72*(1), 7–20. https://doi.org/10.1111/1475-682X.00003
Lima, E. E. C., Zeman, K., Sobotka, T., Nathan, M., & Castro, R. (2018). The emergence of bimodal fertility profiles in Latin America. *Population and Development Review, 0*(1), 1–2. https://doi.org/10.1111/padr.12157
Luppi, F., Arpino, B., & Rosina, A. (2020). The impact of COVID-19 on fertility plans in Italy, Germany, France, Spain, and the United Kingdom. *Demographic Research, 43*(47), 1399–1412. https://doi.org/10.4054/DemRes.2020.43.47
Matysiak, A., Sobotka, T., & Vignoli, D. (2020). The great recession and fertility in Europe: A sub-national analysis. *European Journal of Population, 37*, 29–64. https://doi.org/10.1007/s10680-020-09556-y
Meggiolaro, S., & Ongaro, F. (2010). The implications of marital instability for a woman's fertility: Empirical evidence from Italy. *Demographic Research, 23*, 963–996. https://doi.org/10.4054/DemRes.2010.23.34
Mencarini, L., Vignoli, D., Zeydanli, T., & Kim, J. (2018). Life satisfaction favors reproduction. The universal positive effect of life satisfaction on childbearing in contemporary low fertility countries. *PLoS One, 13*(12), 1–19. https://doi.org/10.1371/journal.pone.0206202
Mikolai, J. (2017). Partnership histories and the transition to motherhood in later reproductive ages in Europe. *Population (English Edition), 72*(1), 123–154. https://doi.org/10.3917/popu.1701.0127

Mills, M. C., Rindfuss, R. R., Mcdonald, P., Velde, E. T., & Force, E. R. S. T. (2011). Why do people postpone parenthood? Reasons and social policy incentives. *Human Reproduction Update, 17*(6), 848–860. https://doi.org/10.1093/humupd/dmr026

Moreau, C., Bouyer, J., Ducot, B., Spira, A., & Slama, R. (2010). When do involuntarily infertile couples choose to seek medical help? *Fertility and Sterility, 93*(3), 737–744. https://doi.org/10.1016/j.fertnstert.2008.10.011

Morgan, S. P. (2003). Is low fertility a twenty-first-century demographic crisis? *Demography, 40*(4), 589–603. https://doi.org/10.1353/dem.2003.0037

Mynarska, M., & Wróblewska, W. (2017). The health of women of reproductive age and their childbearing intentions. *Zdrowie Publiczne i Zarządzanie, 15*(2), 135–143. https://doi.org/10.4467/20842627oz.17.014.6784

Nathan, M., & Pardo, I. (2019). Fertility postponement and regional patterns of dispersion in age at first birth: Descriptive findings and interpretations. *Comparative Population Studies, 44*, 37–60. https://doi.org/10.12765/CPoS-2019-07en

Neels, K., & De Watcher, D. (2010). Postponement and recuperation of Belgian fertility: How are they related to rising female educational attainment? *Vienna Yearbook of Population Research, 8*, 77–106. https://doi.org/10.1553/populationyearbook2010s77

Neels, K., Theunynck, Z., & Wood, J. (2012). Economic recession and first births in Europe: Recession-induced postponement and recuperation of fertility in 14 European countries between 1970 and 2005. *International Journal of Public Health, 58*(1), 43–55. https://doi.org/10.1007/s00038-012-0390-9

Neels, K., Murphy, M., Ní Bhrolcháin, M., & Beaujouan, É. (2017). Rising educational participation and the trend to later childbearing. *Population and Development Review, 43*(4), 667–693. https://doi.org/10.1111/padr.12112

Ní Bhrolcháin, M. (1992). Period paramount? A critique of the cohort approach to fertility. *Population and Development Review, 18*(4), 599–629. https://doi.org/10.2307/1973757

Ní Bhrolcháin, M., & Beaujouan, É. (2012). Fertility postponement is largely due to rising educational enrolment. *Population Studies, 66*(3), 311–327. https://doi.org/10.1080/00324728.2012.697569

Ní Bhrolcháin, M., & Beaujouan, É. (2019). Do people have reproductive goals? Constructive preferences and the discovery of desired family size. In R. Schoen (Ed.), *Analytical family demography* (pp. 27–56). Springer. https://doi.org/10.1007/978-3-319-93227-9_3

Ní Bhrolcháin, M., & Toulemon, L. (2005). Does postponement explain the trend to later childbearing in France? *Vienna Yearbook of Population Research*, 83–107.

Ní Bhrolcháin, M., Beaujouan, É., & Murphy, M. (2011). Sources of error in reported childlessness in a continuous British household survey. *Population Studies, 65*(3), 305–318. https://doi.org/10.1080/00324728.2011.607901

Nicoletti, C., & Tanturri, M. L. (2008). Differences in delaying motherhood across European countries: Empirical evidence from the ECHP. *European Journal of Population – Revue Européenne de Démographie, 24*(2), 157–183. https://doi.org/10.1007/s10680-008-9161-y

Nishikido, M., Cui, Q., & Esteve, A. (2022). Partnership dynamics and the fertility gap. *Genus, 78*, 1–20. https://doi.org/10.1186/s41118-022-00170-w

Olsen, J. R. N., Basso, O., Spinelli, A., & Kuppers-chinnow, M. (1998). Correlates of care seeking for infertility treatment in Europe. *European Journal of Public Health, 8*, 15–20.

Passet-Wittig, J., & Bujard, M. (2021). Medically assisted reproduction in developed countries: Overview and societal challenges. In N. F. Schneider & M. Kreyenfeld (Eds.), *Research handbook on the sociology of the family* (pp. 417–438). Elgar Online. https://doi.org/10.4337/9781788975544.00039

Pifarré i Arolas, H. (2017). A cohort perspective of the effect of unemployment. *Journal of Population Economics, 30*, 1211–1239. https://doi.org/10.1007/s00148-017-0640-5

Rainer, H., Selvaretnam, G., & Ulph, D. (2011). Assisted reproductive technologies (ART) in a model of fertility choice. *Journal of Population Economics, 24*(3), 1101–1132. https://doi.org/10.1007/s00148-010-0320-1

Rallu, J.-L., & Toulemon, L. (1994). Period fertility measures: The construction of different indices and their application to France, 1946-89. *Population, an English Selection, 6*, 59–130. https://www.jstor.org/stable/pdf/2949144.pdf

Régnier-Loilier, A. (2006). Influence of own Sibship size on the number of children desired at various times of life. The Case of France. *Population (English Edition), 61*(3), 165–194. https://doi.org/10.3917/popu.603.0193

Rondinelli, C., Aassve, A., & Billari, F. C. (2006). Socio-economic differences in postponement and recuperation of fertility in Italy: Results from a multi-spell random effect model. *ISER working paper*, Article 2006–46.

Rondinelli, C., Aassve, A., & Billari, F. C. (2010). Women's wages and childbearing decisions: Evidence from Italy. *Demographic Research, 22*, 549–578. https://doi.org/10.4054/DemRes.2010.22.19

Rybińska, A., & Morgan, S. P. (2019). Childless expectations and childlessness over the life course. *Social Forces, 97*(4), 1571–1602. https://doi.org/10.1093/sf/soy098

Saarela, J., & Skirbekk, V. (2019). Childlessness and union histories: Evidence from Finnish population register data. *Journal of Biosocial Science, 2020*, 78–96. https://doi.org/10.1017/S0021932019000257

Schnor, C. (2022). Single mothers by choice? Trends in single mothers' socio-economic profiles and mode of conception in Belgium, 1996-2020. *European Population Conference, 2022*. https://epc2022.eaps.nl/abstracts/210294

Schoen, R. (2004). Timing effects and the interpretation of period fertility. *Demography, 41*(4), 801–819. http://www.ncbi.nlm.nih.gov/pubmed/15622955

Schoen, R., Astone, N. M., Kim, Y. J., Nathanson, C. A., & Fields, J. M. (1999). Do fertility intentions affect fertility behavior? *Journal of Marriage and the Family, 61*(3), 790–799.

Sobotka, T. (2017). Childlessness in Europe: Reconstructing long-term trends among women born in 1900-1972. In M. Kreyenfeld & D. Konietzka (Eds.), *Childlessness in Europe: Contexts, causes, and consequences* (pp. 17–53). Springer.

Sobotka, T. (2021). World's highest childlessness levels in East Asia. *Population & Societies, 595*, 1–4. https://www.ined.fr/fichier/s_rubrique/32255/595_ang.en.pdf

Sobotka, T., & Beaujouan, É. (2014). Two is best? The persistence of a two-child family ideal in Europe. *Population and Development Review, 40*(3), 391–419. http://onlinelibrary.wiley.com/doi/10.1111/j.1728-4457.2014.00691.x/abstract

Sobotka, T., & Beaujouan, É. (2018). Late motherhood in low-fertility countries: Reproductive intentions, trends and consequences. In D. Stoop (Ed.), *Preventing age related fertility loss* (pp. 11–29). Springer International Publishing Switzerland.

Sobotka, T., & Berghammer, C. (2021). Demography of family change in Europe. In N. F. Schneider & M. Kreyenfeld (Eds.), *Research handbook on the sociology of the family* (pp. 162–186). Elgar Online. https://doi.org/10.4337/9781788975544

Sobotka, T., & Toulemon, L. (2008). Changing family and partnership behaviour: Common trends and persistent diversity across Europe. *Demographic Research, 19*(Special Collection 7), 85–138.

Sobotka, T., Hansen, M. A., Jensen, T. K., Pedersen, A. T., Lutz, W., & Skakkebæk, N. E. (2008). The contribution of assisted reproduction to completed fertility: An analysis of Danish data. *Population and Development Review, 34*(1), 79–101.

Sobotka, T., Zeman, K., Lesthaeghe, R. J., Frejka, T., & Neels, K. (2011). Postponement and recuperation in cohort fertility: Austria, Germany and Switzerland in a European context. *Comparative Population Studies, 36*(2–3), 417–452. https://doi.org/10.4232/10.CPoS-2011-16en

Tanturri, M. L., & Mencarini, L. (2008). Childless or childfree? Paths to voluntary childlessness in Italy. *Population and Development Review, 34*(1), 51–77. http://onlinelibrary.wiley.com/doi/10.1111/j.1728-4457.2008.00205.x/abstract

te Velde, E. R., Habbema, J. D. F., Leridon, H., & Eijkemans, M. J. C. (2012). The effect of postponement of first motherhood on permanent involuntary childlessness and total fertility rate in six European countries since the 1970s. *Human Reproduction, 27*(4), 1179–1183. https://doi.org/10.1093/humrep/der455

Thomson, E., Winkler-Dworak, M., Spielauer, M., & Prskawetz, A. (2012). Union instability as an engine of fertility? *A Microsimulation Model for France. Demography, 49*(1), 175–195. https://doi.org/10.1007/s13524-011-0085-5

Toulemon, L., & Mazuy, M. (2001). Les naissances sont retardées mais la fécondité est stable. *Population (French Edition), 56*(4), 611–644.

Trinitapoli, J., & Yeatman, S. (2018). The flexibility of fertility preferences in a context of uncertainty. *Population and Development Review, 44*(1), 87–116. https://doi.org/10.1111/padr.12114

Van Bavel, J., Jansen, M., & Wijckmans, B. (2012). Has divorce become a pro-Natal Force in Europe at the turn of the 21st century? *Population Research and Policy Review, 31*(5), 751–775. https://doi.org/10.1007/s11113-012-9237-6

van de Wiel, L. (2020). The speculative turn in IVF: Egg freezing and the financialization of fertility. *New Genetics and Society, 39*(3), 306–326. https://doi.org/10.1080/14636778.2019.1709430

Wagner, M., Huinink, J., & Liefbroer, A. C. (2019). Running out of time? Understanding the consequences of the biological clock for the dynamics of fertility intentions and union formation. *Demographic Research, 40*, 1–26. https://doi.org/10.4054/DemRes.2019.40.1

Wilkins, E. (2019). Low fertility: A review of the determinants. UNFPA working paper series, 2, 54. https://www.unfpa.org/publications/low-fertility-review-determinants

Winkler-Dworak, M., Beaujouan, É., Di Giulio, P., & Spielauer, M. (2017). Union instability and fertility: A microsimulation model for Italy and Great Britain. VID working paper, 8/2017.

Winkler-Dworak, M., Beaujouan, É., Di Giulio, P., & Spielauer, M. (2019). Simulating family life courses: An application to Italy, Great Britain, and Norway. VID working paper, 08/2019. https://www.oeaw.ac.at/vid/publications/serial-publications/vid-working-papers/

Winkler-Dworak, M., Pohl, M., & Beaujouan, É. (2022). Scenarios of fertility postponement and associated cohort fertility levels. *European Population Conference* 2022. https://epc2022.eaps.nl/abstracts/210345

Wyns, C., De Geyter, C., Calhaz-Jorge, C., Kupka, M. S., Motrenko, T., Smeenk, J., Bergh, C., Tandler-Schneider, A., Rugescu, I., & Goossens, V. (2022). ART in Europe, 2018: Results generated from European registries by ESHRE. *Human Reproduction Open, 2022*, 1–20. https://doi.org/10.1093/hropen/hoac022

Zeman, K., Beaujouan, É., Brzozowska, Z., & Sobotka, T. (2018). Cohort fertility decline in low fertility countries: Decomposition using parity progression ratios. *Demographic Research, 38*, 651–690. https://doi.org/10.4054/DemRes.2018.38.25

Part II
Methodological Analyses of Transforming Families

Chapter 5
Cohort Effects on Fertility as Age-Period Interactions: A Reanalysis of American Birth Rates, 1917–2020

Robert Schoen and Lowell Hargens

5.1 Introduction

Fertility behavior is widely seen as influenced by age, period, and cohort (APC) factors, though specifying the cohort influence has been problematic. Here, a new RBC method is developed to decompose an array of fertility rates into age, period, and cohort = age-period interaction components. The RBC method is then applied to data for the United States over the 1917–2020 interval. No clear evidence of cohort effects is found, as age and period effects have combined to drive American fertility to an all-time low.

Childbearing builds and transforms families. The role played by both period and cohort effects on fertility is thus of great importance, both theoretically and substantively, as it helps shape our understanding of fertility behavior and family dynamics. As a case in point, the widely cited theory for understanding the dramatic changes in family demography over the past half-century, the Second Demographic Transition (cf. Lesthaeghe, 2010), is essentially a period-based explanation.

Variation by age is widely recognized as a fundamental dimension of human fertility, but no consensus exists about the relative importance of variation by time period and birth cohort membership. Some have argued that fertility is fundamentally a cohort phenomenon, and that period variation in fertility is produced by cohort-based variation in quantum and tempo (Hajnal, 1947, Ryder, 1956, Easterlin, 1980, pp. 52–53). Ryder (1980, p41) went so far as to argue that the cohort is the "appropriate focus for causal analysis and what is observed in a period is a distorted manifestation of the underlying cohort behavior." Others have made the opposite

R. Schoen (✉)
Pennsylvania State University, San Francisco, CA, USA

L. Hargens
Department of Sociology, University of Washington, Seattle, WA, USA

R. Schoen (ed.), *The Demography of Transforming Families*, The Springer Series on Demographic Methods and Population Analysis 56,
https://doi.org/10.1007/978-3-031-29666-6_5

argument, that cohort variation in the quantum and tempo of fertility is produced by population wide variation in fertility over time (for an overview, see Ni Bhrolchain, 1992). In Schoen (2022), the fertility of a birth cohort was seen as essentially the period fertility observed about 30 years later, with a modest adjustment for the nature of the trend in fertility.

It is impossible to empirically adjudicate between these positions using standard linear-additive analysis techniques because of the linear dependence of age, period and cohort (APC), i.e.

$$\text{Age} = \text{Period} - \text{Cohort} \tag{5.1}$$

Analysts have proposed various strategies for overcoming the collinearity in Eq. (5.1) (e.g., Mason et al., 1973; Yang et al., 2008; O'Brien, 2015), but this approach, often called the "APC accounting scheme," continues to spark skepticism about the feasibility of producing valid estimates of the size of each of the three effects (Fosse & Winship, 2019). This is because it is necessary to adopt one or more constraints in order to overcome the underidentification problem produced by Eq. (5.1), and it is difficult to provide a strong justification for those constraints, especially if they are viewed as broadly applicable. In addition, choosing different constraints out of a set of equally plausible alternatives often produces widely different values for the effects of age, period and cohort (O'Brien, 2015), a condition that undermines confidence in the results produced by any given choice. As a result, from Glenn (1976), who described the search for a statistical solution to the problem of separating age, period, and cohort effects as "futile, to Fienberg (2013, p. 1981) who flatly stated that "there is no technical way to solve the APC problem," skeptics have doubted that such a solution even exists.

Another reason researchers studying fertility are reluctant to employ the classical APC accounting scheme and its offshoots is because these methods specify a "constant-value" definition of a cohort effect, holding that the size of the effect ascribed to a given cohort remains the same over time. This specification is widely viewed as inappropriate for analysis of fertility insofar as past experience modifies current behavior (Hobcraft et al., 1982, pp. 8–10). For example, if fertility is reduced during wartime, postwar birth rates may surge when couples attempt to make up for their lost fertility. Specifying that a cohort effect for a specific cohort remains constant over time is clearly inconsistent with such phenomena.

In this paper we present a new approach for identifying cohort effects that is not subject to the linear dependence problem and that makes no *a priori* specifications about the form of a cohort effect. Rather than defining a cohort effect as one of three additive effects, as the classical APC accounting scheme does, the method defines cohort effects in terms of a set of cohort-specific age by period interaction effects. This alternative specification has been prominent outside of sociology and demography for many years (Keyes et al., 2010), not only because it avoids the linear dependence problem but also because it is closely related to two-way analysis of variance and is therefore familiar to researchers in a broad range of disciplines. Still, models with age-period interactions have attracted some attention from demographers, going as far back as Clogg (1982) and James and Segal (1982). In a recent paper, Luo and Hodges (2022) present compelling arguments for rejecting the definition of a cohort effect as one of three additive components and in favor of defining it as a set of age by period interaction effects. They reinforce the view that Ryder's abstract verbal descriptions of cohort effects are consistent with the interaction effect specification and inconsistent with the APC accounting scheme.

The "RBC" approach we present below yields a new, theoretically grounded APC decomposition of fertility. As in Luo and Hodges (2022), our method considers a cohort effect to be constituted by several age by period interaction coefficients. Researchers can therefore use our approach to assess the various cohort effect patterns discussed by Hobcraft et al. (1982, pp. 6–11), including Ryder's cohort-target theory of fertility. Our approach breaks new ground in that we express the occurrence-exposure fertility rates via a multiplicative model (see Pullum, 1978), and choose plausible constraints needed to identify model parameters so that those parameters relate to common measures of fertility Doing so allows us to specify the array of age-period interactions. Our method is designed for the analysis of administrative data on age-time-specific fertility rates. Since such data are typically not based on probability samples, sampling variability is not at issue and we emphasize substantive significance

We next describe our RBC method and how it can be used to decompose a table of age-specific fertility rates. We then apply the method to several hypothetical APC tables to show how it can identify cohort effects. From that foundation, we apply the RBC method to United States fertility data over the 1917–1973 and 1974–2020 intervals and describe and discuss the results.

5.2 Modeling Age, Period, and Age by Period Interaction Effects

Our method has two overarching features. First, it is exploratory in that we seek to describe relationships in the data. Second, it is theory based, drawing on Ryder's conceptualization of cohort fertility effects as age-period interactions. We start with an examination of the structure implicit in cross-tabulated rates.

5.2.1 An Exploratory Analysis

Like previous exploratory methods for detecting the presence of cohort effects, we begin with observed data in the form of a two-way table consisting of categories of two independent variables on the table margins and values of a dependent variable in the cells of the table. In the present instance we begin with an age by period matrix (**A**) of fertility rates with ρ rows (for the periods) and κ columns (for the age groups) and ρ times κ entries containing occurrence-exposure fertility rates at period i for persons in age group j. We also specify that the duration of each time period equals the length of each of the age categories. The RBC method extracts any age-by-period interactions from such a table by factoring it into three components: a ρ by ρ diagonal matrix of baseline period coefficients (**R**), a κ by κ diagonal matrix of baseline age group coefficients (**C**), and a ρ by κ matrix (**B**) containing elements that show the extent to which each of the elements of **A** differs from what it would be if only the coefficients in **R** and **C** determined its value. We can state this factorization by the matrix equation

$$\mathbf{A} = \mathbf{R}\,\mathbf{B}\,\mathbf{C} \tag{5.2}$$

which specifies that for each element in the matrix of observed fertility rates,

$$a_{ij} = r_{ii}\, b_{ij}\, c_{jj}. \tag{5.3}$$

The **B** matrix is the central focus in this approach because it shows the extent to which each element in **A** deviates from what one would expect if that element were determined only by the elements in **R** and **C**. Specifically, a given element in **B**, b_{ij}, gives the multiple by which the corresponding element of **A**, a_{ij}, differs from the value that would obtain if $a_{ij} = r_{ii}\, c_{jj}$. For example, if a_{ij} is 50% higher than what it would be if $a_{ij} = r_{ii}\, c_{jj}$, then b_{ij} would equal 1.5, and if it were 20% lower, b_{ij} would equal .8. In the case where $a_{ij} = r_{ii}\, c_{jj}$ holds for all of the elements in **A**, the ρ times κ elements of **B** are all equal to 1.0.

The RBC method follows of a line of work that applies log linear models to tables of rates (c.f. Bishop et al., 1975; Goodman & Kruskal, 1979; Willekens, 1982; and Schoen, 2020). This can be seen by taking logs in Eq. (5.3).

$$\ln(a_{ij}) = \ln(r_{ii}) + \ln\,(b_{ij}) + \ln\,(c_{jj}) \tag{5.4}$$

Note that if all of the elements of **B** equal 1.0, all of the $\ln(b_{ij})$ equal zero and Eq. (5.4) simplifies to Eq. (5.5), indicating that each of the $\ln(a_{ij})$ values is a simple additive function of $\ln(r_{ii})$ and $\ln\,(c_{jj})$, i.e.

$$\ln(a_{ij}) = \ln(r_{ii}) + \ln\,(c_{jj}) \tag{5.5}$$

When the $\ln(a_{ij})$ values in Eq. (5.4) are not simple sums of the coefficients in $\ln(r_{ii})$ and $\ln(c_{jj})$, non-zero $\ln(b_{ij})$ values (from $b_{ij} \neq 1.0$) represent these deviations from simple additivity, and thus represent "interactions."

Given that Eq. (5.4) contains no stochastic term, it is clear that the log linear model it specifies is a saturated model and that the sum of the three quantities on its right side always equals the log of the observed rate in A on its left side. Being based on a saturated model distinguishes the RBC method from other exploratory methods for detecting cohort effects, such as the median and mean polish methods, which begin by estimating an additive age-period model for a two way table and then define interactions as deviations from that model. When there are interactions present in a two-way table, the additive model fits the data poorly and the magnitudes of the derived deviations are in part a function of that lack of fit. Because it is based on a saturated model, the RBC method provides direct measures of the interactions present in a two-way table.

5.2.2 *A Theoretically Motivated Decomposition*

The RBC model of Eqs. (5.2, 5.3, and 5.4) can also be seen as a decomposition of rate matrix **A** into components that suggest age (matrix **C**), period (matrix **R**), and cohort (matrix **B**) factors. Ryder (1965) provides theoretical support for viewing the age-period interactions as potential cohort effects. The RBC decomposition follows from considering rate array **A** as a contingency table that is fit by a saturated log-linear model. While such a decomposition is not unique, the APC interpretation can be reinforced by scaling **C** so that it reflects the average proportional contribution of each age. Then the uniquely specified **R** should approximate the period TFR, a relationship that can be empirically verified. This decomposition perspective is fully consistent with the exploratory perspective, and gives the RBC formulation a strong demographic foundation.

5.2.3 *The Decomposition Procedure*

Given an observed matrix **A**, one can derive matrix **B** using the method of iterative proportional fitting (IPF, also known as biproportional adjustment or the RAS method). The Appendix gives a concrete example of how this is done, but in general we use IPF to rescale **A** into a **B** that has κ for the sum of each row and ρ for the sum of each column. For an array with few zeroes, IPF always converges to a unique solution (Bishop et al., 1975), usually fairly rapidly. It is important to recognize that the various cross-product ratios present in **B** are the same as the corresponding cross-product ratios in **A**. That rescaling is advantageous, however, because it makes it easier to detect possible cohort effects in **A** and provides an interpretable numerical value for the size of such effects.

Once **B** has been calculated, the elements of the **R** and **C** matrices are determined only up to a scalar factor, because multiplying each element of **R** by a constant k and dividing each element of **C** by k leaves the product **RBC** unchanged. In the Appendix we specify a demographically meaningful scaling of these matrices such that the diagonal elements of **C** approximate age-specific fertility proportions and the diagonal elements of **R** approximate period total fertility rates. Strictly speaking, however, the diagonal elements of these two matrices can be interpreted, respectively, as "period effects" and "age effects" only when all of the elements of **B** equal 1.0. If this is not the case, those elements of **B** are only parts of a more complicated specification of the nature of the relationship between the period and age categories and the levels of fertility given in **A** (for a general statement of this point, see Stolzenberg, 1979, p. 472).

Because the RBC method for detecting cohort effects begins with a table of rates rather than the individual level data that were the basis for the calculation of those rates, and because it is a saturated model of those rates, various statistical hypothesis tests concerning the values present in the **B** matrix are not possible. In exploratory analyses and decompositions, statistical hypothesis tests would be inappropriate even if they were possible. The question of whether a given subset of the elements of the **B** matrix shows important deviations from 1.0 is a substantive issue that has no hard and fast answer, and "large" deviations from 1.0 in a given **B** matrix are determined in part by the distribution of values in that matrix.

Non-zero $\ln(b_{ij})$, and $b_{ij} \neq 1.0$, can be produced by many phenomena, not just cohort effects. To assess whether the coefficients in the **B** matrix provide evidence for the existence of a cohort effect, it is necessary to examine the b_{ij} values that are present in diagonals of that matrix (b_{ij}, $b_{i+1, j+1}$, $b_{i+2, j+2}$, . . .$b_{i+n, j+n}$). This is consistent with Ryder's argument that "transformations of the social world modify people of different ages in different ways; the effects of these transformations are persistent" (Ryder, 1965, p. 861).

To summarize, the RBC approach can be applied to any array of fertility rates via iterative proportional fitting. The procedure yields row factors that approximate row sums of **A**, column factors that approximate average column proportions, and a matrix **B** of interactions that can relate to cohort effects. While the statistical significance of the b_{ij} elements cannot be determined, the magnitude of their departure from 1 speaks to their importance.

5.3 Identifying Cohort Effects in Hypothetical Arrays

To illustrate how the RBC method can be used to detect the presence of cohort effects in APC tables, we show the patterns of values in the **B** matrix that are produced by two kinds of cohort effect. The first kind is one in which specific cohorts have elevated fertility rates. Such a pattern might be produced by the those cohorts being exposed to conditions particularly favorable to fertility (e.g., Easterlin, 1980). In the second type of effect, a drop in fertility shown by a cohort in a given time period is followed by an increase in its fertility during the following time period. This is the classic case of a cohort postponing fertility at one age and then making up that missed fertility at the next. In addition to showing how these kinds of cohort effects are reflected in the **B** matrix, we also investigate whether the **B** matrix will reflect the presence of period effects when base matrix **A** is recast as a cohort-by-age array.

Consider a 9-period by 6-age group base matrix **A** with 5-year intervals for both age and time and in which Eq. (5.5) holds. Let all rows of the base matrix have the following elements: .10, .15, .25, .25, .15, and .10. Because there are no interactions in this base matrix, **B** is a 9 by 6 matrix of ones, **C** is a 6 by 6 diagonal matrix with the above elements on its diagonal, and **R** is 9 by 9 identity matrix (because each row of **A** sums to 1.0).

5.3.1 *Interactions When the Level of Cohort Fertility Varies Uniformly Across Age*

To create cohort effects, we manipulate the elements of our base matrix. For the first type of cohort effect we increase the fertility of a single cohort by 20%. Table 5.1 displays the RBC results.

The top panel shows the modified matrix **A**, with the fertility of the cohort age Under 20 at Time 1 increased by 20% at every age (shown in boldface). One column iteration and one row iteration yield the bottom panel showing the **B** matrix of interactions. Interactions related to the cohort with elevated fertility (in boldface) stand out as they are about 16% above unity. During the first 6 periods, all other interactions are slightly below one, and all interactions are one for the last 3 periods. The **C** matrix remains that of the base **C** matrix, while the **R** matrix of row factors spreads that 20% increase over the first 6 periods. In short, a fertility increase in one cohort produces interactions that identify a clear cohort effect.

Table 5.2 presents the matrix of interactions when three cohorts have elevated fertility. The top panel shows the modified matrix **A**, with the three oldest cohorts

Table 5.1 Interactions in a hypothetical population with one cohort having 20% higher fertility

A. Adjusted base model								
Year/Age	Under 20	20–24	25–29	30–34	35–39	40+	Total	**R Elements**
1	**.12**	.15	.25	.25	.15	.10	1.02	**1.03**
2	.10	**.18**	.25	.25	.15	.10	1.03	**1.03**
3	.10	.15	**.30**	.25	.15	.10	1.05	**1.03**
4	.10	.15	.25	**.30**	.15	.10	1.05	**1.03**
5	.10	.15	.25	.25	**.18**	.10	1.03	**1.03**
6	.10	.15	.25	.25	.15	**.12**	1.02	**1.03**
7	.10	.15	.25	.25	.15	.10	1.00	**1.00**
8	.10	.15	.25	.25	.15	.10	1.00	**1.00**
9	.10	.15	.25	.25	.15	.10	1.00	**1.00**
C Elements	**.10**	**.15**	**.25**	**.25**	**.15**	**.10**	**1.00**	
B. Interaction matrix B								
Year/Age	Under 20	20–24	25–29	30–34	35–39	40+	Row sum	
1	**1.16**	.97	.97	.97	.97	.97	6	
2	.97	**1.16**	.97	.97	.97	.97	6	
3	.97	.97	**1.16**	.97	.97	.97	6	
4	.97	.97	.97	**1.16**	.97	.97	6	
5	.97	.97	.97	.97	**1.16**	.97	6	
6	.97	.97	.97	.97	.97	**1.16**	6	
7	1.00	1.00	1.00	1.00	1.00	1.00	6	
8	1.00	1.00	1.00	1.00	1.00	1.00	6	
9	1.00	1.00	1.00	1.00	1.00	1.00	6	
Column sum	9	9	9	9	9	9	54	

Table 5.2 Interactions in a hypothetical population with three cohorts having elevated fertility

A. Adjusted base model								
Year/Age	Under 20	20–24	25–29	30–34	35–39	40+	Total	**R Elements**
1	**.12**	.15	.25	.25	.15	.10	1.02	**1.03**
2	**.13**	**.18**	.25	.25	.15	.10	1.06	**1.08**
3	**.12**	**.195**	**.30**	.25	.15	.10	1.12	**1.12**
4	.10	**.18**	**.325**	**.30**	.15	.10	1.16	**1.12**
5	.10	.15	**.30**	**.325**	**.18**	.10	1.16	**1.12**
6	.10	.15	.25	**.30**	**.195**	**.12**	1.12	**1.12**
7	.10	.15	.25	.25	**.18**	**.13**	1.06	**1.08**
8	.10	.15	.25	.25	.15	**.12**	1.02	**1.03**
9	.10	.15	.25	.25	.15	.10	1.00	**1.00**
C Elements	**.10**	**.15**	**.25**	**.25**	**.15**	**.10**	**1.00**	
B. Interaction matrix B								
Year/Age	Under 20	20–24	25–29	30–34	35–39	40+	Row sum	
1	**1.16**	.97	.97	.97	.97	.97	6	
2	**1.20**	**1.11**	.92	.92	.92	.92	6	
3	**1.07**	**1.16**	**1.08**	.90	.90	.90	6	
4	.89	**1.08**	**1.17**	**1.08**	.90	.90	6	
5	.89	.90	**1.08**	**1.17**	**1.08**	.90	6	
6	.89	.90	.90	**1.08**	**1.17**	**1.07**	6	
7	.92	.92	.92	.92	**1.11**	**1.20**	6	
8	.97	.97	.97	.97	.97	**1.16**	6	
9	1.00	1.00	1.00	1.00	1.00	1.00	6	
Column sum	9	9	9	9	9	9	54	

(in boldface) having their fertility at all ages increased from base values by 20%, 30%, and 20% respectively. Two column iterations and one row iteration yield the bottom panel showing interaction matrix **B**. Interactions related to the three cohorts with elevated fertility, shown in boldface, are markedly above 1. During periods 3 through 6, all of the other cohorts have interactions (italicized) that are at least 10% below 1. The **C** matrix has elements essentially the same as those of the base **C** matrix, while the **R** matrix tracks the period TFRs fairly well. Once more, cohort fertility increases produce **B** matrix interactions that point to clear cohort effects.

5.3.2 Interactions When the Timing of Cohort Fertility Varies

Let us consider the case where the cohorts at ages 25–29 during periods 3 and 4 have a 20% decrease in fertility, while those same cohorts have a 20% increase in fertility at ages 30–34.

The top panel of Table 5.3 shows the modified **A** matrix under that scenario, with the adjusted fertility rates in boldface. One column and one row iteration yield the

Table 5.3 Interactions in a hypothetical population when two cohorts have 20% declines in fertility at ages 25–29 and 20% increases in fertility at ages 30–34

A. Adjusted base model								
Year/Age	Under 20	20–24	25–29	30–34	35–39	40+	Total	**R Elements**
1	.10	.15	.25	.25	.15	.10	1.00	**1.00**
2	.10	.15	.25	.25	.15	.10	1.00	**1.00**
3	.10	.15	**.20**	.25	.15	.10	.95	**.97**
4	.10	.15	**.20**	**.30**	.15	.10	1.00	**1.00**
5	.10	.15	.25	**.30**	.15	.10	1.05	**1.03**
6	.10	.15	.25	.25	.15	.10	1.00	**1.00**
7	.10	.15	.25	.25	.15	.10	1.00	**1.00**
8	.10	.15	.25	.25	.15	.10	1.00	**1.00**
9	.10	.15	.25	.25	.15	.10	1.00	**1.00**
C Elements	**.10**	**.15**	**.24**	**.26**	**.15**	**.10**	**1.00**	

B. Interaction matrix B							
Year/Age	Under 20	20–24	25–29	30–34	35–39	40+	Row sum
1	1.00	1.00	1.05	.96	1.00	1.00	6
2	1.00	1.00	1.05	.96	1.00	1.00	6
3	1.04	1.04	**.87**	.99	1.04	1.04	6
4	1.00	1.00	**.84**	**1.15**	1.00	1.00	6
5	.97	.97	1.01	**1.11**	.97	.97	6
6	1.00	1.00	1.05	.96	1.00	1.00	6
7	1.00	1.00	1.05	.96	1.00	1.00	6
8	1.00	1.00	1.05	.96	1.00	1.00	6
9	1.00	1.00	1.05	.96	1.00	1.00	6
Column sum	9	9	9	9	9	9	54

interaction matrix in the bottom panel. Interactions related to the adjusted fertility rates, in boldface, stand out. Those at ages 25–29 are both more than 10% low, while those at ages 30–34 are both more than 10% high. The elements of the **C** matrix are slightly changed at ages 25–29 and 30–34, while the elements of the **R** matrix again approximate the period TFRs. Calculations done with a 20% "blip" in just one cohort (not shown) yield very similar results. In short, postponement / recuperation changes in cohort timing produce readily interpretable interactions in the **B** matrix.

5.3.3 Interactions in a Cohort-by-Age Fertility Array When Period Fertility Varies

To this point, we have only considered period-by-age arrays. There are cases where either period or cohort effects can account for the variation in such arrays (Glenn, 2005), and in those cases using the RBC method privileges period effects and detects no cohort effects (see also Luo & Hodges, 2022). However, researchers can use the

RBC method to privilege cohort effects over period effects by setting up the **A** matrix as a cohort-by-age array. In this case period effects are defined as a type of cohort-age interaction and the researcher examines the **B** matrix for diagonal patterns of interactions corresponding to periods. As an example, we construct a case in which period fertility varies cyclically, with a cycle length of 8. Starting with base model values at time 1, we increase base fertility by 5% at every age for 4 periods, and then decrease fertility by 5% for the next 4 periods. Period 9 again has base model fertility levels, and begins a new cycle. The top panel of Table 5.4 shows the adjusted base matrix for such a cyclical population. Fourteen periods are shown so that the full experience of the cohort aged Under 20 at time 9 is included. The fertility rates of the first, fourth, and seventh cohorts are indicated in boldface.

That 14 × 6 period-by-age matrix is then translated into a 9 × 6 cohort-by-age array, and that array is decomposed into APC factors by the RBC method. After one column iteration and one row iteration, the interaction matrix shown in the bottom panel of Table 5.4 is obtained. Only 3 elements are noteworthy by a 10% standard. However, with a 5% standard, consistent with the 5% changes, the pattern of the **B** elements becomes quite revealing. Elements that are more than 5% low are indicated by underlined italics, while those that are more than 5% high are in boldface. The bottom panel of Table 5.4 then shows a clear pattern of bands moving from low and left up to high and right. Such diagonal bands follow period lines, and show cycles of approximate length 8. Even though cohort aspects were advantaged in this analysis, the 8-cycle period fluctuations appear in the interaction matrix.

In summary, the **B** matrices produced by the RBC method identify cohort level and timing effects in period-by-age arrays constructed to show such effects. In cohort-by age arrays, the **B** matrices show the existence of period fluctuations. It would be possible to apply the RBC method to period-by-cohort arrays to detect possible age effects, but because age is a fundamental dimension of demographic phenomena, it is routinely given precedence over either of the other two in demographic research.

5.4 RBC Decomposition of Fertility Data for the United States, 1917–2020

Since 1917 American fertility has varied both in overall level and age-pattern. The fertility level generally declined from 1917 to 1940, increased markedly during the 1946–64 Baby Boom, fell to a then record low in 1978 during the Birth Dearth, and subsequently fluctuated around a declining trend to a new record low in 2020 (see Table 5.5). The age-pattern of fertility also varied considerably. Up to the 1960s, there was a dramatic decline in fertility rates at the higher ages and parities (Schoen, 2019), while recent years have seen declines at younger ages and some rebounds at higher ages (Schoen & Hargens, 2020). The trend in the Mean Age of Fertility (MAF), the arithmetic average of the age-specific birth rates, is particularly informative. Table 5.5 shows that from 1917 to 1974 the MAF generally declined, falling

Table 5.4 Interactions in the RBC decomposition of a cohort by age array in a hypothetical population with cyclically varying period fertility

A. Adjusted base model

Year/Age	Under 20	20–24	25–29	30–34	35–39	40+	Total
1	**.100**	.150	.250	.250	.150	.100	1.00
2	.105	**.158**	.263	.263	.158	.105	1.05
3	.110	.165	**.276**	.276	.165	.110	1.10
4	**.116**	.174	.289	**.289**	.174	.116	1.16
5	.122	**.182**	.304	.304	**.182**	.122	1.22
6	.116	.174	**.289**	.289	.174	**.116**	1.16
7	**.110**	.165	.276	**.276**	.165	.110	1.10
8	.105	**.158**	.263	.263	**.158**	.105	1.05
9	.100	.150	**.250**	.250	.150	**.100**	1.00
10	.105	.158	.263	**.263**	.158	.105	1.05
11	.110	.165	.276	.276	**.165**	.110	1.10
12	.116	.174	.289	.289	.174	**.116**	1.16
13	.122	.182	.304	.304	.182	.122	1.22
14	.116	.174	.289	.289	.174	.116	1.16

B. Interaction matrix B

Cohort/ Age	Under 20	20–24	25–29	30–34	35–39	40+	Row sum	R Elements
1	*.909*	*.949*	.991	1.035	**1.081**	1.035	6	**1.11**
2	*.939*	.981	1.025	**1.070**	1.013	.971	6	**1.13**
3	.986	1.030	**1.076**	1.019	.965	*.924*	6	**1.13**
4	**1.051**	**1.098**	1.040	.985	*.933*	*.893*	6	**1.12**
5	**1.121**	**1.063**	1.007	.953	*.903*	.953	6	**1.10**
6	**1.087**	1.030	.976	*.924*	.965	1.019	6	**1.08**
7	1.035	.981	*.929*	.971	1.013	**1.070**	6	**1.08**
8	.969	*.919*	.959	1.002	1.046	**1.105**	6	**1.10**
9	*.9091*	*.949*	.991	1.035	**1.081**	1.035	6	**1.11**
Col. sum	9	9	9	9	9	9	54	
C **Elements**	**.10**	**.15**	**.25**	**.25**	**.15**	**.10**		

from 28.61 years to 25.75 years. From 1974 onward, with one minor exception in 2006, the MAF steadily rose, reaching 29.71 years in 2020. We want to analyze fertility over a time span that allows cohort effects to manifest themselves, but where there is still some consistency in the age pattern of fertility. That suggests a break at the year 1974, when the trend in the MAF reversed. Accordingly, we examine 2 eras, 1917–73 and 1974–2020.

Our fertility rate data come from published vital statistics tabulations. The principal source is Heuser (1976) for the years 1917–1973. The report by Martin et al. (2017) provides the years 1974–2015; Martin et al. (2019) the years 2016–2018; and Hamilton et al. (2021) the years 2019–2020. The full array of 5-year age-specific fertility rates (×1000) is shown in Table 5.5.

Table 5.5 Age-specific fertility rates (×1000) for the United States, 1917–2020

Year/Age	Under20	20–24	25–29	30–34	35–39	40+	Total	TFR
1917	60.3	171.9	172.6	127.5	93.1	40.3	665.7	3.33
1918	59.1	171.2	171.2	126.6	92.2	41.4	661.7	3.31
1919	51.7	150.8	158.7	121.6	90.0	39.1	611.9	3.07
1920	62.6	168.7	167.2	122.9	90.5	40.2	652.1	3.26
1921	67.1	171.3	169.9	125.6	90.0	39.8	663.7	3.33
1922	61.5	160.6	159.0	118.1	84.9	37.1	621.2	3.11
1923	61.7	161.2	158.6	117.5	83.9	36.5	619.4	3.10
1924	64.0	164.7	158.2	116.9	83.2	36.3	623.3	3.12
1925	62.5	158.6	152.4	112.6	80.3	35.0	601.4	3.01
1926	61.2	154.4	146.7	107.6	76.7	32.9	579.5	2.90
1927	60.5	150.0	142.8	104.8	74.5	31.6	564.2	2.82
1928	57.6	142.3	135.0	98.1	68.9	29.6	531.5	2.66
1929	55.4	136.4	129.1	93.5	64.0	27.5	505.9	2.53
1930	56.7	136.8	128.6	93.3	63.3	27.2	505.9	2.53
1931	53.2	130.0	122.9	88.8	59.5	25.4	479.8	2.40
1932	51.4	125.8	118.2	86.0	57.0	24.6	463.0	2.32
1933	47.7	118.2	111.2	80.7	53.0	23.0	433.8	2.17
1934	50.1	123.3	114.5	82.1	53.2	22.5	445.7	2.23
1935	50.8	123.1	111.6	79.0	51.4	21.2	437.1	2.19
1936	50.1	122.9	110.3	76.5	48.9	19.7	428.4	2.15
1937	52.3	126.4	112.3	76.4	47.8	18.7	433.9	2.17
1938	54.1	129.9	116.1	77.3	47.4	18.4	443.2	2.22
1939	52.3	126.7	114.9	76.7	45.8	17.2	433.6	2.17
1940	53.4	131.1	119.7	78.6	45.1	16.6	444.5	2.23
1941	56.0	140.0	126.6	81.1	45.3	16.4	465.4	2.33
1942	60.2	157.7	140.7	87.9	47.2	16.3	510.0	2.55
1943	60.4	156.4	146.4	95.2	51.5	17.3	527.2	2.64
1944	53.7	143.9	136.0	94.2	52.8	17.9	498.5	2.49
1945	50.5	131.9	131.2	96.8	54.7	18.2	483.3	2.42
1946	58.5	172.7	159.1	105.8	56.7	17.9	570.7	2.86
1947	77.2	200.1	173.0	109.3	57.4	18.0	635.0	3.18
1948	79.4	191.1	161.9	101.4	53.9	16.7	604.4	3.03
1949	80.3	192.2	163.1	101.0	53.2	16.5	606.3	3.04
1950	79.4	190.0	164.4	101.7	53.1	16.2	604.8	3.03
1951	85.4	203.6	172.8	106.2	54.6	16.4	639.0	3.20
1952	85.1	208.8	178.9	110.7	56.1	16.7	656.3	3.29
1953	87.8	215.3	180.5	111.8	56.7	17.0	669.1	3.35
1954	90.0	225.4	184.9	115.1	58.4	17.3	691.1	3.46
1955	90.4	231.3	186.4	114.6	58.4	17.3	698.4	3.50
1956	95.0	241.8	190.9	115.7	58.9	17.5	719.8	3.60
1957	97.3	248.0	195.7	117.2	59.6	17.5	735.3	3.68
1958	95.0	245.8	194.3	114.4	58.1	16.9	724.5	3.63

(continued)

Table 5.5 (continued)

Year/Age	Under20	20–24	25–29	30–34	35–39	40+	Total	TFR
1959	94.1	247.1	196.2	114.2	57.9	16.9	726.4	3.64
1960	91.0	246.1	196.0	113.5	56.9	16.7	720.2	3.61
1961	88.7	242.3	194.2	113.0	56.5	16.8	711.5	3.56
1962	85.2	233.2	187.2	108.5	53.6	16.2	683.9	3.42
1963	82.2	222.9	180.5	105.8	51.7	15.5	658.6	3.30
1964	78.4	211.4	174.3	103.1	50.7	14.9	632.8	3.17
1965	73.3	190.0	157.3	94.1	46.7	14.1	575.5	2.88
1966	70.9	178.9	143.9	84.2	42.1	12.8	532.8	2.67
1967	68.5	170.2	137.4	77.7	38.6	11.9	504.3	2.53
1968	67.0	163.6	134.9	73.0	35.8	10.7	485.0	2.43
1969	67.3	162.8	137.2	72.7	33.7	9.8	483.5	2.42
1970	69.7	163.1	138.9	72.0	32.0	9.3	485.0	2.43
1971	66.1	149.1	129.3	66.6	29.0	7.8	447.9	2.25
1972	63.0	128.8	114.6	58.9	25.1	6.7	397.1	1.99
1973	60.4	119.4	108.2	54.6	22.2	6.2	371.0	1.86
1974	58.7	117.7	111.5	53.8	20.2	5.1	367.0	1.84
1975	56.9	113.0	108.2	52.3	19.5	4.9	354.8	1.77
1976	54.0	110.3	106.2	53.6	19.0	4.5	347.6	1.74
1977	54.0	112.9	111.0	56.4	19.2	4.4	357.9	1.79
1978	52.7	109.9	108.5	57.8	19.0	4.1	352.0	1.76
1979	53.5	112.8	111.4	60.3	19.5	4.1	361.6	1.81
1980	54.1	115.1	112.9	61.9	19.8	4.1	367.9	1.84
1981	53.3	112.2	111.5	61.4	20.0	4.0	362.4	1.81
1982	53.5	111.6	111.0	64.1	21.2	4.1	365.5	1.83
1983	52.5	107.8	108.5	64.9	22.0	4.1	359.8	1.80
1984	51.8	106.8	108.7	67.0	22.9	4.1	361.3	1.81
1985	52.2	108.3	111.0	69.1	24.0	4.2	368.8	1.84
1986	51.5	107.4	109.8	70.1	24.4	4.3	367.5	1.84
1987	51.9	107.9	111.6	72.1	26.3	4.6	374.4	1.87
1988	54.3	110.2	114.4	74.8	28.1	5.0	386.8	1.93
1989	58.7	113.8	117.6	77.4	29.9	5.4	402.8	2.01
1990	61.3	116.5	120.2	80.8	31.7	5.7	416.2	2.08
1991	63.2	115.3	117.2	79.2	31.9	5.7	412.5	2.06
1992	61.7	113.7	115.7	79.6	32.3	6.2	409.2	2.05
1993	60.4	111.3	113.2	79.9	32.7	6.4	403.9	2.02
1994	59.6	109.2	111.0	80.4	33.4	6.7	400.3	2.00
1995	57.3	107.5	108.8	81.1	34.0	6.9	395.6	1.98
1996	54.7	107.8	108.6	82.1	34.9	7.1	395.2	1.98
1997	52.4	107.3	108.3	83.0	35.7	7.5	394.2	1.97
1998	51.3	108.4	110.2	85.2	36.9	7.8	399.8	2.00
1999	49.7	107.9	111.2	87.1	37.8	7.8	401.5	2.01
2000	48.6	109.7	113.5	91.2	39.7	8.5	411.2	2.06

(continued)

Table 5.5 (continued)

Year/Age	Under20	20–24	25–29	30–34	35–39	40+	Total	TFR
2001	45.8	105.6	113.8	91.8	40.5	8.6	406.1	2.03
2002	43.3	103.1	114.7	92.6	41.8	8.8	404.3	2.02
2003	41.7	102.3	116.7	95.7	43.9	9.2	409.5	2.05
2004	41.1	101.5	116.5	96.2	45.5	9.5	410.3	2.05
2005	40.3	101.8	116.5	96.7	46.4	9.7	411.4	2.06
2006	41.7	105.5	118.0	98.9	47.5	10.0	421.6	2.11
2007	42.1	105.4	118.1	100.6	47.6	10.2	424.0	2.12
2008	40.8	101.8	115.0	99.4	46.8	10.6	414.4	2.07
2009	38.4	96.2	111.5	97.5	46.1	10.7	400.4	2.00
2010	34.6	90.0	108.3	96.5	45.9	10.9	386.2	1.93
2011	31.7	85.3	107.2	96.5	47.2	11.0	378.9	1.89
2012	29.8	83.1	106.5	97.3	48.3	11.1	376.1	1.88
2013	26.8	80.7	105.5	98.0	49.3	11.2	371.5	1.86
2014	24.5	79.0	105.8	100.8	51.0	11.4	372.5	1.86
2015	22.5	76.8	104.3	101.5	51.8	11.8	368.7	1.84
2016	20.5	73.8	102.1	102.7	52.7	12.3	364.1	1.82
2017	20.0	71.0	98.0	100.3	52.3	12.5	354.1	1.77
2018	17.6	68.0	95.3	99.7	52.6	12.7	345.9	1.73
2019	16.7	66.6	93.7	98.3	52.8	12.9	341.0	1.71
2020	15.3	62.8	90.0	94.8	51.7	12.7	327.3	1.64

Source: See text

We want to examine single year of age rates for single years of time to allow a detailed examination of fertility behavior. Heuser (1976) provides single year of age rates for 1917 through 1973. For the years 1974 through 2020, single year of age birth rates were estimated by linear interpolation.

Specifically, with the fertility level assumed to prevail at the midpoint of each 5-year interval from 15–19 through 45–49, single year rates were estimated by assuming a linear trend from the midpoints of the earlier and later 5-year intervals. For each interval, those rates were then (slightly) adjusted so that the sum of the 5 one-year rates equaled 5 times the 5-year rate and the year's TFR was reproduced.

Table 5.6 presents the RBC decomposition of U.S. fertility over the 1917–1973 era, and Table 5.7 shows the decomposition for the 1974–2020 era. In both tables, the diagonal elements of the R matrix are in the rightmost column, the diagonal elements of the C matrix are in the bottom row, and the elements of interaction matrix B comprise the bulk of the table. In both tables, 3 column iterations and 3 row iterations produced the B values shown. Note that because the **A** matrix rates in these analyses are rates per thousand, the elements in the **R** matrix are also 1000 times the estimated TFR values. Figure 5.1 shows the observed and **R**-estimated TFRs based on the two calculations underlying Tables 5.6, and 5.7. To make it easier to visualize the variation in the **B** matrix elements for each period, we also present shaded contour plots of the **B** matrix values in Figs. 5.2, and 5.3.

In Table 5.6 and Fig. 5.1, the elements of the **R** matrix track each year's TFR fairly well over the 1917–1973 interval. The elements of the **C** matrix are also close to the average fertility proportions over that era. Given the 57 year time span and the over 3 year fall in the MAF, a deviation of 20% from unity in the **B** matrix is considered noteworthy. Values above 1.2 are shown in boldface and values below 0.8 are underlined. Deviations of 40% are considered highly noteworthy, and shown in boldface and italicized. Each r_{ii} b_{ij} c_{jj} product yields the corresponding observed age-time-specific fertility rate.

A striking pattern emerges in Table 5.6 and Fig. 5.2. The noteworthy low interactions are clustered in the upper left and lower right of the B matrix, the noteworthy high interactions are in the lower left and upper right, and the highly noteworthy elements are even more concentrated in the four corners. This pattern reflects the secular shift in birth rates to lower ages over the 1917 to 1973 era. The interactions at the young ages in the earlier years are below one because in those earlier years the observed fertility rates are lower than the average for the era. Thus the product of the TFR and the overall era proportion at those ages yields a value that is above the observed rate, and needs to be adjusted downward by the corresponding value in **B**. In those earlier years, the higher ages have interactions above 1.2 because those ages have higher than average fertility rates for the era. In this case, the product of the relevant **R** and **C** elements must be adjusted upward. The same dynamic is evident during the later years. There, the lower ages have noteworthy high interactions because those age-specific fertility rates are above average for the era. The higher ages have noteworthy low interactions because those fertility rates are below the era average. The shift in fertility to lower ages over the era can also be seen in the columns of the **B** matrix. At ages below 30, the interactions tend to increase over time, while for ages over 30, they tend to decrease. The major exceptions are the war years 1942–1945, and there is little trend at ages 29–31.

Cohort effects are notably absent in Table 5.6 and Fig. 5.2. No cohorts–described by upper-left to lower-right diagonals in the table–stand out as having continuously high or low interaction values, and there are no indications of low cohort elements followed by high cohort elements, or vice versa. Although women in their late teens and early twenties during the late 1950s and early 1960s show high **B** matrix values, they do not maintain those values at later ages, nor do they show low values at those ages. In short, Table 5.6 shows a changing pattern of age-specific fertility, but no sign of cohort effects.

Turning to Table 5.7 and Fig. 5.3, the elements of the **R** matrix once again track the yearly values of the TFR (see Fig. 5.1), and the **C** matrix approximates the overall average fertility proportions for the 1974–2020 era. Again, the product of every r_{ii} b_{ij} c_{jj} equals the corresponding age-time-specific fertility rate.

Table 5.7 and Fig. 5.3 show much the same pattern of interactions as Table 5.6 and Fig. 5.2, except that over the 1974–2020 era the increases in fertility rates went from lower to higher ages. The same 4-corners pattern of 20% deviations is evident, only the direction of the deviations changes. Here, the noteworthy high interactions are at the upper left and lower right, while the noteworthy low interactions are at the lower left and upper right. Once more, no cohort effects are evident in the pattern of

Table 5.6 Elements of B and diagonal elements of R and C matrices for U.S. single age and year fertility rates, 1917–1973

Elements of B Matrix

Year/Age	14-15	16	17	18	19	20	21	22	23	24	25	26	27	28	29
1917	.53	.57	.62	.64	.68	.70	.72	.72	.75	.75	.77	.77	.84	.88	.92
1918	.53	.56	.60	.62	.67	.69	.71	.71	.74	.74	.76	.77	.83	.87	.90
1919	.49	.53	.57	.58	.62	.64	.67	.67	.70	.71	.74	.76	.82	.87	.91
1920	.56	.63	.67	.68	.70	.71	.72	.72	.73	.74	.76	.77	.82	.86	.90
1921	.59	.65	.71	.73	.74	.72	.71	.71	.74	.75	.77	.78	.82	.86	.90
1922	.56	.62	.69	.72	.74	.72	.71	.72	.75	.76	.78	.78	.83	.85	.90
1923	.58	.63	.69	.73	.74	.73	.72	.72	.76	.77	.79	.78	.83	.85	.89
1924	.61	.66	.72	.75	.76	.74	.74	.74	.77	.77	.79	.79	.82	.84	.88
1925	.65	.70	.75	.76	.75	.74	.74	.75	.76	.77	.78	.80	.82	.84	.88
1926	.68	.71	.76	.78	.77	.75	.75	.76	.78	.78	.79	.79	.83	.84	.89
1927	.73	.76	.78	.78	.77	.76	.75	.76	.77	.78	.79	.80	.83	.85	.88
1928	.72	.76	.79	.79	.79	.77	.76	.76	.78	.79	.80	.80	.83	.85	.90
1929	.75	.79	.82	.81	.80	.78	.78	.78	.79	.80	.81	.82	.84	.86	.91
1930	.77	.81	.84	.83	.82	.79	.78	.78	.79	.80	.81	.82	.84	.86	.90
1931	.76	.80	.83	.83	.81	.80	.79	.79	.79	.81	.82	.83	.86	.87	.91
1932	.75	.80	.83	.83	.82	.80	.80	.79	.80	.80	.82	.83	.85	.87	.90
1933	.75	.78	.81	.82	.81	.80	.80	.80	.80	.81	.82	.84	.86	.88	.91
1934	.78	.81	.84	.85	.85	.83	.82	.82	.82	.83	.84	.85	.87	.89	.92
1935	.87	.87	.88	.88	.87	.86	.85	.84	.84	.84	.84	.85	.87	.89	.92
1936	.89	.89	.91	.89	.89	.88	.88	.88	.87	.87	.88	.88	.89	.90	.93
1937	.93	.97	.96	.94	.92	.91	.91	.91	.90	.90	.90	.91	.91	.92	.94
1938	.94	.97	.99	.96	.94	.92	.92	.92	.92	.92	.92	.92	.94	.94	.96
1939	.93	.95	.97	.98	.95	.93	.92	.93	.93	.94	.94	.95	.96	.97	.98
1940	.96	.96	.97	.98	.98	.97	.95	.94	.95	.96	.98	.99	.99	1.00	1.01
1941	1.00	1.00	1.00	.99	1.00	1.00	.99	.99	.98	1.00	1.01	1.02	1.03	1.03	1.03
1942	.97	.97	.99	1.01	1.01	1.01	1.02	1.05	1.07	1.07	1.06	1.06	1.06	1.07	1.05
1943	.94	.95	.96	.97	.97	.96	.97	.99	1.02	1.03	1.04	1.05	1.06	1.07	1.07
1944	.88	.87	.88	.89	.90	.91	.93	.95	.97	.98	.99	1.00	1.02	1.04	1.06
1945	.88	.84	.83	.84	.84	.85	.86	.87	.89	.91	.93	.97	.99	1.03	1.06
1946	.81	.80	.84	.88	.93	.98	1.02	1.05	1.05	1.07	1.08	1.08	1.08	1.08	1.09
1947	.99	1.02	1.04	1.06	1.08	1.09	1.10	1.10	1.09	1.08	1.08	1.09	1.08	1.07	1.05
1948	1.16	1.16	1.15	1.14	1.12	1.11	1.10	1.10	1.08	1.08	1.06	1.06	1.06	1.05	1.03
1949	1.18	1.19	1.17	1.15	1.13	1.12	1.11	1.10	1.09	1.09	1.08	1.07	1.06	1.06	1.05
1950	1.20	1.20	1.17	1.14	1.12	1.11	1.10	1.09	1.08	1.09	1.09	1.09	1.07	1.07	1.06
1951	1.18	1.20	1.19	1.18	1.16	1.16	1.13	1.12	1.10	1.10	1.10	1.10	1.09	1.07	1.05
1952	1.12	1.15	1.15	1.15	1.15	1.15	1.14	1.13	1.11	1.10	1.10	1.11	1.10	1.09	1.07
1953	1.11	1.16	1.17	1.17	1.17	1.17	1.16	1.15	1.12	1.11	1.09	1.10	1.09	1.08	1.06
1954	1.14	1.15	1.15	1.16	1.17	1.19	1.18	1.17	1.14	1.12	1.10	1.09	1.07	1.07	1.06
1955	1.12	1.15	1.14	1.16	1.17	1.20	1.21	1.20	1.17	1.14	1.11	1.10	1.07	1.07	1.05
1956	1.14	1.17	1.17	1.19	1.20	1.23	1.23	1.22	1.19	1.16	1.13	1.10	1.07	1.05	1.04
1957	1.11	1.18	1.18	1.20	1.21	1.23	1.24	1.23	1.20	1.17	1.14	1.12	1.08	1.06	1.03
1958	1.07	1.14	1.17	1.21	1.22	1.25	1.25	1.24	1.22	1.19	1.16	1.14	1.10	1.07	1.04
1959	1.07	1.10	1.13	1.19	1.23	1.26	1.26	1.24	1.22	1.20	1.17	1.14	1.11	1.08	1.05
1960	1.08	1.08	1.10	1.16	1.21	1.26	1.27	1.26	1.23	1.21	1.18	1.16	1.12	1.09	1.06
1961	1.05	1.09	1.09	1.13	1.18	1.24	1.26	1.26	1.23	1.21	1.18	1.16	1.12	1.10	1.07
1962	1.01	1.08	1.10	1.14	1.18	1.24	1.27	1.27	1.23	1.21	1.18	1.17	1.13	1.10	1.07
1963	1.02	1.07	1.10	1.15	1.19	1.23	1.25	1.25	1.23	1.21	1.18	1.17	1.13	1.11	1.08
1964	1.06	1.06	1.09	1.13	1.17	1.21	1.22	1.22	1.21	1.19	1.17	1.16	1.13	1.12	1.08
1965	1.14	1.13	1.12	1.15	1.17	1.19	1.20	1.19	1.18	1.17	1.15	1.15	1.11	1.09	1.07
1966	1.23	1.20	1.18	1.20	1.20	1.22	1.22	1.21	1.19	1.18	1.16	1.13	1.10	1.07	1.04
1967	1.31	1.27	1.22	1.21	1.21	1.22	1.22	1.22	1.21	1.20	1.18	1.16	1.11	1.07	1.03
1968	1.41	1.32	1.26	1.25	1.23	1.23	1.23	1.22	1.21	1.22	1.21	1.20	1.14	1.10	1.05
1969	1.50	1.36	1.29	1.27	1.24	1.23	1.23	1.23	1.24	1.23	1.24	1.23	1.19	1.14	1.08
1970	1.65	1.48	1.37	1.30	1.26	1.24	1.23	1.23	1.24	1.25	1.24	1.24	1.21	1.17	1.10
1971	1.80	1.58	1.43	1.33	1.25	1.22	1.21	1.22	1.23	1.25	1.25	1.25	1.22	1.18	1.12
1972	2.09	1.80	1.56	1.38	1.26	1.18	1.15	1.16	1.17	1.20	1.22	1.23	1.20	1.16	1.10
1973	2.27	1.90	1.62	1.41	1.26	1.18	1.14	1.14	1.16	1.19	1.23	1.24	1.22	1.18	1.11
Diagonal Elements of C	.007	.012	.022	.035	.046	.055	.060	.063	.064	.063	.060	.057	.054	.050	.047

NOTE: All row sums after the third complete iteration differ from 31.0 by no more than .01.

Fertility rate data source: Heuser (1976).

30	31	32	33	34	35	36	37	38	39	40	41	42	43	44	45&up	Diagonal Elements of R
.90	.92	.94	1.01	1.06	1.12	1.17	1.24	1.27	1.34	1.32	1.37	1.40	1.51	1.64	1.95	3890
.89	.91	.93	.99	1.04	1.10	1.15	1.22	1.26	1.33	1.32	1.37	1.39	1.49	1.69	2.27	3913
.91	.94	.96	1.02	1.07	1.15	1.21	1.29	1.33	1.41	1.38	1.43	1.44	1.55	1.66	2.00	3652
.88	.90	.92	.98	1.03	1.09	1.15	1.22	1.26	1.34	1.33	1.39	1.38	1.49	1.62	2.07	3834
.89	.91	.93	.99	1.04	1.10	1.15	1.21	1.25	1.33	1.33	1.38	1.40	1.50	1.58	1.85	3871
.89	.93	.94	1.00	1.05	1.11	1.15	1.21	1.25	1.32	1.32	1.38	1.40	1.50	1.60	1.83	3607
.89	.93	.95	1.01	1.05	1.10	1.15	1.20	1.23	1.31	1.30	1.36	1.40	1.50	1.60	1.86	3591
.88	.92	.94	1.00	1.04	1.09	1.13	1.19	1.22	1.29	1.29	1.35	1.39	1.49	1.59	1.80	3598
.88	.92	.94	1.00	1.05	1.09	1.14	1.19	1.23	1.28	1.29	1.35	1.38	1.48	1.56	1.76	3471
.89	.92	.93	.98	1.03	1.09	1.13	1.19	1.21	1.27	1.26	1.33	1.37	1.46	1.53	1.76	3327
.88	.92	.94	.99	1.03	1.08	1.14	1.19	1.23	1.27	1.28	1.32	1.35	1.43	1.49	1.67	3228
.89	.93	.94	.99	1.02	1.06	1.11	1.18	1.21	1.27	1.26	1.31	1.34	1.42	1.49	1.69	3027
.91	.94	.94	.98	1.02	1.06	1.09	1.14	1.19	1.25	1.25	1.28	1.32	1.37	1.44	1.70	2859
.92	.95	.94	.98	1.01	1.05	1.08	1.13	1.18	1.24	1.25	1.29	1.31	1.38	1.44	1.62	2850
.93	.96	.97	.98	1.01	1.05	1.09	1.13	1.17	1.22	1.24	1.28	1.32	1.36	1.43	1.59	2688
.91	.96	.98	1.02	1.01	1.05	1.08	1.13	1.16	1.21	1.22	1.28	1.32	1.40	1.41	1.58	2592
.91	.94	.97	1.02	1.04	1.04	1.07	1.11	1.16	1.20	1.22	1.28	1.33	1.41	1.45	1.58	2429
.93	.95	.96	1.02	1.05	1.07	1.06	1.09	1.13	1.17	1.19	1.23	1.29	1.38	1.39	1.48	2459
.93	.95	.95	.99	1.03	1.07	1.08	1.08	1.10	1.14	1.16	1.20	1.23	1.30	1.32	1.51	2392
.94	.96	.96	.99	1.00	1.05	1.07	1.09	1.08	1.11	1.12	1.16	1.18	1.25	1.28	1.44	2308
.95	.96	.97	.99	.99	1.02	1.05	1.08	1.08	1.08	1.09	1.11	1.14	1.16	1.17	1.33	2296
.96	.97	.97	.98	.99	1.00	1.01	1.04	1.07	1.08	1.07	1.08	1.11	1.13	1.17	1.27	2323
.99	.99	1.00	1.01	1.00	1.02	1.01	1.03	1.05	1.07	1.08	1.07	1.07	1.08	1.11	1.19	2242
1.02	1.02	1.01	1.02	1.01	1.01	1.01	1.01	1.02	1.02	1.06	1.05	1.04	1.04	1.02	1.06	2259
1.03	1.03	1.02	1.01	1.00	.99	.99	.99	.98	.99	1.00	1.01	1.00	.97	.94	.96	2319
1.05	1.02	1.04	1.04	1.02	.99	.95	.96	.97	.95	.94	.89	.92	.93	1.00	.86	2481
1.08	1.07	1.08	1.09	1.07	1.04	1.00	1.01	1.00	.98	.96	.94	.93	.94	.94	.82	2585
1.08	1.09	1.11	1.12	1.12	1.10	1.08	1.07	1.06	1.03	1.02	1.01	1.02	1.00	.99	.82	2492
1.11	1.13	1.15	1.16	1.17	1.16	1.14	1.11	1.10	1.07	1.07	1.06	1.05	1.02	.99	.91	2474
1.12	1.13	1.14	1.12	1.11	1.10	1.07	1.04	1.01	.98	.96	.94	.92	.90	.86	.77	2747
1.07	1.06	1.07	1.05	1.03	1.01	1.00	.96	.94	.89	.89	.86	.85	.82	.78	.68	3010
1.03	1.04	1.03	1.03	1.01	.99	.97	.95	.92	.88	.87	.85	.83	.79	.72	.62	2875
1.05	1.03	1.03	1.01	1.00	.98	.96	.93	.91	.88	.86	.83	.81	.77	.74	.59	2874
1.07	1.05	1.04	1.02	1.01	.99	.96	.93	.91	.88	.87	.82	.78	.76	.68	.55	2854
1.07	1.05	1.05	1.01	.99	.97	.95	.92	.89	.85	.85	.81	.77	.71	.66	.50	2985
1.08	1.08	1.07	1.04	1.00	.98	.95	.93	.90	.86	.85	.81	.78	.72	.65	.48	3053
1.07	1.06	1.06	1.04	1.01	.97	.95	.92	.90	.85	.84	.80	.77	.72	.66	.47	3106
1.07	1.05	1.05	1.04	1.01	.98	.94	.92	.88	.85	.84	.80	.78	.71	.64	.47	3203
1.06	1.05	1.04	1.02	1.01	.97	.95	.90	.89	.84	.84	.79	.77	.71	.65	.44	3219
1.04	1.04	1.03	1.00	.98	.96	.93	.90	.86	.82	.81	.79	.76	.70	.62	.45	3302
1.04	1.03	1.03	1.01	.98	.95	.93	.89	.86	.81	.81	.78	.75	.68	.60	.45	3358
1.04	1.03	1.02	1.00	.98	.94	.92	.89	.86	.82	.80	.77	.73	.67	.61	.44	3287
1.05	1.03	1.02	.99	.97	.94	.91	.88	.86	.82	.81	.76	.74	.68	.62	.46	3290
1.06	1.04	1.02	.99	.97	.94	.92	.87	.85	.81	.82	.78	.74	.66	.61	.46	3249
1.07	1.04	1.04	.99	.97	.94	.92	.88	.85	.81	.83	.79	.76	.68	.62	.45	3219
1.07	1.05	1.04	1.00	.96	.93	.91	.87	.84	.80	.81	.79	.77	.69	.61	.47	3083
1.08	1.06	1.05	1.01	.98	.93	.91	.87	.85	.81	.81	.78	.78	.69	.64	.40	2971
1.08	1.06	1.06	1.02	.99	.95	.92	.88	.86	.82	.83	.79	.76	.70	.63	.42	2871
1.07	1.06	1.05	1.02	.99	.95	.92	.88	.86	.83	.84	.80	.78	.69	.64	.40	2634
1.04	1.02	1.02	.98	.96	.93	.90	.86	.83	.80	.81	.79	.76	.68	.65	.42	2442
1.03	1.00	.99	.96	.94	.90	.88	.84	.82	.77	.79	.76	.74	.67	.64	.42	2303
1.02	.99	.97	.93	.91	.88	.85	.81	.78	.75	.74	.72	.72	.64	.60	.39	2201
1.05	1.00	.97	.92	.89	.86	.82	.77	.74	.70	.71	.67	.66	.60	.55	.37	2169
1.07	1.01	.96	.90	.86	.82	.78	.73	.70	.67	.67	.63	.61	.53	.51	.34	2169
1.08	1.02	.97	.89	.85	.80	.77	.72	.68	.64	.63	.59	.57	.51	.43	.31	2000
1.07	1.00	.95	.87	.82	.77	.74	.70	.66	.61	.61	.58	.55	.51	.42	.27	1806
1.07	1.00	.94	.85	.80	.73	.70	.65	.62	.58	.58	.55	.54	.47	.43	.25	1689
.041	.038	.034	.031	.028	.025	.022	.020	.017	.014	.011	.008	.006	.004	.003	.004	

Table 5.7 Elements of B and diagonal elements of R and C matrices for U.S. single age and year fertility rates, 1974–2020

Year/Age	Elements of B Matrix																														Diagonal Elements
	14-15	16	17	18	19	20	21	22	23	24	25	26	27	28	29	30	31	32	33	34	35	36	37	38	39	40	41	42	43	44	45&up	of R
1974	1.43	1.47	1.47	1.42	1.39	1.34	1.32	1.31	1.27	1.24	1.22	1.19	1.16	1.09	1.03	.87	.78	.69	.68	.67	.68	.66	.62	.63	.64	.73	.75	.82	.82	.82	.79	1698
1975	1.46	1.47	1.47	1.42	1.38	1.33	1.31	1.30	1.27	1.24	1.22	1.19	1.16	1.10	1.03	.87	.79	.70	.69	.67	.68	.66	.62	.63	.63	.72	.75	.81	.81	.81	.81	1642
1976	1.42	1.44	1.44	1.40	1.38	1.34	1.33	1.32	1.29	1.26	1.24	1.21	1.18	1.13	1.06	.92	.84	.75	.74	.72	.71	.67	.62	.63	.63	.71	.73	.78	.77	.77	.56	1578
1977	1.39	1.41	1.41	1.38	1.37	1.34	1.33	1.33	1.30	1.28	1.26	1.24	1.22	1.16	1.10	.95	.87	.78	.76	.74	.71	.67	.61	.61	.62	.69	.70	.73	.73	.73	.56	1605
1978	1.39	1.41	1.41	1.38	1.36	1.34	1.33	1.32	1.30	1.27	1.26	1.24	1.22	1.16	1.11	.98	.91	.83	.81	.78	.73	.68	.61	.61	.61	.67	.67	.68	.68	.67	.57	1568
1979	1.37	1.39	1.39	1.37	1.36	1.34	1.33	1.33	1.30	1.28	1.26	1.24	1.22	1.17	1.12	.99	.93	.85	.83	.80	.74	.69	.61	.61	.61	.66	.66	.66	.66	.65	.56	1603
1980	1.35	1.39	1.39	1.37	1.36	1.35	1.34	1.34	1.31	1.29	1.26	1.24	1.22	1.17	1.12	1.00	.94	.86	.84	.81	.74	.69	.61	.61	.61	.66	.65	.64	.64	.64	.55	1626
1981	1.35	1.39	1.39	1.37	1.36	1.33	1.32	1.32	1.30	1.27	1.26	1.24	1.22	1.17	1.12	1.01	.94	.87	.84	.82	.76	.71	.63	.63	.63	.66	.65	.63	.62	.62	.56	1603
1982	1.34	1.38	1.38	1.36	1.34	1.31	1.30	1.29	1.27	1.25	1.23	1.21	1.19	1.16	1.11	1.02	.96	.90	.88	.85	.79	.74	.66	.66	.65	.67	.66	.62	.62	.62	.55	1625
1983	1.34	1.37	1.37	1.34	1.32	1.28	1.27	1.26	1.24	1.22	1.21	1.19	1.18	1.14	1.11	1.03	.98	.93	.91	.88	.82	.77	.70	.70	.69	.69	.67	.62	.62	.62	.55	1610
1984	1.33	1.34	1.34	1.31	1.29	1.26	1.25	1.24	1.22	1.21	1.20	1.19	1.17	1.14	1.11	1.05	1.00	.96	.94	.91	.84	.80	.73	.72	.71	.69	.67	.60	.60	.60	.55	1618
1985	1.31	1.32	1.32	1.30	1.28	1.25	1.24	1.23	1.21	1.20	1.20	1.18	1.17	1.15	1.11	1.05	1.01	.97	.95	.92	.86	.82	.75	.74	.73	.70	.67	.60	.60	.60	.54	1653
1986	1.31	1.30	1.30	1.28	1.26	1.23	1.22	1.22	1.20	1.19	1.18	1.17	1.16	1.13	1.11	1.06	1.02	.98	.97	.94	.88	.83	.76	.76	.75	.72	.69	.62	.62	.61	.54	1654
1987	1.28	1.28	1.27	1.25	1.24	1.20	1.19	1.19	1.18	1.17	1.16	1.15	1.14	1.12	1.10	1.05	1.02	.98	.97	.95	.90	.87	.81	.80	.79	.75	.72	.64	.64	.64	.52	1701
1988	1.28	1.29	1.29	1.25	1.23	1.18	1.17	1.16	1.15	1.14	1.14	1.13	1.12	1.10	1.08	1.04	1.01	.98	.97	.95	.91	.88	.84	.83	.82	.78	.75	.68	.68	.67	.50	1776
1989	1.32	1.34	1.33	1.28	1.24	1.17	1.15	1.13	1.12	1.11	1.11	1.10	1.09	1.08	1.06	1.02	.99	.96	.95	.94	.91	.89	.85	.85	.84	.79	.77	.71	.70	.69	.48	1870
1990	1.33	1.35	1.35	1.28	1.24	1.16	1.13	1.11	1.10	1.09	1.09	1.08	1.07	1.06	1.04	1.01	.99	.97	.96	.95	.93	.90	.87	.87	.86	.81	.78	.72	.71	.70	.46	1945
1991	1.37	1.41	1.41	1.32	1.26	1.16	1.13	1.10	1.09	1.08	1.07	1.06	1.05	1.03	1.02	.99	.97	.95	.94	.94	.93	.91	.88	.88	.87	.81	.78	.72	.71	.70	.46	1943
1992	1.34	1.36	1.35	1.28	1.22	1.13	1.10	1.08	1.06	1.05	1.04	1.03	1.02	1.01	1.00	.98	.97	.95	.94	.93	.92	.91	.89	.88	.88	.84	.83	.78	.78	.77	.68	1964
1993	1.32	1.33	1.33	1.25	1.20	1.11	1.08	1.06	1.05	1.03	1.02	1.01	1.00	.99	.99	.98	.97	.96	.95	.95	.94	.92	.90	.90	.89	.87	.86	.82	.81	.81	.68	1956
1994	1.30	1.31	1.31	1.23	1.18	1.08	1.06	1.04	1.02	1.01	1.00	.99	.97	.97	.97	.98	.97	.97	.96	.96	.95	.94	.92	.92	.92	.90	.89	.87	.86	.86	.68	1961
1995	1.25	1.26	1.26	1.19	1.15	1.07	1.05	1.03	1.01	1.00	.98	.97	.96	.96	.96	.98	.98	.98	.98	.98	.97	.96	.95	.94	.94	.93	.92	.90	.90	.89	.68	1951
1996	1.18	1.19	1.19	1.15	1.12	1.06	1.04	1.03	1.02	1.00	.98	.96	.95	.96	.96	.99	.99	1.00	.99	.99	.99	.98	.97	.97	.97	.96	.95	.93	.93	.92	.68	1954
1997	1.11	1.12	1.12	1.09	1.07	1.04	1.03	1.02	1.00	.99	.96	.95	.94	.94	.95	.98	.99	1.00	1.00	1.00	.99	.99	.99	.99	.99	.98	.98	.97	.97	.96	.90	1975
1998	1.06	1.07	1.07	1.05	1.04	1.02	1.02	1.01	1.00	.99	.96	.95	.94	.95	.96	.99	1.00	1.01	1.01	1.01	1.01	1.01	1.01	1.01	1.00	1.00	1.00	1.00	.99	.99	.89	2009
1999	1.01	1.03	1.03	1.02	1.02	1.01	1.01	1.01	1.00	.99	.96	.95	.95	.96	.97	1.00	1.02	1.03	1.03	1.03	1.03	1.03	1.03	1.03	1.03	1.01	1.00	.98	.98	.98	.89	2012
2000	.97	.98	.98	.98	.98	.98	.98	.98	.97	.96	.94	.93	.92	.94	.95	1.00	1.02	1.04	1.04	1.04	1.03	1.04	1.04	1.04	1.04	1.04	1.03	1.03	1.03	1.03	1.06	2099
2001	.88	.88	.88	.91	.92	.94	.95	.96	.96	.96	.94	.94	.94	.96	.98	1.02	1.04	1.06	1.06	1.07	1.07	1.07	1.08	1.08	1.08	1.07	1.06	1.06	1.06	1.06	1.08	2068
2002	.84	.85	.85	.87	.89	.91	.92	.93	.93	.94	.94	.95	.95	.97	.98	1.02	1.04	1.06	1.07	1.08	1.09	1.10	1.11	1.11	1.11	1.09	1.09	1.08	1.08	1.07	1.07	2076
2003	.78	.80	.80	.83	.85	.88	.89	.90	.91	.92	.93	.94	.95	.97	.99	1.03	1.05	1.08	1.09	1.10	1.11	1.13	1.15	1.15	1.15	1.12	1.12	1.11	1.10	1.10	1.05	2116
2004	.76	.78	.78	.81	.83	.86	.87	.88	.90	.91	.92	.93	.94	.96	.98	1.02	1.05	1.07	1.08	1.10	1.13	1.16	1.19	1.19	1.19	1.15	1.15	1.13	1.13	1.13	1.04	2138
2005	.75	.75	.75	.79	.81	.85	.87	.88	.89	.90	.91	.92	.93	.95	.97	1.01	1.04	1.07	1.08	1.09	1.14	1.16	1.21	1.20	1.20	1.15	1.15	1.12	1.13	1.13	1.24	2163
2006	.75	.75	.75	.79	.82	.86	.88	.89	.90	.90	.90	.91	.91	.93	.96	1.01	1.03	1.07	1.08	1.09	1.13	1.16	1.20	1.20	1.20	1.16	1.15	1.14	1.14	1.14	1.20	2220
2007	.75	.76	.76	.79	.82	.86	.87	.88	.89	.89	.89	.90	.90	.93	.95	1.01	1.04	1.08	1.09	1.10	1.13	1.15	1.19	1.19	1.19	1.16	1.16	1.16	1.16	1.16	1.19	2240
2008	.74	.74	.74	.77	.79	.83	.84	.85	.86	.87	.87	.87	.88	.91	.93	1.00	1.03	1.07	1.08	1.09	1.11	1.14	1.17	1.17	1.18	1.18	1.20	1.22	1.23	1.23	1.40	2232
2009	.71	.71	.71	.74	.77	.80	.81	.82	.83	.85	.85	.86	.88	.90	.93	1.00	1.03	1.08	1.09	1.10	1.12	1.14	1.18	1.18	1.19	1.21	1.23	1.28	1.28	1.29	1.43	2183
2010	.65	.65	.65	.69	.72	.76	.77	.78	.80	.82	.84	.85	.87	.90	.93	1.00	1.04	1.09	1.10	1.12	1.14	1.16	1.20	1.21	1.22	1.26	1.28	1.35	1.35	1.35	1.46	2135
2011	.61	.59	.59	.64	.67	.71	.73	.74	.77	.80	.83	.85	.87	.91	.94	1.01	1.05	1.10	1.12	1.13	1.17	1.21	1.26	1.26	1.27	1.29	1.31	1.36	1.37	1.37	1.48	2113
2012	.58	.55	.55	.60	.64	.69	.71	.73	.75	.78	.82	.85	.87	.90	.94	1.01	1.06	1.12	1.13	1.15	1.20	1.24	1.30	1.30	1.31	1.31	1.33	1.37	1.37	1.38	1.48	2109
2013	.52	.49	.49	.55	.59	.66	.69	.71	.74	.77	.81	.84	.87	.90	.94	1.02	1.07	1.13	1.15	1.17	1.22	1.26	1.33	1.33	1.34	1.32	1.33	1.36	1.37	1.38	1.69	2104
2014	.48	.43	.43	.50	.55	.64	.66	.69	.72	.76	.80	.83	.86	.90	.95	1.03	1.09	1.16	1.17	1.20	1.25	1.30	1.37	1.37	1.37	1.34	1.35	1.37	1.38	1.38	1.68	2117
2015	.43	.39	.39	.47	.52	.61	.64	.66	.70	.74	.78	.81	.85	.89	.94	1.03	1.09	1.16	1.18	1.21	1.26	1.31	1.39	1.39	1.40	1.38	1.40	1.43	1.44	1.44	1.68	2122
2016	.40	.34	.35	.42	.47	.58	.61	.63	.67	.71	.75	.78	.82	.87	.92	1.02	1.09	1.17	1.19	1.22	1.27	1.32	1.40	1.41	1.41	1.41	1.43	1.48	1.49	1.50	1.87	2142
2017	.38	.32	.32	.40	.45	.56	.59	.62	.65	.69	.73	.76	.80	.84	.90	1.01	1.08	1.16	1.19	1.22	1.27	1.33	1.42	1.42	1.43	1.44	1.47	1.55	1.55	1.56	1.90	2111
2018	.36	.29	.29	.37	.43	.54	.57	.60	.63	.67	.71	.74	.78	.83	.89	1.00	1.08	1.17	1.19	1.22	1.28	1.34	1.44	1.45	1.46	1.47	1.51	1.59	1.60	1.61	1.91	2096
2019	.35	.28	.28	.36	.41	.53	.56	.58	.62	.66	.70	.73	.77	.82	.88	.99	1.07	1.15	1.18	1.21	1.28	1.35	1.45	1.46	1.47	1.50	1.54	1.63	1.64	1.65	1.92	2090
2020	.34	.26	.26	.34	.39	.51	.54	.57	.61	.65	.69	.72	.76	.81	.87	.98	1.06	1.14	1.17	1.21	1.29	1.36	1.47	1.48	1.49	1.51	1.55	1.66	1.66	1.67	1.98	2028
Diagonal Elements of C	.017	.018	.023	.029	.034	.044	.050	.057	.058	.059	.058	.059	.060	.057	.054	.050	.047	.044	.039	.034	.026	.022	.017	.014	.012	.007	.005	.003	.002	.002	.000	

NOTE: All row sums after the third complete iteration differ from 31.0 by no more than .01.

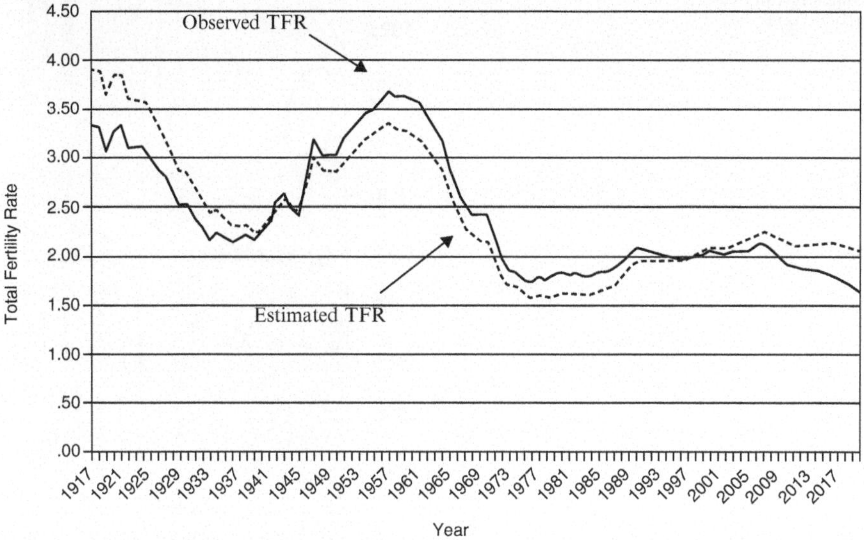

Fig. 5.1 Observed total fertility rates and total fertility rates as estimated by matrix R, United States, 1917–2020

interactions along the diagonals. The columns of **B** show even clearer time trends. At ages below 29, the interactions strongly tend to increase, and at ages over 31 to decrease. While the interactions in Table 5.7 reflect the reversal of the age-pattern of fertility from the previous era, there is no evidence of cohort effects.

As the above analyses indicate, a noteworthy interaction need not represent a cohort effect. The essence of a cohort effect is that it stems from experience earlier in the cohort's life. Tables 5.1, 5.2, 5.3, and 5.4 provide examples of how cohort level and timing changes manifest themselves in interaction matrices. In the **B** matrices of Tables 5.6, and 5.7, none of those characteristic features appear. Instead, as reinforced by the age-specific fertility rates shown in Table 5.5, there was a shift in the age distribution of fertility over those eras. In the 1910s, the Under 20 fertility rates were around 60 per 1000, while the 40+ fertility rates were around 40. In the 1970s, the Under 20 rates were still around 60 while the 40+ rates fell to below 10. In the 2010s, the Under 20 rates were down to around 20, while the 40+ rates still hovered around 10–12. Most of the noteworthy interactions in Tables 5.6, and 5.7 are thus associated with the decrease in the mean age of fertility from 28.61 years in 1917 to 25.74 years in 1974, and the subsequent increase in the MAF to 29.71 years in 2020. Those sizable shifts over time in the age-pattern of fertility produce noteworthy interactions, but they do not suggest that any cohort mechanisms are involved. Socioeconomic and other period factors are likely to be influencing fertility behavior, not previous cohort experience.

Fig. 5.2 Contour plot of B matrix elements, United States fertility rates, 1917–1973

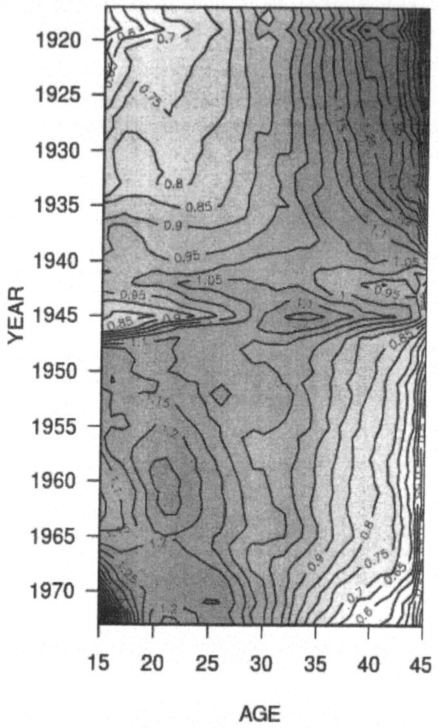

Fig. 5.3 Contour plot of B matrix elements, United States fertility rates, 1974–2020

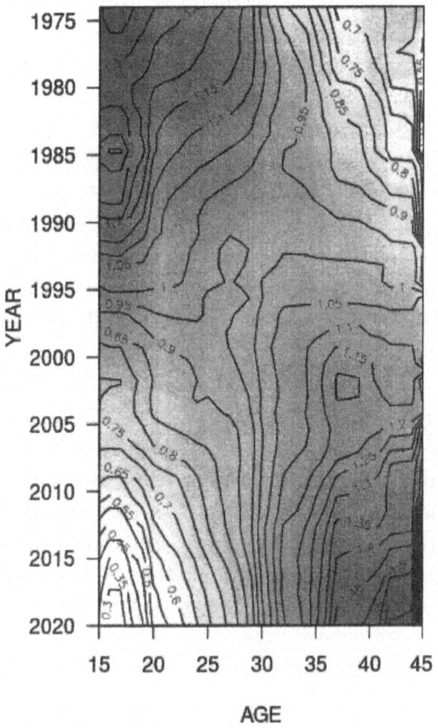

5.5 Summary and Conclusions

Defining cohort effects as specific patterns of age-period interactions, we have analyzed U.S. fertility data from 1917 to 2020 to determine whether cohort effects are present. For this purpose, we used an RBC decomposition method that is equivalent to a saturated log-linear model for age by period arrays. The method decomposes the age-specific fertility rates in such arrays into three factors: period (or row) factors that in our analysis track approximate period TFRs, age (or column) factors that are overall age-specific fertility proportions, and matrix **B**, which shows the deviations (interactions) of each rate in the observed period by age array from what one would expect if period and age were the only factors producing that rate. The elements of the **B** matrix are normalized so that a value of 1 corresponds to the absence of an interaction, and the size of the deviation from 1 indicates the magnitude of the interaction. Thus each rate in the initial period by age array equals (1) a measure of the period fertility level, times (2) an average fertility proportion at that age, times (3) the age-period interaction factor. Viewing cohort effects as interactions avoids the problem of collinear measures, with age, period, and cohort remaining proxy, not causal, variables.

We focus on fertility, first because it is a core demographic variable where cohort effects have long been seen as important, and second because its nature lends itself to the RBC decomposition. The sum of period fertility rates, the TFR, is the principal measure of fertility level. The age-schedule of fertility rates has a characteristic shape that tends to be consistent from period to period (Hobcraft et al., 1982). Finally, Ryder (1965) provides a theoretical basis for interpreting cohort effects in terms of age-period interactions. While the RBC approach, with modifications, may be applicable to other demographic behaviors, we leave such extensions to future work.

By definition, a cohort effect is the result of past influences that continue to affect a cohort's life chances. Age-period interactions can be much broader, however, and may simply reflect the impact of current conditions on current behavior. To show how cohort effects appear in an RBC decomposition, we analyze hypothetical populations. The results, in Tables 5.1, 5.2, 5.3, and 5.4, show that changes in cohort levels and in cohort timing reveal themselves clearly in the matrix of interactions.

We then applied the RBC decomposition approach to fertility data for the United States over the 1917 through 2020 interval. Tables 5.6, and 5.7 examine two meaningful eras, 1917–1973 and 1974–2020. While we found numerous noteworthy interactions, no evidence of cohort effects emerge. Indeed, the relative stability of age patterns of fertility, despite a long term fall in the mean age of fertility during the first era and an even greater long term rise during the second era, argues persuasively for period primacy. Cohort effects would disrupt period age patterns of fertility, but such disruptions are not present.

In recent American experience, many factors can be seen as impacting fertility. Over time, socioeconomic changes such as (1) higher levels of education, (2) the growth of the service sector, and (3) an evolution in gender roles leading to a rise in gender competition (Schoen, 2010) have all produced a marked retreat from marriage and childbearing. The use of effective birth control measures is widespread, childlessness is on the rise (Schoen & Hargens, 2020), and large families have largely disappeared (Schoen, 2019). There have also been numerous period shocks, from the Great Depression, through World War II and the 2008 Great Recession, to the COVID-19 pandemic. Yet no comparable cohort events are evident.

Our conclusion is that, for U. S. fertility from 1917 to 2022, period effects are real; they are not distortions of some more meaningful underlying cohort behavior. The RBC decomposition has allowed an assessment of age, period, and cohort factors over more than a century of American fertility experience, and the results show that age and period influences predominate. Though age-period interactions are common, there is no clear evidence of cohort effects. The times, not the cohorts are driving U.S. fertility, and taking it to new lows. Cohort tempo does not determine period quantum. Instead, period quantum is driving both cohort tempo and cohort quantum. For the data in our analysis, the cohort perspective offers little explanatory or analytical power.

Appendix: Finding the B matrix

We use the method of iterative proportional fitting (IPF) to transform a matrix of observed rates (**A**) into a matrix that shows by what factor an observed element in **A**, a_{ij}, differs from what would be expected if only the baseline coefficients in the **R** and **C** diagonal matrices determined its value. As noted in the text, **B** has the property that all its row sums equal the number of columns (κ) in **A** and all of its column sums equal the number of rows (ρ) in **A**. The IPF method repeats the steps given below until the researcher judges that deviations of row sums from κ and column sums from ρ for a given table are negligible, at which point the iterated sums are accepted and iteration ceases. Table 5.A1 gives a step by step example of this procedure, which is easily implemented in any standard spreadsheet program.

Iteration 1

We begin with the simple 3 by 2 table of hypothetical rates labeled in Table 5.A1 as "Initial A."

We first calculate the mean of the values in each of the ρ rows of **A** and then divide the values in each row by that row's mean. This produces a new matrix, 1a, whose row sums all equal 2 (κ), but this new matrix does not have column sums that equal 3 (ρ). We therefore follow the same procedure to produce a second new matrix, 1b, that has this property. Specifically, we calculate the mean of the values in each column of 1a and then divide all of the values in each column of 1a by that column's mean. This will ensure that matrix 1b has column sums equal to 3, though the row sums of 1b no longer equal 2. Although the new row sums vary between 1.94 and

Table 5.A1 RBC calculations for a simple matrix of hypothetical rates

				Row	Row				
Initial A				Sum	Mean				
	.45	.75		1.2	.6				
	.30	.70		1.0	.5				
	.50	.90		1.4	.7				
				Row				Row	Row
Matrix 1a				Sum		**Matrix 1b**		Sum	Mean
		.750	1.250	2			1.090	.953	2.043	1.021
		.600	1.400	2			.872	1.067	1.939	.970
		.714	1.286	2			1.038	.980	2.018	1.009
Column	Sum	2.064	3.936			Col. Sum	3	3		
Column	Mean	.688	1.312							
				Row					Row	Row
Matrix 2a				Sum		**Matrix 2b**			Sum	Mean
		1.067	.933	2			1.069	.931	2.000	1.000
		.899	1.101	2			.901	1.099	2.000	1.000
		1.029	.971	2			1.030	.970	2.000	1.000
Column	Sum	2.995	3.005			Col. Sum	3	3		
Column	Mean	.998	1.002							
	1st Mean	2nd Mean	3rd Mean	Overall Means						
Row 1	.6	1.021	1.000	.6126						
Row 2	.5	.970	1.000	.4850						
Row 3	.7	1.009	1.000	.7063						
Column 1	.688	.998		.6866						
Column 2	1.312	1.002		1.3146						

2.04, they are much closer to 2.0 than the row sums of **A**, which varied between 1.0 and 1.4. In order to obtain a table whose row and column sums are closer to κ and ρ respectively, we proceed to a second iteration.

Iteration 2

The second iteration repeats the steps followed in the first, but uses the values in the most recent matrix in the process. Thus, the second iteration begins by calculating the row means in matrix 1b and then divides the values in each row of 1b by that row's mean. This produces matrix 2a, which again has row sums equal to 2 but whose column sums do not equal 3, although they are only five one-thousandths off. Desiring greater convergence to the desired sums, we produce matrix 2b by calculating the means of each column of matrix 2a and dividing each value in that matrix by its column mean. We now have column sums equal to 3 again and the row sums are all within three ten-thousandths of 2. That was deemed close enough, but the procedure could be continued further to obtain any desired degree of closeness.

*Assigning Values for the **R** and **C** Matrices*

As we note in the text, determining the **B** matrix in the RBC model does not lead to unique values in the **R** and **C** matrices. Indeed there are an infinite number of combinations of values in the **R** and **C** matrices that will produce the equality **A** = **R B C**. One of these combinations is a byproduct of using IPF to obtain the **B** matrix, however, and we use it to obtain starting values for the subsequent transformations into demographically meaningful quantities.

As outlined above, the IPF method repeatedly divides the values in a series of tables flowing from an observed table of rates by the row and column means of those tables. One way to produce the equality specified by **A** = **R B C** is to incorporate those means into the elements of **R** and **C**. This is done by multiplying the row and column specific means used in the successive steps of the IPF method to produce "summary" or "overall" mean values. Toward the bottom of Table 5.A1 we show the three row and column means used in the IPF solution for **B,** and their product under the heading "Overall Means". Specifically, r11 = .6126, etc. and c11 = .6866, etc. The reader can verify that these values and the elements in **B** produce the values in matrix **A** very closely (to a few ten thousandths). Note that the values for the **R** matrix closely approximate the row means of **A**. This is not true for the values of the **C** matrix however; c11 = .687 whereas the mean of the first column of **A** equals .417, and c22 = 1.315 whereas the mean of the second column of **A** equals.783. The arbitrariness of these values is shown by the fact that if we had begun our IPF procedure by dividing **A**'s columns by their respective means we would have ended up with values in **C** that closely approximate the column means of **A** but with values in **R** that do not closely approximate **A**'s row means.

Given that there are many possible values for the **R** and **C** matrices, we can adopt a scaling of them that conforms to common measures of fertility analysis. In particular, because the categories of **C** represent age groups, the magnitudes the elements in **C** given above may be transformed into the proportional distribution of fertility across the age groups by summing the diagonal elements of **C** and then dividing each of those elements by that sum. In Table 5.A1 the sum of the diagonal elements of **C** equals .6866 + 1.3146 = 2.0012, so the new values of **C** we seek are c11 = .6866/2.0012 = .3431 and c22 = 1.3146/2.0012 = .6569. Because we have divided each of the original elements of **C** by a constant we must multiply all of the elements of the original **R** matrix by a reciprocal of that constant to maintain the equality **A** = **R B C**. We therefore have r_{11} = .6126 * 2.0012 = 1.2259, r_{22} = .4850 * 2.0012 = .9706, and r_{33} = .7063 * 2.0012 = 1.4134. Note that these values approximate the row sums of **A**, which in the context of fertility analysis are period Total Fertility Rates. Our rescaling of the **R** and **C** matrices thus gives us values of the baseline age distribution of fertility and baseline period TFR values that specify the values we would expect to see in the **A** matrix if Eq. (5.5) holds. If in fact Eq. (5.5) does hold, these values in the **R** and **C** matrices will exactly match the corresponding values obtained directly from **A**.

References

Bishop, Y. M., Fienberg, S. E., & Holland, P. W. (1975). *Discrete multivariate analysis*. MIT Press.

Clogg, C. C. (1982). Cohort analysis of recent trends in labor force participation. *Demography, 19*, 459–479.

Easterlin, R. A. (1980). *Birth and fortune: The impact of numbers on personal welfare*. Basic Books.

Fienberg, S. E. (2013). Cohort analysis' unholy quest. *Demography, 50*, 1981–1984.

Fosse, E., & Winship, C. (2019). Analyzing age-period-cohort data: A review and critique. *Annual Review of Sociology, 45*, 467–492.

Glenn, N. D. (1976). Cohort analysts' futile quest: Statistical attempts to separate age, period and cohort effects. *American Sociological Review, 41*, 900–904.

Glenn, N. D. (2005). *Cohort analysis*. Sage.

Goodman, L. A., & Kruskal, W. H. (1979). *Measures of association for cross classifications*. Springer.

Hajnal, J. (1947). The analysis of birth statistics in the light of the recent international recovery of the birth rate. *Population Studies, 1*, 137–164.

Hamilton, B. E., Martin, J. A., & Osterman, M. J. K. (2021). *Births: Provisional data for 2020. Vital statistics rapid release no 12*. National Center for Health Statistics.

Heuser, R. L. (1976). *Fertility tables for birth cohorts by color: United States 1917–1973* (DHEW Pub. No. (HRA) 76-1152). U.S. National Center for Health Statistics.

Hobcraft, J., Menken, J., & Preston, S. (1982). Age, period, and cohort effects in demography: A review. *Population Index, 48*, 4–43.

James, I. R., & Segal, M. R. (1982). On a method of mortality analysis incorporating age-year interaction, with application to prostate cancer mortality. *Biometrics, 38*, 433–443.

Keyes, K. M., Utz, R. L., Robinson, W., & Li, G. (2010). What is a cohort effect? Comparison of three statistical methods for modeling cohort effects in obesity prevalence in the United States, 1971-2006. *Social Science and Medicine, 70*, 1100–1108.

Lesthaeghe, R. (2010). The unfolding story of the second demographic transition. *Population and Development Review, 36*, 211–251.

Luo, L., & Hodges, J. S. (2022). The age-period-cohort-interaction model for describing and investigating inter-cohort deviations and intra-cohort life-course dynamics. *Sociological Methods and Research, 51*, 1164–1210.

Martin, J. A., Hamilton, B. E., Osterman, M. J. K., Driscoll, A. K., & Mathews, T. J. (2017). *Births: Final data for 2015* (National Vital Statistics Reports, Vol. 66, No. 1). National Center for Health Statistics.

Martin, J. A., Hamilton, B. E., Osterman, M. J. K., & Driscoll, A. K. (2019). *Births: Final data for 2018* (National Vital Statistics Reports, Vol. 68, No. 13). National Center for Health Statistics.

Mason, K. O., Mason, W. M., Winsborough, H. H., & Poole, W. K. (1973). Some methodological issues in cohort analysis of archival data. *American Sociological Review, 38*, 242–258.

Ni Bhrolchain, M. (1992). Period paramount? A critique of the cohort approach to fertility. *Population and Development Review, 18*, 599–629.

O'Brien, R. M. (2015). *Age-period-cohort models: Approaches and analyses with aggregate data*. Taylor & Francis.

Pullum, T. W. (1978). Parameterizing age, period, and cohort effects: An application to U.S. delinquency rates, 1964–1973. *Sociological Methodology, 9*, 116–140.

Ryder, N. B. (1956). Problems of trend determination during a transition in fertility. *Milbank Memorial Fund Quarterly, 34*, 5–21.

Ryder, N. B. (1965). The cohort as a concept in the study of social change. *American Sociological Review*, 30, 854–861.

Ryder, N. B. (1980). Components of temporal variations in American fertility. In R. W. Hiorns (Ed.), *Demographic patterns in developed societies* (pp. 15–54). Taylor and Francis.

Schoen, R. (2010). Gender competition and family change. *Genus, 66*, 95–120.

Schoen, R. (2019). Parity progression and the kinship network. In R. Schoen (Ed.), *Analytical family demography* (pp. 189–199). Springer.

Schoen, R. (2020). Dynamic multistate models with constant cross-product ratios: Applications to poverty status. *Demography, 57*, 779–797.

Schoen, R. (2022). Relating period and cohort fertility. *Demography, 59*, 877–894.

Schoen, R., & Hargens, L. (2020). Social capital, gender competition, and the resurgence of childlessness. In R. Schoen (Ed.), *Analyzing contemporary fertility* (pp. 9–24). Springer.

Stolzenberg, R. M. (1979). The measurement and decomposition of causal effects in nonlinear and nonadditive models. In K. F. Schuessler (Ed.), *Sociological Methodology 1980* (pp. 459–488). Jossey-Bass.

Willekens, F. (1982). Multidimensional population analysis with incomplete data. In K. C. Land & A. Rogers (Eds.), *Multidimensional mathematical demography* (pp. 43–111). Academic.

Yang, Y., Schulhofer-Wohl, S., Fu, W. J., & Land, K. C. (2008). The intrinsic estimator for age-period-cohort analysis: What it is and how to use it? *American Journal of Sociology, 113*, 1697–1736.

Chapter 6
The Future of the Italian Family: Evidence from a Household Projection Model

Martina Lo Conte, Gianni Corsetti, Alessandra De Rose, Marco Marsili, and Eleonora Meli

6.1 Introduction

In recent decades, Italy has been experiencing profound transformations in family structures. On the one hand, the intense demographic changes, due to the unstoppable decline in fertility starting from the 1970s, combined with the impressive growth in longevity, have made the Italian family ever smaller and with a growing component of older members. On the other hand, the changes in individual life paths that are increasingly fragmented and complicated, and in couples' behaviors, as well as in the social legitimization of forms of relationships previously considered unacceptable, have made the family system increasingly heterogeneous. Marriage no longer marks the transition from adolescence to adulthood, it is no longer the event that legitimizes the beginning of sexual and reproductive life, and it no longer lasts for life; cohabitating couples have become a widespread phenomenon; children born to unmarried parents have increased; same-sex couples are recognized and legitimized. The most striking result of these dynamics is that, if at the beginning of the new millennium the nuclear family consisting of a couple with children was still the most frequent type of family, today it has been superseded by the one-member family. That is, by people who, for different reasons, live alone during a phase of their life, frequently corresponding with an older age. This last evidence arouses a certain amount of concern from the public policy viewpoint, in terms of the need for care and services, which cannot be entrusted exclusively to the kinship network, increasingly reduced in size, and weakened in interpersonal ties (Reher, 1998). In

M. Lo Conte · G. Corsetti · M. Marsili · E. Meli
Italian National Institute of Statistics, Rome, Italy

A. De Rose (✉)
Sapienza University of Rome, Rome, Italy
e-mail: alessandra.derose@uniroma1.it

R. Schoen (ed.), *The Demography of Transforming Families*, The Springer Series on Demographic Methods and Population Analysis 56,
https://doi.org/10.1007/978-3-031-29666-6_6

prospective terms, the situation can become extremely worrying, especially in a country like Italy, where fertility shows no signs of increasing and the aging rate of the population is expected to grow (Istat, 2022a). For these reasons, monitoring the evolution of households in forecasting terms is of particular importance.

This Chapter illustrates the household projections performed for Italy from 2021 to 2041 by the Italian National Institute of Statistics (Istat). A static method has been applied to the projected population estimates, which are annually updated. The approach is based on the *Propensity rate model* that has proven to meet the requirements of parsimony, simplicity, replicability and quality. The method also provides future time series data of the population by household position (child, living with a partner with or without children, lone parent, living alone and other position), age and sex.

Results show that, in a framework of continuation of the ongoing trend of progressive population decline and aging, we can expect an increase in the number of households by one million in 20 years, and a decrease in their average size, which would drop from 2.3 members per household to 2.1. Furthermore, we forecast a diminishing number of couples with children, while couples without children and above all, single people, especially older people, will increase.

Household projections show the future trend in the number and type of households that will characterize the forthcoming population. The purpose is to provide stakeholders, both public and private, with an integrated system of information that can be useful when dealing with goods and services intended for families rather than for individuals. Given the importance of the role of the family in Italian society, both at the protective level and for the determination of individual choices and paths, the demand for information on households arises from planning needs in various areas. Among them, we can consider the decisions to be taken in economic and social policies, such as those relating to housing, social and welfare systems for the young and the older population. Improving the knowledge base for the perspective productive strategies of durable goods for households and energy consumption is another potential task.

The chapter is organized as follows: first, we frame the projections of the Italian households in the context of recent demographic trends and in the changes occurred in the family system and in living arrangement behaviors in the country. We will then go into the details of data and methods used by Istat to perform medium-term household projections, and motivate the strategic choices made in the range of possible methodologies for households forecasting. Finally, we will illustrate the main results and discuss their implications in terms of the future shape of Italian society.

6.2 Changes of the Family System in Italy

To grasp the salient features of the transformations of the family system that have occurred in Italy in recent decades, it is necessary to place them in the broader process of change of the patterns of union formation and dissolution that have occurred throughout Europe since the beginning of the 1960s, according to the *Second Demographic Transition* (SDT) conceptual framework (Lesthaeghe & van de Kaa, 1986; Lesthaeghe & Surkyn, 1988). The first aspect of this process is the crisis of marriage, especially religious marriage, which until the middle of the century had been the founding institution of the family. The number of marriages celebrated by single women decreased in all European countries, while the mean age at marriage increased, especially for women. At the same time, "paperless" cohabitations became widespread. Another distinctive feature of SDT is the growth of marital instability. The indissolubility of conjugal unions ceased to be a cornerstone of the family. Couples who dissolve voluntarily due to conflicts between partners or simply due to the end of the sentimental understanding became increasingly numerous everywhere in the Western world. These changes in the life of the couple contributed to the further reduction of family size, already caused by the intense reduction in fertility that had begun in the previous decades. This is especially true in countries like Italy, where, as we will discuss shortly, cohabitation has struggled to replace traditional marriage until recent years and the increase in divorce has not been matched by a significant increase in the so-called stepfamilies (De Rose & Vignoli, 2011).

Indeed, as consequences of conjugal dissolution, complex family forms have emerged throughout Europe such as: a) stepfamilies, resulting from a second marriage or, more frequently, from an informal union, eventually with children born to at least one of the two partners in the previous unions; b) lone-parent households, almost always formed by the mother and children; c) multi-nuclear families, which are formed when one of the two partners, possibly with the children, joins his/her family of origin and shares resources and housing.

Although these changes have occurred all over Western European societies after World War II, there has been a great deal of cross-country variations in the intensity and speed of the changes themselves, due to the different initial conditions or different political and economic contexts (Sobotka, 2008; Carlson, 2019). The process has been most advanced in the Nordic European countries, followed by Western, Central and Eastern countries. The laggard cluster includes the Southern European regions, where the diffusion of new attitudes and behaviors did not start until the mid-1970s (Liefbroer & Dourleijn, 2006; Lesthaeghe, 2014).

Italy is a clear example in this respect. The most relevant cultural and societal changes, reflected in legislation innovations, occurred late in the 1970s. Indeed, the laws innovating family rules appeared only in that decade: the divorce law was approved in 1970, the new law regulating family ties in 1975, and voluntary abortion was legalized in 1978. Gender system changes – which are at the origin of the partnership revolution and the decline in fertility (Lesthaeghe & Surkyn, 1988) – that had already occurred in Northern and Central Europe, became relevant in Italy only starting from the 1970s, with the massive entry of women into secondary and tertiary education and then into labor forces. Indeed, with a female employment rate equal to 50.9% in 2022, women's participation in the labor market is still below European standards and Lisbon's EU targets (Istat, 2022b).

Italy was characterized by a very rigid union dynamic pattern until the mid-1970s. The evolution of the family system was mainly marked by the decline in fertility and population aging, while the ways of entering and leaving the family changed little (De Rose et al., 2008). Stable cohabitation between partners of the opposite sex still took place almost exclusively through marriage, albeit rarer and later, and the *de facto* cohabitations were rare. Informal unions were not widespread among young people, who instead remain in the parental family for a long time; births, few and late, still took place predominantly in marriage; separations and divorces were infrequent, although in constant increase and therefore, single-parent families and reconstituted families were not numerically relevant. However, things began to change rapidly starting from the 1980s, so that a progressive and inexorable process of change has been underway in the times and ways of making a family.

With the beginning of the new Millennium, the process of change accelerates (Tomassini & Vignoli, 2023). The reduction in the number of marriages intensified during the 1990s and especially from the first decade of the twenty-first century. Between 2000 and 2020, the total first marriage rate drops from 652 marriages per 1000 in 2000 to 475 in 2019, and to 236 in 2020 (also because of the restrictions imposed during the COVID-19 pandemic). Among people aged 25–54 living as a couple, the percentage of them cohabiting but not married grows from 4% to 16% between 2000 and 2020. The majority of these unions are premarital cohabitations, but the number of never married cohabiting couples has increased considerably in recent years, also due to important legal advances in the recognition of the rights and duties of *de facto* families.

In this regard, the introduction of a law in 2016 which allows the recognition in Italy of civil unions also between persons of the same sex is noteworthy. From July 2016 to December 2020, over 13,000 civil unions were celebrated in Italy, concentrated above all in the northern and central regions, and in particular, in large urban areas (Istat, 2022c).

Not only are the ways of union formation changing, but also the dissolution patterns changed. Separations and divorces show a growing trend in recent years, both in absolute and relative terms, also due to some recent regulatory changes that have simplified the law in force (Guarneri et al., 2021). A real boom in divorces has been observed after 2015: 99,000 in 2016, against 54,000 in 2008 (a peak of about 350 per 1000 marriages in relative terms), barely declining in subsequent years.

These changes are deeply intertwined with population demographic dynamics, which is the decline in fertility and the progressive aging of the population that has occurred in the last 20 years. The TFR reached 1.25 in 2021, showing a progressive further decline after the tempo and illusory peak of 1.44 in 2008, this latter achieved as a partial recovery from postponed births and contribution given to fertility by immigrant women. In the same time span, the mean age of the population, equal to 45.9 years in 2021, has gained 4 years. On the one hand, the decline in fertility has as a direct consequence the decrease in size of households with children, which is only partly counteracted by the prolonged permanence of young people in the parental home. On the other hand, the result of population aging can be seen in the conspicuous increase in people living alone. Due to the persistent gender gap between men and women in terms of survival, there are more women who live alone among the older people, even if the gain in life expectancy of both females and males has also led to more and more old people living as a couple.

Because of the demographic dynamics mentioned above, the natural balance has been negative since 2007, so that the Italian population has lost its capacity to grow; it was only thanks to the positive contribution of immigration that the resident population has grown, scoring a record of 60.3 million on January 1, 2014. The widening deficit between births and deaths and the contraction of the migratory balance has triggered a trend reversal since 2014. As of January 1, 2021, the population has dropped to 59.2 million inhabitants.

As the number of inhabitants declined, the number of households has been growing. In 2020, there were over 25 million households in Italy, about four million more than in 2000. The average size declined from 2.7 in the early 2000s to 2.3 in 2020; households with four or more members went from 30% of the total in 2000 to just under 19% in 2020, and those with five or more members from 8% in 2000 to just over 4% in 2020. In 2020, 33% of households is made up of only one person, it was 22% in 2000 (Fig. 6.1). The reasons driving the increase in the number of people living alone differ depending on age and, in some cases, reverse trends can be observed (Tomassini & Vignoli, 2023). The share of people aged less than 45 and living alone is decreasing (20% in 2020, 24% in 2000), due to the prolonged stay in the family of origin and because, in this age group, cohabitation is increasingly taking place. On the contrary, between the ages of 45 and 64, we observe a substantial increase in the number of people living alone (21% in 2000 and 31% in 2020); this increase can be ascribed to marital instability, which is particularly concentrated in this latter age group. Notwithstanding these dynamics, depending on the age considered, the largest share of people living alone is still that of the individuals aged 65 and older (48% in 2020, 55% in 2000).

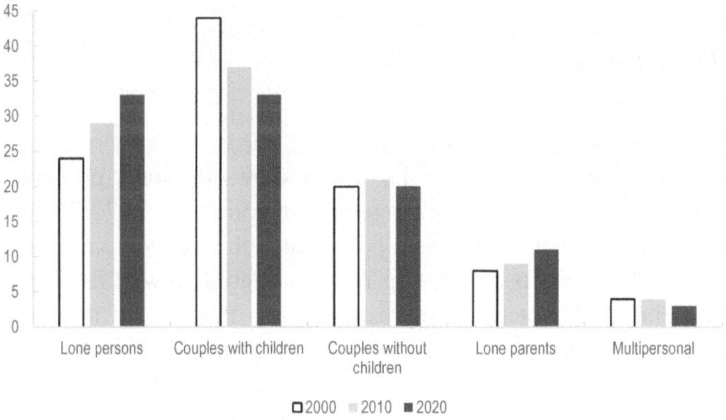

Source: Authors' elaborations of multi-purpose household surveys "Aspects of Daily Life" Istat, Istat, various years.

Fig. 6.1 Distribution of Italian households by type. Years 2000, 2010 and 2020, percentage values

The household typology represented by a couple with children decreased from 44% in 2000 to 36% in 2010, to 30% in 2020. Following the drop in fertility, this type of family is increasingly made up of couples with a lone child (54%). Furthermore, the increase in separations and divorces means that single-parent families in 2020 represent 10% of the total (they were 8% in 2000). These mainly consist of single mothers (about 80%), although in the last 20 years the number of lone fathers living with at least one child has also increased (from 350,000 in 2000 to over 532,000 in 2020). Extended households with or without children, with at least one aggregate member, have gone from over 3% in 2000 (almost 676,000) to 2% in 2020 (over 596,000). Finally, people living together not linked by parental or affiliation relationships are stable over time and represent less than 4% of families in 2020.

In Italy, it is also important to highlight the territorial differences in the diffusion of the household change processes. In fact, different Italian contexts present peculiar features related to history, cultural influences, attractiveness of domestic or foreign immigration, availability of services, labor market flexibility and overall citizens' wellbeing, which result in different demographic processes, such as declining fertility and aging in the different Italian regions (Salvati et al., 2020).

The Southern area has been traditionally characterized by higher fertility and larger families, but in recent years has witnessed a more rapid decline in fertility and, consequently, in the distribution of the different household types. In 2020, the North-west and Central regions recorded a high concentration of lone-person households, 35% and 34%, respectively. Childless couples are also over-represented in the North-west and North-east (23%) compared to the Italian average (21%). On the contrary, in the Southern regions the couple with children continues to represent the most widespread type of family, despite a strong decline in the 20 years considered (from 50% in 2000, to 42% in 2010, to 33% in 2020).

6.3 Data and Definitions

The reference point of our household predictions is the median scenario of the official probabilistic projections (base 1.1.2021), which shows the most probable future of the population, broken down by sex, age and region (Istat, 2022d). The official figures on population include all people fulfilling the concept of usual residence in the country, therefore, people living in a household as well as living in an institutional household.[1] These latter, representing less than 1% of the total resident population, are not the real object of our exercise, thus, we exclude them from this analysis. The distinction between people living in a household and living in an institution is conducted using appropriate constant proportions that come from the

[1]People cohabiting for religious, caretaking, military, punitive, religious and other reasons, and therefore living in institutions such as hospitals, barracks, prisons, nursing homes, religious buildings, etc.

Permanent Census of Population and Housing. Since 2018, it has replaced the decennial population census, being based on the information available from an integrated system of administrative sources and sample surveys.

Information on household structures and individual household position was obtained from the Italian Multipurpose Survey *Aspects of Daily Life* (AVQ),[2] which provided a long time series (2002 to 2021). This is an annual cross-sectional sample survey conducted by interviewing a sample of 20,000 households (about 50,000 people in total), ensuring consistent and accurate estimates at the regional level.

The definition of family and household refers to the *de facto* situation. A household consists of all people habitually living in the same dwelling and bound by marriage, kinship, affinity, adoption, guardianship or affectional ties. A family (or nucleus) is formed by people in a couple or a parent-child relationship living together. This includes a married, civilly united or cohabiting couple, with or without children, or a single parent with one or more children.

A household may contain one or more families (family households), but also none, as in the case of lone people (one-person household) or several isolated members (multi-person household). Each individual can be classified according to the position he/she occupies in the household.

In this study, we consider the following household positions:

- Lone person: a person living alone.
- Partner in couple with children: person in a (married or cohabiting) couple with at least one child.
- Partner in couple without children: person in a (married or cohabiting) couple with no children.
- Lone parent: one parent living with one or more children.
- Child: never married biological, step/adopted son or daughter (regardless of age), who lives with at least one of the parents, and who has no partner or own children in the same household.
- Other person: a person living in a one-family household, not having a couple relationship or parent-child relationship with other members, such as, for example, a cousin or a friend.
- Person in multi-person household: a person living with others not forming a family (for instance, two siblings living together or a divorced person who has returned home to a parent).
- Person in household with two or more families: person living in a household where two or more families are present.

Partners, lone parents, children and other persons refer to individuals living in one-family households. People living in households with two or more families are

[2] AVQ is the Italian acronym of the survey, coming from the abbreviation of "*Aspetti della vita quotidiana*".

considered in a single category, since this typology constitutes a small share of the total number of households (approximately 1.5% over the last two decades).

In addition, since we know that fertility and delayed transition to adulthood are affecting family composition, we decided to include an additional detail for families with children, based on the age of sons and daughters. Partners with children and lone parents were then distinguished according to the presence of children aged up to 19 years ("with at least one child under 20" or "with all children 20 and over"). The choice of this age was made because in Italy high school generally ends at 19 years of age and information on cohabiting children under age 20 is useful for policies on families with children. Another practical reason is that, since we work with 5-year age groups, the choice of 18 years (the age at which one becomes an adult in Italy), would have led to complications in the projection method.

6.4 Method

Several alternative models for projecting households have been developed worldwide (Keilman et al., 1988; Keilman, 2019). Following the classification proposed by Gill and Keilman (1990), household forecasting models can be distinguished according to the approach followed (static or dynamic) and/or to the basic unit of analysis (micro or macro).

In a static approach, projections are carried out through the application of proportions or rates that allow shifting from the projected population to the corresponding families and households. The best known is the *Headship rate method* (UN, 1973; Kono, 1987; Linke, 1988), widely applied due to the extreme simplicity of the procedure. However, this model is rather weak because it is based only on the head of household's characteristics, which is often defined vaguely and differently from country to country (Murphy, 1991). Moreover, it produces results with little detail.

Dynamic methods explicitly model family events, thus providing a more realistic representation of population development due to demographic and social processes (births, deaths, marriages, divorces, migration events, etc.). Among these methods, macro or micro dynamic models are defined according to the basic unit used. Macro models proceed by aggregates, defined by several characteristics, depending on the application. Rates for demographic events and household formation and dissolution are applied to the population disaggregated into groups, modeling transitions between states until the end of the projection period. In contrast, micro models consider the individual as the basic unit of prediction. Starting from a sample of the population, the entire life cycle of each individual is simulated separately, introducing consistency constraints for events involving more than one individual. However, modeling family dynamics may be complicated, in particular when many different family positions are used, and a large amount of data is required (Keilman, 2019).

Some research tried to combine both static and dynamic approaches. For example, De Beer and Alders (1999) developed a probabilistic forecast model, which first projects the population by marital status on the basis of a multistate model and then applies propensity rates to obtain households.

In this range of possible methodologies for projecting households, we sought a model that was consistent with demographic projections, parsimonious (with detailed, high-quality results versus costs) and replicable each year, thus based on not too burdensome data.

With this objective in mind, we chose a static approach based on the *Propensity rate model*, which has been used in recent years by the Australian Bureau of Statistics (ABS) to project households in Australia and New Zealand (ABS, 2019). It is a static method that goes beyond the classic *Headship rate model,* overcoming the concept of 'head of household' and providing a more detailed set of information. Predictions of the number of future households, their average size and composition can be easily obtained (Cooper et al., 1995; Blangiardo et al., 2012).

This model best met our needs. In fact, it links easily to the demographic projections; no complex data are needed; it is quick to apply and provides detailed results. However, some drawbacks are also present, which arise mainly from the static nature of the method, not allowing the reproduction of the process of household formation and dissolution (Wilson, 2013). In some situations, the application of propensity rates to the population may determine inconsistencies in terms of global results, for example between sexes or for household positions within age-classes.

The method consists of five steps:

- Step 1. Estimate of the projected population living in private households
- Step 2. Calculate the household propensity rates
- Step 3. Model future trends of household propensity rates
- Step 4. Derive the projected population by household position
- Step 5. Calculate the number, type and size of projected households.

In **Step 1**, we estimate the projected population living in private households from the official population projections, excluding individuals residing in institutional households. The necessary information on these types of households was taken from the Permanent Census of Population and Housing (1.1.2020–1.1.2021 mean values).

Despite the ongoing aging process in Italy, the share of people living in institutional households has remained constant in recent decades. Possible reasons can be found in the lengthening of healthy life expectancy and in the typical Italian family system, in which the older people are often cared for by family members or dedicated caregivers at home.

Given their substantial stability over time, the percentage incidences of the population living in institutions by sex, 5-year age group and region have been assumed as constant throughout the time horizon of the projection. Excluding institutional households, we obtained the population living in private households from 2021 to 2041.

Step 2 of the model consists of calculating the propensity rates to live in a given household position. These rates are constructed as the proportion of persons of age x in category i. In this context, the age variable was considered in 5-year classes and the rates were also disaggregated by sex, as this latter variable is very discriminating in household behavior. Hereinafter, the rates are referred to as *Living Arrangement Propensities* (LAP):

$$\text{Propensity Rate}_{x,i,s,t} = \frac{P_{x,i,s,t}}{P_{x,s,t}} = LAP_{x,i,s,t}$$

where x = 5-year age group 0–4, 5–9, ..., 80–84, 85+, i = household position, s = sex, t = time.

LAPs are calculated for the period 2002–2021 using data from the annual AVQ survey. Since regional estimates by sex and age groups result in a sparsity of data in small regions, we decided to group regions into "macro-regions".

To identify homogeneous groups of regions in terms of common family structures and similar trends over time, a dynamic principal component analysis was conducted using STATIS methodology (Lavit et al., 1994). The results identified the following five groups of regions:

- Group 1 – North-west (Piemonte, Valle d'Aosta, Lombardia, Liguria);
- Group 2 – East Adriatic (Veneto, Emilia-Romagna, Trentino-Alto Adige, Friuli-Venezia Giulia, Marche);
- Group 3 – Tyrrhenian (Toscana, Lazio);
- Group 4 – South (Campania, Puglia, Calabria, Sicilia);
- Group 5 – Central (Umbria, Sardegna, Abruzzo, Molise, Basilicata).

In **Step 3**, we need to make assumptions about the evolution of household propensities from 2021 to 2041. To model future household propensity rates, we introduce a synthetic indicator, constructed as the sum by age of the LAP, weighted by the years lived in each age class (L_x), as proposed in Sullivan's methodology (Sullivan, 1971).

We refer to this indicator as Total Household Position Intensity Rate (TPR):

$$TPR_{i,s,t} = \sum_{x=0-4}^{85+} LAP_{x,i,s,t} * L_{x,s,t} = \sum_{x=0-4}^{85+} \frac{P_{x,i,s,t}}{P_{x,s,t}} * 100 * L_{x,s,t}$$

where i = household position, s = sex, x = 5-year age class, t = time.

The $L_{x,\,s,\,t}$ represent the number of years lived in the age class x by sex s in year t and are collected from the official Life tables in all years 2002 to 2019.[3]

Although people living in different family positions (for example "lone person" vs "partner in couple") have different death risks, mortality and household position are assumed to be independent, in the sense that no further distinctions are introduced. We assume that the error made by attributing the same mortality to different family types has a limited impact. In fact, in old age, where mortality is higher, the

[3] Source: Istat, Life tables of the resident population, https://demo.istat.it/app/?i=TVM&a=1974&l=en.

prevailing family condition is living alone. On the contrary, in adulthood, where there is greater heterogeneity between family positions, the risk of death is low and therefore the impact of the error is rather negligible.

The TPR for a given household position would represent approximately how many years on average a cohort of individuals expects to live in that position, experiencing along the course of life the family behaviors and the mortality conditions as observed in a given calendar year. The TPR indicator, despite the limitations described above, allowed the construction of forecast assumptions that make logical sense and that can be kept under control. Actually, under the previous hypothesis, the sum of the TPRs by household position corresponds to the life expectancy at birth, in other words, for a given calendar year and sex we have:

$$e_{0,s,t} = \sum_{i} TPR_{i,s,t}$$

that is a very useful element to keep Households projections linked to Population projections.

To hypothesize future trends in propensities, we proceeded to project the total intensity rates by single household position, and then to estimate their distribution broken down by age group ($LAP_{x,\ i,\ s,\ t}$) in each projected year. Predicting total intensity has made it possible, on the one hand, to easily translate the assumptions about family behavior and, on the other, to keep the trends in the various household positions together.

Moreover, to obtain a regional level detail, while taking control of the small regions' pattern, we performed two sub-steps, first running the projections at the macro-region level and then moving on to regional detail.

The total time spent in each household position and sex ($TPR_{i,\ s,\ t}$) at a macro-region level was predicted through a trend extrapolation over the period 2021–2041. We used time-series analysis models (Box et al., 2015). A best ARIMA optimization procedure was applied to find the models for each household position and sex (Table 6.1).

Figure 6.2 shows the future evolution of the TPRs in the North-west territorial group taken as an example. In general, the variation in the time spent in different household positions reflects the social and demographic changes occurring in Italy in recent decades. In fact, we note:

- an increase in "lone persons",
- a decrease in "partners with children",
- a slight increase in "partners without children",
- a small increase of people in "child" position,
- a slight increase in "lone parents", especially fathers,
- a substantial stability of "other people" living in a family household,
- a slight increase in "persons in households with two or more families".

At this stage, we derive the specific rates of LAPs from the synthetic indicators of TPRs. Estimates of expected LAPs (representing age distributions) were obtained

Table 6.1 Predictive models of total household position rates by position and sex[a]

Household position	Men	Women
Lone person	RWD ǁ ARIMA (1,0,0)	RWD
Person in a childless couple	ARIMA (2,0,0)	RWD
Person in a couple with at least one child under 20	RWD	RWD
Person in a couple with only children 20 and over	RWD ǁ ARIMA (2,1,0)	RWD ǁ ARIMA (2,1,0)
Lone parent with at least one child under 20	Linear trend	Linear trend
Lone parent with only children 20 and over	RWD	RWD
Child under 20	RWD	RWD
Child 20 and over	AR2	ARIMA (2,1,0)
Other person living in a one-family household	RWD	ARIMA (1,0,0)
Person in multi-person household	RWD	RWD
Person in a household with two or more families	ARIMA (1,1,0)	ARIMA (1,1,0)

[a]Prevailing model among the five territorial groups. *RWD* Random Walk with Drift model, *ARIMA* Auto Regressive Integrated Moving Average model

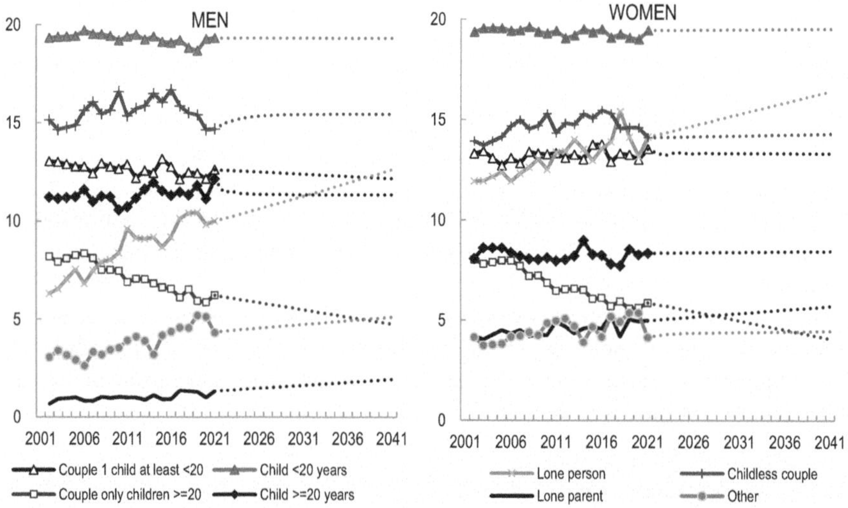

(a) Despite being projected separately, "lone parent with at least one child aged <20 years" and "lone parent with only children aged > 20 years" are taken together in the Figure. At the same time, the category "Other" in the Figure includes people "living in multi-personal households" as well as people "living in households with two or more families".

Fig. 6.2 Total household position rates by household position and gender. North-west area, years 2002–2041

using the distributions from the AVQ survey, as observed on average in the 2019–21 period. Two specific weights are then introduced in combination, one to account for the expected TPR in year t versus that in 2019–21 ($WP_{s,\ i,\ t}$), another for the changes in mortality over time ($WL_{x,\ s,\ t}$):

$$WP_{s,i,t} = \frac{TPR_{s,i,t}}{TPR_{s,i,2019-21}} \qquad t = 2021, \ldots, 2041$$

$$WL_{x,s,t} = \frac{L_{x,s,2019-21}}{L_{x,s,t}} \qquad t = 2021, \ldots, 2041$$

Therefore, household propensities throughout the projection horizon were calculated using the formula:

$$LAP_{x,s,i,t} = LAP_{x,s,i,2019-21} * WP_{s,i,t} * WL_{x,s,t} \qquad t = 2021, \ldots, 2041$$

where: x = age groups 0–4, …,85+, s = sex, i = household position.

Since no annual changes in the age distribution of the LAPs were assumed, it was implicitly assumed that the behavior in terms of household position will in the future maintain a distribution by age group proportional to that observed over the 3-year period 2019–2021.

At the end of the procedure, the sum of the LAPs by household position in each age group approximates but does not always equal the value 100. The problem occurred mainly at the open-aged group (85+). However, because of low absolute frequencies, the impact proved to be not significant. Some ex-post adjustments, consisting in pro-rating the distributions to the value 100, were therefore carried out.

To project households at the regional level, it is important to ensure that each region retains its socio-demographic specificity within the projecting group to which it belongs. Thus, we defined a regional correction factor (RFC) to be applied to the LAP projections of the various territorial groups:

$$RFC_{r,i} = \frac{TPR_{2019-21,i,r}}{TPR_{2019-21,i,G}}$$

where i = household position, r = region, G = group to which region r belongs.

The series of regional LAPs from 2021 to 2041 is therefore obtained by multiplying the projected LAPs at the spatial group level by the above regional correction factors. To make an example, for the male single-person household position, the TPR found in Piemonte is 11.06, while in group 1 it is equal to 10.08. In this case, the correction factor is therefore equivalent to 1.10. This means that, since Piemonte has a TPR higher than that of the group to which it belongs, it is necessary to make an adjustment by multiplying all the LAPs at the various ages and the various projection years by 1.10, increasing the level slightly. More explicitly, it is assumed that in the forecast period the differences in terms of general intensity between regions within the groups remain constant and equal to those observed in 2019–2021.

In **Step 4**, regional propensities are applied to the projected population living in private households obtained in Step 1. The projected population by household position, sex, age group and region from 2021 to 2041 is thus derived.

Finally, **Step 5** aims at computing the number, type and size of the future households. We consider the Household Representative Rate (HRR), defined as the probability of a person from a specific group (based on geography, age group, sex and type of household) being a household reference person. From the population by household position, gender and age, we have that each *lone person* represents 1 household (HRR = 1), a *single parent* acts as 1 household (HRR = 1), *partners in couple* constitute 0.5 of a household (HRR = ½). *Children* and *other persons* do not count in the calculation of households (HRR = 0).

For multi-person households and households with two or more families, the HRR is the ratio between 1 and the average number of people in a multi-person household or in a household with two or more families, as observed from data in 2019–2021. Therefore, the multi-person households were obtained by dividing the number of *people living in multi-person households* by the average size of this type of household, which has remained broadly stable over time at about 2.1 members. Similarly, the households containing two or more families have been derived from dividing the number of *persons living in households with two or more families* by the average size, which assumed values between 5 and 5.4, depending on the territorial reference group. Applying these coefficients to the population of sex s and age x yields as a final product the number of households by type. For dissemination purposes, multi-person households and those with two or more families are considered together in the "other type of household" category.

Finally, the average household size is calculated by dividing the population living in households by the number of households. It can be worked out for total households and for those with at least one family (excluding single persons and multi-person households).

6.5 Main Results

6.5.1 Projected Population by Household Position

Italy is a country with a progressively declining population: from 59.2 million in 2021 it is expected to consist of 56.2 million in 2041. People living in private households (excluding institutional households) will fall from 58.9 to 55.8 million (−5%). Such a decline stems mainly from the significant reduction of younger generations, both in absolute and relative terms. Older generations are the predominant part in the population as early as 2021, and there are no factors suggesting a change of direction. Demographic projections show that a reversal in the number of births in the coming years is unlikely, even under favorable fertility assumptions (Istat, 2022d). In fact, the decline in the number of women of childbearing age, on

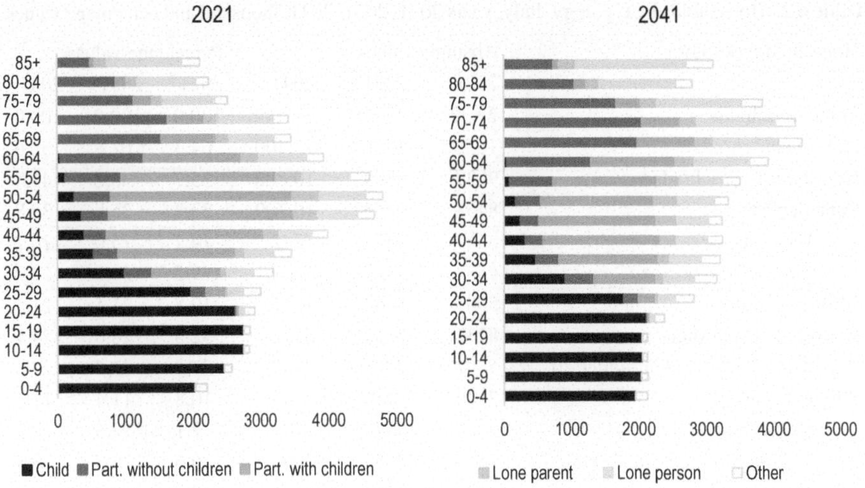

Fig. 6.3 Projected population by age and household position. Italy, years 2021 and 2041, thousand

the one hand, and the tendency to postpone parenthood, on the other, are expected to take on increasing weight in the near future.

The predicted population by age and role in the family expected by 2041 highlights both the aging process and the changes in family positions. Pyramids in Fig. 6.3 show the decrease of people in couples with children, the increase of those without children and of people living alone, this latter especially among older persons. Among individuals aged 65 and older, there will be an increase of nearly two million single people (+44%) over the next two decades. Younger age groups are thinning in size, but the family position as a "child" remains prevalent until age 30, due to the prolonged stay of young people in the family of origin.

6.5.2 *Number and Size of Households*

Between 2021 and 2041, the number of households in Italy is expected to continue the upward trend that has been in place in the past decades. From 25.3 million in 2021, they are estimated to grow to 26.3 million in 2041, with an increase of 3.8% (Table 6.2). Such a growth hides a specific feature of the evolution of families: their fragmentation.

The rise in the total number of households in the next 20 years is driven by households without nuclei, i.e., single persons or several people who do not have a parent-child or marital relationship with each other (*non-family households*). This type of household, which now accounts for 35.7% of total households, will come to make up 41.4% in 2041 (from nine million to nearly 11 million, an increase of 20.5%). In contrast, households with at least one nucleus (*family households*) follow

Table 6.2 Households by typology. Italy, years 2021, 2031, 2041, thousand and percentage values

Household typology	Absolute values			Percentage values		
	2021	2031	2041	2021	2031	2041
Total households	25,323	25,895	26,289	100.0	100.0	100.0
Family households	16,285	15,996	15,400	64.3	61.8	58.6
Non-family households	9039	9899	10,888	35.7	38.2	41.4
Lone persons	8458	9263	10,209	33.4	35.8	38.8
Male lone persons	*3584*	*3883*	*4242*	*14.2*	*15.0*	*16.1*
Female lone persons	*4874*	*5380*	*5967*	*19.2*	*20.8*	*22.7*
Childless couples	5003	5463	5657	19.8	21.1	21.5
Couples with children	8232	7253	6332	32.5	28.0	24.1
With at least 1 child under 20	*5301*	*4413*	*3931*	*20.9*	*17.0*	*15.0*
Single parents	2729	2956	3088	10.8	11.4	11.7
Single fathers	532	667	770	2.1	2.6	2.9
With at least 1 child under 20	*162*	*186*	*206*	*0.6*	*0.7*	*0.8*
Single mothers	2197	2289	2318	8.7	8.8	8.8
With at least 1 child under 20	*902*	*909*	*951*	*3.6*	*3.5*	*3.6*
Other type of household	902	959	1003	3.6	3.7	3.8

the opposite trend, decreasing by 5.4% over the 20 years: falling from 16.3 to 15.4 million, they represent 64.3% of the total number of households in 2021 and 58.6% in 2041 (Table 6.2). Such a reduction is due to the consequences of long-term socio-demographic dynamics (De Rose et al., 2008; Blangiardo & Rimoldi, 2014; Istat, 2022e). The last 50 years have witnessed an acceleration of socio-demographic processes that have substantially reshaped family structures. As mentioned in the introduction, the aging of the population, the very low birth rate and the increase in the dissolution of unions are processes that implied both a rise in the number of families and a decline in the number of members. In particular, the increase in life expectancy has generated more lone persons; declining birth rates have increased the number of childless couples, while growing marital instability has driven both the number of people living alone and as single parents.

Therefore, alongside the increase in number of households, we expect a decrease in their average size, which will drop from 2.3 members in 2021 to 2.1 in 2041. Taking into consideration only family households, the mean size will change from 3 to 2.8 components.

6.5.3 *People Living Alone*

The increase of people living alone is mainly responsible for the absolute growth of the total number of households. Lone men will increase from 3.6 million in 2021 to 4.2 million in 2041, recording a growth of 18%. Lone women, on the other hand, will pass from 4.9 to six million (+22%). In total, lone persons, which in 2021

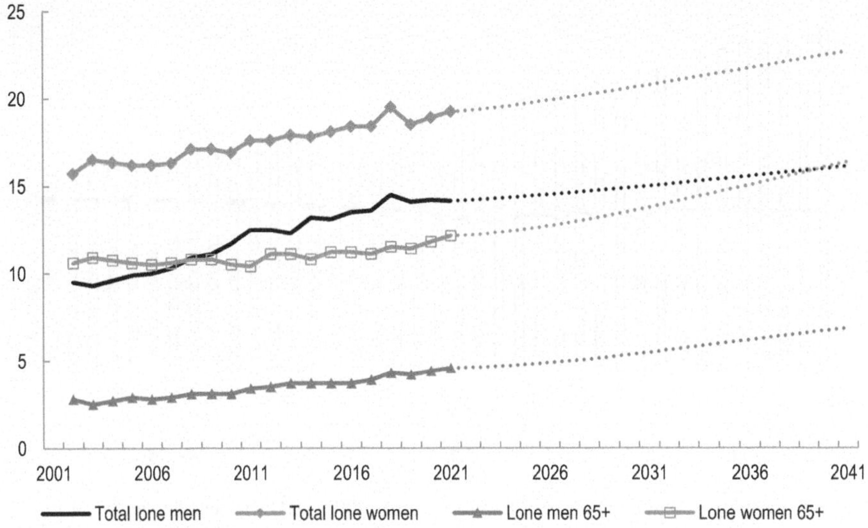

Fig. 6.4 Lone persons by gender and age (total and 65 and older). Italy, years 2002–2041, percentage values

account for one in three households (33.4%), will represent nearly 40% of all households in 2041 (38.8%) (Fig. 6.4).

Between 2021 and 2041, the rise in the number of single people occurs mainly over the age of 65, while between the ages of 45 and 65 their number decreases (due to the reduction of those generations). In addition, there will be a slight increase in men aged between 30 and 40 years living alone; this trend is linked, for younger men, to leaving their family of origin to live on their own and for older men to marital instability.

However, the largest part of this family type will consist of older people. If in 2021 single persons over 65 accounts for 50% of all lone persons, by 2041 this proportion will rise to nearly 60%. Older women, in particular, represent a very important share of women living alone already in 2021 (63.1%) and will reach an even higher level in 2041 (72.2%).

6.5.4 *Couples with and without Children*

For decades, the most common family type in Italy has been the couple with children, but current trends are about to lead to a significant change. Due to fertility levels observed in recent years, as well as to the consequent assumptions adopted in the population projection median scenario (Istat, 2022d), couples with children are expected to decrease substantially. Between 2021 and 2041, their consistency will drop by 23%, from 8.2 million to 6.3 million. Because of this demographic scenario,

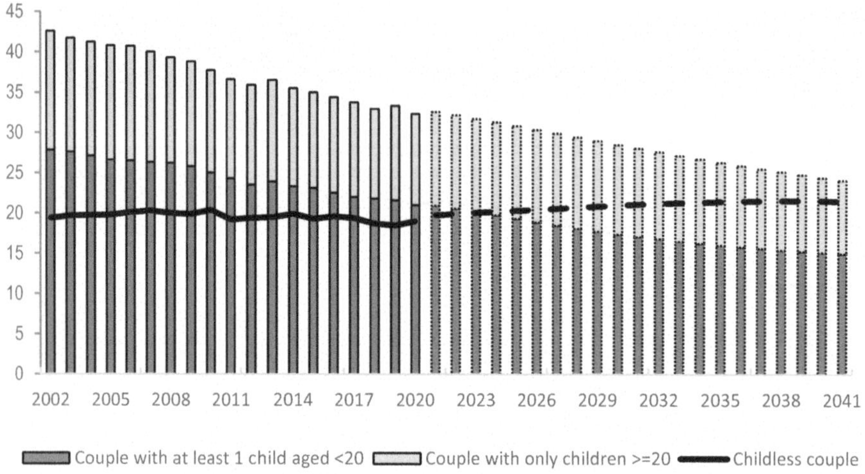

Fig. 6.5 Couples with and without children. Italy, years 2002–2041, percentage values

couples with at least one child under 20 will decline by more than one million units (from 5.3 to 3.9 million) (Fig. 6.5).

At the same time, childless couples will rise slightly from 5.1 to 5.7 million, for an increase of 13%. If these trends were to proceed with the same expected intensity until 2041, especially as regards the rate of decrease of couples with children, the overtaking by couples without children could already take place by 2045.

Thus, while in 2021 one in three households (32.5%) will be a couple with children, in 2041 it will be less than one in four (24.1%). Moreover, couples with at least one child up to the age of 19 will drop from 20.9% to 15%, and those with children over 20 from 11.6% to 9.1%.

6.5.5 *Single Parents*

Although marital disruption in Italy is still less widespread than in other countries, its growing trend will lead to an increase in single-parent households. In past decades, after a breakup of the couple, children were generally entrusted to their mothers. However, social and legislative changes in recent years have led to an increase in the number of custodial fathers in separation or divorce judgments (also due to the enactment of the 2006 law on joint custody[4]). Thus, single fathers, while remaining a minority, are expected to increase more than single mothers do.

[4]The 2006 law on joint custody (February 8, 2006, no. 54) provides regulations on the separation of parents and the shared custody of children in Italy.

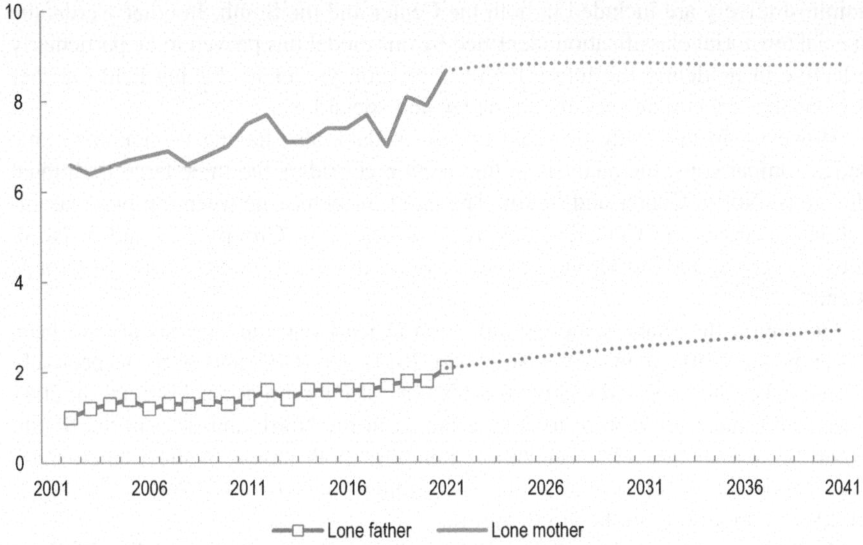

Fig. 6.6 Single parents by gender. Italy, years 2002–2041, percentage values

In 2021, there are 2.7 million single parents, more mothers (2.2 million) than fathers (about 530,000), accounting for 8.7% and 2.1% of total households, respectively (Fig. 6.6). By 2041, single fathers will reach about 800,000 (2.9% of total households) while single mothers will remain numerically unchanged at 2.3 million (8.8% of the total), so that the total number of single parents will be just over three million.

6.5.6 *Territorial Specificities*

Italy is characterized by significant territorial heterogeneity. The specificities of the Italian regions are visible both in present and future developments. In particular, the dualism between the Center-North and the South, which distinguishes the Country, is also reflected in the structure of households. In parallel, further heterogeneity is also substantial within the three main administrative aggregations, to the point that a complete analysis of territorial differences should only be addressed in the framework of geographical divisions that go beyond the simple administrative border. This is the case, for example, of the Northern division, where different demographic and social behaviors lead to separating the North-west (Group 1 of our cluster analysis) from the North-east and merging this latter with the Marche region (Group 2), which belongs to the Center on an administrative level. Similar considerations have led to the identification of a homogeneous territorial group (Group 5), characterized by a more advanced aging process, even if the regions that are part of it administratively are included in both the Center and the South. In other words, the special territorial classification identified by our model has proven to be particularly effective in modeling the future family formation processes, having held together regions that are similar on a demographic and social level.

However, in line with the usual release of data, also having to guarantee time series comparisons, the analysis in this section considers the three large traditional divisions: North, Center and South. The main difference between the two classifications concerns the Center, whose regions belong to Groups 2, 3 and 5. North roughly corresponds to Groups 1 and 2, while the South refers mostly to Groups 4 and 5.

Generally, the share of households with at least one nucleus has always been lower in the North than in the South: in 2021, it is 64% and 67%, respectively (Table 6.3). The expected change for this type of household is substantial: in 2041 they could make up 58% of total households in the North and 61% in the South, reporting a reduction of 6 percentage points in both cases. In the Center, these households would decrease by about 5 percentage points (from 62% in 2021 to 57% in 2041), converging to the North values.

The most pronounced change over the next two decades is expected in the share of couples with children. In the South, the predicted decline is around 9 percentage points (from 37% in 2021 to 28% in 2041), while in the North (from 31% to 23%) and in the Center (from 30% to 22%) it is about 8%. Despite experiencing the larger

Table 6.3 Households by typology and territorial area. Years 2021, 2031, 2041, percentage values

	North			Center			South		
Household typology	2021	2031	2041	2021	2031	2041	2021	2031	2041
Male lone persons	14.5	15.9	17.3	15.6	16.1	17.0	12.7	13.0	13.7
Female lone persons	19.8	21.1	22.6	20.3	21.5	23.0	17.8	19.9	22.7
Childless couples	21.9	23.1	23.4	18.4	19.5	19.8	17.4	19.0	19.7
Couples with children	30.7	26.1	22.5	29.5	25.2	21.5	37.2	32.8	28.3
With at least 1 child under 20	*20.6*	*17.0*	*15.5*	*19.3*	*15.5*	*13.4*	*22.5*	*18.1*	*15.1*
Single fathers	2.1	2.6	3.0	2.4	3.0	3.3	1.9	2.3	2.6
With at least 1 child under 20	*0.6*	*0.6*	*0.7*	*0.8*	*0.9*	*1.0*	*0.7*	*0.8*	*0.9*
Single mothers	7.9	7.9	7.8	9.6	10.2	10.4	9.2	9.4	9.4
With at least 1 child under 20	*3.3*	*3.2*	*3.4*	*3.9*	*3.8*	*3.8*	*3.7*	*3.7*	*3.7*
Other type of household	3.2	3.3	3.5	4.2	4.6	4.9	3.7	3.7	3.6
Family households	63.6	60.8	57.8	61.6	59.6	56.7	67.0	64.7	61.1
Non-family households	36.4	39.2	42.2	38.4	40.4	43.3	33.0	35.3	38.9
Total households	100.0	100.0	100.0	100.0	100.0	100.0	100.0	100.0	100.0

contraction, the South would still maintain the larger proportion of couples with children.

Analyzing the couples with children by macro classes of children's age, it is noticeable that most of the reduction will affect the "couple with at least one child under the age of 20". Although generally in the North, couples with children will experience a contraction of 8 percentage points, those with "young" children will decrease by 5 percentage points (from 21% to 16%). A greater reduction will occur in the Central regions, where couples with children under 20 will drop from 19% to 13%, with 6 percentage points lost out of all couples with children in this area. In the South, projections point to a wider demographic crisis. Here, couples with at least one child under the age of 20 would decrease by 7 percentage points out of the 9 overall of couples with children. The result, therefore, is that for couples with "young" children there is a process of territorial convergence. The same cannot be said for couples with "mature" children, where a difference remains in favor of the South, partly because in this area of the country the timing for leaving the family of origin is longer than elsewhere in Italy (Istat, 2022e).

Different territorial and gender trends are also expected for single-person households. For Italy as a whole, women living alone could make up about 23% of total households by 2041, from a current value of 19%. In the Center and in the North, females living alone will increase from 20% to 23%. At the same time, in the South as well, they will rise faster, from 18% to 23%, setting off a process of convergence in the years to come.

Compared to women, there are far fewer men living alone. This is due to two factors. On the one hand, it is accounted for due to the presence of territorial differences in life expectancy. On the other, there is a greater predisposition on behalf of men, especially in the South, to enter a second union in the event of widowhood or following the dissolution of a previous union (Meggiolaro & Ongaro, 2008; De Rose & Meli, 2022). Therefore, unlike women, among men living alone the convergence process affects only the North and the Center. Both geographical areas are projected to have a 17% share of lone-men households in 2041, compared to a national average of 16%. The South maintains its territorial specificity, presenting a small upward trend, such that in 2041 the share of lone-men households would be less than 14% of total households.

Due to lower fertility levels, childless couples are more prevalent in the North than in the rest of Italy, showing a modest increase over the 20 years (from 22% to over 23%). A somewhat sharper change is expected in the South, where, from a less widespread situation, childless couples would rise from 17% to about 20% of all households, catching up with the values in the Center (from over 18% to about 20%).

Finally, lone-parent households are more frequent in the Center than in other regions, increasing their share to about 14% in 2041, while in the North and South, the levels reached in 2041 would be about 11% and 12% of households, respectively.

The family changes analyzed above clearly show that it is all over the national territory that small families are increasing. Then, the mean household size is expected to continue to decrease, not only nationally (from 2.3 to 2.1 members),

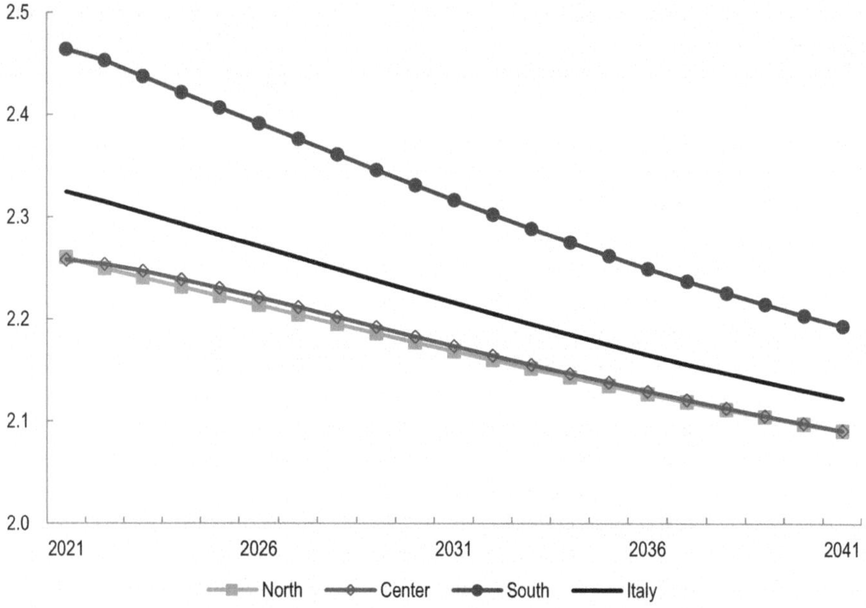

Fig. 6.7 Average household size by territorial area. Years 2021–2041

but also with differences among the geographical areas. On the one hand, the North and the Center, with very similar current values and future trajectories, will reach an average value of members close to the national value. On the other hand, the South, due to past higher fertility rates, has historically been characterized by larger families compared to the rest of the Country. Today, with lower reproductive levels even in the South, this record (2.5 members per household) is trending downward, and in 2041, it is expected to decline further to 2.2 members on average. The result of this tendency will be a convergence of the mean household size to a level of around 2.2 components (Fig. 6.7).

6.6 Final Remarks

During the most recent decades, living arrangements and household structures in Italy and in most Western countries have been undergoing profound transformations. Only a few decades ago, the nuclear family – composed of married parents and their biological children – appeared as the prevalent living arrangement of Western societies. However, since the 1970s, households and families have been deeply changing, with the nuclear family losing its centrality to a more complex mix of living arrangements (Heuveline & Timberlake, 2002).

Italy is a low-fertility country and, at the same time, ensures high longevity levels to its citizens. The aging process is running continuously, significantly affecting the overall population change. In a demographic situation like the Italian one, population and household projections are of great interest and utility for planning special policies to help families and the most fragile individuals. In 2021, the Italian National Institute of Statistics started to release official household projections alongside population projections.

In this chapter, we described the methodology used for the last release that occurred in 2022. The method is static and based on the *Propensity Rate Model*. Among its advantages is the fact that it links easily to demographic projections; it provides detailed results; it is quick to apply, and not too burdensome data are needed, so that it can be replicated each year. However, the static nature of the method does not allow the processes of household formation and dissolution to be reproduced and involves some drawbacks. The application of propensity rates to the population can, in some cases, lead to inconsistencies in terms of overall results, for example, between the sexes or for family positions within age groups. Some adjustments were therefore necessary during the projection process.

Moreover, there are still some open issues. One is the two-sex problem, which arises when males and females are modelled separately, so that the predicted number of male partners is not equal to the number of female partners. This has proven to be a rather difficult problem, because it has both conceptual and methodological aspects, and there is no simple way to bring empirical data to bear on it. Although there are several interesting proposals (Schoen, 1988), we had to overlook them as it was essential to maintain numerical consistency between the population by household position and the total predicted population by age and sex. Furthermore, it is meant to provide measures of the uncertainty of the estimates, which are important for better understanding phenomena and making appropriate decisions.

The results show a continuity in trends taking place over the past 50 years, which have substantially reshaped the Italian family structure. An aging population, a very low birth rate and an increase in union dissolutions have resulted in a growth in the number of households and a decrease in the number of household members.

Couples with children are expected to decrease: while in 2021 one in three households is a couple with children, in 2041 it will be less than one in four. Meanwhile, childless couples will rise slightly. Should this trend proceed with the same intensity as predicted until 2041, couples without children could outnumber couples with children within a few years.

The increase of people living alone is mainly responsible for the absolute growth of the total number of households. Lone persons, which in 2021 account for one in three households, will represent nearly 40% of all households in 2041. A very relevant issue is that most of these households will be composed of older people. If in 2021 single people aged 65 and older account for 50% of all single people, by 2041 this percentage will rise to nearly 60%. Especially older women account for a very large share of women living alone in 2021 (63.1%) and will reach an even higher level in 2041 (72.2%).

This phenomenon is of great interest to policy makers, as the need for formal and informal care is expected to grow. Spending an increasing part of one's life as an old person, moreover alone and perhaps with health problems related to aging and social isolation, raises new questions from the perspective of social and economic sustainability. Additionally, the impact of aging on economic sustainability concerns the progressive reduction of the workforce, the high incidence of pension spending in the overall resources allocated to welfare and the growing issue of "non-self-sufficiency" in the last part of an adult life (Mazzola et al., 2016). However, a wider presence of lone older people can also have positive implications. A longer survival, when in a good quality of life, could allow these people to play an active role in society, for example, by providing their children with the care of grandchildren and guaranteeing them economic support, as well as participating in the economic cycle as consumers of welfare services or as money investors (Istat, 2020; Van Nimwegen, 2013).

Single-parent households are also growing, and single fathers, while remaining a minority, are expected to increase more than single mothers do. Lone parents are among the families most at risk of poverty and social exclusion because of the greater difficulty in reconciling work and family and the lack of support from a partner/caregiver with whom to share responsibility for the children (Riederer, 2017).

In conclusion, the results offer a picture that provides the policy makers with a great deal of useful inputs for their prospective actions, such as: a growing number of people and families at risk of vulnerability (lone older people and single parents); a long stay in child status; a steep decline in families with children with all the consequences it brings to future economic and caregiving conditions; unequal territories.

A key aspect for family law and social policy is to prevent and reduce vulnerability and ensure future well-being of households, particularly those with older people and those with children. Wide-ranging and long-term policies are needed, with targeted interventions to ensure balance in the new social, demographic and economic system.

References

ABS – Australian Bureau of Statistics. (2019). *Household and family projections, Australia methodology*. Reference period: 2016–2041. https://www.abs.gov.au/methodologies/household-and-familyprojections-australia-methodology/2016-2041

Blangiardo, G. C., & Rimoldi, S. (2014). Portraits of the Italian family: Past, present and future. *Journal of Comparative Family Studies, 45*(2), 201–219. http://www.jstor.org/stable/24339606

Blangiardo, G. C., Barbiano di Belgiojoso, E., & Bonomi, P. (2012). Le previsioni demografiche delle famiglie. In P. Donati (Ed.), *La famiglia in Italia. Sfide sociali e innovazioni nei Servizi. Osservatorio Nazionale sulla Famiglia. Rapporto biennale 2011–2012* (Vol. Volume I, pp. 91–123). Aspetti demografici, sociali e legislativi.

Box, G. E. P., Jenkins, G. M., Reinsel, G. C., & Ljung, G. M. (2015). *Time series analysis: Forecasting and control* (5th ed., p. 712). Wiley. ISBN: 978-1-118-67502-1.

Carlson, E. (2019). Reformulating second demographic transition *theory*. In R. Schoen (Ed.), *Analytical family demography* (The springer series on demographic methods and population analysis, vol 47). Springer. https://doi.org/10.1007/978-3-319-93227-9_2

Cooper, J., Bell, M., & Les, M. (1995). *Household and family forecasting models: A review. Review of IPC long-term projections model.* Paper no. 3. Australian Housing and Urban Research Institute in conjunction with demographics.

De Beer, J., & Alders, M. (1999, May 3–7). *Probabilistic population and household forecasts for The Netherlands.* Working paper 45, joint ECE-Eurostat work session on demographic projections, Perugia.

De Rose, A., & Meli, E. (2022). Still believe it? An analysis of partnership trajectories after first union dissolution in Italy. *Rivista Italiana di Economia, Demografia e Statistica, LXXV*(1), 167–178.

De Rose, A., & Vignoli, D. (2011). *Families all'italiana*: 150 years of history. *Rivista Italiana di Economia, Demografia, Statistica, LXV*(2), 121–144.

De Rose, A., Racioppi, F., & Zanatta, A. (2008). Italy: Delayed adaptation of social institutions to changes in family behaviour. *Demographic Research, 19*(19), 665–704. https://doi.org/10.4054/DemRes.2008.19.19

Gill, R., & Keilman, N. (1990). On the estimation of multidimensional demographic models with population registration data. *Mathematical Population Studies, 22*, 119–143.

Guarneri, A., Rinesi, F., Fraboni, R., & De Rose, A. (2021). On the magnitude, frequency, and nature of marriage dissolution in Italy: Insights from vital statistics and life-table analysis. *Genus, 77*, 28. https://doi.org/10.1186/s41118-021-00138-2

Heuveline, P., & Timberlake, J. M. (2002). *The dynamics of fertility and partnership in Europe: Insights and lessons from comparative research.* UNECE.

Istat. (2020). *Invecchiamento attivo e condizioni di vita degli anziani, Letture Statistiche – Temi.* ISTAT.

Istat. (2022a). *Demographic indicators – Year 2021*, Statistiche report, April 8th. Istat Demographic indicators_year_2021 (istat.it).

Istat. (2022b). Labour market statistics, Statistiche Flash, Istat Mercato-del-lavoro-III-trim_2022.pdf (istat.it).

Istat. (2022c), Matrimoni, unioni civili, separazioni e divorzi. Anno 2020. https://www.istat.it/it/archivio/266545

Istat. (2022d). *Household and population projections – Base 1.1.2021*, Statistiche report, September 2022. Istat Households and population projections (istat.it).

Istat. (2022e). *Famiglie, reti familiari, percorsi lavorativi e di vita, Letture Statistiche – Temi.* Istat. https://www.istat.it/it/archivio/275924

Keilman, N. (2019). Family projection methods: A review. In R. Schoen (Ed.), *Analytical family demography* (The springer series on demographic methods and population analysis, vol 47). Springer. https://doi.org/10.1007/978-3-319-93227-9_12

Keilman, N., Kuijsten, A., & Vossen, A. (Eds.). (1988). *Modelling household formation and dissolution.* University Press.

Kono, S. (1987). The headship rate method for projecting households. In J. Bongaarts, T. Burch, & K. Wachter (Eds.), *Family demography, methods and their applications.* Clarendon Press.

Lavit, C., Escoufier, Y., Sabatier, R., & Traissac, P. (1994). The ACT (STATIS) method. *Computational Statistical Data Analysis., 18*, 97–119.

Lesthaeghe, R. (2014). The second demographic transition: A concise overview of its development. *Proceedings of the U.S. National Academy of Sciences, 111*(51), 18112–18115.

Lesthaeghe, R., & Surkyn, J. (1988). Cultural dynamics and economic theories of fertility change. *Population and Development Review, 14*(1), 1–45.

Lesthaeghe, R., & van de Kaa, D. (1986). Twee demographischetransities? In R. Lesthaeghe & D. van de Kaa (Eds.), *Bevolking-Groei en Krim, Mens en Mattschappij* (pp. 9–24). Van LoghumSlaterus.

Liefbroer, A. C., & Dourleijn, E. (2006). Unmarried cohabitation and union stability: Testing the role of diffusion using data from 16 European countries. *Demography, 43*(2), 203–221. https://doi.org/10.1353/dem.2006.0018

Linke, W. (1988). The headship rate approach in modelling households: The case of the Federal Republic of Germany. In N. Keilman, A. Kuijsten, & A. Vossen (Eds.), *Modelling household formation and dissolution*. Clarendon Press.

Mazzola, P., Rimoldi, S. M. L., Rossi, P., Noale, M., Rea, F., Facchini, C., et al. (2016). Aging in Italy: The need for new welfare strategies in an old country. *The Gerontologist, 56*(3), 383–390.

Meggiolaro, S., & Ongaro, F. (2008). Repartnering after marital dissolution: Does context play a role? *Demographic Research, 19*, 1913–1934.

Murphy, M. (1991). Household modelling and forecasting-dynamic approaches with use of linked census data. *Environment and Planning A: Economy and Space., 236*, 885–902. https://doi.org/10.1068/a230885

Reher, D. S. (1998). Family ties in western Europe: Persistent contrasts. *Population and Development Review, 24*(2), 203–234.

Riederer, B. (2017). *Vulnerability and the future of families with children in Europe: Nine questions and corresponding answers*. Families and societies Published by the Vienna Institute of Demography. ISBN 978-3-7001-8223-8.

Salvati, L., Benassi, F., Miccoli, S., Rabiel-Dastjerdi, H., & Matthews, S. A. (2020). Spatial variability of total fertility rate and crude birth rate in a low-fertility country: Patterns and trends in regional and local scale heterogeneity across Italy, 2002–2018. *Applied Geography, 124*, 1–8. https://doi.org/10.1016/j.apgeog.2020.102321

Schoen, R. (1988). *Modelling multigroup population* (The plenum series on demographic methods and population analysis). Plenum Press.

Sobotka, T. (2008). Overview chapter 6: The diverse faces of the second demographic transition in Europe. *Demographic Research, 19*(8), 171–224.

Sullivan, D. F. (1971). A single index of mortality and morbidity. *HSMHA Health Reports, 86*, 347–354.

Tomassini, C., & Vignoli, D. (2023). Introduction. In C. Tomassini & D. Vignoli (Eds.), *AISP-Rapporto sulla popolazione. Le famiglie in Italia. Forme, ostacoli, sfide*. Il Mulino.

United Nations. (1973). *Methods of projecting households and families, Manual VII*. United Nations.

Van Nimwegen, N. (2013). Population changes in Europe: Turning challenges into opportunities. *Genus, 69*(1), 103–125. https://doi.org/10.4402/genus-456

Wilson, T. (2013). The sequential propensity household projection model. *Demographic Research, 28*(24), 681–712., http://www.demographic-research.org/Volumes/Vol28/24/. https://doi.org/10.4054/DemRes.2013.28.24

Chapter 7
A Multistate Analysis of United States Marriage, Divorce, and Fertility, 2005–10 and 2015–20: The Retreat from Marriage Continues

Robert Schoen

Demographic models can help capture the profound changes in marriage, divorce, and fertility behavior that began around 1960 and have yet to run their course (Andersson et al., 2017; Lesthaeghe, 2010; Manning et al., 2014). Here, augmented marital status life tables are prepared and examined for the United States over the 2005–10 and 2015–20 intervals. Summary measures derived from those life tables show a clear continuation of the retreat from marriage. Between 2005–10 and 2015–20, the probability of marrying by age 50 fell from 80% to 70%, the average age at first marriage increased by 1.1 years, and the nonmarital proportion of all births increased to 41%. Despite those broad trends, the continuing retreat of marriage was not a rout, and marriage may well strengthen as better ways are found to reconcile gender equality with the demands of childrearing.

In past work, my colleagues and I have calculated Marital Status Life Tables (MSLTs) to describe changes in family formation and dissolution. Those MSLTs showed the four states Never Married (S), Presently Married (M), Widowed (W), and Divorced (V), and followed hypothetical cohorts as their members moved between those 4 marital states over the course of their lives (cf. Schoen & Nelson, 1974; Schoen & Baj, 1984; Schoen et al., 1985; Schoen & Weinick, 1993; Schoen & Standish, 2001; and Schoen, 2016).

Recent years have seen the fertility of many Western nations fall well below replacement levels, while the rise in cohabitation and nonmarital fertility have reduced the centrality of marriage. Moreover, in the United States, national data on marriage and divorce have been very limited since 1995. The present chapter, using published data for women supplemented by estimates, expands a 3-state MSLT model by adding fertility statuses, and presents a new approach to unifying the analysis of marriage, divorce, and fertility.

R. Schoen (✉)
Pennsylvania State University, San Francisco, CA, USA

R. Schoen (ed.), *The Demography of Transforming Families*, The Springer Series on Demographic Methods and Population Analysis 56,
https://doi.org/10.1007/978-3-031-29666-6_7

7.1 The Augmented Marital Status Life Table Model

Combining marital and fertility states requires a restructured model. There is now little mortality in the United States between the ages of 15 and 50, the main ages of female reproduction. Accordingly, let us consider three marital states, Never Married (S), Presently Married (M), and Divorced (V). With no attrition from mortality, there is no widowhood.

Adding fertility implies a focus on females. Fertility data are typically provided based on the mother's characteristics, and data on male fertility are generally incomplete. Few contemporary American women have six or more children, so let us consider the 6 parity (number of children ever borne) states of 0 through 5.

Life tables are typically calculated from occurrence/exposure rates, and such rates can be found (or estimated) for the present tables as described below. Combined with the three marital states, the 6 parity states produce the 18 state model of Fig. 7.1. In that augmented model, there are 33 possible interstate transitions, 15 resulting from parity changes and 18 from changes in marital status. Ever married persons cannot enter an S state, nor can a person move to a lower parity state.

For each age group and time period, the rates are assembled in 18-by-18 **M** matrices of the form shown in Table 7.1. Rate matrix **M**(x,n) contains the rates for the x to x + n age group. The fertility rates are of the form f_{ijk} (x,n) where $\underline{i} = \underline{s}$ or $\underline{m}$ indicates whether the origin state is unmarried (S or V) or married (M), $\underline{j}$ indicates the beginning parity, $\underline{k} = \underline{j} + 1$ indicates the ending parity, and (x,n) indicates ages x to x + n. Marital status transition rates are of the form m_{ijk} (x,n), where $\underline{i}$ denotes the origin state (e.g. $\underline{s}$ for Never Married), $\underline{j}$ denotes the destination state, $\underline{k}$ denotes the beginning and ending parity, and (x,n) indicates ages x to x + n. The diagonal elements of **M** are negative as they reflect movements out of a state. The rate matrix is column stochastic, that is each column sums to zero, reflecting the absence of mortality. The augmented life tables are prepared for the multi-year intervals 2005–10 and 2015–20 to avoid the instabilities associated with single years.

To construct an augmented life table, we need to calculate probabilities and use them to "survive" or project the initial cohort population to find the number of persons in each state at the next exact age. The life table begins at exact age 15, where all persons are in state S_0, i.e. are never married and at parity zero. The survivorship vector for exact age x, $\boldsymbol{\ell}(x)$, has dimension 18-by-1, with elements of the compound form $\ell_{(uv)}$, where $\underline{u}$ denotes marital status and $\underline{v}$ denotes parity. At age 15, the (1,1) element is set at 100,000 persons, with all other elements zero. The first 6 elements of $\boldsymbol{\ell}$ reflect the 6 parities of the S states (from 0 through 5), the next 6 elements show the 6 parities of the M states, and the last 6 elements give the 6 parities of the V states.

Since the input rates are partially estimated and hence inexact, it is reasonable to proceed in 5-year steps and use the linear calculation assumption, that is to assume that survivorship is linear within those 5-year age intervals. Then the matrix **P**(x,n) of probabilities of state changes between the ages of x and x + n can be written as

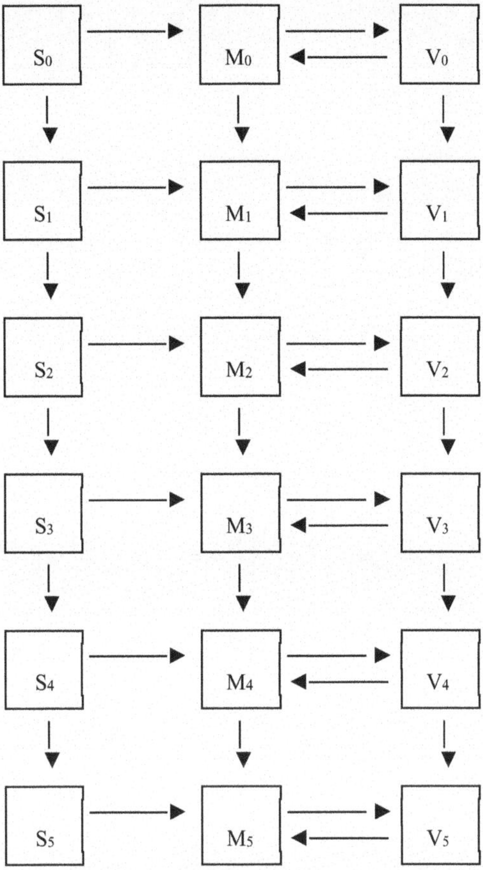

NOTE: The letters S, M, and V denote the states Never Married, Married, and Divorced, respectively. The numerical subscripts indicate parity. The arrows are directional, and show the possible transitions between states. There are 33 possible transitions, 15 from changes in parity, and 18 from changes in marital status.

Fig. 7.1 The 18-state augmented marital status life table model

$$\mathbf{P}(x, n) = [\mathbf{I}-(n/2)\mathbf{M}(x, n)]^{-1}[\mathbf{I} + (n/2)\mathbf{M}(x, n)] \tag{7.1}$$

where $n = 5$, **I** is the 18-by-18 identity matrix, and the (i,j)th element of **P**, p_{ji}, is the probability that a person who begins the interval in marital-parity state j ends the interval in marital-parity state i (cf Schoen, 2006).

The number in each marital-parity state at the end of an n-year interval that begins at exact age x is given by

Table 7.1 The 18 × 18 rate array for the augmented marital status life table

Destination	Origin State																	
State	S_0	S_1	S_2	S_3	S_4	S_5	M_0	M_1	M_2	M_3	M_4	M_5	V_0	V_1	V_2	V_3	V_4	V_5
S_0	$-f_{s01}$ $-m_{sm0}$	0	0	0	0	0	0	0	0	0	0	0	0	0	0	0	0	0
S_1	f_{s01}	$-f_{s12}$ $-m_{sm1}$	0	0	0	0	0	0	0	0	0	0	0	0	0	0	0	0
S_2	0	f_{s12}	$-f_{s23}$ $-m_{sm2}$	0	0	0	0	0	0	0	0	0	0	0	0	0	0	0
S_3	0	0	f_{s23}	$-f_{s34}$ $-m_{sm3}$	0	0	0	0	0	0	0	0	0	0	0	0	0	0
S_4	0	0	0	f_{s34}	$-f_{s45}$ $-m_{sm4}$	0	0	0	0	0	0	0	0	0	0	0	0	0
S_5	0	0	0	0	f_{s45}	$-m_{sm5}$	0	0	0	0	0	0	0	0	0	0	0	0
M_0	m_{sm0}	0	0	0	0	0	$-f_{m01}$ $-m_{mv0}$	0	0	0	0	0	m_{vm0}	0	0	0	0	0
M_1	0	m_{sm1}	0	0	0	0	f_{m01}	$-f_{m12}$ $-m_{mv1}$	0	0	0	0	0	m_{vm1}	0	0	0	0
M_2	0	0	m_{sm2}	0	0	0	0	f_{m12}	$-f_{m23}$ $-m_{mv2}$	0	0	0	0	0	m_{vm2}	0	0	0
M_3	0	0	0	m_{sm3}	0	0	0	0	f_{m23}	$-f_{m34}$ $-m_{mv3}$	0	0	0	0	0	m_{vm3}	0	0
M_4	0	0	0	0	m_{sm4}	0	0	0	0	f_{m34}	$-f_{m45}$ $-m_{mv4}$	0	0	0	0	0	m_{vm4}	0
M_5	0	0	0	0	0	m_{sm5}	0	0	0	0	f_{m45}	$-m_{mv5}$	0	0	0	0	0	m_{vm5}
V_0	0	0	0	0	0	0	m_{mv0}	0	0	0	0	0	$-f_{s01}$ $-m_{vm0}$	0	0	0	0	0
V_1	0	0	0	0	0	0	0	m_{mv1}	0	0	0	0	f_{s01}	$-f_{s12}$ $-m_{vm1}$	0	0	0	0
V_2	0	0	0	0	0	0	0	0	m_{mv2}	0	0	0	0	f_{s12}	$-f_{s23}$ $-m_{vm2}$	0	0	0
V_3	0	0	0	0	0	0	0	0	0	m_{mv3}	0	0	0	0	f_{s23}	$-f_{s34}$ $-m_{vm3}$	0	0
V_4	0	0	0	0	0	0	0	0	0	0	m_{mv4}	0	0	0	0	f_{s34}	$-f_{s45}$ $-m_{vm4}$	0
V_5	0	0	0	0	0	0	0	0	0	0	0	m_{mv5}	0	0	0	0	f_{s45}	$-m_{vm5}$

Note: Symbol f_{ijk} is a fertility rate for $\underline{i} = \underline{s}$ or $\underline{m}$ from parity $\underline{j}$ to parity $\underline{k} = \underline{j} + 1$; m_{ijk} is a transition rate from state $\underline{i}$ to state $\underline{j}$ at parity $\underline{k}$

$$\boldsymbol{\ell}(x+n) = \mathbf{P}(x,n)\boldsymbol{\ell}(x) \tag{7.2}$$

Equation (7.2) is used to project the number in each state, in 5-year steps, from age 15 to age 50.

The remaining life table functions can readily be calculated from the $\boldsymbol{\ell}(x)$ and $\mathbf{M}(x,n)$ matrices. In particular, $\mathbf{L}(x,n)$, the 18-by-1 vector containing the number of person-years lived between the ages of x and x + n in each marital-parity state, is given by

$$\mathbf{L}(x,n) = (n/2)[\boldsymbol{\ell}(x) + \boldsymbol{\ell}(x+n)] \tag{7.3}$$

where the (j,1) element of $\mathbf{L}$, $L_{(uv)}$ (x,n), is the number of years lived in the uth marital state and the vth parity state between the ages of x and x + n.

The number of decrements (transfers) between the ages of x and x + n from marital state $\underline{i}$ to marital state $\underline{j}$ for persons of parity $\underline{k}$, d_{ijk}, is then given by

$$d_{ijk}(x,n) = m_{ijk}(x,n)L_{(ik)}(x,n) \tag{7.4}$$

where $L_{(ik)}$ (x,n) is the number of person-years lived in marital state $\underline{i}$ at parity $\underline{k}$ between the ages of x and x + n. The number of fertility generated movements between the ages of x and x + n from marital state $\underline{i}$ and parity state $\underline{j}$ to parity state $\underline{k} = \underline{j} + 1$, is.

$$D_{ijk}(x,n) = f_{hjk}(x,n)L_{(ij)}(x,n) \tag{7.5}$$

where $\underline{h} = \underline{s}$ or $\underline{m}$ depending on whether state $\underline{i}$ is an unmarried or married state, and $L_{(ij)}$ denotes the element of $\mathbf{L}$ representing marital state $\underline{i}$ and parity state $\underline{j}$. All of the summary measures presented below are derived from those values.

7.2 The Input Data

Let us consider each time period in turn. The marriage and divorce rates used for the 2005–10 augmented MSLTs are the same as those used for the female tables in Schoen (2016). Those rates were derived from Census Bureau population and survey data, National Center for Health Statistics (NCHS) vital statistics data, and divorce rates modified from those presented in Kennedy and Ruggles (2014).

The 2005–10 fertility rates for all women and for unmarried women are from Osterman et al. (2022; Tables 2 and 10). The fertility rate, f, for married women was then found using the relationship

$$f(\text{total}) = f(\text{unmarried}) * \text{proportion unmarried} + f(\text{married}) * \text{proportion married} \quad (7.6)$$

where the 2010 population proportions married and unmarried were taken from U.S. Census Bureau (2010; Table 57). Single and divorced women are assumed to have the same age-specific fertility, and those age-specific fertility rates are assumed to hold at all parities. Thus, for a given age group, two distinct fertility rates were calculated, one for single and divorced women of all parities, and one for married women of all parities.

The fertility data for 2015–20 were found in a similar fashion. The total and marital fertility rates were taken from Osterman et al. (2022; Tables 2 and 10). The unmarried fertility rates were derived, using Eq. (7.6), with population figures averaged from U.S. Census Bureau (2021; Table A1), which provided populations by age and marital status for 2021, and U.S. Census Bureau (2018; Table 2) which provided those figures for 2016.

The marital status data required a good deal of approximation because of the lack of age-specific data on marriages and divorces in the U.S. The same age-specific marriage and divorce rates were assumed to apply to women of all parities. For marriages, the starting point was the total annual number of U.S. marriages reported in Curtin and Sutton (2020) for the years 2015 to 2018, and figures downloaded in 2022 from the CDC/NCHS National Vital Statistics System for 2019 and 2020. The average of the number of marriages in the 2015–19 interval was used, as the year 2020 showed an abrupt drop in marriages, likely produced by the COVID epidemic. The NCHS figures, which include marriages at ages 50 and over, were adjusted by excluding estimated marriages at those ages. From the 2005–10 MSLTs, 12% of marriages occurred at ages over 50. However, the MSLT population was older than the corresponding U.S. population by approximately 12%. Accordingly the number of NCHS marriages was reduced by a factor of 1 − (.12)(.88) = (.902). Indirect Standardization was then used to estimate the 2015–2019 interval marriage rates, separately for first marriages and remarriages, from that total number of marriages and the age pattern of the 2005–10 rates. The result indicated that the 2005–10 rates should be reduced by a factor of (.741) at every age in order to estimate the 2015–20 rates.

The 2015–19 divorce rates were estimated in a similar fashion using the provisional number of divorces in the years 2015 through 2020 provided by the CDC/NCHS National Vital Statistics System (2022). With 2020 an aberrant year, NCHS divorce figures were averaged over the years 2015–19. The reported figures were then reduced by a factor of (.812) to remove divorces to persons 50 and over. A further adjustment was needed as the NCHS divorce figures did not include 5 states that likely accounted for some 20% of all U.S. divorces during that period. The NCHS figures were accordingly adjusted by a factor of (.812)(1.25) = 1.015, essentially returning the original NCHS figure. Again, Indirect Standardization was applied, using the age-pattern of the 2005–10 divorce rates to estimate the age-specific divorce rates. The result indicated that the 2005–10 rates should be reduced by a factor of (.866).

We should step back and consider the results of those approximations. Because of data limitations, the 2015–20 period MSLT uses fertility rates for 2016–20 and marital status rates for 2015–19. For simplicity, transparency, and interpretability let us take the augmented 2015–20 MSLT marriage and divorce rates to be the 2005–10 MSLT age-specific marriage rates reduced by 25% and the 2005–10 MSLT age-specific divorce rates reduced by 12.5%. Substantively, those reductions seem both reasonable and a bit conservative. Divorce rates under age 50 have indeed been falling (cf Kennedy & Ruggles, 2014; Brown & Lin, 2022), and a one-eighth drop is quite plausible. Marriages are now coming later and less often (Westrick-Payne, 2022), and a one-quarter drop in marriage rates is not at all unreasonable. Readers who hesitate to interpret the results as reflecting 2015–20 rates of marriage and divorce, can instead interpret them as reflecting 2016–20 fertility rates along with marriage rates at three-quarters of those during 2005–10 and divorce rates at seven-eighths of those in 2005–10.

7.3 Calculating Summary Measures of Marriage, Divorce, and Fertility

A number of informative summary measures can be derived from the 2005–10 and 2015–20 augmented MSLTs. For 2005–10 and 2015–20 respectively, **Appendix Tables A1** and **A2** show the rates (f and m), the survivorship (**ℓ**) values, and the person-year (**L**) values for ages 15 to 50, from which the summary measures were derived.

Let us begin with measures of first marriage. The proportion ever marrying by age 50, psm50, is given by

$$\text{psm50} = 1 - \Sigma_j\, \ell_{(sj)}(50)/100{,}000 \tag{7.7}$$

where the sum over index j ranges over all parity states and $\ell_{(sj)}$ (50) is the number of never married persons of parity j at age 50. The proportion of life lived Never Married between ages 15 and 50 at all parities, $P_{(s\cdot)}$ (15,35) is given by

$$P_{(s\cdot)}(15, 35) = \Sigma_j \Sigma_i L_{(sj)}(i, n)/3{,}500{,}000 \tag{7.8}$$

where the sum over j ranges over all 6 parities, the sum over i ranges over the seven 5-year age groups 15–20 through 45–50, and 3,500,000 is the total number of person-years lived by the life table cohort of 100,000, in all states, between the ages of 15 and 50. Analogous expressions provide the proportions lived Married and Divorced.

The mean age at first marriage during the 15 to 50 age interval can be found from

$$A_{m1} = \Sigma_i d_{sm\cdot}(i, n) * (i + 2.5)/\Sigma_i d_{sm\cdot}(i, n) \quad (7.9)$$

where the age weights are taken at the midpoint of each of the seven 5-year age intervals and the subscripted dot (·) indicates all parity states. Similar expressions yield the mean age at divorce and the mean age at remarriage.

The age 50 parity distribution follows from the $\ell_{(\cdot j)}$ (50) distribution. The proportion of life at ages 15 to 50 lived childless is given by

$$P_{(\cdot 0)}(15, 35) = \Sigma_i L_{(\cdot 0)}(i, n)/3,500,000 \quad (7.10)$$

where the subscripted (·0) indicates all marital statuses at parity 0.

Turning to measures of fertility, the Total Fertility Rate (TFR) is

$$\mathrm{TFR} = \Sigma_i f \ldots (i, n) \quad (7.11)$$

or the sum of the all age-specific fertility rates. The nonmarital proportion of all births is provided by

$$P_{(nmf)} = \left[\Sigma_i \Sigma_j D_{sjk}(i, n) + \Sigma_i \Sigma_j D_{vjk}(i, n)\right]/\Sigma_h \Sigma_i \Sigma_j D_{hjk}(i, n) \quad (7.12)$$

where summation over h spans all three marital statuses.

The mean age at first birth is found from

$$A_{f01} = \Sigma_h \Sigma_i D_{h01}(i, n) * (i + 2.5)/\Sigma_h \Sigma_i D_{h01}(i, n) \quad (7.13)$$

Other mean ages at birth can be found by analogous expressions. The probability of a person having a first marriage after having one or more births is given by

$$P_{f<m} = \Sigma_i \Sigma_j d_{smj}(i, n)/100,000 \quad (7.14)$$

where the sum over j goes from parity 1 through parity 5. The probability of having a child but never marrying is.

$$P_{s>0} = \Sigma_j \ell_{(sj)}(50)/100,000 \quad (7.15)$$

where the sum over j again goes from parity 1 through parity 5.

The augmented MSLT also allows the calculation of some measures of kinship. Sibsize, C, the average number of children in a family, is given (Preston, 1976) by

$$C = \mathrm{TFR} + \mathrm{VarP}/\mathrm{TFR} \quad (7.16)$$

where VarP, the variance of the age 50 parity distribution, is calculated in the usual manner from the $\ell_{(\cdot j)}$ (50) distribution. The number of "Close Kin", that is a person's average number of parents, children, siblings, nieces, and nephews, can be found, from Schoen (2019), as.

$$\text{NrKin} = 1 + C(\text{TFR} + 1) \tag{7.17}$$

7.4 Results

The summary measures from the augmented MSLTs are presented in Table 7.2. The proportion of women ever marrying fell from about 80% during 2005–10 to 70% during 2015–20. The proportion of life at ages 15 to 50 spent Never Married increased by 20%, while the average age at first marriage increased by 1.1 years. In contrast, the proportion of life spent Married fell by 15%.

With the fall in divorce rates, the proportion spent in the Divorced state at ages 15–50 fell to 7%, while the ratio of age 15–50 divorces to marriages dropped 9%. Still, the divorces/ marriages ratio was at 40%, and the mean age at divorce changed little. The remarriage ratio fell by 14%, as the mean age at remarriage increased slightly.

The proportion of women remaining childless at age 50 increased from 15% during 2005–10 to nearly 20% during 2015–20. During both periods, parity 1 was most common, and in 2015–20 that proportion exceeded the proportion at parity 2 by some 25%. The old 2–4 child range appears to have been replaced by a 0–2 child range, with one child families the most common. During 2015–20, close to half of women's lives between the ages of 15 and 50 was spent childless.

The augmented MSLT TFRs were 1.96 for 2005–10 and 1.71 for 2016–20. Those levels approximate the figures published by NCHS. During 2005–10, 37% of births were nonmarital, a bit below the NCHS level of about 40% for that period. The MSLT proportion nonmarital increased to 40% during 2015–20, as the mean age of mother at nonmarital birth increased by a year and a quarter.

The mean age at all first births increased by over a year and a half over the decade studied, with the mean age at all births increasing by 1.2 years. The probability of marrying after having one or more births fell from over a quarter to about a fifth, mostly because of less marriage. However, the probability of having a child and never marrying rose from one-seventh to over a fifth.

A further implication of the fall in fertility is the smaller kinship network. Average sibsize fell 9%, while the number of Close Kin dropped by 13%.

Table 7.2 Summary measures of marriage, divorce, and fertility, augmented marital status life tables for United States females, 2005–10 and 2015–20

Measure	Years 2005–10	Years 2015–20
1. Proportion ever marrying by age 50	.805	.705
2. Proportion of ages 15–50 lived never married	.424	.510
3. Mean age at first marriage	24.59	25.69
4. Proportion of ages 15–50 lived married	.491	.417
5. Ratio of divorces at ages 15–50 over marriages ages 15–50	.434	.397
6. Proportion of ages 15–50 lived divorced	.085	.073
7. Mean age at divorce	34.71	34.97
8. Mean age at remarriage	35.96	36.30
9. Ratio of remarriages at ages 15–50 over divorces ages 15–50	.655	.565
10. Age 50 proportion at parity		
0	.150	.195
1	.276	.306
2	.256	.246
3	.165	.141
4	.086	.067
5	.067	.045
11. Proportion of ages 15–50 lived childless	.389	.458
12. Total Fertility Rate	1.96	1.71
13. Nonmarital proportion of all births	.371	.410
14. Mean age at first birth	24.86	26.44
15. Never married mean age at first birth	22.99	25.14
16. Mean age, all births	27.87	29.08
17. Mean age of nonmarital births	25.65	26.90
18. Mean age of marital births	29.17	30.06
19. Probability of a first marriage after having one more births	.277	.206
20. Probability of having a child and never marrying	.147	.209
21. Average sibsize	2.973	2.772
22. Number of Close Kin	9.806	8.519

Note: Based on 18 state augmented marital status life tables spanning ages 15 to 50. See text

7.5 Discussion

The results in Table 7.2 clearly show a continuing retreat of marriage. The proportion ever marrying is down from about 80% in 2005–10 to 70% in 2015–20, the mean age of first marriage is up from 24.6 to 25.7 years, and the level of remarriage fell. The only contrary sign is a modest decline in the high level of divorce.

The connection between marriage and fertility continues to weaken. The proportion of nonmarital births is up to 41%, and the likelihood a woman will have one or more children but never marry is 21%. The 2015–20 augmented MSLT finds that one woman in five will be childless, a record level for the United States. In 2020, American fertility hit an all-time low of 1.64. The MSLTs show that only children, once infrequent, are now the modal parity, while the kinship web is contracting.

The transformation of family life associated with the large-scale economic activity of women and the accompanying demand for gender equality is continuing to evolve. Men and women live more independent, autonomous lives, and increasingly seek to establish themselves before marrying. Children are still seen as being closer to their mothers, a reality reinforced by the high levels of divorce and nonmarital fertility. With no clear normative guidance, parents are largely left on their own to reconcile desires for autonomy and gender equality with the heavy and differential demands of childrearing.

Despite all of those changes, the continuing retreat of marriage is not a rout. Some 70% of women still marry. The housework differential is diminishing as more couples outsource cooking, cleaning, and even some childcare. The strengths of a stable partnership---companionship, mutual assistance, economies of scale, and a longer planning horizon---remain strong. The future course of fertility is not clear, but marriage may well strengthen as progress is made to reduce, or to better balance, the demands of parenting.

Acknowledgements Helpful comments from Lowell Hargens are gratefully acknowledged.

Appendix

Table A1 2005–2010 rates and survivor-ship values

Age	Surv L S0	Surv L S1	Surv L S2	Surv L S3	Surv L S4	Surv L S5	Surv L M0	Surv L M1
15	100000	0	0	0	0	0	0	0
20	69624.49	11185.3	737.57	48.64	3.21	0.23	13035.13	3493.12
25	30209.88	17379.09	3903.89	603.45	83.21	12.55	19387.31	15017.52
30	13534.52	13265.25	5587.31	1459.16	295.63	62.47	14488.19	19724.99
35	7533.75	9691.85	5624.98	2040.5	547.94	150.52	9811.74	18044.72
40	5718.52	8219.16	5435.4	2268.71	696.38	219.31	8156.07	16533.72
45	5028.56	7429.46	5073.69	2192.48	696.2	227.42	7970.88	16239.42
50	4729.95	6997.75	4786.4	2071.85	659	215.66	8084.31	16311.46
Age	P-Y LL S0	P-Y LL S1	P-Y LL S2	P-Y LL S3	P-Y LL S4	P-Y LL S5	P-Y LL M0	P-Y LL M1
15	424061.2	27963.25	1843.925	121.6	8.025	0.575	32587.83	8732.8
20	249585.9	71410.98	11603.65	1630.225	216.05	31.95	81056.1	46276.6
25	109361	76610.85	23728	5156.525	947.1	187.55	84688.75	86856.28
30	52670.68	57392.75	28030.73	8749.15	2108.925	532.475	60749.83	94424.28
35	33130.68	44777.53	27650.95	10773.03	3110.8	924.575	44919.53	86446.1
40	26867.7	39121.55	26272.73	11152.98	3481.45	1116.83	40317.38	81932.85
45	24396.28	36068.03	24650.23	10660.83	3388	1107.7	40137.98	81377.2
Total	*920073.5*	*353344.9*	*143780.2*	*48244.33*	*13260.35*	*3901.65*	*384457.4*	*486046.1*
Age	fs01	fm01	msm	mmv	mvm			
15	0.0311	0.1061	0.04053	0.0303	0.18182			
20	0.07	0.174167	0.08792	0.0364	0.25114			
25	0.0692	0.151343	0.08328	0.0347	0.17826			
30	0.0563	0.119309	0.05763	0.0295	0.12371			
35	0.0296	0.053087	0.02519	0.0281	0.11665			
40	0.008	0.011138	0.01768	0.026	0.08561			
45	0.0004	0.000839	0.01184	0.0208	0.0633			
Total								

Surv L M2	Surv L M3	Surv L M4	Surv L M5	Surv L V0	Surv L V1	Surv L V2	Surv L V3	Surv L V4	Surv L V5	
0	0	0	0	0	0	0	0	0	0	
762.99	158.07	32.22	8.2	644.4	205.38	48.14	10.26	2.11	0.54	100000
6411.77	2266.58	738.52	332.01	1707.01	1185.04	502.38	176.95	57.31	25.53	100000
13293.53	6486.13	2690.83	1565.77	2217.69	2560.65	1574.78	732.79	294.53	165.78	100000
16431.71	10311.86	5203.93	3763.58	2077.06	3309.11	2678.92	1545.2	734.47	498.26	100000
16735.36	11617.82	6386.51	5099.37	1889.15	3530.88	3321.25	2171.03	1138.74	862.62	100000
16573.48	11624.8	6459.26	5236.72	2022.08	3981.32	3937.78	2689.5	1462.23	1154.72	100000
16508.34	11505.32	6365.11	5142.55	2159.65	4297.63	4293.71	2958.67	1620.67	1291.98	100000
P-Y LL M2	P-Y LL M3	P-Y LL M4	P-Y LL M5	P-Y LL V0	P-Y LL V1	P-Y LL V2	P-Y LL V3	P-Y LL V4	P-Y LL V5	Total
1907.475	395.175	80.55	20.5	1611	513.45	120.35	25.65	5.275	1.35	500000
17936.9	6061.625	1926.85	850.525	5878.525	3476.05	1376.3	468.025	148.55	65.175	500000
49263.25	21881.78	8573.375	4744.45	9811.75	9364.225	5192.9	2274.35	879.6	478.275	500000
74313.1	41994.98	19736.9	13323.38	10736.88	14674.4	10634.25	5694.975	2572.5	1660.1	500000
82917.68	54824.2	28976.1	22157.38	9915.525	17099.98	15000.43	9290.575	4683.025	3402.2	500000
83272.1	58106.55	32114.43	25840.23	9778.075	18780.5	18147.58	12151.33	6502.425	5043.35	500000
82704.55	57825.3	32060.93	25948.18	10454.33	20697.38	20578.73	14120.43	7707.25	6116.75	500000
392315.1	*241090*	*123469.1*	*92884.63*	*58186.08*	*84605.98*	*71050.5*	*44025.33*	*22498.63*	*16767.2*	3500001

Table A2 2015–2020 rates survivor-ship values

Age	Surv L S0	Surv L S1	Surv L S2	Surv L S3	Surv L S4	Surv L S5	Surv L M0	Surv L M1
15	100000	0	0	0	0	0	0	0
20	79099.93	6527.62	237.91	8.67	0.32	0.01	11404.17	1791.99
25	42906.67	15942.37	2413.04	274.16	28.92	3.32	18613.02	11376.1
30	22425.15	16158.66	5106.7	1044.11	173.04	29.91	15559.77	17192.27
35	13286.32	13777.67	6549.8	1990.85	459.81	108.52	10552.61	16914.17
40	10078.71	12301.48	7033.48	2585.74	711.18	199.42	8605.42	15665.02
45	8942.21	11391.76	6835.07	2642.27	762.21	224.56	8422.07	15403.06
50	8536.7	10892.25	6546.89	2535.53	732.71	216.27	8537.44	15421.18
Age	P-Y LL S0	P-Y LL S1	P-Y LL S2	P-Y LL S3	P-Y LL S4	P-Y LL S5	P-Y LL M0	P-Y LL M1
15	447749.8	16319.05	594.775	21.675	0.8	0.025	28510.43	4479.975
20	305016.5	56174.98	6627.375	707.075	73.1	8.325	75042.98	32920.23
25	163329.6	80252.58	18799.35	3295.675	504.9	83.075	85431.98	71420.93
30	89278.68	74840.83	29141.25	7587.4	1582.125	346.075	65280.95	85266.1
35	58412.58	65197.88	33958.2	11441.48	2927.475	769.85	47895.08	81447.98
40	47552.3	59233.1	34671.38	13070.03	3683.475	1059.95	42568.73	77670.2
45	43697.28	55710.03	33454.9	12944.5	3737.3	1102.08	42398.78	77060.6
Total	*1155037*	*407728.4*	*157247.2*	*49067.83*	*12509.18*	*3369.38*	*387128.9*	*430266*
		Rates						
Age	fs01	fm01	msm	mmv	mvm			
15	0.01628	0.057423	0.030398	0.026513	0.136365			
20	0.05272	0.153746	0.06594	0.03185	0.188355			
25	0.06294	0.140126	0.06246	0.030363	0.133695			
30	0.05914	0.126153	0.043223	0.025813	0.092783			
35	0.03602	0.060601	0.018893	0.024588	0.087488			
40	0.01064	0.012254	0.01326	0.02275	0.064208			
45	0.0004	0.001142	0.00888	0.0182	0.047475			

Surv L M2	Surv L M3	Surv L M4	Surv L M5	Surv L V0	Surv L V1	Surv L V2	Surv L V3	Surv L V4	Surv L V5	
0	0	0	0	0	0	0	0	0	0	100000
231.56	28.52	3.47	0.48	547.11	102.09	14.12	1.78	0.22	0.03	100000
3938.23	1164.87	325.52	121.88	1626.95	858.32	289.65	84.71	23.51	8.76	100000
9753.69	4100.14	1488.4	725.76	2293.62	2160	1113.92	444.88	156.19	73.79	100000
13640.07	7686.72	3517.56	2210.9	2252.19	3053.1	2153.39	1101.33	470.01	274.98	100000
14455.11	9241.07	4703.78	3333.21	2016.12	3311.89	2787.49	1652.02	792.41	526.45	100000
14347.23	9287.03	4790.41	3457.84	2196.32	3850.68	3449.15	2158.65	1082.86	756.62	100000
14220.78	9139.8	4693.41	3377.49	2415.95	4284.16	3879.93	2452.5	1240.86	876.16	100000
P-Y LL M2	P-Y LL M3	P-Y LL M4	P-Y LL M5	P-Y LL V0	P-Y LL V1	P-Y LL V2	P-Y LL V3	P-Y LL V4	P-Y LL V5	Total
578.9	71.3	8.675	1.2	1367.775	255.225	35.3	4.45	0.55	0.075	500000
10424.48	2983.475	822.475	305.9	5435.15	2401.025	759.425	216.225	59.325	21.975	500000
34229.8	13162.53	4534.8	2119.1	9801.425	7545.8	3508.925	1323.975	449.25	206.375	500000
58484.4	29467.15	12514.9	7341.65	11364.53	13032.75	8168.275	3865.525	1565.5	871.925	500000
70237.95	42319.48	20553.35	13860.28	10670.78	15912.48	12352.2	6883.375	3156.05	2003.58	500000
72005.85	46320.25	23735.48	16977.63	10531.1	17906.43	15591.6	9526.675	4688.175	3207.68	500000
71420.03	46067.08	23709.55	17088.33	11530.68	20337.1	18322.7	11527.88	5809.3	4081.95	500000
317381.4	*180391*	*85879.23*	*57694.08*	*60701.43*	*77390.8*	*58738.4*	*33348.1*	*15728.15*	*10393.6*	3500000

References

Andersson, G., Thomson, E., & Duntava, A. (2017). Life table representations of family dynamics in the 21st century. *Demographic Research, 37*, 1081–1230.

Brown, S. L., & Lin, I.-F. (2022). *The graying of divorce: A half century of change*. Paper presented at the April Meeting of the Population Association of America in Atlanta.

CDC/NCHS National Vital Statistics System. (2022). Downloaded 6/19/2022 from cdc.gov/nchs/data/dvs/national-marriage-divorce-rates-00-20.pdf

Curtin, S. C., & Sutton, P. D. (2020). *Marriage rates in the United States, 1900–2018*. NCHS Health E-Stat.

Kennedy, S., & Ruggles, S. (2014). Breaking up is hard to count: The rise in divorce in the United States, 1980–2010. *Demography, 51*, 587–598.

Lesthaeghe, R. (2010). The unfolding story of the second demographic transition. *Population and Development Review, 36*, 211–251.

Manning, W. D., Brown, S. L., & Stykes, J. B. (2014). Family complexity among children in the United States. *The Annals of the American Academy of Political and Social Science, 654*(1), 48–65.

Osterman, M. J. K., Hamilton, B. E., Martin, J. A., Driscoll, A. K., & Valenzuela, C. P. (2022). Births: Final data for 2020. National Vital Statistics Reports (Vol. 70, no 17). National Center for Health Statistics.

Preston, S. H. (1976). Family sizes of children and family sizes of women. *Demography, 13*, 105–114.

Schoen, R. (2006). *Dynamic population models*. Springer.

Schoen, R. (2016). The continuing retreat of marriage: Figures from marital status life tables for United States females, 2000–2005 and 2005–2010. In R. Schoen (Ed.), *Dynamic demographic analysis* (pp. 203–215). Springer.

Schoen, R. (2019). On the implications of age-specific fertility for sibships and birth spacing. In R. Schoen (Ed.), *Analytical family demography* (pp. 201–214). Springer.

Schoen, R., & Baj, J. (1984). Twentieth century cohort marriage and divorce in England and Wales. *Population Studies, 38*, 439–449.

Schoen, R., & Nelson, V. E. (1974). Marriage, divorce and mortality: A life table analysis. *Demography, 11*, 267–290.

Schoen, R., & Standish, N. (2001). The retrenchment of marriage: Results from marital status life tables for the United States, 1995. *Population and Development Review, 27*, 555–563.

Schoen, R., & Weinick, R. M. (1993). The slowing metabolism of marriage: Figures from 1988 U.S. marital status life tables. *Demography, 30*, 737–746.

Schoen, R., Urton, W., Woodrow, K., & Baj, J. (1985). Marriage and divorce in twentieth century American cohorts. *Demography, 22*, 101–114.

United States Census Bureau. (2010). *Table 57. Marital status of the population by sex and age: 2010*. Downloaded 6/10/2022 from www.census.gov/population/www/socdemo/hh-fam/cps2010.html

United States Census Bureau. (2018). *Table 2. Marital status of the population 15 years and over by sex and age: 2016*. Current Population Survey, Annual Social and Economic Supplement, 2016. Released August 2018.

United States Census Bureau. (2021) *Table A1. Marital status of people 15 years and over, by age, sex, and personal earnings: 2021*. Downloaded 7/3/2022 from www.census.gov/data/tables/2021/demo/families/cps-2021.html

Westrick-Payne, K. (2022). *A profile of national and state-level marriage rates in the U.S., 1880–2018: A research note*. Paper presented at the April Meeting of the Population Association of America in Atlanta.

Chapter 8
Heterogeneity in Hispanic Fertility: Confronting the Challenges of Estimation and Disaggregation

Rhiannon A. Kroeger, Courtney E. Williams, Elizabeth Wildsmith, and Reanne Frank

8.1 Introduction

The U.S. has witnessed record declines in fertility since 2007, particularly among Hispanics[1] (Kearney et al., 2022; Smock & Schwartz, 2020). Between 2006 and 2017, fertility rates for women[2] ages 15–44 decreased by 31% for Hispanics, compared with 5% for Non-Hispanic Whites and about 11% for Non-Hispanic Blacks (Alvira-Hammond, 2019). Nonetheless, Hispanic women retained higher fertility rates than Non-Hispanic Whites and Non-Hispanic Blacks during this

[1]We acknowledge the importance of specifying the appropriate ethnonym in the case of the Hispanic/Latin/o/a/x population (García, 2020). However, as there is not yet a consistently agreed upon term (Lopez et al., 2022), we choose to use the term Hispanic as it is in accordance with how the NVSS labels this population and agrees with much of the literature reviewed in this chapter.

[2]While we acknowledge there are diverse reproductive capabilities across various genders, we use the term woman/women or mother as it is in accordance with labels used by the NVSS (which collects information on the mother, "defined as the woman who gave birth to or delivered the infant") and neither the NVSS nor the ACS ask respondents about gender identity (https://www.cdc.gov/nchs/nvss/revisions-of-the-us-standard-certificates-and-reports.htm; https://www.census.gov/acs/www/about/why-we-ask-each-question/sex/).

R. A. Kroeger (✉)
Department of Sociology, Louisiana State University, Baton Rouge, LA, USA
e-mail: rkroeger@lsu.edu

C. E. Williams
Louisiana State University, Baton Rouge, LA, USA

E. Wildsmith
Child Trends, Bethesda, MD, USA

R. Frank
The Ohio State University, Columbus, OH, USA

R. Schoen (ed.), *The Demography of Transforming Families*, The Springer Series on Demographic Methods and Population Analysis 56,
https://doi.org/10.1007/978-3-031-29666-6_8

same period. While Hispanics' greater declines in fertility, on the one hand, and sustained higher fertility rates, on the other hand, have received considerable attention in the literature, efforts to understand these aggregate trends are hindered by the complex heterogeneity in the Hispanic population.

In this chapter, we investigate variation in Hispanic fertility in the United States over a decade, beginning the year before the initiation of national fertility declines (i.e., 2006) and continuing through 2016.[3] Echoing prior research, our core argument is that before we begin to assess the reasons and demographic consequences behind trends in Hispanic childbearing, we must first describe the phenomenon we are trying to explain (Sweeney & Raley, 2014). We first discuss important sources of heterogeneity in Hispanic fertility identified in prior literature as well as challenges and potential solutions to correctly estimating variation in Hispanic fertility. Next, we use birth counts from the national vital statistics system (NVSS) and population distributions from the American Community Survey (ACS) adjusted to U.S. Census population totals to estimate Hispanic age-specific fertility rates (ASFR) from 2006–2016 by nativity, region of origin, and marital status. Finally, we demonstrate how decomposition analysis can be applied to Hispanic fertility rates cross-classified by multiple factors over time to better understand the extent to which observed changes in fertility are due to changes in the composition of population sub-groups that have differential childbearing risk.

8.2 Background

8.2.1 Sources of Heterogeneity in Hispanic Fertility

Seminal work by Emilio Parrado and colleagues made clear that Hispanic fertility levels are not nearly as high as they are conventionally depicted, once various demographic sub-group differences in fertility and population composition are taken into account (Parrado, 2011; Parrado & Flippen, 2012; Parrado & Morgan, 2008). Collectively, their work provides an analytic blueprint for scholars to comprehensively describe changes in Hispanic fertility, emphasizing the necessity of disaggregating the Hispanic population by nativity, among other dimensions, in the context of fertility. In particular, Parrado and colleagues argue that fertility rates should be estimated separately for U.S.-born and foreign-born Hispanic women. There are stark differences in fertility between the U.S.-born and foreign-born, and both the higher levels of and greater declines in fertility among Hispanic women are confounded by these differences (Castro Torres & Parrado, 2022; Parrado & Flippen, 2012; Smock & Schwartz, 2020). Fertility rates are generally higher for foreign-born Hispanic women relative to their U.S.-born counterparts, though this gap has grown smaller in recent years (Lichter et al., 2012; Livingston, 2019).

[3] 2016 is the final year that mother's marital status is available for births in California in the NVSS.

Moreover, there are compositional differences in age and marital status between U.S. and foreign-born Hispanic women that have implications for fertility rates (Parrado, 2011). For example, among Hispanic women aged 15–44, a larger percentage of U.S.-born women are in the youngest age group (15–19) relative to their foreign-born counterparts, and hence not yet in their peak childbearing years (Parrado). Moreover, relative to the U.S.-born, a greater percentage of foreign-born Hispanic women ages 15–44 are married, both overall and within each 5-year age group. Indeed, marital status is strongly linked to fertility. Although this association has weakened in recent decades, delays in marriage are partially responsible for the observed declines in childbearing (Hayford et al., 2014; Smith, 2019). Even though marriage is still normative and relatively common among Hispanic populations, marriage rates have declined in recent decades. For example, the percentage of Hispanic women aged 18–34 who report being married declined from 59% in 1990 to 35% in 2017; these declines were most pronounced among U.S. born Hispanic women, with very little change observed among foreign-born women (Ju, 2022). There is also some variation in marriage by region of origin, with Puerto Rican women being somewhat less likely than Mexican, Cuban, and Salvadoran women to be married.

Region of origin is another important source of heterogeneity in Hispanic fertility rates. For instance, higher fertility among Mexican-origin women is a significant component of the higher fertility rates observed among Hispanic women overall (Lichter et al., 2012). This is in part due to compositional differences in age and nativity; a greater proportion of Mexican-origin women are of child-bearing age when compared with Hispanic women from other countries of origin (Pew Research Center, 2011, 2015). Among foreign-born Hispanics in particular, a larger share of births are to Mexican-origin women than to women in other region-of-origin groups (Driscoll & Valenzuela, 2022; Livingston, 2016).

Considering sources of heterogeneity in Hispanic fertility identified in prior research, in this study we disaggregate Hispanic fertility rates for women aged 15–44 by nativity, region of origin, marital status, and age.

8.2.2 Challenges to Correctly Estimating Variation in Hispanic Fertility

Accurate sub-group estimates for births and population counts are critical to comprehensive analyses of variation in Hispanic fertility. Some estimates greatly differ across different sources even for the same year and same subgroups, mainly because of differences in the data used to capture births (numerators) and estimate population totals (denominators). Studies on Hispanic fertility either derive fertility estimates from national surveys in which information on births *and* population counts come from the same source (e.g., the American Community Survey (ACS), the Current Population Survey (CPS) June Fertility supplement, the National Survey of Family

Growth (NSFG), etc.), or estimate fertility rates based on vital registration systems which pair birth certificate data with population estimates from an external source (e.g., DeLeone et al. (2009) paired birth certificate data with population estimates derived from 3-year moving averages of the March CPS to examine changes in the non-marital fertility ratio for Latinas versus other racial-ethnic groups).

There are multiple advantages to relying on large national surveys for Hispanic fertility estimates. When the numerator and denominator are sourced from the same data, one does not have to be concerned about mismatches between categorization schemas for Hispanic subpopulations. Additionally, surveys that collect data on retrospective birth histories allow for analyses of completed fertility which avoids the well-known issues related to tempo distortions in period fertility measures. In the case of the CPS June supplement and ACS, an additional advantage is that questions on both immigration timing and childbearing allow for an assessment of the relationship between migration and fertility timing (Lichter et al., 2012; Parrado & Flippen, 2012). A third advantage is that researchers can examine trends in fertility by indicators either not included in birth certificate data or measured inconsistently over time/across states. For example, Lichter et al. (2012) examine the effects of educational attainment on fertility rates derived from the ACS. Had the authors relied on birth registration system data for this analysis instead, they might have had to limit their study to a subset of states or faced additional limitations; While educational attainment is collected in birth certificate data, how it is assessed has evolved and varies across states depending on when they adopted the new recommended measure. All states did not use the same measure of education until 2016; thus, birth certificate data on educational attainment are not comparable across all states until 2016.[4]

At the same time, there are clearly advantages to estimating fertility rates based on vital registration systems, especially when assessing heterogeneity. First, because birth certificate registration in the U.S. is at nearly 100%, birth counts coming from the national vital statistics system are more accurate than those derived from national surveys. For instance, birth counts derived from the ACS rely on self-reporting[5] of whether female household members had a birth in the prior year. Consequently, the birth counts are less accurate and have been shown to over-estimate fertility of older women (Cai & Morgan, 2019). Second, the sheer volume of births captured in the

[4]"The format of the education item on the 2003 revised standard certificate differs substantively from that of the 1989 unrevised standard certificate. The 1989 certificate asks for the number of years of school completed by the mother. In contrast, the revised 2003 certificate item asks for the highest degree or level of school completed at the time of the birth (e.g., high school diploma, some college credit but no degree, bachelor's degree, etc.). Education data for the states that have implemented the revised 2003 certificate are not directly comparable with data for the states that are not yet using the revised certificate. Accordingly, revised and unrevised educational attainment data are not combined in the natality data files." (p. 24 of the *Detailed Technical Notes – natality: United States, 2006*; https://ftp.cdc.gov/pub/Health_Statistics/NCHS/Dataset_Documentation/DVS/natality/UserGuide2006.pdf).

[5]For women ages 15–50, ACS asks "Has this person given birth to any children in the past 12 months?" (Lichter et al., 2012).

vital registration system (over 3.5 million in 2021) provides sufficient subpopulation counts to assess the true extent of heterogeneity in Hispanic fertility. This is in contrast to national surveys for which the sample sizes are often not large enough to allow for the degree of differentiation that we are arguing is necessary for accurately characterizing Hispanic fertility. For instance, in prior work assessing fertility change in the Hispanic population using the CPS, Parrado and Morgan (2008) only had sufficient sample size to disaggregate trends for Mexican-origin women and none of the other region-of-origin subgroupings. Similarly, some of the national fertility/family surveys, such as the NSFG, which are rich in questions on childbearing and fertility intentions, are limited by their small sample size in their ability to represent the true extent of heterogeneity in the broader Hispanic population (Castro Torres & Parrado, 2022).

U.S. fertility rates based on vital statistics generally use population estimates produced by the U.S. Census Bureau as denominators (U.S. Census Bureau, Population Division, 2022).[6] Yet sub-group population estimates provided by the U.S. census are only available by race, ethnicity, sex, and age. This creates challenges for correctly estimating yearly population counts by nativity, region of origin, marital status, and other factors not included in U.S. census population estimates but essential for providing an accurate assessment of Hispanic fertility trends. It is perhaps because of these data constraints that the practice of Hispanic population disaggregation is often limited in analyses of fertility rates from vital registration systems. In the realm of fertility, however, subgroup differences are too consequential to ignore.

Scholars commonly manage these constraints by using data from the Current Population Survey (CPS), American Community Survey (ACS), or Decennial Census public use microdata samples (PUMS) to obtain sub-group population estimates. However, to obtain accurate denominators for sub-groups, researchers should rely on the population *distributions* rather than the population *totals* estimated from surveys like the ACS or CPS. The ACS provides clear guidance on this, noting in their 2020 user guide that "The ACS was designed to provide estimates of the characteristics of the population, not to provide counts of the population in different geographic areas or population subgroups. For basic counts of the U.S. population by age, sex, race, and Hispanic origin, visit the Census Bureau's Population and Housing Unit Estimates Web page." (U.S. Census Bureau, 2022). In other words, to estimate fertility rates for women ages 15–44 by nativity using the ACS, population distributions by nativity for women ages 15–44 estimated from the ACS should be adjusted to population totals from the U.S. Census for women ages 15–44.

Researchers can take various approaches to adjusting survey-based population distributions to U.S. Census population totals. While some of these approaches are surely very complicated, for the purposes of using survey distributions to obtain

[6]See also population estimates released by NCHS (https://www.cdc.gov/nchs/nvss/bridged_race.htm) and NCI/SEER (https://seer.cancer.gov/popdata/) produced in collaboration with U.S. Census Bureau.

sub-group population counts, one essentially just needs to use the survey distributions to weight the population totals. To do this manually (e.g., in excel), examples of clear explanations on what steps to follow include studies by Zavodny and Bitler (2010), DeLeire et al. (2011), and Palmer, 2020. If analyzing survey data like the ACS in Stata, one can use poststratification techniques to adjust a person's sampling weight to population totals (for an excellent resource on calculating survey weights in Stata, see Valliant & Dever, 2018).

When adjusting survey-based population distributions to U.S. Census population totals for Hispanic sub-groups, there are multiple factors to consider when choosing between sources for the population distributions. For example, analyses of Hispanic fertility by nativity are possible with the CPS or ACS but are limited in the Decennial Census PUMS (i.e., Census questions on nativity were included in 2000 but not 2010). The focal study period is another important consideration—the CPS allows for analysis of trends in Hispanic fertility starting in the 1990s, whereas the ACS allows for analysis of trends starting in the mid-2000s. Finally, for assessments of heterogeneity in Hispanic fertility across multiple sub-groups, one must consider sample size and level of representation of the U.S. population (which favor the ACS over the CPS). Indeed, while U.S. fertility estimates for Hispanic sub-groups published by the NCHS are based on population distributions from the March CPS prior to 2010, they are based on the 1-year ACS from 2010 onward. In their annual user guide for the birth certificate data, the NVSS explains the reason for this switch: "The change to the ACS-based rates was made because ACS estimates are more statistically reliable and represent the entire United States population. ACS estimates are based on an approximately 3 million annual sample of the U.S. population, including all households (civilian and military) and the institutionalized population (persons living in group quarters)." In contrast, they note that the "CPS estimates are based on an approximate 200,000 sample of only the civilian, non-institutionalized U.S. population. The larger ACS sample allows the possibility to show rates in more detail than in previous years, especially for Cuban and Puerto Rican women." (page 75, Natality 2016 User Guide).

Because denominators for the birth rates are based on survey distributions adjusted to population totals, differences in Hispanic subgroup distributions across sources can lead to vast differences in the estimated birth rates for those sub-groups. Regardless of the source chosen for estimating the Hispanic subgroup distributions used to weigh the population totals, researchers can cross-check the accuracy of their estimates using multiple sources. If a researcher uses birth rates published by the NCHS to cross-check their own computations, it is important to note which sources were used for each year in a given publication since U.S. fertility estimates for Hispanic sub-groups published by the NCHS are based on population distributions from the CPS for some years and the ACS for others.[7] If a decennial census took

[7]In some reports published by the NCHS, CPS distributions are used to estimate Hispanic sub-group population counts even when other estimates are based on decennial census data. For example, Sutton and Matthews (2006) explain why they use CPS distributions for Hispanic

place during the study period, census summary file data can be used to evaluate discrepancies in rates based on different survey distributions. For example, the estimated birth rate for Mexican women ages 15–19 in 2000 differs depending on whether one uses survey distributions from the CPS versus Census PUMS. Specifically, birth rates published by the NCHS for 2000, which were based on population distributions from the CPS, indicate that the birth rate for Mexican women ages 15–19 in 2000 was 95.4 (Martin et al., 2005; Sutton & Matthews, 2006). In contrast, the birth rate for Mexican women ages 15–19 in 2000 using distributions from the Census 2000 1% PUMS is 108.6 (Ruggles et al., 2022). While these rates are based on the same number of births for Mexican women ages 15–19 (97,101) and the same April 1 population for Hispanic women ages 15–19 (1,483,090), distributions from the CPS indicate a higher percentage of 15–19-year-old Hispanic women in 2000 who were Mexican (68.6%) when compared with distributions from the Census PUMS (60.3%). Counts for the number of Hispanic women ages 15–19 overall and by region of origin from Summary File 2 of the 2000 Decennial Census[8] show that 59.5% of 15–19-year-old Hispanic women were Mexican (implying a birth rate of 110 for Mexican women ages 15–19), which suggests that the 60% population distribution/birth rate of 108.6 (from the Census 1% PUMS) is more accurate than the 68% population distribution/birth rate of 95.4 (from the CPS).

8.3 Variation in Hispanic Fertility from 2006–2016

8.3.1 Data and Sample

To disaggregate Hispanic fertility rates for women ages 15–44 by nativity, region of origin, marital status, and age, we use data from three sources: the National Vital Statistics System (NVSS), the U.S. Census Bureau's Population Estimates Program (PEP), and the American Community Survey (ACS). The 2006–2016 birth counts (i.e., the numerators) come from the NVSS, which aggregates and harmonizes birth certificate data across all 50 states, the District of Columbia, and U.-S. territories. Birth certificate registration in the U.S. is estimated at near 100% (National Center for Health Statistics, 2021). We use the natality microdata files for years 2006–2016 to get yearly birth counts for Hispanic women ages 15–44 that are cross classified by each of our factors. Regarding *nativity*, we distinguish between births to mothers born in the U.S. and outside of the U.S. Following protocol, for

---

subgroups in a paper that otherwise compares estimates from 1990 and 2000 census data: "Additionally, national population estimates for 2000 for Hispanic subgroups (Mexican, Puerto Rican, Cuban, and other and unknown Hispanic) were adjusted to be consistent with the 2001 Current Population Survey and previously published birth and fertility rates" (p. 94).

[8] https://api.census.gov/data/2000/dec/sf2?get=PCT003122,PCT003123,PCT003124,PCT003125,PCT003126,POPGROUP_LABEL&POPGROUP=400&POPGROUP=401&POPGROUP=402&POPGROUP=403&POPGROUP=404&for=us:*

Puerto Rican women, we distinguish between mainland vs. island born (Landale et al., 2000). Next, we differentiate between births to mothers in five *region-of-origin* categories, including Mexican, Puerto Rican, Cuban, Central & South American, and Other Hispanic. Concerning *marital status*, we distinguish between births to married and unmarried mothers. Finally, we differentiate between births to mothers ages 15–19, 20–24, 25–29, 30–34, 35–39, and 40–44.

For the 2006–2016 population counts (i.e., the denominators), population distributions from the ACS are adjusted to July 1 population totals from the U.S. Census Bureau's PEP (National Center for Health Statistics, 2012, 2021; Ruggles et al., 2022). We first estimate yearly population totals from the PEP for Hispanic women ages 15–19, 20–24, 25–29, 30–34, 35–39, and 40–44, resulting in population totals for 66 unique groups stratified by year and 5-year age category. Population totals from the PEP are based on intercensal estimates for 2006–2009 and Vintage 2020 postcensal estimates for 2010–2016. Next, we pool data from the ACS single-year files for years 2006–2016 to get population distributions for Hispanic women ages 15–44 that are cross-classified by each of our factors. Finally, we merge the July 1 population totals with the ACS data and use survey post-stratification techniques in Stata 17.0 to calibrate the ACS person weights to population control totals that are stratified by year and 5-year age category.[9]

Given our focus on nativity, one factor to consider in evaluating the quality of our data for ascertaining trends in Hispanic childbearing concerns the size of the undocumented population. The number of unauthorized immigrants in the U.S. has fluctuated over the decade we are examining, from an estimated high of 12.2 million in 2007 to 10.7 million in 2016 (Passel & D'Vera, 2018). Although region of origin patterns are in flux, the unauthorized population in the U.S. continues to be disproportionately made up of immigrants from Mexico and Central America (68% in 2018) (Capps et al., 2020) and disproportionately male (54% in 2016) (Passel & D'Vera, 2018). Broken down by age and gender, the Pew Research Center estimates that there were 3.5 million unauthorized female immigrants between the ages 18–44 residing in the U.S. in 2007 and 3.1 million in 2016 (Passel & D'Vera, 2018).

The large size of the female unauthorized population of childbearing age in the U.S. (~3.1–3.5 M over the period) and the disproportionate representation of Mexican and Central American immigrants among the undocumented population could impact our estimates in two ways. First, if births to undocumented women are not captured in the vital statistics. To our knowledge, there is no evidence that this is the case, despite some anecdotal accounts that women without documentation status were more fearful of accessing prenatal care during the Trump presidency (Dickerson & Addario, 2020). Regarding missing data on nativity, there were no missing values for the population counts, but for each year there was a small number of missing values for the birth counts (on average, for each year in the study period less than one-fifth of a percent—i.e., 0.18% of all births—were missing on nativity).

[9]svyset [iw = perwt], jkrweight(repwtp1-repwtp80, multiplier(.05)) vce(jackknife) mse poststrata (popgroup) postweight(pop).

It is possible that the data missing on nativity are concentrated in part among births to undocumented mothers. Given the minimal number of births with missing data on nativity, however, we do not anticipate this having an impact on results.

Second, if undocumented women are less likely to be captured in the population counts (i.e., the denominators of the birth rates). This is called “coverage error” and has been most extensively assessed with respect to the Mexican-origin population (Van Hook et al., 2014, 2021). According to Van Hook et al., 2014, coverage error for the Mexican-origin population declined substantially from 2000–2009 due to declines in shorter term undocumented migrants. By 2010, coverage-error rates were estimated to be around 8%. A recent update found that from 2010–2017, there were further declines in coverage error, particularly for women, resulting in an estimated rate of 4% in 2015 (Van Hook et al., 2021). When separated by gender and age, the rate for women ages 15–64 was even lower- only 1% from 2015–2018. If we follow Van Hook et al. (2021) and assume similar coverage error for other Hispanic origin groups as for Mexican women, then we do not anticipate coverage error having a significant impact on our estimation of Hispanic birth rates, particularly from 2010 onwards.

Another factor to consider in evaluating the quality of our data for ascertaining trends in Hispanic childbearing concerns changes during the study period to the categorization of the region-of-origin denominator and numerator. Regarding the denominators, the categorization for Central/South American and Other Hispanic women changed in 2008 in the American Community Survey (Ennis et al., 2011). In 2006 and 2007, respondents to the Hispanic heritage question on the American Community Survey were asked if they were “Mexican,” “Cuban,” “Puerto Rican,” or “Other” under which they were instructed to “print group.” In 2008, the question changed such that after the initial three groups (Mexican, Cuban, Puerto Rican), respondents were further instructed to “print origin, for example, Argentinean, Colombian, Dominican, Nicaraguan, Salvadoran, Spaniard.” The addition of the example origin countries greatly increased the number of “Other respondents” who listed their origin country. As a result, beginning in 2008, the number of women classified as “Central/South American” increased (by roughly 50,000) and the number of those categorized as “Other” decreased (by 119,000). Regarding the numerators, changes in the measurement of region of origin in the NVSS birth data impacted the number of births to mothers categorized as “Other Hispanic” (Fig. 8.1). First, the percentage of Hispanic births accounted for by states using the 2003 revised birth certificate steadily increased over the study period, from 63% in 2006, to 91% in 2013, to 100% in 2014. This is important because there were differences between the 1989 and 2003 revised birth certificates in: 1) the Hispanic origin question wording and 2) guidelines on how to categorize births to mothers specifying more than one Hispanic origin. Regarding question wording for whether mothers are “of Hispanic origin,” the 1989 revised birth certificate includes options for “No” and “Yes.” If respondents choose “Yes,” they are instructed to “specify Cuban, Mexican, Puerto Rican, etc.” The 2003 revised birth certificate includes options for “No,” “Yes, Mexican, Mexican American, Chicana,” “Yes, Puerto Rican,” “Yes, Cuban,” and “Yes, other Spanish/Hispanic/Latina (Specify).” Regarding categorization guidelines, the 1989 revised birth certificate assigns Hispanic

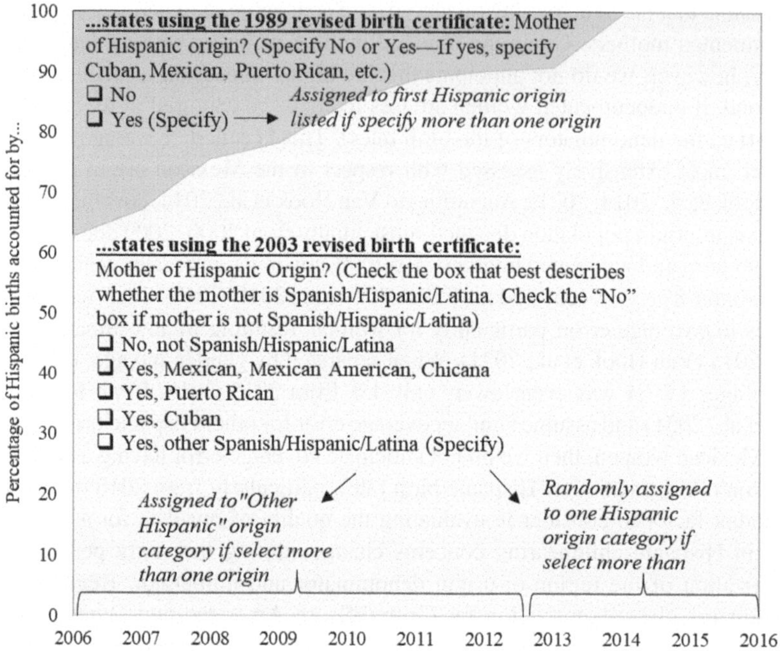

Fig. 8.1 Changes in the measurement of region of origin in the NVSS birth data: 2006–2016

mothers listing more than one origin to the first origin listed. For the 2003 revised birth certificate, Hispanic mothers selecting more than one origin are assigned to the "Other Hispanic" category from 2006–2012 and randomly assigned to one of their selected categories from 2013–2016.[10]

Taken together, changes in the measurement of the region-of-origin denominator and numerator during the study period led to a *decrease* in the percentage of *women* categorized as "Other Hispanic" in the ACS (denominator) and an *increase* in the percentage of *births* categorized to "Other Hispanic" mothers in the NVSS (numerator), potentially inflating fertility rates to "Other Hispanic" mothers (Fig. 8.2).[11] These changes warrant caution in interpreting fertility trends over the study period by region of origin, especially for "Other Hispanic" women.

[10]Per the 2016 User Guide: "This change was implemented to be consistent with the coding methods of the American Community Survey, on which the rates for the specified Hispanic groups from 2010 on are based." (https://ftp.cdc.gov/pub/Health_Statistics/NCHS/Dataset_Documentation/DVS/natality/UserGuide2016.pdf)

[11]Yearly increases in the percentage of births to "Other Hispanic" mothers have continued even after 100% of states were using the 2003 revised birth certificate (in 2014) and randomly assigning mothers with more than one Hispanic origin to a single category (in 2013). Per NVSS, "factors that may have influenced this rise are not clear but may include less specificity in respondent reporting of Hispanic origin and increases in the populations of groups included in the "other Hispanic" category" (https://ftp.cdc.gov/pub/Health_Statistics/NCHS/Dataset_Documentation/DVS/natality/UserGuide2016.pdf).

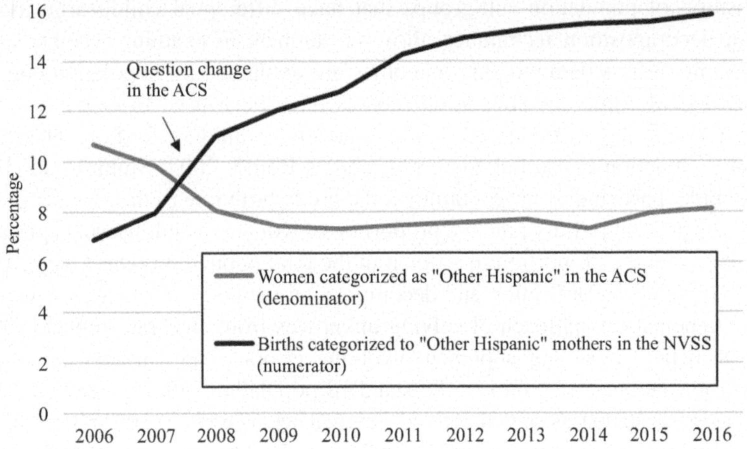

Fig. 8.2 Changes in the percentage of women and births categorized as "Other Hispanic" origin: 2006–2016

8.3.2 Analytic Method

We first estimate age-specific fertility rates (ASFR) and the TFR for each year between 2006–2016, both overall and for U.S.-born and foreign-born Hispanic women. We then further stratify the age-specific fertility rates from 2006–2016 for U.S.-born and foreign-born women by region of origin and marital status. We also estimate age-specific first-birth rates and the first birth order TFR (TFR1) by nativity and region of origin to evaluate the severity of temporal distortions in the ASFRs across groups. One limitation to period estimates of fertility is that they cannot differentiate between the timing of births and overall births. This is problematic in analyses of Hispanic fertility because migration directly impacts the timing of childbearing, resulting in period fertility estimates that contain pronounced tempo distortions (Bongaarts & Feeney, 1998; Parrado, 2011). Specifically, immigrant women typically delay births in anticipation of migrating and experience a rise in fertility that peaks in the first five years after arrival (Ford, 1990; Parrado, 2011). While focusing on completed fertility is one way to avoid tempo distortions (Schoen, 2004), period estimates at least permit us to assess the severity of temporal distortions over time by disaggregating the total fertility rate (TFR) into birth-order components and focusing on first births. After evaluating differences in fertility rates by nativity and how these estimates differ by region of origin and marital status, we underscore important sources of heterogeneity in Hispanic fertility by comparing rates of specific Hispanic subgroups with overall trends in U.S. fertility.

Finally, we demonstrate how Das Gupta's standardization and decomposition methods for cross-classified data can be applied to Hispanic birth rates and population counts disaggregated by multiple factors over time to better understand the extent to which observed changes in the Hispanic birth rate are due to changes in the composition of population sub-groups that have differential childbearing risk. In general, decomposition techniques allow researchers to examine whether and to what extent various demographic outcomes are explained by population composition factors. Multiple decomposition models have been used to examine fertility behavior at the aggregate level, such as models examining fertility rates as the product or function of various factors (Canudas Romo, 2003; Smith et al., 1996). For example, past studies have examined the crude birth rate as the product of three factors: the general fertility rate; the proportion of women of childbearing age among all women; and the proportion of women in the total population (Das Gupta, 1993).

Das Gupta's standardization and decomposition methods for cross-classified data use "a mathematical approach of solving unknowns from algebraic equations rather than a statistical modeling approach involving errors," and—instead of choosing values from one year or group as the standard population—use the average of two "populations as standards such that the difference between two rates can be expressed as the sum of only the main effects." (1993, page 3). The cross-classification model requires cell-specific rates and population counts across all combinations of the composition factors to decompose the difference in two rates into a rate effect and, for each compositional factor assessed, a composition effect. For our analysis, we first decompose the change in the Hispanic birth rate between 2006 and 2016 into a rate effect and compositional effects for age, marital status, and nativity, where the difference in the Hispanic birth rate between 2006 and 2016 is the sum of the rate effect, the age composition effect, the marital status composition effect, and the nativity composition effect (equations shown in Appendix 1). Because we know that the compositional shifts have been different for U.S.-born and foreign-born Hispanic women, we also conduct separate analyses by nativity, where the change in the U.S.-born or foreign-born Hispanic birth rate is the sum of the rate effect, the age composition effect, and the marital status composition effect. Because the aforementioned changes in the measurement of the region-of-origin denominator and numerator during the study period (discussed in Sect. 8.3.1) may have impacted the accuracy of the estimated birth rates and population counts, especially for "Other Hispanic" women, we do not include region of origin as a factor in the decomposition analysis. That is, the cross-classification model is a powerful descriptive tool, but its validity depends on the accuracy of the cell-specific rates and population counts, especially considering that the birth rates are standardized by the average population composition and each composition factor is standardized by the average population composition of the other factors and the average cell-specific birth rates.

8.3.3 Fertility Rates and Population Composition from 2006–2016

Table 8.1 presents the fertility of Hispanic women ages 15–44 in the United States from 2006–2016, both overall and by nativity. Panel A of Table 8.1 shows the age-specific fertility rates (ASFRs) and total fertility rate (TFR). Over the 11-year

Table 8.1 Fertility of Hispanic women, overall and by nativity: 2006–2016

Panel A Age-specific fertility rates (ASFR) and the total fertility rate (TFR)					**Panel B** Age-specific first-birth rates (ASFR1) and the first birth order total fertility rate (TFR1)				
		Overall	U.S.-born	Foreign-born			Overall	U.S.-born	Foreign-born
Year	**Age**				**Year**	**Age**			
2006	15–19	0.077	0.056	0.139	**2006**	15–19	0.060	0.044	0.107
	20–24	0.167	0.121	0.231		20–24	0.072	0.050	0.103
	25–29	0.150	0.109	0.186		25–29	0.038	0.028	0.046
	30–34	0.108	0.079	0.125		30–34	0.020	0.017	0.022
	35–39	0.055	0.040	0.062		35–39	0.008	0.008	0.008
	40–44	0.013	0.008	0.016		40–44	0.002	0.002	0.002
	TFR	**2.846**	**2.068**	**3.792**		**TFR1**	**1.000**	**0.746**	**1.439**
2007	15–19	0.075	0.057	0.132	**2007**	15–19	0.058	0.045	0.102
	20–24	0.165	0.121	0.228		20–24	0.072	0.051	0.101
	25–29	0.149	0.112	0.183		25–29	0.038	0.030	0.045
	30–34	0.109	0.082	0.125		30–34	0.020	0.018	0.021
	35–39	0.055	0.040	0.063		35–39	0.008	0.008	0.008
	40–44	0.013	0.009	0.015		40–44	0.002	0.002	0.002
	TFR	**2.830**	**2.103**	**3.736**		**TFR1**	**0.989**	**0.765**	**1.395**
2008	15–19	0.070	0.056	0.121	**2008**	15–19	0.055	0.044	0.093
	20–24	0.154	0.114	0.217		20–24	0.067	0.050	0.093
	25–29	0.142	0.105	0.181		25–29	0.036	0.028	0.044
	30–34	0.105	0.079	0.123		30–34	0.019	0.017	0.021
	35–39	0.054	0.039	0.063		35–39	0.008	0.008	0.008
	40–44	0.013	0.008	0.016		40–44	0.002	0.002	0.002
	TFR	**2.697**	**2.004**	**3.604**		**TFR1**	**0.937**	**0.747**	**1.305**
2009	15–19	0.064	0.053	0.103	**2009**	15–19	0.050	0.042	0.078
	20–24	0.140	0.107	0.197		20–24	0.061	0.048	0.084
	25–29	0.134	0.102	0.167		25–29	0.034	0.029	0.040
	30–34	0.101	0.078	0.116		30–34	0.019	0.017	0.019
	35–39	0.052	0.039	0.060		35–39	0.008	0.008	0.008
	40–44	0.013	0.009	0.015		40–44	0.002	0.002	0.002
	TFR	**2.522**	**1.943**	**3.295**		**TFR1**	**0.866**	**0.727**	**1.156**
2010	15–19	0.056	0.047	0.087	**2010**	15–19	0.044	0.038	0.066
	20–24	0.125	0.100	0.173		20–24	0.055	0.046	0.072
	25–29	0.125	0.098	0.154		25–29	0.032	0.028	0.036
	30–34	0.096	0.077	0.110		30–34	0.018	0.017	0.018
	35–39	0.052	0.038	0.059		35–39	0.008	0.007	0.008
	40–44	0.013	0.009	0.015		40–44	0.002	0.002	0.002
	TFR	**2.333**	**1.850**	**2.987**		**TFR1**	**0.789**	**0.692**	**1.010**
2011	15–19	0.050	0.043	0.077	**2011**	15–19	0.039	0.034	0.059
	20–24	0.116	0.095	0.163		20–24	0.052	0.044	0.068
	25–29	0.121	0.097	0.149		25–29	0.032	0.028	0.035
	30–34	0.095	0.078	0.108		30–34	0.018	0.018	0.018

(continued)

Table 8.1 (continued)

Panel A Age-specific fertility rates (ASFR) and the total fertility rate (TFR)					**Panel B** Age-specific first-birth rates (ASFR1) and the first birth order total fertility rate (TFR1)				
		Overall	U.S.-born	Foreign-born			Overall	U.S.-born	Foreign-born
Year	**Age**				**Year**	**Age**			
	35–39	0.051	0.040	0.058		35–39	0.008	0.008	0.007
	40–44	0.013	0.009	0.015		40–44	0.002	0.002	0.002
	TFR	**2.233**	**1.803**	**2.853**		**TFR1**	**0.749**	**0.672**	**0.946**
2012	15–19	0.046	0.040	0.072	**2012**	15–19	0.037	0.033	0.055
	20–24	0.111	0.092	0.159		20–24	0.050	0.043	0.067
	25–29	0.119	0.096	0.147		25–29	0.031	0.028	0.034
	30–34	0.094	0.078	0.107		30–34	0.018	0.018	0.017
	35–39	0.051	0.040	0.058		35–39	0.007	0.008	0.007
	40–44	0.013	0.009	0.015		40–44	0.002	0.002	0.002
	TFR	**2.176**	**1.774**	**2.791**		**TFR1**	**0.726**	**0.659**	**0.916**
2013	15–19	0.042	0.036	0.063	**2013**	15–19	0.033	0.029	0.050
	20–24	0.107	0.092	0.147		20–24	0.049	0.043	0.065
	25–29	0.118	0.099	0.143		25–29	0.031	0.029	0.034
	30–34	0.094	0.078	0.108		30–34	0.018	0.019	0.018
	35–39	0.052	0.040	0.060		35–39	0.008	0.008	0.008
	40–44	0.013	0.009	0.015		40–44	0.002	0.002	0.002
	TFR	**2.132**	**1.773**	**2.683**		**TFR1**	**0.708**	**0.648**	**0.881**
2014	15–19	0.038	0.033	0.061	**2014**	15–19	0.031	0.027	0.048
	20–24	0.105	0.091	0.144		20–24	0.049	0.043	0.065
	25–29	0.119	0.102	0.142		25–29	0.032	0.030	0.035
	30–34	0.097	0.080	0.112		30–34	0.019	0.019	0.020
	35–39	0.054	0.042	0.062		35–39	0.008	0.008	0.008
	40–44	0.014	0.010	0.016		40–44	0.002	0.002	0.002
	TFR	**2.133**	**1.791**	**2.681**		**TFR1**	**0.705**	**0.644**	**0.890**
2015	15–19	0.035	0.030	0.056	**2015**	15–19	0.028	0.025	0.045
	20–24	0.103	0.088	0.147		20–24	0.048	0.042	0.067
	25–29	0.120	0.101	0.148		25–29	0.033	0.029	0.039
	30–34	0.099	0.081	0.116		30–34	0.020	0.019	0.021
	35–39	0.055	0.044	0.063		35–39	0.008	0.008	0.008
	40–44	0.014	0.010	0.017		40–44	0.002	0.002	0.002
	TFR	**2.127**	**1.768**	**2.735**		**TFR1**	**0.701**	**0.628**	**0.911**
2016	15–19	0.032	0.027	0.056	**2016**	15–19	0.026	0.022	0.045
	20–24	0.098	0.084	0.143		20–24	0.047	0.040	0.067
	25–29	0.117	0.097	0.151		25–29	0.033	0.029	0.041
	30–34	0.099	0.081	0.118		30–34	0.021	0.019	0.022
	35–39	0.056	0.045	0.063		35–39	0.009	0.009	0.009
	40–44	0.015	0.010	0.017		40–44	0.002	0.002	0.002
	TFR	**2.084**	**1.718**	**2.740**		**TFR1**	**0.687**	**0.606**	**0.924**

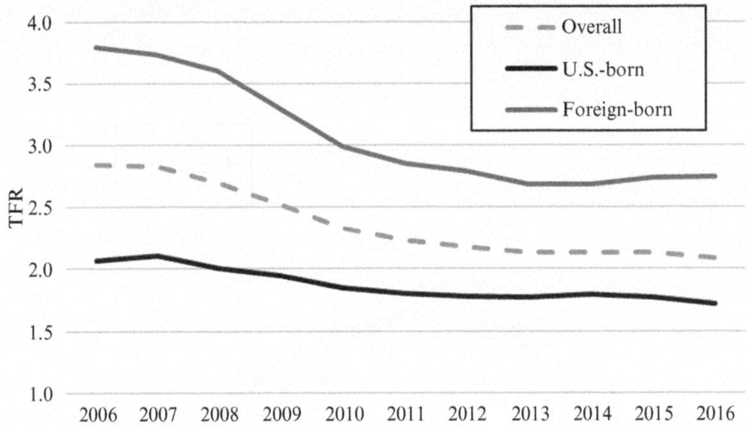

Fig. 8.3 TFR of Hispanic women, overall and by nativity: 2006–2016

period, Hispanic fertility declined dramatically (Fig. 8.3), with the overall period TFR for Hispanic women falling from 2.846 to 2.084 (a 26.8% decline in the TFR). Given that the national TFR only declined by 13.7% during this period, an overall decline of nearly 27% for Hispanics is quite large. Distinguishing by nativity, we see that, as expected, over the entire period, foreign-born fertility was higher than U.S.-born fertility. However, the disparity narrows near the end of the period (from a 1.724 difference in TFR to 1.022) due to larger declines in immigrant fertility—a 27.7% decrease in immigrant fertility relative to the 17% decrease in the native-born TFR. Beyond differences in the overall TFR, the age-specific fertility rates in Table 8.1 allow us to assess the degree that fertility timing varies by nativity in (Fig. 8.4). Both native- and foreign-born Hispanic women demonstrate a fairly similar timing schedule with similar changes occurring over the 11-year period, although immigrant AFSRs are consistently higher throughout. In 2006, fertility rates for both native and foreign-born women peaked at 20–24 years old. By the end of the period (2016), peak fertility rates shift to 25–29 years old, albeit this shift occurred earlier for U.S.-born (2011) versus foreign-born (2015) women. The largest nativity gap in ASFRs also shifts over the period, becoming smaller overall and occurring among 20–24 years at the beginning of the period and equally among 20–24 and 25–29 years old by the end of the observation window.

The age-specific first-birth rates (ASFR1) and the first birth order total fertility rate (TFR1) of Hispanic women, overall and by nativity, are shown in Panel B of Table 8.1. The TFR1 for Hispanic women overall declined from 1.000 in 2006 to 0.687 in 2016. For U.S.-born Hispanic women, the TFR1 was below 1.00 for the entire study period, ranging from .746 in 2006 to .606 in 2016. Yet for foreign-born women, the TFR1 was above 1.00 from 2006 (1.439) to 2010 (1.010). How is it possible that the TFR1 indicates that the average woman can have more than 1 first birth, when that is clearly impossible? The answer lies in the way that the ASFR1s are calculated; where, for each age category, first births are divided by the total

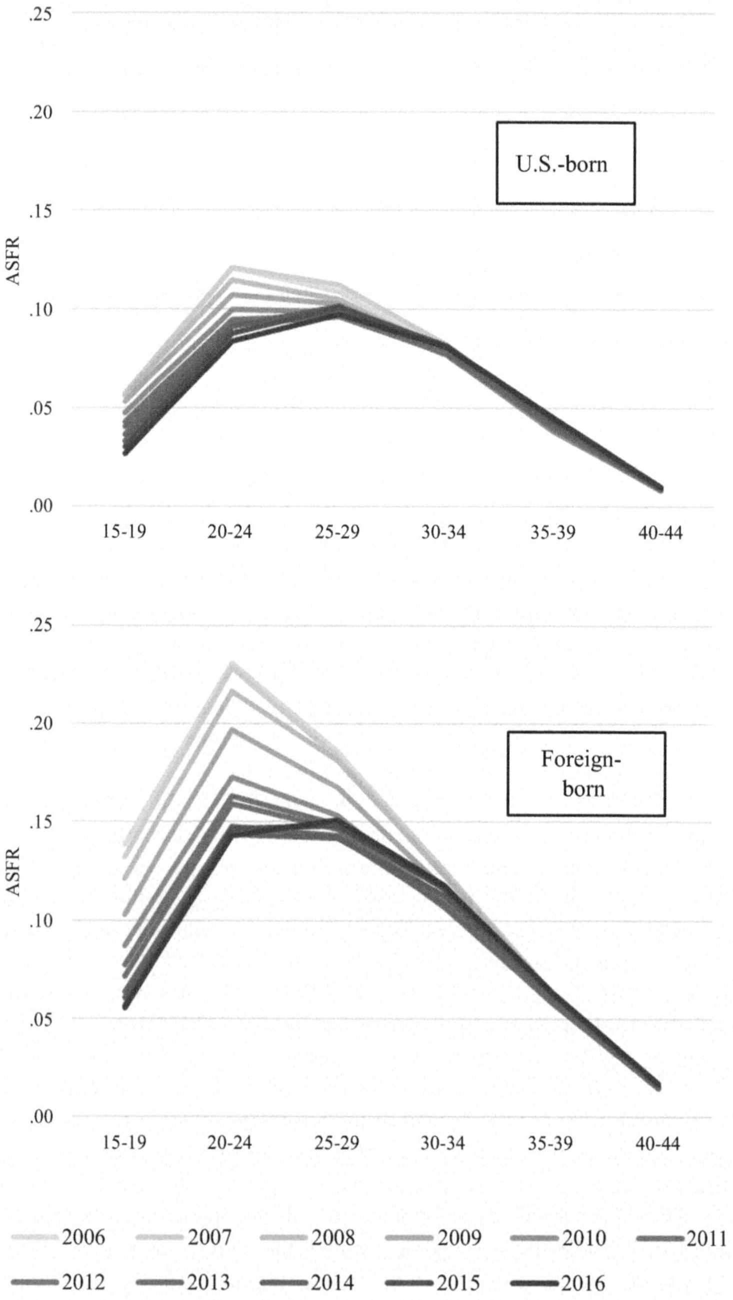

Fig. 8.4 Age-specific fertility rates of Hispanic women, overall and by nativity: 2006–2016

number of women in that category instead of by the total number of women at parity zero (i.e., at risk of having a first birth) (Kohler & Ortega, 2002; Schoen, 2006; Whelpton, 1946). As Kohler and Ortega (2002) note, "this lack of disaggregation in the denominator ... can lead to severe distortions in the inferences of the level and particularly the timing of fertility from period data.... because the population distribution by parity fluctuates over time, and these fluctuations induce changes in both the level and age-pattern of period incidence rates." (p. 95). Looking at the ASFR1s, the TFR1 values surpassing 1 for foreign-born women seem primarily driven by higher fertility at younger ages, especially ages 15–19 and 20–24 (whereas the rates for 35–39 and 40–44 are remarkably stable over the study period). The ASFR1 for foreign-born Hispanic women peaked at 15–19 in 2006 and 2007, at 15–19 and 20–24 in 2008, and at 20–24 from 2009 onward. In 2006 and 2007, just summing the ASFR1s (multiplied by 5) for ages 15–19 and 20–24 results in a TFR1 above 1. In 2008 and 2009, the sums of the ASFR1s (multiplied by 5) for the three youngest age categories results in a TFR1 that surpasses 1.

The decline in the TFR1 for foreign-born women was steepest at the beginning of the period (2006–2010), stabilized during the middle of the period (2011–2013), and then slightly increased at the end of the period (2014–2016). As previously mentioned, immigrant women typically delay births in anticipation of migrating and experience a rise in fertility that peaks in the first five years after arrival (i.e., a disruption effect) (Ford, 1990; Parrado, 2011). The dramatic decline in the immigrant TFR1 at the beginning of the period (through 2010) may be reflecting this disruption. Relatedly, the 2007–2010 period also corresponds to the Great Recession when immigration inflows, particularly from Mexico, dropped precipitously (Gonzalez-Barrera, 2015). The degree that the decline in immigrant first births in this pre-2010 period is due to immigration-related disruption versus recession-related tempo distortions versus changes in the size and composition of the immigrant population, cannot be discerned from these period data.

Table 8.2 shows the fertility of U.S.-born and foreign-born Hispanic women ages 15–44 by region of origin. Because of the methodological changes in measurement of the denominator starting in 2008 (discussed in Sect. 8.3.1), we discuss fertility trends from 2008 onwards for Central/South American and "Other Hispanic" women. Panel A of Table 8.2 (Fig. 8.5) shows that the magnitude of the nativity differences in the TFR varies considerably by region of origin. Puerto Rican women, who have U.S. citizenship and are free to travel between the mainland and island, have the smallest difference in TFRs between those who are mainland versus island-born women. Similarly, the nativity differences are smaller for Cuban women. Larger nativity differences are evident for the other three groups, although most narrow over the study period. The most dramatic decline in fertility over the period occurred for Mexican immigrant women; they saw a 35% decrease in the TFR from 2006–2016 compared to a 27 percent decrease for their native-born counterparts. Cuban women (U.S. and foreign-born), who begin the period with the lowest TFRs, display the opposite pattern, with the fertility of the U.S.-born experiencing a larger percent decline than immigrant women (20% vs. 12%). The same is true for Central/South American women—from 2008–2016, the U.S.-born experienced a larger

Table 8.2 Fertility of U.S.-born and foreign-born Hispanic women, by region of origin: 2006–2016

Panel A Age-specific fertility rates (ASFR) and the total fertility rate (TFR)											
		Mexican		Puerto Rican		Cuban		Central/South American		Other	
		U.S.-born	Foreign-born	U.S.-born	Foreign-born	U.S.-born	Foreign-born	U.S.-born	Foreign-born	U.S.-born	Foreign-born
Year	**Age**										
2006	15–19	0.060	0.169	0.057	0.102	0.025	0.029	0.038	0.115	0.055	0.031
	20–24	0.125	0.261	0.118	0.165	0.067	0.119	0.092	0.215	0.128	0.071
	25–29	0.108	0.201	0.102	0.112	0.102	0.128	0.114	0.194	0.119	0.076
	30–34	0.078	0.131	0.067	0.070	0.091	0.095	0.114	0.147	0.082	0.056
	35–39	0.039	0.067	0.033	0.030	0.055	0.040	0.077	0.073	0.040	0.025
	40–44	0.008	0.017	0.008	0.008	0.010	0.008	0.014	0.019	0.009	0.006
	TFR	**2.092**	**4.231**	**1.927**	**2.431**	**1.755**	**2.093**	**2.250**	**3.817**	**2.167**	**1.323**
2007	15–19	0.059	0.158	0.055	0.073	0.022	0.035	0.037	0.115	0.073	0.044
	20–24	0.122	0.257	0.122	0.133	0.064	0.106	0.084	0.212	0.152	0.098
	25–29	0.108	0.194	0.109	0.094	0.082	0.112	0.114	0.198	0.142	0.105
	30–34	0.079	0.130	0.075	0.064	0.087	0.091	0.096	0.142	0.097	0.070
	35–39	0.037	0.067	0.035	0.029	0.050	0.045	0.074	0.073	0.050	0.031
	40–44	0.008	0.017	0.008	0.006	0.008	0.008	0.016	0.019	0.010	0.007
	TFR	**2.064**	**4.120**	**2.014**	**1.998**	**1.557**	**1.979**	**2.104**	**3.803**	**2.618**	**1.776**
2008	15–19	0.052	0.149	0.060	0.079	0.019	0.033	0.030	0.087	0.115	0.071
	20–24	0.105	0.237	0.122	0.155	0.059	0.116	0.062	0.190	0.241	0.169
	25–29	0.094	0.188	0.096	0.115	0.079	0.113	0.086	0.178	0.216	0.193
	30–34	0.069	0.126	0.072	0.066	0.079	0.099	0.081	0.132	0.160	0.115
	35–39	0.033	0.065	0.039	0.029	0.041	0.044	0.053	0.066	0.069	0.067
	40–44	0.007	0.018	0.008	0.006	0.009	0.008	0.011	0.016	0.015	0.014
	TFR	**1.793**	**3.915**	**1.984**	**2.251**	**1.432**	**2.061**	**1.615**	**3.348**	**4.084**	**3.147**

2009	15–19	0.049	0.121	0.050	0.067	0.019	0.028	0.027	0.080	0.129	0.081
	20–24	0.097	0.214	0.114	0.124	0.052	0.121	0.059	0.173	0.234	0.204
	25–29	0.089	0.177	0.106	0.093	0.086	0.121	0.067	0.156	0.235	0.193
	30–34	0.069	0.121	0.070	0.063	0.072	0.099	0.074	0.115	0.172	0.126
	35–39	0.033	0.062	0.035	0.027	0.038	0.045	0.049	0.063	0.088	0.070
	40–44	0.007	0.016	0.009	0.006	0.011	0.008	0.014	0.017	0.017	0.017
	TFR	**1.714**	**3.552**	**1.923**	**1.892**	**1.388**	**2.108**	**1.446**	**3.016**	**4.370**	**3.454**
2010	15–19	0.044	0.105	0.042	0.061	0.016	0.024	0.022	0.062	0.129	0.072
	20–24	0.090	0.189	0.103	0.118	0.051	0.081	0.049	0.157	0.244	0.164
	25–29	0.086	0.165	0.090	0.088	0.076	0.087	0.065	0.140	0.251	0.180
	30–34	0.065	0.113	0.071	0.062	0.086	0.078	0.068	0.110	0.192	0.137
	35–39	0.032	0.059	0.035	0.030	0.038	0.041	0.047	0.067	0.079	0.069
	40–44	0.007	0.016	0.009	0.006	0.008	0.008	0.013	0.016	0.019	0.015
	TFR	**1.626**	**3.231**	**1.745**	**1.825**	**1.379**	**1.591**	**1.321**	**2.763**	**4.572**	**3.189**
2011	15–19	0.039	0.089	0.039	0.057	0.013	0.028	0.019	0.060	0.120	0.075
	20–24	0.083	0.182	0.101	0.149	0.040	0.080	0.046	0.136	0.259	0.150
	25–29	0.085	0.155	0.088	0.099	0.071	0.101	0.054	0.135	0.249	0.206
	30–34	0.064	0.109	0.069	0.056	0.076	0.084	0.070	0.115	0.209	0.133
	35–39	0.032	0.058	0.033	0.031	0.045	0.041	0.049	0.064	0.100	0.073
	40–44	0.007	0.015	0.009	0.007	0.012	0.008	0.012	0.016	0.022	0.018
	TFR	**1.560**	**3.043**	**1.695**	**1.986**	**1.286**	**1.706**	**1.252**	**2.630**	**4.800**	**3.268**
2012	15–19	0.037	0.082	0.037	0.070	0.012	0.024	0.017	0.052	0.115	0.070
	20–24	0.082	0.175	0.088	0.144	0.039	0.089	0.044	0.129	0.259	0.176
	25–29	0.083	0.155	0.086	0.093	0.064	0.100	0.059	0.135	0.265	0.185
	30–34	0.067	0.109	0.066	0.061	0.074	0.072	0.062	0.106	0.190	0.156
	35–39	0.032	0.060	0.037	0.030	0.042	0.037	0.039	0.061	0.105	0.072
	40–44	0.007	0.016	0.009	0.007	0.009	0.009	0.011	0.016	0.018	0.019
	TFR	**1.541**	**2.978**	**1.624**	**2.024**	**1.198**	**1.650**	**1.162**	**2.501**	**4.762**	**3.392**

(continued)

Table 8.2 (continued)

2013	15–19	0.033	0.076	0.034	0.052	0.013	0.021	0.015	0.048	0.104	0.056
	20–24	0.083	0.163	0.088	0.124	0.042	0.090	0.041	0.126	0.246	0.150
	25–29	0.085	0.149	0.093	0.087	0.072	0.098	0.056	0.138	0.284	0.182
	30–34	0.065	0.110	0.074	0.060	0.079	0.079	0.066	0.110	0.202	0.140
	35–39	0.033	0.058	0.035	0.032	0.048	0.046	0.041	0.066	0.101	0.084
	40–44	0.008	0.016	0.009	0.006	0.009	0.008	0.010	0.017	0.021	0.018
	TFR	**1.535**	**2.852**	**1.663**	**1.808**	**1.314**	**1.706**	**1.146**	**2.521**	**4.790**	**3.152**
2014	15–19	0.030	0.069	0.031	0.043	0.012	0.021	0.015	0.053	0.099	0.062
	20–24	0.081	0.155	0.093	0.100	0.045	0.112	0.042	0.127	0.257	0.167
	25–29	0.087	0.148	0.099	0.084	0.080	0.115	0.058	0.131	0.303	0.196
	30–34	0.067	0.113	0.074	0.053	0.080	0.087	0.062	0.117	0.217	0.159
	35–39	0.035	0.061	0.037	0.031	0.046	0.045	0.042	0.065	0.108	0.093
	40–44	0.008	0.016	0.009	0.007	0.011	0.009	0.013	0.018	0.020	0.021
	TFR	**1.541**	**2.810**	**1.719**	**1.584**	**1.376**	**1.944**	**1.156**	**2.557**	**5.012**	**3.491**
2015	15–19	0.028	0.060	0.028	0.047	0.012	0.018	0.013	0.056	0.082	0.064
	20–24	0.078	0.157	0.097	0.117	0.045	0.085	0.039	0.134	0.230	0.173
	25–29	0.089	0.152	0.097	0.086	0.077	0.126	0.057	0.150	0.258	0.179
	30–34	0.069	0.118	0.077	0.057	0.094	0.085	0.065	0.122	0.187	0.154
	35–39	0.037	0.062	0.039	0.029	0.046	0.046	0.041	0.068	0.105	0.087
	40–44	0.008	0.016	0.009	0.008	0.013	0.009	0.010	0.019	0.022	0.022
	TFR	**1.542**	**2.825**	**1.732**	**1.721**	**1.432**	**1.845**	**1.130**	**2.744**	**4.417**	**3.397**
2016	15–19	0.025	0.058	0.024	0.039	0.011	0.018	0.011	0.062	0.074	0.060
	20–24	0.076	0.150	0.091	0.124	0.042	0.098	0.036	0.133	0.206	0.175
	25–29	0.087	0.150	0.095	0.110	0.077	0.115	0.052	0.153	0.229	0.203
	30–34	0.070	0.117	0.074	0.060	0.086	0.081	0.062	0.122	0.184	0.181
	35–39	0.038	0.060	0.041	0.031	0.051	0.047	0.041	0.073	0.105	0.095
	40–44	0.008	0.017	0.009	0.008	0.012	0.009	0.013	0.020	0.023	0.024
	TFR	**1.518**	**2.763**	**1.667**	**1.857**	**1.396**	**1.840**	**1.072**	**2.816**	**4.112**	**3.687**

Panel B Age-specific first-birth rates (ASFR1) and the first birth order total fertility rate (TFR1)

		Mexican		Puerto Rican		Cuban		Central/South American		Other	
		U.S.-born	Foreign-born	U.S.-born	Foreign-born	U.S.-born	Foreign-born	U.S.-born	Foreign-born	U.S.-born	Foreign-born
Year	**Age**										
2006	15–19	0.046	0.130	0.046	0.075	0.021	0.026	0.033	0.093	0.042	0.024
	20–24	0.050	0.111	0.053	0.066	0.037	0.079	0.053	0.113	0.051	0.035
	25–29	0.026	0.043	0.028	0.029	0.047	0.060	0.047	0.064	0.031	0.023
	30–34	0.015	0.017	0.015	0.017	0.031	0.032	0.040	0.037	0.017	0.015
	35–39	0.007	0.007	0.007	0.006	0.015	0.010	0.022	0.014	0.008	0.006
	40–44	0.001	0.001	0.002	0.001	0.003	0.002	0.004	0.003	0.002	0.001
	TFR1	**0.728**	**1.541**	**0.749**	**0.974**	**0.771**	**1.049**	**0.993**	**1.626**	**0.758**	**0.523**
2007	15–19	0.046	0.120	0.044	0.055	0.018	0.030	0.031	0.094	0.056	0.035
	20–24	0.050	0.108	0.056	0.053	0.035	0.072	0.047	0.111	0.063	0.047
	25–29	0.027	0.041	0.029	0.025	0.037	0.053	0.046	0.066	0.038	0.032
	30–34	0.016	0.017	0.017	0.015	0.030	0.032	0.033	0.035	0.020	0.018
	35–39	0.006	0.007	0.007	0.006	0.013	0.011	0.021	0.014	0.009	0.006
	40–44	0.001	0.001	0.001	0.001	0.002	0.002	0.005	0.003	0.002	0.001
	TFR1	**0.729**	**1.466**	**0.770**	**0.777**	**0.678**	**1.002**	**0.914**	**1.617**	**0.941**	**0.698**
2008	15–19	0.041	0.112	0.049	0.060	0.016	0.029	0.026	0.070	0.090	0.056
	20–24	0.044	0.096	0.056	0.064	0.034	0.081	0.035	0.094	0.106	0.087
	25–29	0.024	0.039	0.027	0.033	0.034	0.054	0.035	0.057	0.060	0.063
	30–34	0.014	0.016	0.017	0.016	0.029	0.034	0.027	0.032	0.035	0.028
	35–39	0.006	0.006	0.008	0.006	0.012	0.011	0.014	0.013	0.013	0.013
	40–44	0.001	0.002	0.002	0.001	0.003	0.002	0.003	0.003	0.003	0.003
	TFR1	**0.649**	**1.354**	**0.789**	**0.899**	**0.636**	**1.062**	**0.699**	**1.346**	**1.533**	**1.249**

(continued)

Table 8.2 (continued)

2009	15–19	0.038	0.091	0.041	0.050	0.016	0.024	0.022	0.063	0.100	0.064
	20–24	0.042	0.084	0.053	0.052	0.029	0.081	0.034	0.085	0.105	0.106
	25–29	0.024	0.035	0.030	0.027	0.038	0.061	0.028	0.049	0.065	0.064
	30–34	0.014	0.015	0.016	0.015	0.027	0.036	0.026	0.028	0.038	0.031
	35–39	0.006	0.006	0.007	0.006	0.011	0.012	0.015	0.012	0.016	0.013
	40–44	0.001	0.001	0.002	0.001	0.003	0.002	0.004	0.003	0.004	0.003
	TFR1	**0.623**	**1.160**	**0.746**	**0.753**	**0.616**	**1.085**	**0.646**	**1.200**	**1.639**	**1.406**
2010	15–19	0.035	0.079	0.035	0.047	0.013	0.021	0.019	0.049	0.101	0.058
	20–24	0.040	0.073	0.049	0.050	0.028	0.055	0.028	0.075	0.110	0.083
	25–29	0.023	0.032	0.025	0.025	0.034	0.044	0.028	0.042	0.072	0.060
	30–34	0.014	0.014	0.016	0.015	0.032	0.026	0.025	0.026	0.042	0.032
	35–39	0.006	0.005	0.007	0.006	0.010	0.010	0.013	0.013	0.015	0.013
	40–44	0.001	0.001	0.002	0.001	0.002	0.001	0.004	0.003	0.004	0.002
	TFR1	**0.596**	**1.020**	**0.668**	**0.720**	**0.589**	**0.790**	**0.580**	**1.039**	**1.722**	**1.239**
2011	15–19	0.032	0.067	0.032	0.044	0.011	0.026	0.016	0.048	0.096	0.061
	20–24	0.038	0.069	0.049	0.065	0.023	0.055	0.027	0.065	0.119	0.078
	25–29	0.024	0.031	0.026	0.027	0.031	0.051	0.022	0.040	0.072	0.066
	30–34	0.014	0.013	0.016	0.014	0.028	0.031	0.025	0.026	0.047	0.031
	35–39	0.006	0.005	0.007	0.006	0.012	0.010	0.015	0.012	0.019	0.014
	40–44	0.001	0.001	0.002	0.001	0.003	0.002	0.004	0.003	0.004	0.003
	TFR1	**0.571**	**0.926**	**0.656**	**0.783**	**0.543**	**0.879**	**0.538**	**0.967**	**1.789**	**1.264**
2012	15–19	0.030	0.062	0.031	0.054	0.010	0.021	0.015	0.042	0.092	0.058
	20–24	0.038	0.067	0.043	0.061	0.022	0.060	0.025	0.062	0.119	0.091
	25–29	0.023	0.030	0.025	0.025	0.028	0.050	0.025	0.040	0.076	0.057
	30–34	0.015	0.013	0.016	0.014	0.027	0.025	0.022	0.024	0.043	0.036
	35–39	0.006	0.005	0.008	0.006	0.012	0.010	0.011	0.011	0.020	0.012
	40–44	0.001	0.001	0.002	0.002	0.003	0.002	0.003	0.003	0.003	0.003
	TFR	**0.562**	**0.890**	**0.619**	**0.809**	**0.504**	**0.846**	**0.505**	**0.910**	**1.766**	**1.288**

2013	15–19	0.027	0.058	0.028	0.040	0.011	0.019	0.012	0.039	0.083	0.046
	20–24	0.038	0.065	0.043	0.053	0.025	0.062	0.024	0.062	0.114	0.078
	25–29	0.024	0.029	0.027	0.024	0.032	0.050	0.024	0.042	0.080	0.058
	30–34	0.015	0.013	0.018	0.014	0.028	0.030	0.024	0.025	0.045	0.033
	35–39	0.006	0.005	0.007	0.006	0.013	0.013	0.011	0.012	0.018	0.016
	40–44	0.001	0.001	0.002	0.001	0.003	0.002	0.003	0.003	0.004	0.003
	TFR1	**0.553**	**0.859**	**0.622**	**0.693**	**0.560**	**0.881**	**0.492**	**0.916**	**1.724**	**1.168**
2014	15–19	0.024	0.054	0.025	0.033	0.011	0.018	0.012	0.044	0.080	0.051
	20–24	0.037	0.065	0.045	0.042	0.026	0.079	0.024	0.064	0.119	0.089
	25–29	0.024	0.030	0.029	0.023	0.035	0.059	0.024	0.040	0.087	0.063
	30–34	0.015	0.014	0.017	0.013	0.029	0.033	0.023	0.028	0.049	0.037
	35–39	0.006	0.006	0.007	0.007	0.013	0.013	0.013	0.012	0.019	0.016
	40–44	0.001	0.001	0.002	0.002	0.003	0.002	0.004	0.003	0.004	0.003
	TFR1	**0.543**	**0.847**	**0.624**	**0.593**	**0.580**	**1.019**	**0.502**	**0.955**	**1.783**	**1.294**
2015	15–19	0.023	0.047	0.023	0.037	0.010	0.016	0.011	0.045	0.067	0.053
	20–24	0.036	0.067	0.048	0.052	0.026	0.060	0.022	0.066	0.109	0.093
	25–29	0.025	0.033	0.028	0.023	0.035	0.063	0.023	0.046	0.072	0.061
	30–34	0.015	0.016	0.018	0.014	0.034	0.032	0.023	0.028	0.042	0.038
	35–39	0.007	0.006	0.008	0.006	0.013	0.013	0.012	0.012	0.019	0.015
	40–44	0.001	0.002	0.002	0.002	0.003	0.002	0.003	0.003	0.004	0.003
	TFR1	**0.536**	**0.848**	**0.635**	**0.670**	**0.609**	**0.935**	**0.473**	**1.002**	**1.567**	**1.319**
2016	15–19	0.020	0.046	0.020	0.031	0.010	0.016	0.009	0.051	0.061	0.050
	20–24	0.036	0.065	0.046	0.055	0.025	0.070	0.021	0.064	0.100	0.098
	25–29	0.024	0.033	0.028	0.030	0.035	0.062	0.021	0.047	0.068	0.070
	30–34	0.016	0.016	0.018	0.015	0.031	0.032	0.022	0.028	0.042	0.043
	35–39	0.007	0.006	0.008	0.006	0.014	0.014	0.012	0.013	0.020	0.018
	40–44	0.001	0.001	0.002	0.001	0.003	0.002	0.004	0.003	0.004	0.004
	TFR1	**0.523**	**0.840**	**0.604**	**0.693**	**0.589**	**0.980**	**0.447**	**1.031**	**1.467**	**1.409**

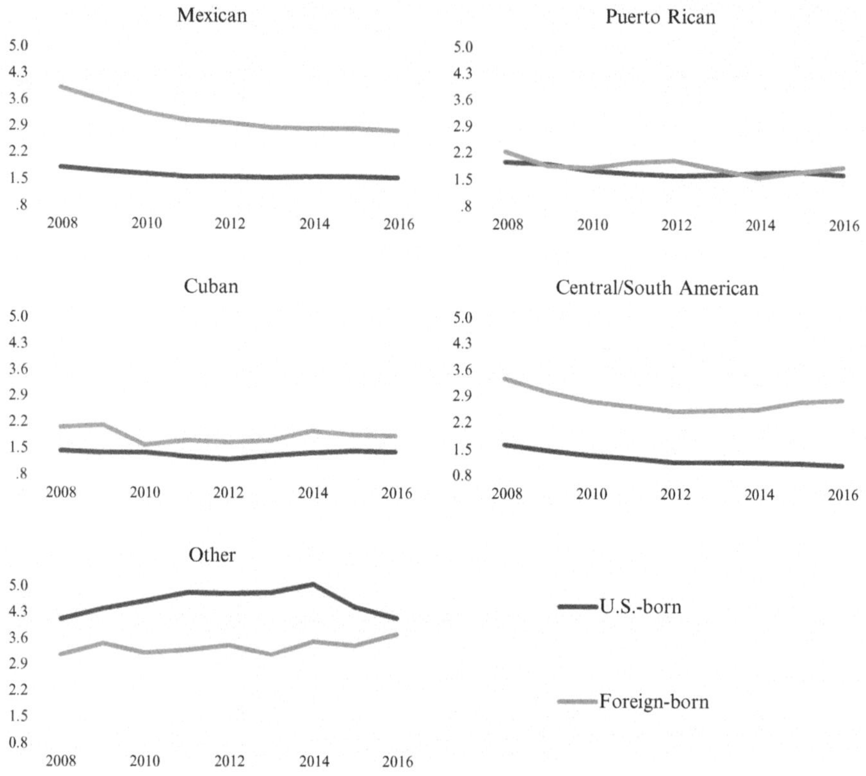

Fig. 8.5 TFR of Hispanic women, by nativity and region of origin: 2006–2016

percent decline than immigrant women (33.6% vs. 15.9%), ultimately ending the period with the lowest TFR of all nativity/origin sub-groups (1.072). The declines in fertility for Puerto Rican women, both island and mainland born, were also quite large, but fluctuated over the period. Women categorized as "Other" were the only ones to experience an increase in the TFR over the 9-year period (2008–2016), evident for both foreign-born and U.S.-born women. However, as discussed in Sect. 8.3.1, changes in the measurement of the region-of-origin numerator during the study period leading to an *increase* in the percentage of *births* categorized to "Other Hispanic" mothers are potentially inflating the fertility rates for "Other Hispanic" mothers.

The degree that nativity and region-of-origin sub-groups differ in fertility timing is addressed in the age-specific fertility rates. In 2006, fertility rates peaked at 20–24 years old for Mexican and Puerto Rican women and at 25–29 years old for Cuban women, regardless of nativity. By the end of the period (2016), peak fertility rates shifted to 25–29 years old for Mexican and "Other Hispanic" women, for Puerto Rican mainland-born women, and for Central/South American foreign-born women, and to 30–34 years old for Cuban and Central/South American U.S.-born women. Subgroup differences started off large at the beginning of the childbearing years, with dramatically different levels of adolescent fertility. For example, adolescent childbearing is over 6 times higher for foreign-born Mexican women than for native-born Cuban women in 2006 (.169 vs .025) and remains about 5 times higher (0.058 vs. 0.011) in 2016. Overall, sub-group differences are largest during the peak childbearing years and then narrow at the oldest ages, when fertility rates are at their lowest.

Panel B of Table 8.2 shows the ASFR1s and TFR1s for U.S.-born and foreign-born Hispanic women by region of origin. Similar to foreign-born women overall, the TFR1 for Mexican women was above 1.00 from 2006 (1.541) to 2010 (1.020) and seemed primarily driven by higher fertility at ages 15–19 and 20–24. Central/South American foreign-born women had TFR1s that surpassed 1 from 2008–2010 and again in 2015–2016, which also seemed primarily driven by higher ASFR1s in the three youngest age groups. In contrast, when Cuban foreign-born women had TFR1 values over 1.00 (prior to 2010 and in 2014), they seemed primarily driven by higher fertility in the middle three age categories (20–34). For both mainland- and island born Puerto Rican women, the TFR1 was below 1.00 for the entire study period. Whereas most region-of-origin subgroups clearly differed in the TFR1/ASFR1 trends observed for U.S.-born vs. foreign-born women, for U.S.- and foreign-born "Other Hispanic" women alike the TFR1 was well above 1.000 from 2008–2016 and the trends for the ASFR1s were remarkably similar (Fig. 8.6). While our analysis cannot distinguish between the potential causes, the results for "Other Hispanic" women likely reflect both temporal distortions as well as effects due to the aforementioned measurement changes in region of origin over the study period. This is supported by sensitivity analyses estimating differences in the 2010 ASFRs/TFR and ASFR1s/TFR1 using region-of-origin population distributions from the ACS vs Census 2010 10% PUMS.[12] The Census PUMS indicated a higher percentage of "Other Hispanic" women compared to the 2010 ACS, which would result in lower fertility rates (Fig. 8.7).

Table 8.3 shows age-specific fertility rates of married and unmarried U.S.-born and foreign-born Hispanic women from 2006–2016. The unmarried to married ASFR ratios (Fig. 8.8) show that from 2006 to 2016, unmarried women (both U.S.- and foreign-born) had considerably lower fertility levels than the married at ages 15–19 and 20–24. Similarly, over the study period U.S.-born unmarried women had lower fertility levels than their married counterparts at ages 25–29, 30–34, 35–39, and 40–44. In contrast, in 2006 foreign-born unmarried women had similar fertility levels when compared with married women at ages 25–29, 30–34, 35–39, and 40–44. By 2016, the unmarried to married ASFR ratios remained at around 1.00 for foreign-born women in the oldest age groups, but dropped for foreign-born

[12]Population counts from the 2010 Census Summary File 2 suggest population distributions for "Other Hispanic" women are more accurate in the Census 2010 PUMS vs ACS, but the Census 2010 PUMS does not include information on nativity.

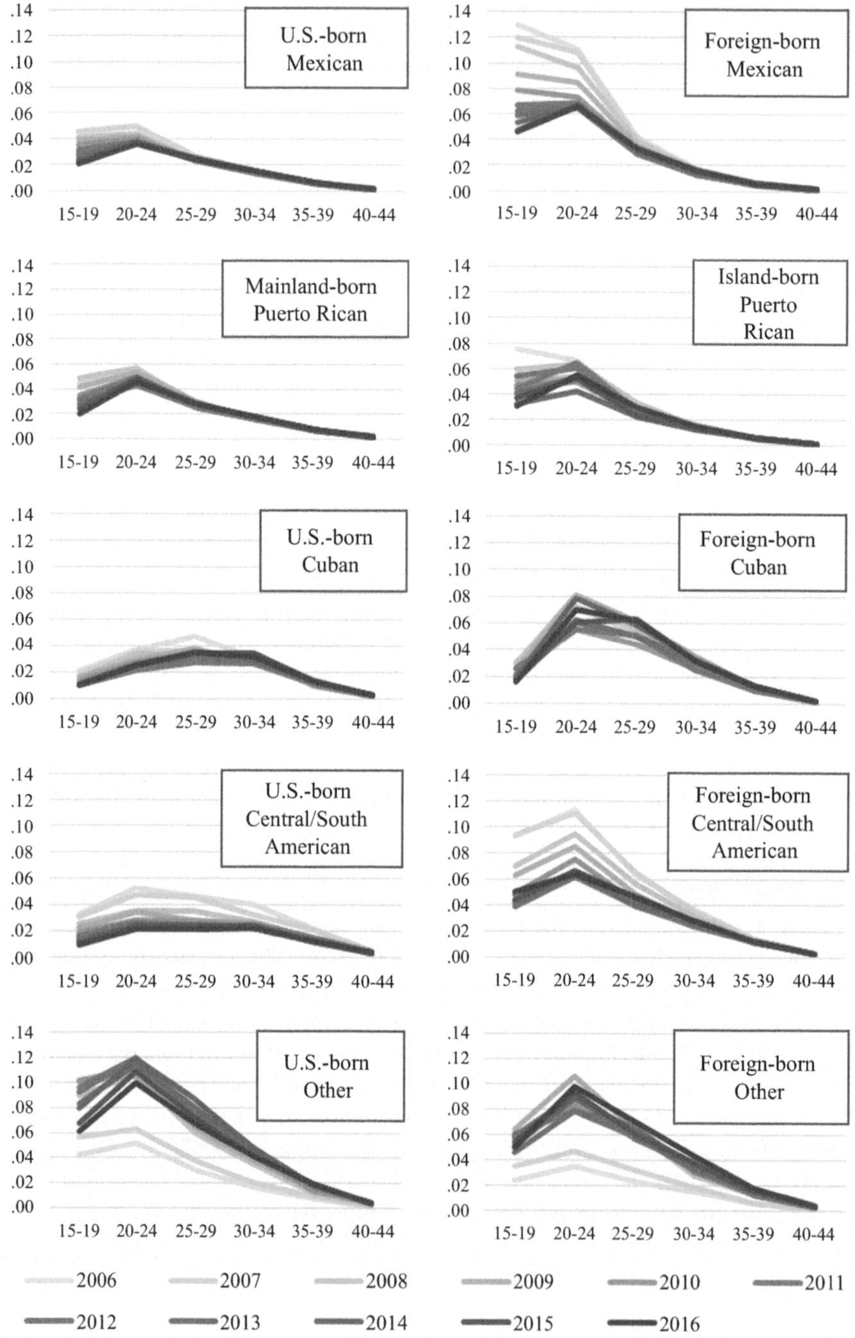

Fig. 8.6 Age-specific first-birth rates (ASFR1) of U.S.-born and foreign-born Hispanic women, by region of origin: 2006–2016

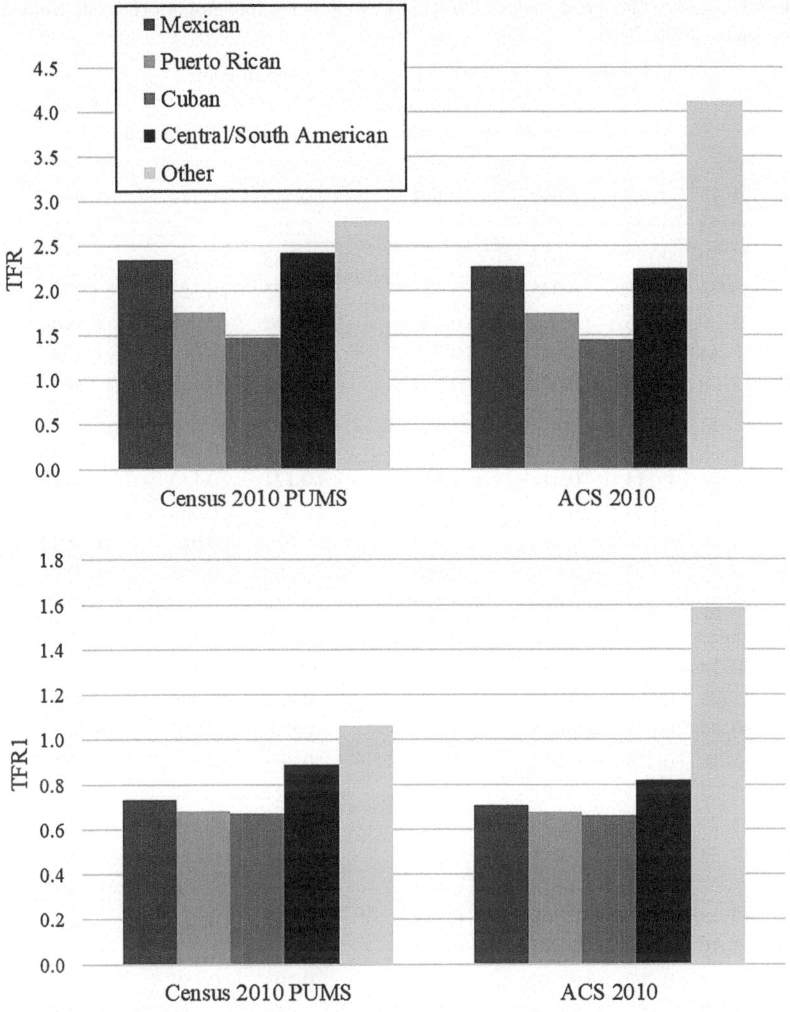

Fig. 8.7 TFR and TFR1 with population totals weighted by ACS versus Census 10% PUMS, by region of origin: 2010

women ages 25–29 and 30–34, indicating a greater decline in unmarried versus married fertility levels for foreign-born women in those age groups.

In Fig. 8.9, we underscore important sources of heterogeneity in Hispanic fertility by comparing rates of specific Hispanic subgroups with overall trends in U.S. fertility. Panel A shows comparisons between Non-Hispanic Whites, Non-Hispanic Blacks, U.S.-born Hispanics, and foreign-born Hispanics. The results indicate that foreign-born Hispanics had the highest TFR in 2006 and experienced the greatest decline in the TFR over the study period. Moreover, the results for U.S.-born Hispanic women look more similar to Non-Hispanic Black and

Table 8.3 Age-specific fertility rates (ASFR) of U.S.-born and foreign-born Hispanic women, by marital status: 2006–2016

		U.S.-born			Foreign-born		
		Married	Unmarried	Unmarried ÷ Married	Married	Unmarried	Unmarried ÷ Married
Year	Age						
2006	15–19	0.284	0.049	0.174	0.415	0.114	0.275
	20–24	0.244	0.092	0.377	0.254	0.216	0.851
	25–29	0.159	0.075	0.468	0.185	0.188	1.016
	30–34	0.108	0.045	0.421	0.125	0.127	1.020
	35–39	0.055	0.022	0.406	0.062	0.062	0.990
	40–44	0.011	0.005	0.515	0.016	0.016	0.999
2007	15–19	0.289	0.051	0.175	0.387	0.111	0.287
	20–24	0.241	0.094	0.389	0.258	0.212	0.823
	25–29	0.170	0.076	0.450	0.180	0.187	1.036
	30–34	0.114	0.048	0.422	0.121	0.133	1.097
	35–39	0.054	0.023	0.423	0.062	0.066	1.064
	40–44	0.011	0.005	0.500	0.016	0.015	0.988
2008	15–19	0.297	0.050	0.168	0.300	0.105	0.351
	20–24	0.231	0.090	0.390	0.244	0.202	0.828
	25–29	0.158	0.073	0.460	0.176	0.187	1.062
	30–34	0.108	0.048	0.450	0.121	0.127	1.054
	35–39	0.052	0.023	0.448	0.062	0.064	1.026
	40–44	0.011	0.005	0.507	0.016	0.017	1.044
2009	15–19	0.258	0.048	0.184	0.304	0.089	0.292
	20–24	0.203	0.087	0.427	0.227	0.182	0.801
	25–29	0.156	0.072	0.459	0.170	0.165	0.967
	30–34	0.109	0.048	0.443	0.117	0.115	0.990
	35–39	0.051	0.024	0.469	0.060	0.060	0.995
	40–44	0.011	0.006	0.523	0.015	0.016	1.034
2010	15–19	0.246	0.043	0.175	0.306	0.075	0.245
	20–24	0.202	0.080	0.398	0.203	0.159	0.781
	25–29	0.151	0.069	0.456	0.156	0.151	0.972
	30–34	0.106	0.049	0.458	0.108	0.112	1.034
	35–39	0.051	0.023	0.455	0.059	0.059	0.990
	40–44	0.011	0.006	0.523	0.015	0.016	1.064
2011	15–19	0.271	0.039	0.142	0.239	0.068	0.284
	20–24	0.200	0.076	0.381	0.209	0.144	0.689
	25–29	0.160	0.066	0.411	0.158	0.140	0.886
	30–34	0.110	0.048	0.438	0.111	0.105	0.942
	35–39	0.053	0.024	0.458	0.059	0.056	0.951
	40–44	0.012	0.006	0.546	0.015	0.015	1.009
2012	15–19	0.214	0.037	0.171	0.222	0.063	0.285
	20–24	0.194	0.075	0.384	0.209	0.139	0.668
	25–29	0.162	0.066	0.404	0.155	0.139	0.899

(continued)

Table 8.3 (continued)

		U.S.-born			Foreign-born		
		Married	Unmarried	Unmarried ÷ Married	Married	Unmarried	Unmarried ÷ Married
Year	Age						
	30–34	0.113	0.048	0.423	0.107	0.106	0.990
	35–39	0.052	0.025	0.482	0.058	0.059	1.006
	40–44	0.011	0.006	0.579	0.015	0.016	1.106
2013	15–19	0.211	0.033	0.157	0.246	0.055	0.225
	20–24	0.206	0.074	0.357	0.212	0.125	0.589
	25–29	0.159	0.070	0.439	0.153	0.133	0.871
	30–34	0.116	0.048	0.415	0.110	0.104	0.946
	35–39	0.054	0.026	0.486	0.059	0.060	1.008
	40–44	0.011	0.007	0.588	0.015	0.016	1.030
2014	15–19	0.208	0.030	0.144	0.261	0.053	0.203
	20–24	0.209	0.073	0.350	0.205	0.122	0.594
	25–29	0.166	0.072	0.433	0.162	0.125	0.775
	30–34	0.115	0.051	0.446	0.117	0.106	0.901
	35–39	0.057	0.027	0.474	0.061	0.064	1.052
	40–44	0.012	0.007	0.552	0.015	0.017	1.080
2015	15–19	0.207	0.027	0.133	0.250	0.049	0.198
	20–24	0.207	0.071	0.341	0.237	0.120	0.508
	25–29	0.163	0.073	0.446	0.166	0.133	0.800
	30–34	0.116	0.052	0.452	0.122	0.108	0.885
	35–39	0.058	0.029	0.495	0.063	0.062	0.983
	40–44	0.012	0.007	0.592	0.016	0.018	1.155
2016	15–19	0.184	0.024	0.133	0.298	0.049	0.164
	20–24	0.198	0.067	0.340	0.229	0.118	0.514
	25–29	0.163	0.070	0.429	0.173	0.132	0.764
	30–34	0.116	0.052	0.448	0.123	0.110	0.892
	35–39	0.058	0.030	0.524	0.063	0.064	1.025
	40–44	0.012	0.007	0.590	0.016	0.019	1.181

Non-Hispanic White women than to foreign-born Hispanic women; In 2006, the TFR for U.S.-born Hispanic women was similar to the TFR for Non-Hispanic black women. In 2016, their TFR was more similar to Non-Hispanic White women. In Panel B, the TFRs for Non-Hispanic White and Non-Hispanic Black women are compared to the TFRs for U.S./mainland born Mexican, Puerto Rican, and Cuban women. In Panel C, the TFRs for Non-Hispanic White and Non-Hispanic Black women are compared to the TFRs for foreign/island born Mexican, Puerto Rican, and Cuban women. Taken together, the results from Panels B and C show that the 2006 TFR and subsequent decline in the TFR over the study period was greatest for foreign-born Mexican women and lowest for U.S.-born Cuban women.

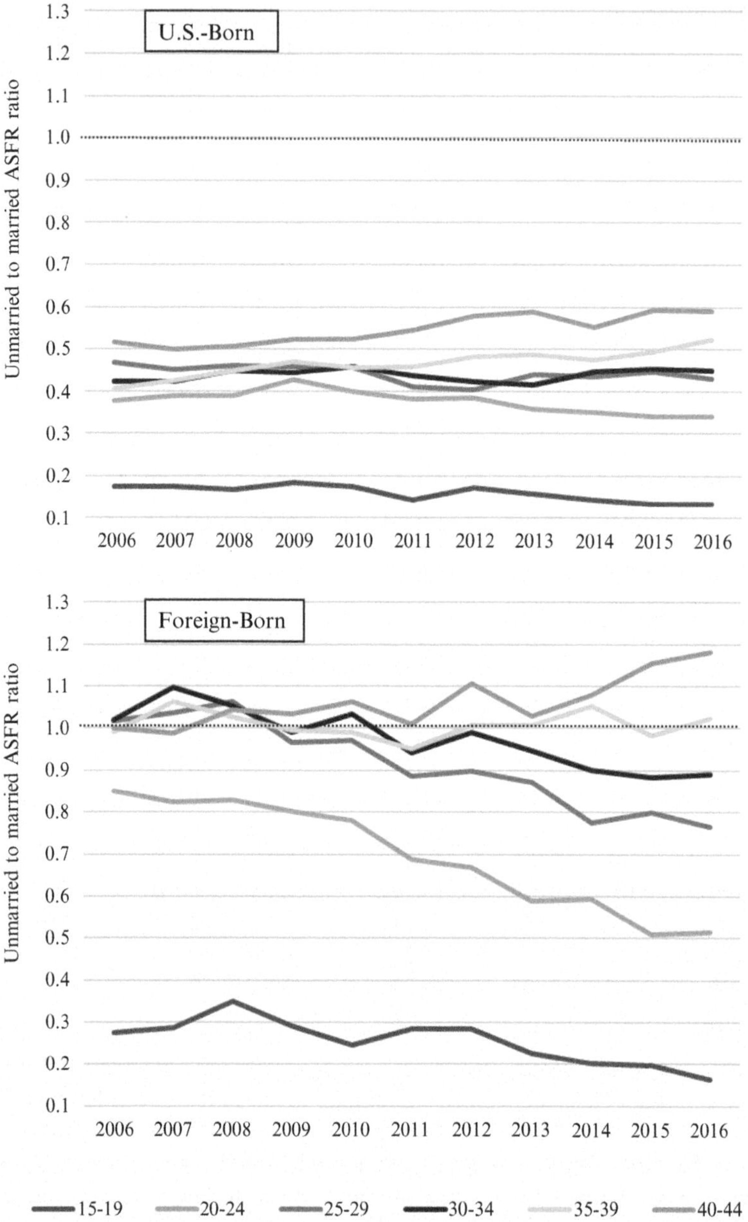

Fig. 8.8 Unmarried to married ASFR ratio for U.S.-born and foreign-born Hispanic women

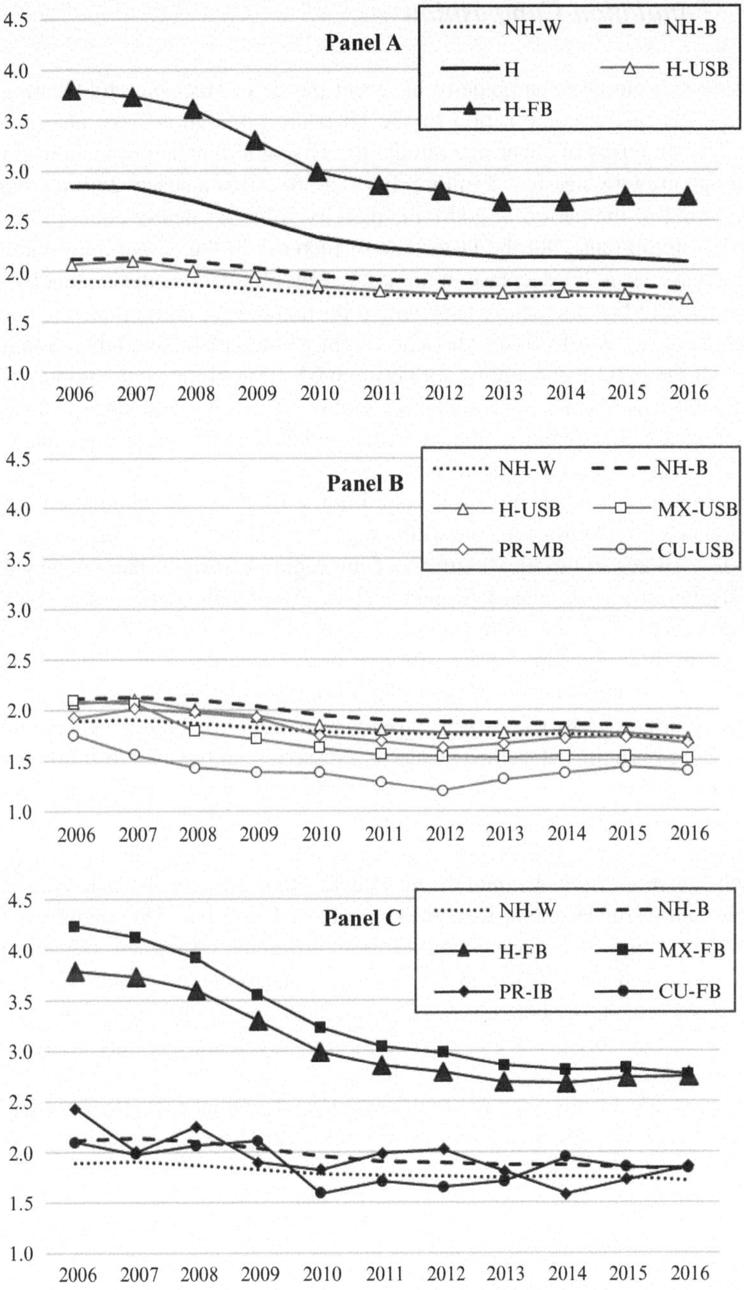

Fig. 8.9 TFR by race-ethnicity for women ages 15–44: 2006–2016. Note: H Hispanic, USB U.S.-born, FB Foreign-born, NH-W Non-Hispanic white, NH-B Non-Hispanic black, MX Mexican, PR Puerto Rican, CU Cuban

8.3.4 Population Composition

Alongside substantial heterogeneity in recent trends in Hispanic childbearing, significant shifts in the composition of the Hispanic population have also occurred (Table 8.4). In terms of sheer magnitude, the Hispanic female population of childbearing age grew by nearly 2.5 million from 2006–2016- a nearly 25% increase. At the beginning of the period in 2006, the nativity split was nearly equal (49% U.S.-born, 51% immigrant), but the faster rate of increase in the native-born population (50% increase vs. a 2% decrease in the immigrant population) means that by 2016, the nativity split became nearly 60% native-born and 40% immigrant.

In terms of region-of-origin, Mexican-origin women maintained their dominance throughout the period, accounting for between 63–65% of the population across the years. Puerto Rican women accounted for another 9% each year. Cuban women are a consistently small segment of the overall population at between 2–3% across the years. The Central/South American category accounts for another 14–15%. The "Other" grouping starts the period accounting for 10.7% of the population but ends the period at 8.7% (some of the proportional shift in the latter two categories is likely related to changes in the measurement of the region-of-origin denominator during the study period, as discussed in Sect. 8.3.1). Among the native-born, Mexican-origin dominance is even more pronounced, accounting for 68% of all U.S.-born Hispanics in 2016 but only 58% of foreign-born Hispanics. Central/South Americans account for another 25% of the foreign-born population.

By 2006, the majority of Hispanic women were unmarried (56.3%), a pattern that became more pronounced as the decade progressed, with nearly two-thirds (64.4%) of Hispanic women ages 15–44 unmarried in 2016. Of course, pronounced nativity differentials are also present. Among immigrant women, the opposite pattern occurs with the majority of women being married throughout the observation period, although the proportion declines from 55.8 to 50.4. Among the native-born, just over one-quarter of Hispanic women were married in 2016. This pattern is likely related to the age and marital composition differences between U.S.-born and foreign-born women, as shown in Fig. 8.10. Similar to the trends noted by Parrado (2011), Hispanic foreign-born women have an older age composition relative to their U.S.-born counterparts, and this trend grew in magnitude over the study period. Moreover, relative to the U.S.-born, a greater percentage of foreign-born Hispanic women ages 15–44 are married, both overall and within each 5-year age group (though this trend grew smaller in magnitude over the study period for the two smallest age groups).

8.3.5 Decomposition Results

Whether and to what extent the observed changes in the fertility rates described in Tables 8.1, 8.2, and 8.3 are due to compositional shifts in the population over time

Table 8.4 Population composition of Hispanic women ages 15–44, overall and by nativity: 2006–2016

Panel A Overall	2006	2007	2008	2009	2010	2011	2012	2013	2014	2015	2016
Nativity											
U.S.-born	48.97	49.57	51.58	51.98	53.06	54.17	55.57	56.48	57.57	58.55	59.46
Foreign-born	51.03	50.43	48.42	48.02	46.94	45.83	44.43	43.52	42.43	41.45	40.54
Region of origin											
Mexican	63.21	63.67	65.41	65.38	64.68	64.55	64.26	64.19	64.39	63.87	63.63
Puerto Rican	9.23	9.31	8.84	9.22	9.35	9.34	9.33	9.44	9.63	9.47	9.47
Cuban	2.85	2.95	2.87	2.80	3.06	3.08	3.19	3.14	3.04	3.05	3.21
Central/South American	14.00	14.22	14.81	15.15	15.60	15.57	15.64	15.53	15.61	15.64	15.59
Other	10.70	9.84	8.07	7.44	7.32	7.46	7.58	7.69	7.33	7.96	8.11
Marital status											
Married	43.68	42.69	41.55	40.28	39.53	37.88	37.81	36.94	36.44	35.98	35.64
Unmarried	56.32	57.31	58.45	59.72	60.47	62.12	62.19	63.06	63.56	64.02	64.36
Age											
15–19	17.81	18.10	18.33	18.53	18.53	18.35	18.13	18.00	17.92	17.97	18.06
20–24	17.22	17.01	16.93	16.97	17.19	17.42	17.70	17.89	18.04	17.97	17.80
25–29	17.71	17.66	17.59	17.45	17.20	17.00	16.76	16.61	16.58	16.70	16.92
30–34	17.13	17.02	16.89	16.82	16.81	16.82	16.83	16.82	16.73	16.52	16.36
35–39	15.86	15.97	16.03	16.05	16.00	15.92	15.89	15.86	15.82	15.90	15.95
40–44	14.28	14.24	14.23	14.18	14.27	14.49	14.69	14.83	14.92	14.95	14.91
N (million)	10.57	10.91	11.24	11.55	11.84	12.04	12.23	12.42	12.61	12.81	13.02

(continued)

Table 8.4 (continued)

Panel B U.S.-born

	2006	**2007**	**2008**	**2009**	**2010**	**2011**	**2012**	**2013**	**2014**	**2015**	**2016**
Region of origin											
Mexican	64.09	64.54	67.95	68.24	67.60	67.61	67.60	67.73	68.42	68.17	68.31
Puerto Rican	13.18	13.11	12.23	12.50	12.79	12.47	12.27	12.05	12.25	11.68	11.29
Cuban	2.79	2.94	2.88	2.90	2.91	3.03	3.15	3.03	2.82	2.68	2.73
Central/South American	6.02	6.62	7.06	7.30	8.20	8.52	8.45	8.85	8.59	8.91	8.96
Other	13.93	12.79	9.87	9.07	8.50	8.37	8.52	8.35	7.92	8.56	8.71
Marital status											
Married	31.07	29.71	29.43	28.67	27.86	26.62	26.43	26.22	26.02	25.99	25.61
Unmarried	68.93	70.29	70.57	71.33	72.14	73.38	73.57	73.78	73.98	74.01	74.39
Age											
15–19	27.14	27.79	27.70	28.03	27.79	27.26	26.51	25.89	25.54	25.22	25.14
20–24	20.56	20.42	20.18	20.78	21.26	22.12	22.83	23.08	23.17	23.05	22.54
25–29	17.03	17.04	17.44	17.20	16.78	16.68	16.49	16.39	16.49	17.17	17.98
30–34	13.53	13.29	13.32	13.28	13.34	13.59	13.76	14.08	14.29	14.03	14.03
35–39	11.41	11.56	11.48	11.24	11.19	10.93	10.91	11.09	11.24	11.22	11.17
40–44	10.33	9.91	9.89	9.46	9.63	9.42	9.49	9.46	9.27	9.31	9.14
N (million)	5.18	5.41	5.80	6.00	6.28	6.52	6.80	7.02	7.26	7.50	7.74

Panel C Foreign-born

	2006	**2007**	**2008**	**2009**	**2010**	**2011**	**2012**	**2013**	**2014**	**2015**	**2016**
Region of origin											
Mexican	62.37	62.82	62.70	62.30	61.37	60.95	60.09	59.60	58.94	57.79	56.76
Puerto Rican	5.44	5.59	5.23	5.68	5.45	5.63	5.64	6.07	6.07	6.36	6.80
Cuban	2.92	2.96	2.86	2.70	3.23	3.14	3.24	3.30	3.33	3.58	3.91
Central/South American	21.67	21.69	23.07	23.65	23.96	23.90	24.64	24.20	25.13	25.16	25.30
Other	7.60	6.95	6.14	5.67	5.98	6.39	6.40	6.83	6.54	7.11	7.23

Marital status											
Married	55.78	55.45	54.46	52.85	52.73	51.18	52.03	50.84	50.59	50.11	50.36
Unmarried	44.22	44.55	45.54	47.15	47.27	48.82	47.97	49.16	49.41	49.89	49.64
Age											
15–19	8.85	8.57	8.35	8.25	8.05	7.82	7.65	7.76	7.57	7.73	7.66
20–24	14.02	13.65	13.46	12.85	12.58	11.86	11.28	11.15	11.07	10.79	10.84
25–29	18.37	18.27	17.75	17.71	17.68	17.38	17.10	16.89	16.69	16.03	15.37
30–34	20.57	20.68	20.70	20.64	20.74	20.64	20.67	20.37	20.05	20.03	19.78
35–39	20.13	20.31	20.88	21.26	21.43	21.81	22.12	22.05	22.03	22.51	22.96
40–44	18.06	18.51	18.86	19.28	19.52	20.49	21.18	21.78	22.59	22.91	23.39
N (million)	5.39	5.50	5.44	5.55	5.56	5.52	5.44	5.41	5.35	5.31	5.28

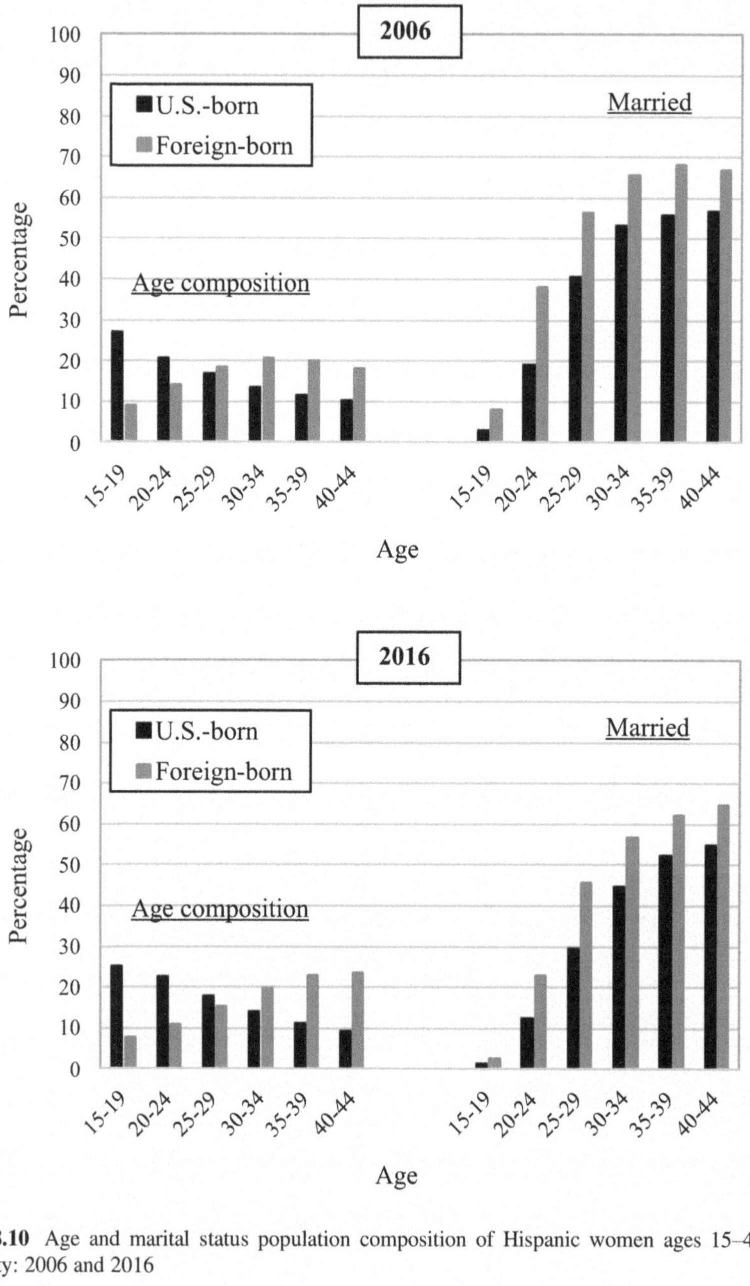

Fig. 8.10 Age and marital status population composition of Hispanic women ages 15–44, by nativity: 2006 and 2016

(as shown in Table 8.4) by factors such as age, marital status, and nativity—is addressed in Table 8.5, which presents the results from the decomposition analysis for Hispanic women ages 15–44 between 2006 and 2016.

In Panel A of Table 8.5, we decompose the change in the Hispanic birth rate into a rate effect and three composition effects, where the difference in Hispanic birth rate between 2006 and 2016 is the sum of the rate effect, the age composition effect, the marital status composition effect, and the nativity composition effect. As the equations show in Appendix 1, to get the rate effect, the birth rates for 2006 and 2016 are standardized by the average population composition; to get the composition effects, the 2006 and 2016 population composition for each factor is standardized by the average population composition of the other factors and the average age-marital status-nativity-specific birth rates. It is important to note that this is a descriptive endeavor—we will always be able to attribute differences between two rates either to one of the composition factors or the rate effect. As Das Gupta (1994) notes, "The effects of factors do not necessarily imply any causal relationships. They simply

Table 8.5 Standardization and decomposition of the change in the Hispanic birth rate from 2006 to 2016

Panel A Change in overall Hispanic birth rate = rate effect + age effect + marital status effect + nativity effect				
	Standardization		Decomposition	
	2006	2016	Absolute difference	Percent distribution
Crude change in birth rate	97.82	70.27	−27.55	100
Composition effects	89.22	77.74	−11.49	41.69
Age effect	84.86	81.11	−3.75	13.60
Marital status effect	84.86	81.34	−3.52	12.78
Nativity effect	85.22	81.00	−4.22	15.31
Rate effect	91.51	75.45	−16.07	58.31
Panel B Change in U.S.-born Hispanic birth rate = rate effect + age effect + marital status effect				
	Standardization		Decomposition	
	2006	2016	Absolute difference	Percent distribution
Crude change in birth rate	74.82	60.35	−14.47	100
Composition effects	69.00	65.97	−3.03	20.95
Age effect	66.81	67.96	1.14	−7.89
Marital status effect	69.47	65.30	−4.17	28.84
Rate effect	73.20	61.76	−11.44	79.05
Panel C Change in foreign-born Hispanic birth rate = rate effect + age effect + marital status effect				
	Standardization		Decomposition	
	2006	2016	Absolute difference	Percent distribution
Crude change in birth rate	119.90	84.83	−35.07	100
Composition effects	108.63	95.00	−13.63	38.86
Age effect	107.52	95.31	−12.22	34.83
Marital status effect	102.12	100.71	−1.41	4.03
Rate effect	112.54	91.09	−21.44	61.14

indicate the nature of the association of the factors with the phenomenon being measured. There might be some hidden forces behind the factors that are actually responsible for the numbers we allocate to different factors as effects, but identifying those forces is beyond the scope of the decomposition analysis." (p. 193).

Looking at the bottom row of Panel A in Table 8.5, we see that if the age-marital status-nativity-specific rates had changed but the population composition had not changed between 2006 and 2016, the decline in the birth rate would have been 16.07 (about 58% of the observed change of −27.55). In contrast, if the population composition had changed and the cell-specific rates had not changed, the decline in the birth rate would have been 11.49 (about 42% of the crude change of −27.55). Change in the nativity composition (i.e., increases in the percentage of U.S.-born Hispanic women, who have considerably lower rates of childbearing than their foreign-born counterparts, contributed to about 15% of the change (−4.22 ÷ −27.55). Changes in the age compositon (to slightly older ages, on average) and in the marital compositon (to relatively less married) over this time contributed to approximately 14 percent and 13 percent of the change, respectively.

In Panels B and C of Table 8.5, we decompose the change in the Hispanic birth rate into a rate effect and two composition effects, where the change in the U.S.-born or foreign-born Hispanic birth rate between 2006 and 2016 is the sum of the rate effect, the age composition effect, and the marital status composition effect. The results show there are large differences in the magnitude of the overall decline in fertility during this time (−14.47 for U.S.-born versus −35.07 for foreign-born Hispanic women). In addition, different factors emerge as more important across the groups in contributing to the overall decline in the birth rate. Specifically, changes in marital status account for 4.17 points (or almost 30 percent) of the 14.47 decline in birth rates among U.S.-born Hispanic women. Moreover, changes in the age structure actually worked to supress the decline in birth rates somewhat (by 1.14 points or almost 8%). In other words, if only the age composition had changed over this time period, with marital status composition and the cell-specific birth rates held constant, the birth rate for U.S.-born Hispanics would have actually increased slightly between 2006 and 2016. For foreign-born Hispanic women, on the other hand, changes in age structure accounted for −12.22 points (nearly 35%) of the 35.07 decline in birth rates, while changes in marital status accounted for −1.41 points (about 4%) of the decline in birth rates.

8.4 Conclusion

Our analysis identified with greater accuracy the fertility patterns of different Hispanic subgroups over a 10-year period. In doing so, we deepened what has all too often been an overly general conversation that ignores the complex heterogeneity in the Hispanic population, particularly around family formation processes and behaviors.

Taken together, this chapter has demonstrated the critical importance of attending to the role of Hispanic population heterogeneity in patterning demographic outcomes- in this case fertility. While the perils of relying on pan-ethnic groupings are frequently acknowledged, the practice of population disaggregation is often limited due to data limitations and an absence of practical guidance for how to best estimate the variation. We aimed to elucidate how to foreground the complex variability within the Hispanic population in the realm of fertility and family formation.

Future research can further disaggregate Hispanic fertility rates for U.S. born and foreign-born women by other factors, specifically educational attainment (with cross-classification by age, region-of-origin, and marital status, as appropriate). Research has long documented a link between education and fertility, although it is complex and contingent on context. Generally, however, in the U.S., increased levels of education are associated with a delay in first births and lower completed fertility (Hamilton, 2021). This is particularly true for people who come from more disadvantaged backgrounds (Brand & Davis, 2011). While Hispanic adults have among the lowest levels of education compared to other racial-ethnic groups overall, levels of completed education vary substantially within the Hispanic population along multiple domains, including region of origin and nativity. The level of completed education is higher for those of Cuban-origin, on average, than for Puerto Ricans or Mexicans. Additionally, even though levels of education among Hispanic immigrant groups have increased quite dramatically in recent years (in part reflecting changes in migration streams and the expansion of education in origin countries), they remain lower among foreign-born Hispanics than U.S.-born Hispanics. Notwithstanding measurement challenges with education in the vital statistics (see Sect. 8.2.2), future research must attend to this important component of population heterogeneity as it is highly consequential for family formation patterns generally and is often overlooked in the case of the Hispanic population.

One of our central arguments is that just because period estimates are prone to error does not mean we should not use them. In fact, it is important to note that there is some level of error in all of these estimates (i.e., CPS, ACS, Census PUMS, etc.). While there are clear advantages to using Census population counts, population counts are continuously updated and require researchers to revise their estimates once new data become available. For example, in this chapter, our population totals from the PEP were based on intercensal estimates for 2006–2009 and Vintage 2020 postcensal estimates for 2010–2016. The estimates from 2010–2016 will need revision once the 2010–2020 intercensal estimates are released in 2023 and "become the official estimates for the 2010–2020 decade" (U.S. Census Bureau, Population Division, 2022).[13] Echoing prior research, our core argument is that before we begin

[13]"The 2010 to 2020 Intercensal Estimates will become the official estimates for the 2010–2020 decade and are currently scheduled to become available in 2023 (specific timeline for release forthcoming). They are produced by modifying the Vintage 2020 estimates to account for differences between these estimates and the results of the 2020 Census. The result is a consistent time series from the 2010 Census to the 2020 Census. For more information on the Intercensal Estimates, please see the 2000–2010 Methodology Statement."

to assess the reasons and demographic consequences behind trends in Hispanic childbearing, we must first describe the phenomenon we are trying to explain (Sweeney & Raley, 2014). Period estimates are essential to accurately describing trends in Hispanic fertility.

Taken together, we hope that this chapter has demonstrated the utility and continued relevance of the vital registration birth data for capturing heterogeneity in Hispanic fertility patterns. Prior work relying on national surveys for estimates of both numerators and denominators has advantages, including the ability to discern fertility and migration timing, to capture cohort change over time, to more comprehensively assess predictors of fertility, and to model intentionality and wantedness. However, a major disadvantage characterizing this work is that national surveys approximate fertility but are not able to capture it directly (Schoen, 2022). As we have shown, the vital statistics system, although not without its challenges, is the only data source that accurately captures the entire universe of U.S. births. Hence, returning to our core argument—that before we can assess the reasons and consequences behind trends in Hispanic childbearing, we must first describe the phenomenon we are trying to explain—the vital statistics system is the best option for these descriptive endeavors. Equipped with the information on methodological decision-making that we have detailed in this chapter, we hope that future scholars and policy makers will consider using vital statistics to estimate ongoing trends in Hispanic fertility alongside ongoing work using national surveys.

Funding Information Support for this project was provided by Eunice Kennedy Shriver National Institute of Child Health and Human Development Grant/Award Numbers R03-HD102740 and P2C-HD058484-Ohio State University, Department of Sociology.

Appendix 1

Adhering to notation conventions in Das Gupta (1993, 1994), we use upper-case letters to identify values in 2006 and lower-case letters to identify values in 2016:

$$t\ldots - T\ldots = \left[R(\bar{t}) - R(\overline{T})\right] + \left[I(\bar{a}) - I(\overline{A})\right] + \left[J(\bar{b}) - J(\overline{B})\right] + \left[K(\bar{c}) - K(\overline{C})\right]$$

where the difference in Hispanic birth rate between 2006 ($T\ldots$) and 2016 ($t\ldots$) is the sum of the rate effect ($\left[R(\bar{t}) - R(\overline{T})\right]$), the age composition effect ($\left[I(\bar{a}) - I(\overline{A})\right]$), the marital status composition effect ($\left[J(\bar{b}) - J(\overline{B})\right]$), and the nativity composition effect ($\left[K(\bar{c}) - K(\overline{C})\right]$). $R(\overline{T})$ and $R(\bar{t})$ represent the birth rate in 2006 and 2016, respectively, standardized by age (I), marital status (J), and nativity (K):

$$R(\overline{T}) = \sum_{ijk} \frac{\frac{n_{ijk}}{n\ldots} + \frac{N_{ijk}}{N\ldots}}{2} T_{ijk}, \quad R(\bar{t}) = \sum_{ijk} \frac{\frac{n_{ijk}}{n\ldots} + \frac{N_{ijk}}{N\ldots}}{2} t_{ijk}$$

For the three composition factors—age (I), marital status (J), and nativity (K)—the values for each composition factor in 2006 and 2016 are standardized by the other composition factors and the cell-specific birth rates (Table 8.A1):

Table 8.A1 Population counts and birth rates of Hispanic Women, cross-classified by nativity, marital status, and age: 2006 and 2016

			2006		2016	
Nativity	Marital status	Age	Number of women	Birth rate	Number of women	Birth rate
k	*j*	*i*	*N_ijk*	*T_ijk*	*n_ijk*	*t_ijk*
U.S.-Born	Married	15/19	41,394	284.1	28,599	183.9
U.S.-Born	Married	20/24	202,784	243.6	215,709	198.2
U.S.-Born	Married	25/29	358,252	159.2	410,876	162.6
U.S.-Born	Married	30/34	373,135	108.1	487,015	116.1
U.S.-Born	Married	35/39	329,713	54.7	452,853	58.2
U.S.-Born	Married	40/44	302,927	10.6	388,004	12.5
U.S.-Born	Unmarried	15/19	1,363,381	49.5	1,917,704	24.5
U.S.-Born	Unmarried	20/24	861,134	91.8	1,529,576	67.4
U.S.-Born	Unmarried	25/29	522,889	74.5	981,162	69.8
U.S.-Born	Unmarried	30/34	327,293	45.5	599,156	52.0
U.S.-Born	Unmarried	35/39	260,605	22.2	411,939	30.5
U.S.-Born	Unmarried	40/44	231,770	5.5	319,358	7.4
Foreign-Born	Married	15/19	38,935	414.9	11,184	297.7
Foreign-Born	Married	20/24	286,959	254.3	131,285	229.1
Foreign-Born	Married	25/29	560,017	184.6	369,850	173.2
Foreign-Born	Married	30/34	728,742	124.5	593,698	123.3
Foreign-Born	Married	35/39	741,892	62.5	753,355	62.8
Foreign-Born	Married	40/44	651,888	15.6	798,441	16.1
Foreign-Born	Unmarried	15/19	438,221	114.0	393,292	48.7
Foreign-Born	Unmarried	20/24	469,078	216.3	441,013	117.8
Foreign-Born	Unmarried	25/29	430,681	187.6	441,202	132.4
Foreign-Born	Unmarried	30/34	380,937	127.0	450,229	110.0
Foreign-Born	Unmarried	35/39	343,908	61.9	458,268	64.4
Foreign-Born	Unmarried	40/44	322,328	15.6	436,101	19.0

Age (I):

$$I(\overline{A}) = \sum_{ijk} \frac{t_{ijk} + T_{ijk}}{2} \left[\frac{b_{ijk}c_{ijk} + B_{ijk}C_{ijk}}{3} + \frac{b_{ijk}C_{ijk} + B_{ijk}c_{ijk}}{6} \right] A_{ijk}$$

$$I(\overline{a}) = \sum_{ijk} \frac{t_{ijk} + T_{ijk}}{2} \left[\frac{b_{ijk}c_{ijk} + B_{ijk}C_{ijk}}{3} + \frac{b_{ijk}C_{ijk} + B_{ijk}c_{ijk}}{6} \right] a_{ijk}$$

Marital Status (J):

$$J(\overline{B}) = \sum_{ijk} \frac{t_{ijk} + T_{ijk}}{2} \left[\frac{a_{ijk}c_{ijk} + A_{ijk}C_{ijk}}{3} + \frac{a_{ijk}C_{ijk} + A_{ijk}c_{ijk}}{6} \right] B_{ijk}$$

$$J(\overline{b}) = \sum_{ijk} \frac{t_{ijk} + T_{ijk}}{2} \left[\frac{a_{ijk}c_{ijk} + A_{ijk}C_{ijk}}{3} + \frac{a_{ijk}C_{ijk} + A_{ijk}c_{ijk}}{6} \right] b_{ijk}$$

Nativity (K):

$$K(\overline{C}) = \sum_{ijk} \frac{t_{ijk} + T_{ijk}}{2} \left[\frac{a_{ijk}b_{ijk} + A_{ijk}B_{ijk}}{3} + \frac{a_{ijk}B_{ijk} + A_{ijk}b_{ijk}}{6} \right] C_{ijk}$$

$$K(\overline{c}) = \sum_{ijk} \frac{t_{ijk} + T_{ijk}}{2} \left[\frac{a_{ijk}b_{ijk} + A_{ijk}B_{ijk}}{3} + \frac{a_{ijk}B_{ijk} + A_{ijk}b_{ijk}}{6} \right] c_{ijk}$$

where,

$$A_{ijk} = \left(\frac{N_{ijk}}{N_{.jk}}\right)^{\frac{1}{3}} \times \left(\frac{N_{ij.}}{N_{.j.}} \times \frac{N_{i.k}}{N_{..k}}\right)^{\frac{1}{6}} \times \left(\frac{N_{i..}}{N_{...}}\right)^{\frac{1}{3}}, \quad a_{ijk} = \left(\frac{n_{ijk}}{n_{.jk}}\right)^{\frac{1}{3}} \times \left(\frac{n_{ij.}}{n_{.j.}} \times \frac{n_{i.k}}{n_{..k}}\right)^{\frac{1}{6}} \times \left(\frac{n_{i..}}{n_{...}}\right)^{\frac{1}{3}}$$

$$B_{ijk} = \left(\frac{N_{ijk}}{N_{i.k}}\right)^{\frac{1}{3}} \times \left(\frac{N_{ij.}}{N_{i..}} \times \frac{N_{.jk}}{N_{..k}}\right)^{\frac{1}{6}} \times \left(\frac{N_{.j.}}{N_{...}}\right)^{\frac{1}{3}}, \quad b_{ijk} = \left(\frac{n_{ijk}}{n_{i.k}}\right)^{\frac{1}{3}} \times \left(\frac{n_{ij.}}{n_{i..}} \times \frac{n_{.jk}}{n_{..k}}\right)^{\frac{1}{6}} \times \left(\frac{n_{.j.}}{n_{...}}\right)^{\frac{1}{3}}$$

$$C_{ijk} = \left(\frac{N_{ijk}}{N_{ij.}}\right)^{\frac{1}{3}} \times \left(\frac{N_{i.k}}{N_{i..}} \times \frac{N_{.jk}}{N_{.j.}}\right)^{\frac{1}{6}} \times \left(\frac{N_{..k}}{N_{...}}\right)^{\frac{1}{3}}, \quad c_{ijk} = \left(\frac{n_{ijk}}{n_{ij.}}\right)^{\frac{1}{3}} \times \left(\frac{n_{i.k}}{n_{i..}} \times \frac{n_{.jk}}{n_{.j.}}\right)^{\frac{1}{6}} \times \left(\frac{n_{..k}}{n_{...}}\right)^{\frac{1}{3}}$$

References

Alvira-Hammond, M. (2019). *Hispanic women are helping drive the recent decline in the US fertility rate*. National Research Center on Hispanic Children and Families.

Bongaarts, J., & Feeney, G. (1998). On the quantum and tempo of fertility. *Population and Development Review, 24*(2), 271. https://doi.org/10.2307/2807974

Brand, J. E., & Davis, D. (2011). The impact of college education on fertility: Evidence for heterogeneous effects. *Demography, 48*(3), 863–887. https://doi.org/10.1007/s13524-011-0034-3

Cai, Y., & Morgan, S. P. (2019). Persistent low fertility among the East Asia descendants in the United States: Perspectives and implications. *China Population and Development Studies, 2*(4), 384–400. https://doi.org/10.1007/s42379-019-00024-7

Canudas Romo, V. (2003). *Decomposition methods in demography*. Rozenberg.

Capps, R., Gelatt, J., Ruiz Soto, A. G., & Van Hook, J. (2020). *Unauthorized immigrants in the United States: Stable numbers, changing origins*, (December), 23. https://www.migrationpolicy.org/sites/default/files/publications/mpi-unauthorized-immigrants-stablenumbers-changingorigins_final.pdf

Castro Torres, A. F., & Parrado, E. A. (2022). Nativity differentials in first births in the United States: Patterns by race and ethnicity. *Demographic Research, 46*, 37–64. https://doi.org/10.4054/DemRes.2022.46.2

Das Gupta, P. (1993). *Standardization and decomposition of rates: A user's manual* (p. 145). U.S. Department of Commerce, Economics and Statistics Administration, Bureau of the Census.

Das Gupta, P. (1994). Standardization and decomposition of rates from cross-classified data. *Genus*, 171–196.

DeLeire, T., Lopoo, L. M., & Simon, K. I. (2011). Medicaid expansions and fertility in the United States. *Demography, 48*(2), 725–747. https://doi.org/10.1007/s13524-011-0031-6

DeLeone, F. Y., Lichter, D. T., & Strawderman, R. L. (2009). Decomposing trends in nonmarital fertility among Latinas. *Perspectives on Sexual and Reproductive Health, 41*(3), 166–172. https://doi.org/10.1363/4116609

Dickerson, C., & Addario, L. (2020, November 22). Undocumented and pregnant: Why women are afraid to get prenatal care. *The New York Times*. https://www.nytimes.com/2020/11/22/us/undocumented-immigrants-pregnant-prenatal.html. Accessed 17 Nov 2022.

Driscoll, A. K., & Valenzuela, C. P. (2022). Maternal characteristics and infant outcomes of women born in and outside the United States: United States, 2020. *Vital and Health Statistics Series, 3*(48), 1–6. https://stacks.cdc.gov/view/cdc/116002

Ennis, S. R., Ríos-Vargas, M., & Albert, N. G. (2011). *The hispanic population: 2010*. US Department of Commerce, economics and statistics administration, US ....

Ford, K. (1990). Duration of residence in the United States and the fertility of U.S. immigrants. *International Migration Review, 24*(1), 34–68. https://doi.org/10.1177/019791839002400102

García, I. (2020). Cultural insights for planners: Understanding the terms Hispanic, Latino, and Latinx. *Journal of the American Planning Association, 86*(4), 393–402. https://doi.org/10.1080/01944363.2020.1758191

Gonzalez-Barrera, A. (2015, November 19). More Mexicans Leaving Than Coming to the U.S. *Pew Research Center's Hispanic Trends Project*. https://www.pewresearch.org/hispanic/2015/11/19/more-mexicans-leaving-than-coming-to-the-u-s/. Accessed 28 Mar 2022.

Hamilton, B. (2021). *Total fertility rates, by maternal educational attainment and race and Hispanic origin: United States, 2019*. National Center for Health Statistics. https://doi.org/10.15620/cdc:105234

Hayford, S. R., Guzzo, K. B., & Smock, P. J. (2014). The decoupling of marriage and parenthood? Trends in the timing of marital first births, 1945-2002. *Journal of Marriage and the Family, 76*(3), 520–538. https://doi.org/10.1111/jomf.12114

Ju, D. H. (2022). *A portrait of partnership statuses in the United States between 1990 and 2017*. Center for Latin American, Caribbean and Latino Studies at the CUNY Graduate Center.

Kearney, M. S., Levine, P. B., & Pardue, L. (2022). The puzzle of falling US birth rates since the great recession. *Journal of Economic Perspectives, 36*(1), 151–176. https://doi.org/10.1257/jep.36.1.151

Kohler, H.-P., & Ortega, J. A. (2002). Tempo-adjusted period parity progression measures, fertility postponement and completed cohort fertility. *Demographic Research, 6*, 91–144. https://doi.org/10.4054/DemRes.2002.6.6

Landale, N. S., Oropesa, R. S., & Gorman, B. K. (2000). Migration and infant death: assimilation or selective migration among puerto ricans? *American Sociological Review, 65*(6), 888–909. https://doi.org/10.2307/2657518

Lichter, D. T., Johnson, K. M., Turner, R. N., & Churilla, A. (2012). Hispanic assimilation and fertility in new U.S. destinations. *International Migration Review, 46*(4), 767–791. https://doi.org/10.1111/imre.12000

Livingston, G. (2016). *Births outside of marriage decline for immigrant women.* Washington D.C. https://www.pewsocialtrends.org/2016/10/26/fertility-methodology/

Livingston, G. (2019). *Hispanic women no longer account for the majority of immigrant births in the U.S.* Pew Research Center. https://pewrsr.ch/2YzvLa8

Lopez, M. H., Krogstad, J. M., & Passel, J. S. (2022). Who is Hispanic? *Pew Research Center.* https://www.pewresearch.org/fact-tank/2022/09/15/who-is-hispanic/. Accessed 18 Nov 2022.

Martin, J., Hamilton, B., Sutton, P., Ventura, S., Menacker, F., & Munson, M. (2005). *Births: Final Data for 2003.* National Center for Health Statistics (U.S.). https://www.cdc.gov/nchs/data/nvsr/nvsr54/nvsr54_02.pdf. Accessed 7 Mar 2022.

National Center for Health Statistics. (2012). *Intercensal estimates of the resident population of the United States for July 1, 2000-July 1, 2009, by year, county, single-year of age (0, 1, 2, …, 85 years and over), bridged race, Hispanic origin, and sex.* Prepared under a collaborative arrangement with the U.S. Census Bureau. Available from: http://www.cdc.gov/nchs/nvss/bridged_race.htm as of October 26, 2012, following release by the U.S. Census Bureau of the revised unbridged intercensal estimates by 5-year age group on October 9, 2012.

National Center for Health Statistics. (2021). Vintage 2020 postcensal estimates of the resident population of the United States (April 1, 2010, July 1, 2010-July 1, 2020), by year, county, single-year of age (0, 1, 2, …, 85 years and over), bridged race, Hispanic origin, and sex. Prepared under a collaborative arrangement with the U.S. Census Bureau. Available from: http://www.cdc.gov/nchs/nvss/bridged_race.htm as of September 22, 2021 following release by the U.S. Census Bureau of the unbridged Vintage 2020 postcensal estimates by 5-year age group on June 17, 2021.

Palmer, M. (2020). Does publicly subsidized health insurance affect the birth rate? *Southern Economic Journal, 87*(1), 70–121. https://doi.org/10.1002/soej.12436

Parrado, E. A. (2011). How high is Hispanic/Mexican fertility in the United States? Immigration and tempo considerations. *Demography, 48*(3), 1059–1080. https://doi.org/10.1007/s13524-011-0045-0

Parrado, E. A., & Flippen, C. A. (2012). Hispanic fertility, immigration, and race in the twenty-first century. *Race and Social Problems, 4*(1), 18–30. https://doi.org/10.1007/s12552-012-9063-9

Parrado, E. A., & Morgan, S. P. (2008). Intergenerational fertility among Hispanic women: New evidence of immigrant assimilation. *Demography, 45*(3), 651–671. https://doi.org/10.1353/dem.0.0023

Passel, J., & D'Vera, C. (2018). *U.S. unauthorized immigrant Total dips to lowest level in a decade.* Pew Research Center. https://www.pewresearch.org/hispanic/wp-content/uploads/sites/5/2019/03/Pew-Research-Center_2018-11-27_U-S-Unauthorized-Immigrants-Total-Dips_Updated-2019-06-25.pdf

Pew Research Center. (2011). *The Mexican-American boom: Births overtake immigration.* https://www.pewresearch.org/hispanic/2011/07/14/the-mexican-american-boom-brbirths-overtake-immigration/

Pew Research Center. (2015). *More Mexicans leaving than coming to the US.* Washington D.C.

Ruggles, S., Flood, S., Goeken, R., Schouweiler, M., & Sobek, M. (2022). *IPUMS USA: Version 12.0.* IPUMS. https://doi.org/10.18128/D010.V12.0

Schoen, R. (2004). Timing effects and the interpretation of period fertility. *Demography, 41*(4), 801–819. https://doi.org/10.1353/dem.2004.0036

Schoen, R. (2006). Insights from parity status life tables for the 20th century U.S. *Social Science Research, 35*(1), 29–39. https://doi.org/10.1016/j.ssresearch.2004.06.002

Schoen, R. (2022). Relating period and cohort fertility. *Demography, 59*(3), 877–894. https://doi.org/10.1215/00703370-9936991

Smith, R. D. (2019). Marital fertility patterns and nonmarital birth ratios: An integrated approach. *Genus, 75*(1), 9. https://doi.org/10.1186/s41118-019-0056-z

Smith, H. L., Morgan, S. P., & Koropeckyj-Cox, T. (1996). A decomposition of trends in the nonmarital fertility ratios of blacks and whites in the United States, 1960–1992. *Demography, 33*(2), 141–151. https://doi.org/10.2307/2061868

Smock, P. J., & Schwartz, C. R. (2020). The demography of families: A review of patterns and change. *Journal of Marriage and Family, 82*(1), 9–34. https://doi.org/10.1111/jomf.12612

Sutton, P. D., & Matthews, T. J. (2006). *Birth and fertility rates by Hispanic origin subgroups: United States, 1990 and 2000.* (No. 21 (57)). National Center for Health Statistics.

Sweeney, M. M., & Raley, R. K. (2014). Race, ethnicity, and the changing context of childbearing in the United States. *Annual Review of Sociology, 40*(1), 539–558. https://doi.org/10.1146/annurev-soc-071913-043342

U.S. Census Bureau. (2022). *Comparing ACS Data.* https://www.census.gov/programs-surveys/acs/guidance/comparing-acs-data.html

U.S. Census Bureau, Population Division. (2022). *Population and Housing Unit Estimates, Schedule.* https://www.census.gov/programs-surveys/popest/about/schedule.html

Valliant, R., & Dever, J. A. (2018). *Survey weights: A step-by-step guide to calculation* (1st ed.). Stata Press, A Stata Press Publication, StataCorp LLC.

Van Hook, J., Bean, F. D., Bachmeier, J. D., & Tucker, C. (2014). Recent trends in coverage of the Mexican-born population of the United States: Results from applying multiple methods across time. *Demography, 51*(2), 699–726. https://doi.org/10.1007/s13524-014-0280-2

Van Hook, J., Morse, A., Capps, R., & Gelatt, J. (2021). Uncertainty about the size of the unauthorized foreign-born population in the United States. *Demography, 58*(6), 2315–2336. https://doi.org/10.1215/00703370-9491801

Whelpton, P. K. (1946). Reproduction rates adjusted for age, parity, fecundity, and marriage. *Journal of the American Statistical Association, 41*(236), 501–516. https://doi.org/10.1080/01621459.1946.10501893

Zavodny, M., & Bitler, M. P. (2010). The effect of Medicaid eligibility expansions on fertility. *Social Science & Medicine, 71*(5), 918–924. https://doi.org/10.1016/j.socscimed.2010.05.046

Part III
Case Studies of Family Transformation

Chapter 9
The Gender War and the Rise of Anti-family Sentiments in South Korea

Joeun Kim

9.1 Introduction

The emergence of "lowest-low fertility" (total fertility rates at or below 1.3) and a rapid rise in never marrying—what some commentators have called a "crisis of family"—in multiple industrialized countries have generated great interest among demographers and family researchers (Kohler et al., 2002; Lesthaeghe, 2010). Some European scholars expected a recovery of union formation and fertility rates to near-replacement level across postindustrial countries (Esping-Andersen & Billari, 2015; Goldstein et al., 2009). Union formation and fertility rates in most very low-fertility societies have not rebounded as expected, however. South Korea (Korea, hereafter) is particularly interesting. Korea continues to record one of the most-sustained lowest-low fertility rates in the world (Kim & Luke, 2020). In recent years, total fertility rates in Korea dropped even further below 1.0 since 2017, with no sign of recovery (World Bank, 2019).

At the heart of this phenomenon is the recent increase in the number of young adults eschewing marriage in Korea. In Korea, marriage was almost universal until the 1990s. Since then, the proportion of men and women never married by age 50 has increased more than 20-fold (see Fig. 9.1). According to the population projections, never marrying will substantially increase in the coming decades (see Fig. 9.1). In contrast to Western countries, in Korea, never marrying almost always results in a lifetime childlessness, as nonmarital childbearing in Korea is rare (Raymo et al. 2015). Since the 1970s, the proportion of nonmarital childbirths has remained at around 2%, significantly lower than the OECD average of 42% (OECD, 2022).

J. Kim (✉)
KDI School of Public Policy and Management, Sejong City, South Korea
e-mail: joeunkim@kdischool.ac.kr

R. Schoen (ed.), *The Demography of Transforming Families*, The Springer Series on Demographic Methods and Population Analysis 56,
https://doi.org/10.1007/978-3-031-29666-6_9

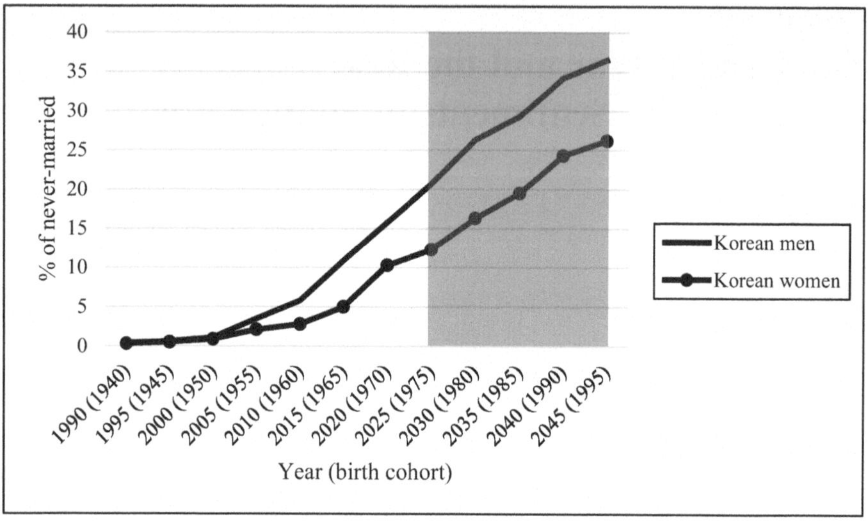

Fig. 9.1 The proportion of never-married men and women by age 50 in Korea, 1990–2045. *Note*. Shaded area indicates projected figures. (*Source*: Official Statistics Korea)

This chapter attributes the recent rise in anti-family sentiments among young adults to the gender war in Korea. Schoen (2010) have argued that the ideological divergence between men and women over gender issues may be an important force undermining family formation in a postindustrial context. Compared to women, men have been slow—even reluctant—to fully embrace gender egalitarian ideals, leading to incompatible ideas about gender and sometimes to conflict (Schoen, 2010; Schoen & Hargens, 2020, p. 11). Building on this perspective, I argue that, on the one hand, public awareness of entrenched gender inequality and ideological support for gender equality has recently increased, particularly among young women in Korea. On the other hand, there has been backlash against feminism among young men online and offline, resulting in a dramatic ideological clash between men and women. As such, many young women are choosing to forgo marriage and parenthood altogether.

I identify an ideological battle between men and women that has played out online in Korea, which then spilled over into the mainstream media, in the last 5 years. This "gender war" has increased public interest and awareness of both deep-seated misogyny and feminism in Korea. The war first received significant public attention in 2015 with feminists' outcries over the online grievances and slurs against young Korean women being voiced by a small group of right-wing men and other examples of entrenched misogyny in society. The online war intensified in May 2016, when a young woman was stabbed to death in public. In what became known as the "Gangnam Murder," her male killer justified the act based on his hatred of women and how they always looked down on him. With this murder, the gender war became a nationwide debate that spilled over from online forums into mainstream media and public discourse.

I take advantage of the timing of the Gangnam Murder (May 2016) to examine trends in three focal variables before and after the event. First, using a novel combination of archival and internet data, I am the first (to my knowledge) to explicitly examine shifts in public discourse about gender issues, as measured by results from Internet searches and mass media coverage of the terms "misogyny" and "feminism." Second, I use survey data from a nationally representative sample to examine trends in egalitarian gender attitudes after 2016. Third, I examine shifts in views about marriage after 2016.

9.2 Background

9.2.1 Uneven Gender Revolution by Gender in South Korea

In South Korea, equality has recently advanced in the public sphere; today, young women in their 20s now achieve higher levels of education and labor force participation than young men of the same age group (KOSIS, 2019). Accordingly, egalitarian gender views that support women's and men's equal participation in work and family has increased over time. The proportion of women and men who believe that women's employment should not be interrupted by family responsibilities such as marriage and childbearing has increased in recent cohorts, as seen in Table 9.1. However, men's embrace of egalitarian attitudes about gender lags behind women's acceptance of gender egalitarian ideals, producing a widening gender gap in gender attitudes among recent cohorts. The majority of young women, including Millennials and Generation Z, support egalitarian gender ideals while less than a majority of men of the same generation remains supportive of egalitarian gender ideals (see Table 9.1).

In addition to men's slow acceptance of egalitarian gender ideals, institutions, norms, and practices in the South Korean family and workplace remain resistant to cultural pressure to fully embrace gender equality. Confucian patriarchal ideology

Table 9.1 Descriptive statistics in egalitarian gender attitudes by gender and by Cohort (1998–2019)

Generation	Women (%)	Men (%)	Gender differences (Women-Men)
Silent generation (born between 1928 and 1945)	35.81	32.45	3.36
Baby-Boomer generation (born between 1946 and 1964)	42.16	36.08	6.08
Generation X (born between 1965 and 1980)	45.05	38.08	6.97
Millennial (born between 1981 and 1996)	59.71	48.30	11.41
Generation Z (born after 1997)	68.26	48.56	19.70

Note: N = 428,488. Egalitarian gender attitudes include support of women's continued employment uninterrupted by familial responsibilities. *Source*: Social Survey (1998–2019)

also continues to underpin family institutions in South Korea (Sung, 2003). Despite greater support for female breadwinning (Park & Lee, 2017), traditional gender norms of motherhood and domestic work remain resilient (Oh, 2018; Raymo et al., 2015). Moreover, marriage in Korea often involves a "marriage package," in which wives care for in-laws in addition to their children and husbands (Bumpass et al., 2009). Despite women's advancements in the public sphere, the gender gap in unpaid labor hours is widest in South Korea among the high-income OCED countries (OCED, 2020). As such, a substantial proportion of women continue to withdraw from employment upon marriage and childbearing (Brinton & Oh, 2019).

South Korea has sustained its lowest-low fertility rates along with a rapid rise in never marrying over two decades. In response to the sustained very low fertility, the South Korean government dramatically expanded public support for parental leave and daycare services. It now provides one of the most generous work-family reconciliation provisions in the world. However, in recent years, South Korea experienced an even more rapid decline in marriage and fertility rates (World Bank, 2019).

To address this puzzle, this study argues that increasing public awareness and egalitarian gender ideals drive further declines in family formation in South Korea, where men and the marriage institution remain persistently patriarchal (Coontz, 2004). Young adults' growing desire for gender equality is at odds with this traditional view of men and the institution of marriage, leading many to forgo marriage altogether. To empirically test this explanation, I identify a distinct cultural event, the "gender war," which has recently expanded public awareness of deep-seated misogyny and gender inequality in South Korea.

9.2.1.1 The Origins and Diffusion of the Gender War in South Korea

Despite its ongoing gender revolution in the public sphere, South Korea has experienced a rise in far-right male dominance and misogyny, especially in online communities, since the early 2000s (Kim, 2018). A group of far-right men began posting online grievances, slurs, and diatribes against young Korean women for being selfish, rude, and materialistic. In this context, the term *Kimchi-nyeo* ("Kimchi woman") became a common slur that then spilled into public discourse. According to Um (2016), *Kimchi-nyeo* refers to a woman who uses her gender to exploit men while demanding gender equality. These women are perceived as materialistic (because they aspire to own luxury goods), selfish (because they do not fulfill the perceived social responsibilities of marriage and childbearing), and sexually promiscuous (because they have no shame about abortions). A 2015 survey showed that 84% of young Korean adults reported exposure to misogynistic content on the Internet, and 94% knew the term *Kimchi-nyeo* (Ahn, 2015).

Although precise sources of the rise in online misogyny are unclear, Kim (2018) interprets this phenomenon as patriarchal backlash against young women gaining economic and political power in Korea. Middle-class-based hegemonic masculinity is increasingly difficult to achieve for many Korean men, whose economic stability

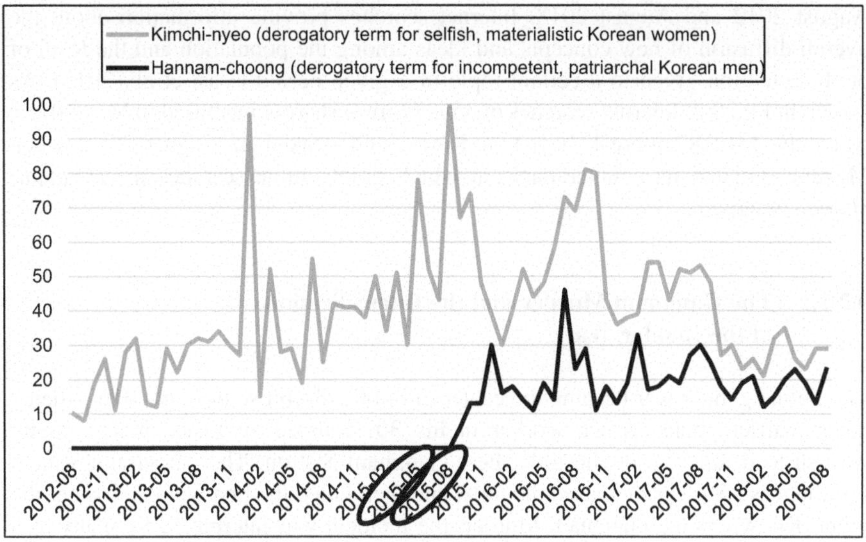

Fig. 9.2 Origins and trajectories of the Gender War. *Note.* The figure shows the relative percentages of Google search volume for "*Kimchi-nyeo*" and "*Hannam-choong*" (in Korean and in South Korea) to the highest number of searches between August 2012 and August 2018. The first MERS outbreak occurred in May 2015; the feminist website Megalia launched in August 2015; and the Gangnam Murder occurred in May 2016. (*Source*: Google Trends)

and prospects have declined over time (Park & Lee, 2017; Shin, 2013). Some men's anxiety over changing gender relations thus converts into misogynistic attacks (Kim, 2018), perhaps in an attempt to control the behaviors and attitudes of women, especially young women, and to reinstate men's hegemonic gender status.

In response to the *Kimchi-nyeo* and other attacks, a feminist online community called "Megalia" openly declared war on misogyny. In May 2015, the Middle East Respiratory Syndrome (MERS) coronavirus outbreak generated enormous fear among Koreans.[1] Misogynistic attacks, particularly those targeting *Kimchi-nyeo*, sharply increased in response to a rumor that two Korean women suspected of testing positive for MERS refused to quarantine and instead went on a shopping trip to Hong Kong. The MERS outbreak reveled deepening misogyny in Korea that, in turn, fueled the online feminist activism of Megalia, in August 2015. Megalia initiated multiple anti-misogyny campaigns, including popularizing a new slur, *Hannam-choong* ("Korean male pest"), to mock the dominant misogynistic attacks using *Kimchi-nyeo* slurs.

Figure 9.2 illustrates the trajectories of this online war. Figure 9.2 shows the popularity of Google searches for *Kimchi-nyeo* and *Hannam-choong* between

[1]MERS is an infectious viral respiratory illness with high mortality rates (35%), causing 186 confirmed cases and 38 deaths between May 2015 and July 2015 in Korea (World Health Organization accessed on December 2022).

August 2012 and August 2018. Internet searches provide information about the overall diffusion of new concepts and ideas among the population and the level of public attention given to a certain topic in a given period (Vasi et al., 2015). As shown in Fig. 9.2, Internet searches of *Kimchi-nyeo* sharply increased in May 2015,[2] when the MERS outbreak began in Korea, and peaked in August 2015, when Megalia initiated its counterattack, at which point online searches for *Hannam-choong* emerged.

9.2.1.2 The Gangnam Murder and the Intensification of the Gender War

The online gender war became the center of public discourse in May 2016, when a never-married male service worker in his 30s stabbed an unacquainted young woman to death in a public toilet near Gangnam Station. The perpetrator waited for hours as six other men used the toilet and then killed the first woman to enter the toilet. Known as the Gangnam Murder, the incident was interpreted by many as a hate crime (Kim, 2021), though police initially denied this claim (e.g., see *The Korea Herald* article titled "Gangnam murder was not a hate crime: police" in 22 May 2016). The assailant stated that he targeted and murdered a woman he had never met out of hatred for all women who "ignored and humiliated him all his life" (Park. "The Reason Why Gangnam Murder is a Female-Hatred Crime." *The Hankyoreh*, 19 May 2015). By revealing the deep-seated misogyny in Korea, I argue, the Gangnam Murder and its aftermath fueled a burgeoning feminist movement.

The Gangnam Murder served as a flashpoint, igniting new public discourse over gender issues in South Korea. First, the randomness of the attack created enormous fear among Korean women, particularly because it occurred in a crowded public area—meaning that any woman anywhere could be a target of violence, not just women in situations of domestic abuse or other dangerous circumstances (Stout, 1991). Second, the murder occurred when tension over gender issues had been rising and thus perpetuated and increased public contentiousness over issues of misogyny and feminism in South Korea.

This study provides novel quantitative evidence showing how the gender war affected public awareness in South Korea. I first show how the murder brought gender issues into sharp focus as a public issue. I measured the salience of gender issues in public discourse using results from Internet searches and mass media coverage of the terms "misogyny" and "feminism." As previously mentioned, Internet searches are valuable measures of issue salience and disagreement among populations. Additionally, mass media coverage of certain issues provides important ways for issues to "enter the public sphere" (Oliver & Myers, 2003). Because multiple issues compete for public attention, events (e.g., Gangnam Murder)

[2] The prior surge in searches of *Kimchi-nyeo* in December 2013 coincides with the establishment of another right-wing male-dominant online community, sukkot ("male")-dot-com in Korea.

generally show a spike in attention in the short term, which diminishes over time. However, I also argue that the Gangnam Murder sparked longer-term effects. I therefore propose the following hypotheses:

Hypothesis 1. Online searches and mass media coverage of the Gangnam Murder spiked immediately after the event and quickly diminished thereafter.
Hypothesis 2a. Public attention and mass media coverage of the terms *misogyny* and *feminism* increased after the Gangnam Murder.
Hypothesis 2b. Public attention and mass media coverage of the terms *misogyny* and *feminism* remained high after the Gangnam Murder.

Whether increased public attention over gender contention leads to more conservative or more progressive gender ideology remains an empirical question. If the Gangnam Murder created an intense public and media focus on misogyny and feminism, topics that have been largely ignored by the public, it is plausible that the public became more cognizant of gender inequality in Korea and progressed toward greater support for gender equality. Hypothesis 3 is formulated as follows:

Hypothesis 3. Egalitarian gender attitudes increased after the Gangnam Murder.

Finally, I argue that the rise of new feminist awareness and egalitarian attitudes will be associated with rising anti-family sentiments. Hypotheses 4 and 5 are thus formulated as follows:

Hypothesis 4. Negative attitudes toward marriage increased after the Gangnam Murder.
Hypothesis 5. Negative intentions toward marriage increased after the Gangnam Murder.

9.3 Analytical Approach and Data

The main analytical goal of this study was to examine associations between the timing of the Gangnam Murder and trends in three key dependent variables: public discourse over gender issues, trends in egalitarian gender attitudes, and trends in marital attitudes. I conducted three separate sets of analyses using varying data sources. First, I explored how the murder influenced the public discourse on gender issues in South Korea by analyzing Internet searches and mass media coverage of "misogyny" and "feminism" separately. I obtained Internet search data from Google Trends, which provides data on the relative frequency of Google search terms across time and geographical units. I searched for the terms "Gangnam Murder," "misogyny," and "feminism" simultaneously but individually in Korean within the geographic region of South Korea between August 2012 and August 2018. I also looked at news article archives available through the Factiva platform, one of the largest databases of free and licensed news articles in the world, containing millions of news articles from almost all countries in the last 35 years. I searched for and counted all

Korean language articles from August 2012 to August 2018 in Factiva containing the terms "Gangnam murder," "misogyny," or "feminism." In total, I extracted 3258 articles from 48 different news sources.

Second, I examined key trends in gender attitudes before and after the Gangnam Murder for women and men, separately. I use data from the Social Survey in Korea from 1998 to 2019. This large, cross-sectional, biannual questionnaire surveys a nationally representative sample of Koreans over 13 years old. Approximately 39,000 individuals were interviewed in each survey, totaling 428,488 respondents for the study period. Because the entire population could have learned about the Gangnam Murder through online and media discussion, the sample of this study includes the entire population. The survey asked respondents over age 16, "What is the most ideal work-family arrangement for women?" Respondents were asked to choose one "most ideal work-family arrangement for women" out of six options. The six options were: "Women should not work and just focus on family work"; "Women should work until marriage"; "Women should work until the first birth"; "Women should work after childrearing"; "Women should work before the first birth and after childrearing"; and "Women's employment should continue regardless of marriage, childbearing, and childrearing." Egalitarian gender attitudes were coded as dichotomous variable, indicating one if respondents agreed that "Women's employment should continue regardless of marriage, childbearing, and childrearing," and zero for the remaining responses, which suggest support for women's domestic duties over market work.

I measured trends in egalitarian attitudes by estimating logistic regression models with a dichotomous variable of survey year after 2016 and a linear spline of survey year after 2016, accounting for the period after the Gangnam Murder, as the key independent variable, controlling for time trends and other variables. The first independent variable of the survey year after 2016 estimates the change in gender attitudes in 2016. The second independent variable of a linear spline of survey year after 2016 shows the change in the slope in gender attitudes after 2016. The linear spline allows the slope of the survey year variable to take on different values during the given period (e.g., the spline for after survey year 2016 is coded 0 for before 2016 and then increased by 1 for each subsequent survey year, such that 2017 = 2, 2019 = 3). In addition to linear spline of survey year after 2016, I include linear spline for surveys from 2009–2015 to account for a period when online misogyny emerged.

I included several control variables both on the individual and national levels. As for the individual-level controls, I included respondents' generation codes as five categories, Silent (born 1928–1945), Baby Boomer (born 1946–1964), X (born 1965–1980), Millennial (born 1981–1996), and Z (born 1997 and later). I also included education level (ever attended 4-year university or not[3]), marital status

[3]Given that the sample includes a substantial proportion of young adults who are still in college, I included enrollment of 4-year university rather than graduation of 4-year university as a proxy for educational level.

(ever married or not), and place of residence (living in Seoul vs. non-Seoul area). The national-level controls are important correlates of gender attitudes. These included GDP, men's unemployment rates, female college education rates, and the proportion of young adults of those aged 20–44. All variables are reported at each year. Information for these national-level controls are from Korean Statistical Information Service (https://kosis.kr/index/index.do). All variables are reported at each year.

Last, I examined trends in attitudes toward marriage and marital intentions before and after the Gangnam Murder for women and men, separately. I use data from the National Survey on Fertility and Family Health and Welfare from 2005 to 2018. This is a cross-sectional, triannual survey on a nationally representative sample of Koreans in childbearing age (from 20 to 44). The survey asked never-married respondents on their attitudes and intentions toward marriage. Regarding attitudes toward marriage, the survey asked respondents to choose one option out of five choices based on the question "What do you think of marriage?". Options include: (1) Must marry, (2) Better to marry, (3) It makes no difference whether you marry or not, (4) Better not to marry, (5) Don't know. I created a dummy variable indicating negative attitudes toward marriage if respondents chose "Better not to marry" over others. Additionally, the survey asked respondents "Do you intend to marry in the future?". I also created a dummy variable indicating negative intentions to marry if respondent reported "No, I have no intention to marry in the future" over other options (including "Yes," "Don't know," and "Haven't decided").

I included several control variables: (a) respondents' age as three categories (1. 20–29 years old, 2. 30–39 years old, and 3. 40–44 years old); (b) education level (ever attended 4-year university); (c) employment status; and (d) place of residence (living in Seoul vs. non-Seoul area).

9.4 Results

9.4.1 *Gangnam Murder's Influence on Public Discourse About Gender Issues*

Figure 9.3 shows trends in Google searches for the key terms "Gangnam (station) murder," "misogyny," and "feminism" from August 2012 to August 2018 in the Korean language and in the geographical unit of South Korea. Searches for "Gangnam murder" skyrocketed in May 2016, the month of the murder, accounting for almost 65% of the highest value of overall public attention to gender issues.[4] Searches for "misogyny" and "feminism" also increased notably in the month of the murder.

[4]In Fig. 9.2, the highest number of searches between August 2012 and August 2018 includes "feminism" in June 2018. This timing coincides with the intensification of the #MeToo movement.

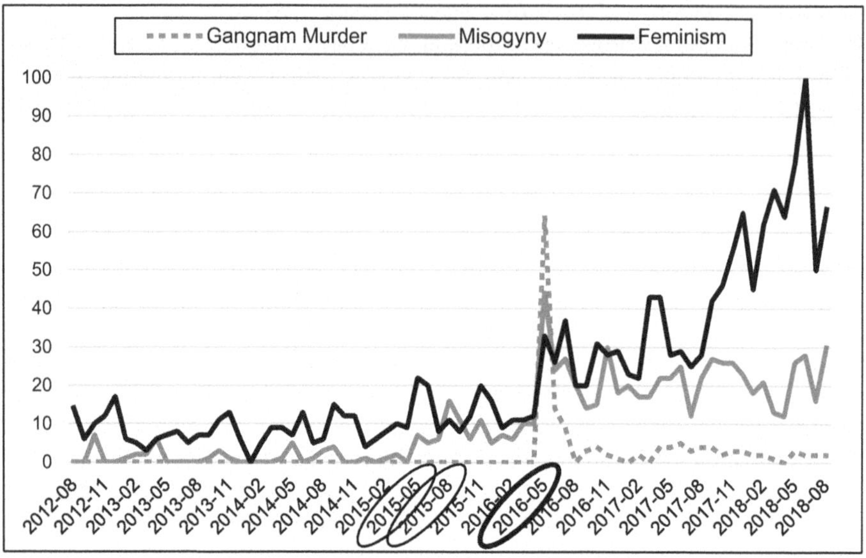

Fig. 9.3 Gangnam murder's influence on online public attention. *Note:* The figure shows the percentage of Google searches for "Gangnam (station) murder," "misogyny," and "feminism," relative to the highest number of searches between August 2012 and August 2018. The first MERS outbreak occurred in May 2015; the feminist website Megalia launched in August 2015; and the Gangnam Murder occurred in May 2016. (*Source*: Google Trends)

Figure 9.3 also illustrates trends in overall public attention to gender issues before and after the Gangnam murder. For example, although searches for "Gangnam murder" quickly declined within a month of the event, which is consistent with the literature showing that multiple issues compete for public attention (Vasi et al., 2015), searches for "misogyny" and "feminism" remained relatively high after sharp increases in the month of the murder and compared to search levels before the murder. Specifically, after May 2016, searches for "Gangnam murder" remained at or below 5% of the highest searches. Searches for "misogyny" fluctuated but remained above 10%, with no sign of decline until the last observation period (August 2018). Prior to the Gangnam Murder, searches for "misogyny" consistently fell below 5% of the highest search volume, except in May 2015, when misogynistic attacks intensified during the MERS outbreak in Korea. Likewise, searches for "feminism" were around 10% of the highest search volume and similarly increased after May 2015. Overall, the results suggest that the Gangnam Murder helped diffuse these gender issues into the public discourse in Korea in the short and long term.

Figure 9.4 shows the number of newspaper articles that mention "Gangnam Murder," "misogyny," or "feminism" per month in Korea between August 2012 and August 2018. The results are similar to those shown in Fig. 9.3 for online searches: mentions of these terms in mass media coverage rose sharply in the month of the Gangnam Murder. More than 350 newspaper articles mentioned the Gangnam Murder in May 2016, indicating substantial public attention, which declined in

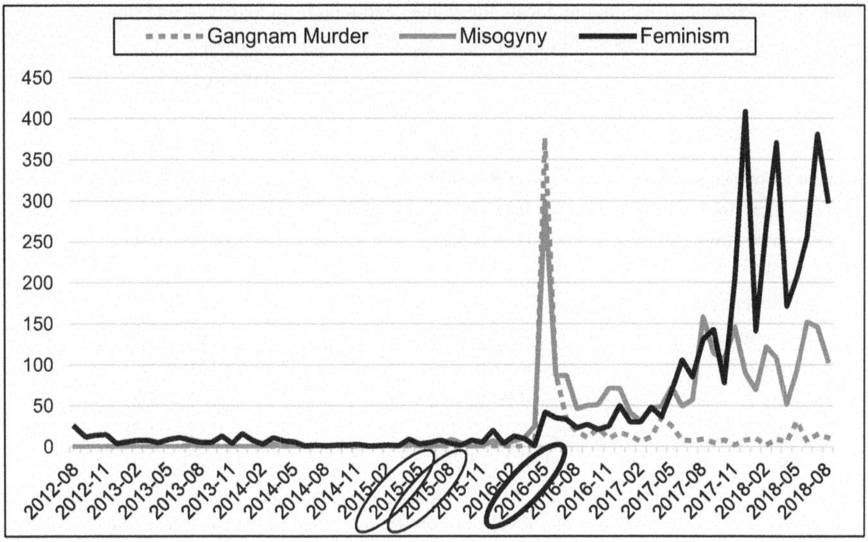

Fig. 9.4 Gangnam murder's influence on mass media coverage. *Note:* The figure shows the number of newspaper articles that mentioned "Gangnam Murder," "misogyny," or "feminism" separately between August 2012 and August 2018. (*Source*: Factiva (Dow Jones). The first MERS outbreak occurred in May 2015; the feminist website Megalia launched in August 2015; and the Gangnam Murder occurred in May 2016)

subsequent months. Mentions of "misogyny" also sharply increased in May 2016. Virtually no newspaper article mentioned misogyny before the Gangnam Murder, whereas nearly 300 articles discussed it in May 2016. Similarly, mentions of "feminism" increased in the same month, though not as many as for "Gangnam Murder" or "misogyny." Also consistent with the findings from Fig. 9.3, mass media coverage of "misogyny" and "feminism" did not decrease as rapidly as coverage of "Gangnam Murder." Mentions of "misogyny" declined dramatically in the months after May 2016, but a moderately high number of articles (50–150 per month) continued to mention this term. Similar to online public attention to feminism, which increased even further after the Gangnam Murder, mass media coverage of "feminism" increased over time. This persistent increase may suggest a shift in public discourse and increased attention to the topics of misogyny and feminism.

9.4.2 Gender Attitudes After the Gangnam Murder

Table 9.2 presents the results of a logistic regression model estimating trends in egalitarian gender attitudes for women and men, separately, controlling for covariates. For women, Model 1 shows a positive (0.06) and significant trend in the main annual trend in egalitarian attitudes, which suggests an overall increase in

Table 9.2 Estimates of egalitarian ideals for women and men from logistic regression

	Model 1: Women		Model 2: Men	
	B (se)		B (se)	
Trends				
Survey year	0.06 (0.001)	***	0.07 (0.002)	***
Year slope (knot 2009)	−0.09 (0.003)	***	−0.07 (0.004)	***
Year after 2016	0.18 (0.27)	***	0.12 (0.03)	***
Year slope (knot 2016)	0.08 (0.01)	***	0.06 (0.01)	***
Generation				
Silent generation				
Baby Boomers	0.22 (0.01)	***	0.07 (0.02)	***
Generation X	0.34 (0.01)	***	0.20 (0.02)	***
Millennials	0.90 (0.02)	***	0.48 (0.02)	***
Generation Z	1.19 (0.03)	***	0.42 (0.03)	***
Intercept	−120.41 (3.20)	***	−136.30 (3.55)	***

Note: N = 428,488. Models include both individual-level (generation, educational, marital status, and place of residents) and national-level controls (men's unemployment rates, female college education, GDP and the proportion of young adults [aged 20–44]). Egalitarian ideals include support of women's continued employment uninterrupted by familial responsibilities. *Source*: Social Survey (1998–2019)

egalitarian support for women over time (between 1998 and 2019). Despite an overall rising trend in egalitarian attitudes, the slope of egalitarian ideals between 2009 and 2015 is negative (−0.09) and significant, suggesting a downward trend in egalitarian attitudes after the 2009 survey. The coefficient for the year after 2016 presents the predicted change that occurs in 2016. The coefficient is positive and significant (0.18), suggesting the occurrence of a jump in egalitarian attitudes by 0.18 in 2016 (in this case, in the 2017 survey). Additionally, the second slope after 2016, which includes the surveys conducted after the Gangnam Murder, is positive (0.08), indicating a rebounding trend toward more egalitarian attitudes. Additionally, the coefficient size for the linear spline for the period after 2016 is substantial (0.08), suggesting a full recovery from the slightly downward trend after 2009 and further support for egalitarian gender ideals after 2016.

Figure 9.5 reports the predicted values of egalitarian gender attitudes for women by generation before and after 2016. Overall, Fig. 9.5 shows that support for egalitarian gender attitudes increased notably after 2016 across all generations. Despite the increase after 2016, less than half of women of the older generations, including the Silent generation and Baby Boomers, believe that women's employment should not be interrupted by domestic responsibilities. On the other hand, the majority of women in the younger generation, including Millennials and Generation Z, have supported egalitarian gender attitudes since early 2000. The proportion of women of the younger generation who support egalitarian gender ideals increased further after 2016 reaching almost 65% for Millennials and 70% for Generation Z in 2019.

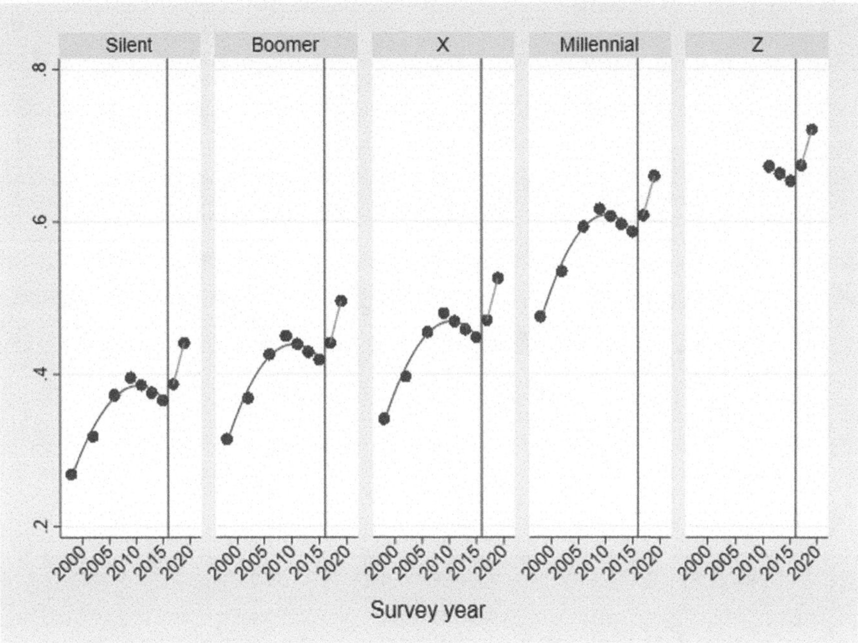

Fig. 9.5 Predicted values of egalitarian gender attitudes by generation before and after 2016, Korean Women

Model 2 in Table 9.2 shows the results for men. The main annual trend in egalitarian attitudes is positive (0.07) and significant, suggesting increased support for egalitarian attitudes among men over time. The slope of egalitarian attitudes after 2009 for men is negative (−0.07) and significant, suggesting a downward trend in egalitarian support for men after 2009. However, similar to the results for women, men's support for egalitarian attitudes increased considerably in 2016, by approximately 0.06 point. In addition, as indicated by the positive coefficient of the year slope after 2016, trends in egalitarian attitudes became positive again after 2016. Overall, Table 9.2 shows the notable rise of egalitarian attitudes after 2016, the year when the Gangnam Murder occurred.

Figure 9.6 shows the predicted values of egalitarian gender attitudes for men by generation before and after 2016. Men's support for egalitarian gender attitudes increased substantially after 2016. Similar to the results of women, the majority of men of the older generation, including the Silent generation and Baby Boomers, are unsupportive of egalitarian gender attitudes even after 2016. Interestingly, unlike women, prior to 2016, the majority of men of the younger generation, including Millennials and Generation Z, did not support the idea that women's employment should continue regardless of their domestic responsibilities. This mindset changed after 2016. Although less than women, almost 55% of men of the younger generation (Millennials and Generation Z) expressed egalitarian gender attitudes in 2019.

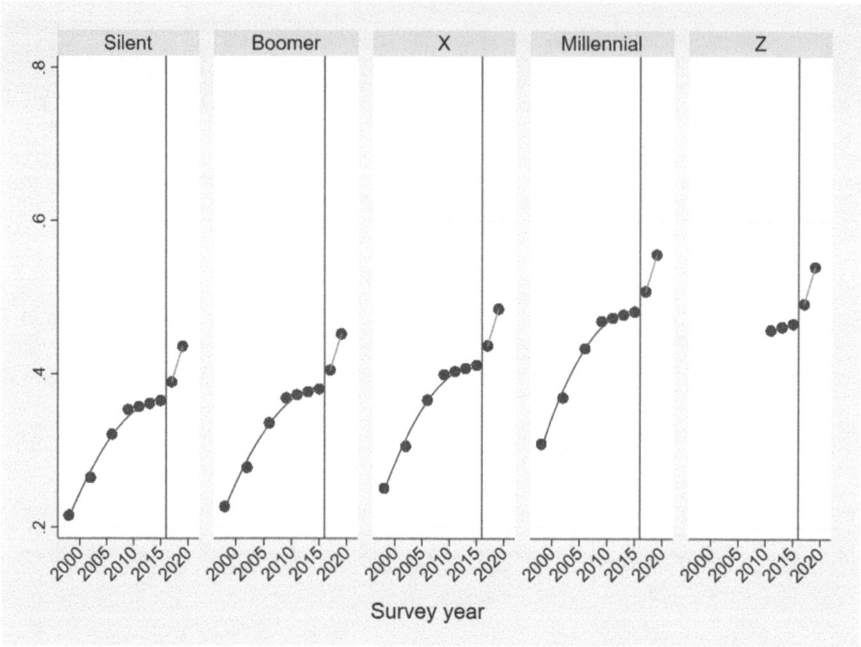

Fig. 9.6 Predicted values of egalitarian gender attitudes by generation before and after 2016, Korean Men

9.4.3 Attitudes and Intentions Toward Marriage After the Gangnam Murder

Table 9.3 displays the results of a logistic regression model that predicted negative attitudes toward marriage ("It is better not to marry") among never-married women and men in South Korea (ages 20–44). Model 1 in Table 9.3 indicates that women's hostile attitudes toward marriage increased by 0.02 per year between 2006 and 2018. The coefficient for "year slope after 2016" is 0.08, indicating that hostile attitudes toward marriage rose by 0.10 percentage points per year after 2016. Model 2 in Table 9.3 depicts comparable trends in men's and women's marital attitudes. From 2005 to 2018, negative attitudes toward marriage increased by a logarithmic rate of 0.02 per year. Although less dramatic than the changes in women's attitudes toward marriage, the increase in men's negative attitudes since the 2016 survey is notable. The log odds of slope after 2016 is 0.04, indicating that negative attitudes toward marriage increased by 0.04 per year after 2016.

Table 9.4 presents the results of a logistic regression model that predicts negative marital intentions ("I have no intentions to marry in the future") among never-married women and men (aged 20–44). Model 1 in Table 9.4 demonstrates that never-married women's desire to avoid marriage increased over time. Table 9.4 shows that negative marital intentions among women have increased steadily by an

Table 9.3 Estimates of negative attitudes toward marriage for never-married women and never-married men from logistic regression

	Model 1: Women		Model 2: Men	
	B (se)		B (se)	
Trends				
Survey year	0.02 (0.01)	*	0.02 (0.01)	*
Year slope (knot 2009)	0.01 (0.03)		0.01 (0.04)	
Year after 2016	0.28 (0.04)	***	0.13 (0.03)	***
Year slope (knot 2016)	0.08 (0.01)	***	0.04 (0.01)	***
Age group				
20–29				
30–39	−0.38 (0.31)		0.007 (0.20)	
40–44	0.56 (0.20)	**	0.46 (0.20)	**
Intercept	−2.65 (3.20)	***	−1.83 (0.09)	***

Note: N = 9507. Models include individual-level (age, educational, and place of residents). Negative attitudes toward marriage include those reporting "It is better not to marry." *Source*: The National Survey on Fertility and Family Health and Welfare (2005–2018)

Table 9.4 Estimates of negative intentions to marry for never-married women and never-married men from logistic regression

	Model 1: Women		Model 2: Men	
	B (se)		B (se)	
Trends				
Survey year	0.02 (0.01)	*	0.02 (0.01)	*
Year slope (knot 2009)	0.05 (0.02)	**	0.03 (0.01)	**
Year after 2016	0.41 (0.07)	***	0.16 (0.05)	**
Year slope (knot 2016)	0.10 (0.03)	***	0.04 (0.02)	**
Age group				
20–29				
30–39	0.98 (0.14)	***	0.92 (0.17)	***
40–44	1.96 (0.20)	***	1.77 (0.26)	**
Intercept	−2.53 (0.10)	***	−2.63 (0.11)	***

Note: N = 9507. Models include individual-level (age, educational, and place of residents). Negative marital intentions those who reported having no intentions to marry in the future. *Source*: The National Survey on Fertility and Family Health and Welfare (2005–2018)

average of 0.02 points per year. The coefficient for "year after 2016" is 0.41, indicating a surge in women's negative marriage intentions in 2016. After 2016, trends toward negative marital intentions accelerate: women's intentions to eschew marriage increased by 0.10% per year following 2016. Similarly, Model 2 in Table 9.4 indicates that men's negative intentions to marry increased over time, particularly after 2016. Adjusting for overall rising trends in marital disinterest, male marital disinterest increased by 0.16% in 2016. Moreover, the rise in unfavorable marital intentions is notable and dramatic even after 2016.

Overall, Table 9.3 supports hypothesis 4, which predicts an increase in hostile attitudes toward marriage. In addition, Table 9.4 supports hypothesis 5, which predicts an increase in hostile intentions toward marriage.

9.5 Discussion

Some postindustrial regions have experienced rapid declines in marriage and fertility rates, leading to what some call a "crisis of family" (Brinton & Lee, 2016). South Korea is a country with one of the most-sustained lowest-low fertility rates in the world as well as a recent dramatic decline in marriage rates. This study is the first to recognize the "gender war" as an explanation for recent changes in public attention to gender issues and gender attitudes in Korea. Taking advantage of the timing of the Gangnam Murder (May 2016), which intensified the gender war, this study identifies three important trends associated with this timeframe. First, using archival and internet search data, I find dramatic shifts in the public discourse surrounding gender issues, as measured by results from internet searches and mass media coverage of the terms "misogyny" and "feminism" after May 2016. Second, using survey data from a nationally representative sample, this study also finds increasing trends toward egalitarian gender attitudes for both women and men after 2016. Lastly, the results also reveal significant, increasing trends in negative attitudes and intentions toward marriage, especially among Korean women, after 2016.

Findings from this study yield two new insights. First, rising trends in egalitarian gender attitudes after 2016 coincide with a growing trend in negative sentiments toward marriage in Korea. Yet despite evidence of changing gender attitudes, gendered expectations of the marriage institution did not shift; in fact, they declined. Prior research suggests that patriarchal ideology and practices are maintained by traditional gender beliefs of the parental generation (Kim et al., 2015), who continue to have a strong influence on young adults' decisions over marriage. I find evidence that older generations (Silent and Baby Boomer) do continue to hold more traditional gender beliefs than the younger generations (Millennial and Gen Y). Taken together, these findings suggest that young adults with more egalitarian views may perceive the current institution of marriage as unequal and may decide to avoid marriage altogether.

Second, my findings suggest the gender revolution is neither irreversible nor self-reinforcing. Despite women's continued movement into the public sphere, Korea first experienced a decline in egalitarian gender attitudes for both women and men between 2009 and 2015. It is beyond the scope of this study to explain the cause of the retreat from egalitarian gender attitudes after 2009; however, this period coincides with the 2007–2008 financial crisis and the rise of misogynistic attacks in far-right online communities, especially toward young women who are gaining economic and political power. This arc suggests that the pathway to the gender revolution can be stalled or even reversed. Similar trends were found in other postindustrial countries, such as the United States, where egalitarian gender ideals stalled in the mid-1990s (Cotter et al., 2011; England, 2010). Research in the United States also documented the rise of a gender backlash in the 1990s in the form of media criticism against the "working mom" (Faludi et al., 2020; Motro & Vanneman, 2015).

Scholars of the gender revolution framework often highlight women's work-family conflict and promote the expansion of family policies as an important solution for gender inequality at home in an effort to boost very low fertility rates. Although prior studies have shown that individual access to these family polices is positively associated with fertility outcomes in Korea (Kim & Luke, 2020), macro-level trends in fertility and marriage rates have not rebounded despite both the substantial expansion of national policy support for family leave and the growing gender equitability attitudes. This study underscores the need for more fundamental changes to the normative and institutional factors that continue to enforce traditional gender relations and behaviors among young adults to promote family formation in Korea. In addition, future research ought to investigate the factors that motivate young men's misogynistic reactions to women's advancement.

This study has several limitations. First, the causal relationships between the Gangnam Murder and trends in egalitarian attitudes and anti-marriage sentiments are tentative. In the case of the Gangnam Murder, plausible control groups do not exist, as the murder was a media event with nationwide impact (rates of internet use are over 90% in South Korea). Nevertheless, this study provides evidence of the notable changes in egalitarian gender attitudes of a nationally representative sample of the Korean population and changes in attitudes toward marriage after the time of the Gangnam Murder. Second, my current analytic models did not account for institutional factors relating to marriage and assumed that the marriage institution did not change during the study period. Indeed, my evidence suggests that during a time of great social upheaval and change, awareness of misogyny and feminism grew in public prominence, Koreans became increasingly egalitarian, and young (increasingly egalitarian) Korean adults may have developed distaste toward marriage. Future research should consider the gender attitudes of the older generation that continues to influence the marriage institution in Korea, to examine whether it changes or interacts with young adults' gender beliefs in influencing marriage rates. Third, this study did not directly explore changes in marriage rates before and after the Gangnam Murder. While the gender revolution in attitudes may have discouraged marriage formation, this study does not connect the two. An analysis of trends in marriage rates around the time of the Gangnam Murder would corroborate the findings of this study.

Despite this limitation, this study makes significant theoretical contributions to the literature on gender and family demography. This study highlights that the ideological conflict over the gender issue between men and women may play a significant role in discouraging marriage and fertility. In addition, findings suggest that in contexts where the institution of traditional marriage remains resistant to change while young adults' ideals do not, the relationship between progress toward egalitarian values and family formation may be negative, according to the findings of this study. The ongoing gender war in South Korea signals a continuing decline in family formation in Korea. Lastly, the implications of this study should be extended to and examined in other Asian nations, where patriarchal family systems persist and attitudes and gender roles are not changing as rapidly as in Western nations.

References

Ahn, S.-s. (2015). *Basic study on Men's life in Korea*. Korea Women's Development Institute. Retrieved from https://kwdi.re.kr/publications/reportView.do?p=37&idx=115027

Brinton, M. C., & Lee, D.-J. (2016). Gender-role ideology, labor market institutions, and post-industrial fertility. *Population and Development Review, 42*, 405–433.

Brinton, M. C., & Oh, E. (2019). Babies, work, or both? Highly educated Women's employment and fertility in East Asia. *American Journal of Sociology, 125*(1), 105–140. https://doi.org/10.1086/704369

Bumpass, L. L., Rindfuss, R. R., Choe, M. K., & Tsuya, N. O. (2009). The institutional context of low fertility: The case of Japan. *Asian Population Studies, 5*(3), 215–235.

Coontz, S. (2004). The world historical transformation of marriage. *Journal of Marriage and the Family, 66*, 974–979.

Cotter, D., Hermsen, J. M., & Vanneman, R. (2011). The end of the gender revolution? Gender role attitudes from 1977 to 2008. *American Journal of Sociology, 117*(1), 259–289.

England, P. (2010). The gender revolution: Uneven and stalled. *Gender & Society, 24*(2), 149–166.

Esping-Andersen, G., & Billari, F. C. (2015). Re-theorizing family demographics. *Population and Development Review, 41*(1), 1–31. https://doi.org/10.1111/j.1728-4457.2015.00024.x

Faludi, S., Shames, S., Piscopo, J. M., & Walsh, D. M. (2020). A conversation with Susan Faludi on Backlash, Trumpism, and #MeToo. *Signs: Journal of Women in Culture and Society, 45*(2), 336–345. https://doi.org/10.1086/704988

Goldstein, J. R., Sobotka, T., & Jasilioniene, A. (2009). The end of 'lowest-low' fertility? *Population and Development Review, 35*(4), 663–699.

Kim, J. (2018). Misogyny for male solidarity: Online hate discourse against women in South Korea. In J. R. Vickery & T. Everbach (Eds.), *Mediating misogyny* (pp. 151–169). Springer.

Kim, J. (2021). Sticky activism: The Gangnam Station murder case and new feminist practices against misogyny and Femicide. *JCMS: Journal of Cinema and Media Studies, 60*(4), 37–60. https://doi.org/10.1353/cj.2021.0044

Kim, J., & Luke, N. (2020). Lowest-low fertility in South Korea: Policy and domestic labor supports and the transition to second birth. *Social Forces, 99*(2), 700–731. https://doi.org/10.1093/sf/soz159

Kim, K., Zarit, S. H., Fingerman, K. L., & Han, G. (2015). Intergenerational exchanges of middle-aged adults with their parents and parents-in-law in Korea. *Journal of Marriage and Family, 77*(3), 791–805.

Kohler, H.-P., Billari, F. C., & Ortega, J. A. (2002). The emergence of lowest-low fertility in Europe during the 1990s. *Population and Development Review, 28*(4), 641–680. https://doi.org/10.1111/j.1728-4457.2002.00641.x

Korean Statistical Information Service. (2019). https://kosis.kr/statHtml/statHtml.do?orgId=101&tblId=DT_1DA7012S&conn_path=I2. Accessed on June 2019.

Lesthaeghe, R. (2010). The unfolding story of the second demographic transition. *Population and Development Review, 36*(2), 211–251.

Motro, J., & Vanneman, R. (2015). The 1990s shift in the media portrayal of working mothers. *Sociological Forum, 30*(4), 1017–1037. https://doi.org/10.1111/socf.12206

OCED. (2020). *Time spent in paid and unpaid work by sex*. https://stats.oecd.org/index.aspx?queryid=54757. Accessed on March 2020.

OCED. (2022). *Family database. SF2.4 Share of births outside of marriage.* https://www.oecd.org/els/family/SF_2_4_Share_births_outside_marriage.pdf. Accessed on April, 2023.

Oh, E. (2018). Who deserves to work? How women develop expectations of child care support in Korea. *Gender & Society, 32*(4), 493–515.

Oliver, P. E., & Myers, D. J. (2003). Networks, diffusion, and cycles of collective action. In *Social movements and networks: Relational approaches to collective action* (p. 173). Oxford Academic.

Park, H., & Lee, J. K. (2017). Growing educational differentials in the retreat from marriage among Korean men. *Social Science Research, 66*, 187–200. https://doi.org/10.1016/j.ssresearch.2016.10.003

Raymo, J. M., Park, H., Xie, Y., & Yeung, W.-j. J. (2015). Marriage and family in East Asia: Continuity and change. *Annual Review of Sociology, 41*(1), 471–492. https://doi.org/10.1146/annurev-soc-073014-112428

Schoen, R. (2010). Gender competition and family change. *Genus, 66*(3), 95–120.

Schoen, R., & Hargens, L. (2020). Social capital, gender competition, and the resurgence of childlessness. In *Analyzing contemporary fertility* (pp. 9–24). Springer.

Shin, K.-Y. (2013). Economic crisis, neoliberal reforms, and the rise of precarious work in South Korea. *American Behavioral Scientist, 57*(3), 335–353.

Stout, K. D. (1991). Intimate Femicide: A national demographic overview. *Journal of Interpersonal Violence, 6*(4), 476–485.

Sung, S. (2003). Women reconciling paid and unpaid work in a Confucian welfare state: The case of South Korea. *Social Policy & Administration, 37*(4), 342–360.

Taewoo Park. (2015, May 19). The reason why Gangnam Murder is a Female-Hatred Crime. *The Hankyoreh*, retrieved from https://www.hani.co.kr/arti/society/society_general/744707.html

Vasi, I. B., Walker, E. T., Johnson, J. S., & Tan, H. F. (2015). 'No fracking way!' Documentary film, discursive opportunity, and local opposition against hydraulic fracturing in the United States, 2010 to 2013. *American Sociological Review, 80*(5), 934–959.

World Bank. (2019). https://data.worldbank.org/indicator/SP.DYN.TFRT.IN. Accessed on May 2019.

World Health Organization. MERS outbreak in the Republic of Korea 2015. https://www.who.int/westernpacific/emergencies/2015-mers-outbreak. Accessed on December 2022.

In Korean

Um, J. (2016). Strategic misogyny and its contradiction: Focusing on the analysis of the posts on the internet community site Ilgan Best Jeojangso (Daily Best Stroage). *Media, Gender, & Culture, 31*(2), 193–236.

Chapter 10
Cohort Change in Family Life Course Complexity of Adults and Children

Carla Rowold and Zachary Van Winkle

10.1 Introduction

Scholarly and public interest in the complexity of family lives has increased in recent decades as a response to family demographic change (Cherlin, 2010; Frejka & Sobotka, 2008; Lesthaeghe, 2014). Across many western industrial democracies, early family formation has shifted from a relatively simple and contracted pattern of marriage and parenthood to more complex and protracted patterns of family life (Billari & Liefbroer, 2010; Buchmann & Kriesi, 2011). For example, divorce and remarriage as well as non-marital and multi-partner childbirth have become more common (Cherlin, 2017; Guzzo, 2014). In sum, the family life courses of adults have become more complex, meaning that they consist of more family demographic transitions and greater unpredictability (Van Winkle, 2018; Van Winkle & Fasang, 2021). However, since family complexity tends to be measured at the end of the life course, we know less about the temporal dynamics of life course complexity, such as periods of relative stability (Pelletier et al., 2020).

Research on the complexity of family lives is commonly motivated by its potential consequences for children (McLanahan, 2004; McLanahan & Jacobsen, 2015; McLanahan & Percheski, 2008). However, studies on the consequences of

C. Rowold (✉)
Nuffield College, University of Oxford, Oxford, UK

Department of Sociology, University of Oxford, Oxford, UK
e-mail: carla.rowold@nuffield.ox.ac.uk

Z. Van Winkle
Nuffield College, University of Oxford, Oxford, UK

Sciences Po, Centre for Research on Social Inequalities (CRIS), CNRS, Paris, France

Department of Sociology, University of Oxford, Oxford, UK
e-mail: zachary.vanwinkle@sciencespo.fr

R. Schoen (ed.), *The Demography of Transforming Families*, The Springer Series on Demographic Methods and Population Analysis 56,
https://doi.org/10.1007/978-3-031-29666-6_10

family life for children mostly focus on individual events, such as parental separation (Härkönen et al., 2017). In line with the notion that family stability is important for children's wellbeing (Waldfogel et al., 2010), we argue that it is pertinent to take a holistic perspective. This means assessing the role of family events across the life courses of adults and children measured as family life course complexity.

Despite the open questions revolving around family complexity and children's wellbeing, there are no studies that have directly assessed whether the family life courses of parents tend to be more complex than those of childless adults. Kalmijn and Leopold (2021) recently demonstrated that the divorce revolution – the dramatic increase in divorce rates across the twentieth century – was concentrated mostly among adults without children. Thus, children were affected less by the increase in divorce than was previously assumed to be the case. Similarly, family life course complexity could be concentrated among childless adults and its increase over time may have had little effect on children. It is important that research on family complexity and its impact on children first describe the extent that life course complexity has increased among children.

In this study, we address this important gap by assessing three research questions: First, how has family complexity evolved over the life courses of adults in the United Kingdom? We go beyond standard approaches in the literature that measure life course complexity at a single point in time. Specifically, family complexity – measured based on the partnership lives – is analysed as a dynamic process that unfolds as individuals grow older (Pelletier et al., 2020). This allows us to understand when in the life course family complexity tends to increase, for example through numerous partnership transitions, and when family lives become more stable and predictable.

Second, how does family life course complexity vary by birth cohort, gender, and parenthood status? This is important to understand whether and when in the life course parents have more complex family lives than childless adults. For example, it is possible that parents' family lives are more complex before entering parenthood followed by a period of stability. In addition, it's important to know whether these trends have changed across birth cohorts.

Third, how does family complexity vary across the early life courses of children by birth cohort? We are the first to investigate to what extent children are exposed to family complexity based on their mothers' and fathers' life courses. Children may not be affected by the life course complexity of their parents if family transitions occur either before children are born or after they leave the parental home.

We make theoretical, methodological, and empirical contributions to the family sociological and demographic literature. Theoretically, we integrate three lines of literature that although similar have evolved separately: family life course complexity, relational family complexity, and family instability. Our conceptualization of family complexity integrates these three perspectives by demonstrating how adults' life course complexity translates into complexity for children, both in kinship networks and household instability.

Methodologically, we present a method for analysing the family complexity of adults and children dynamically over the life course. To measure family complexity for individuals and their children in the United Kingdom, we use rich retrospective data on partnership histories from the UK Household Longitudinal Study (UKHLS) and the British Household Panel Survey (BHPS). Specifically, we reconstruct adults' family life courses, concentrating on processes of union formation and dissolution, such as cohabitation, marriage, separation, and divorce. We then use techniques developed in sequence analysis to calculate the complexity – incorporating both the number of family transitions and their unpredictability – of men and women born across the twentieth century. In a second step, we transpose mothers' and fathers' family sequences to reflect the experiences of their children. Therefore, we are able to trace how children's family complexity evolved from birth to age 16. This reveals whether parents' family lives are more or less stable when their children are young.

Empirically, we find considerable differences in family complexity across age groups, birth cohorts, gender, and parenthood status. We show not only that average levels of complexity have increased across birth cohorts, but that complexity increases faster during young adulthood and stabilizes later in the life course for cohorts born after the mid-1960s compared to those born before. Across all cohorts, we show that mothers have considerably higher family complexity followed by fathers and childless adults. One of our most important contributions is to show how family complexity develops from children's point of view. We find that for children of the baby boomer cohort born between 1946–64 levels of complexity were low and increased only to a minor degree. However, especially for children born after 1980, family complexity begins to increase dramatically in their first year of life and, for millennials, continues to increase as they grow older. These findings demonstrate not only that children are indeed exposed to increasing levels of family complexity, but that family transitions and unpredictability accumulate across their early life course.

10.2 Conceptualizing Family Complexity

10.2.1 Previous Literature on Family Complexity

Family complexity has been conceptualized and studied in various manners across disciplines, especially in sociology and demography. In this section, we briefly review three distinct strands of literature on family complexity: life course family complexity, relational family complexity, and family instability. Each strand of literature defines and operationalizes family complexity differently, and is motivated by varying public and scholarly debates.

The first strand of literature on life course complexity revolves around debates on whether and to what extent family formation has become more differentiated and de-standardized across birth cohorts. There is general agreement that life course complexity should be conceptualized in terms of life course differentiation (Van Winkle, 2018; Van Winkle & Fasang, 2017). Brückner and Mayer (2005) define differentiation as an increase in the number of life course states experienced across the life course. As a result, complexity has often been operationalized using a simple count measure of the number of life course states or transitions experienced across individuals' lives. However, complexity is also associated with an increase in life course uncertainty (Mills & Blossfeld, 2013). Composite metrics developed in sequence analysis incorporate both the number of life course states as well as the degree of unpredictability (Elzinga & Liefbroer, 2007; Gabadinho et al., 2010). Sequence based complexity measures have the advantage that they can incorporate a large number of life course states, i.e. the intersection of different life course dimensions, as well as a small number of simple states.

While research on the complexity of family trajectories using sequence-based complexity metrics is becoming more common, the bulk of studies on life course complexity are interested in the differentiation of education-work-retirement trajectories (Biemann et al., 2011; Ciganda, 2015; Riekhoff, 2018). Although many studies apply sequence and cluster analysis to family trajectories, Elzinga and Liefbroer (2007) first studied the complexity of early family life courses in a number of countries and across birth cohorts. They found that average early family life course complexity had only increased moderately across a small number of their study countries. Otherwise, average complexity had remained relatively stable. Van Winkle (2018) analyzed long-life family trajectories in a number of European countries and cohorts, and concluded that although complexity had increased across cohorts, cross-national variation was considerably larger (see also Van Winkle, 2019; Van Winkle & Fasang, 2021).

A limitation of previous studies is their static conceptualization and measurement of the complexity of family life courses. The studies reviewed above all estimate the complexity of life course sequences at the end of the process. For example, researchers studying early adulthood might calculate the complexity of family trajectories between ages 18–35 at age 35 (e.g., Elzinga & Liefbroer, 2007), while others studying longer segments of the life course might measure the complexity of sequences between ages 18–50 at age 50 (e.g. Van Winkle, 2018). Recently, Pelletier et al. (2020) proposed a dynamic life course approach to complexity. Specifically, they argued that family complexity should be conceptualized as an aspect of the life course that evolves as individuals grow older. Thus, family complexity will be low when the process begins, e.g. at age 18, but will increase quickly as adults transition into new family demographic states, such as cohabitation or marriage. As individuals grow older, complexity may continue to increase, for example due to divorce or remarriage, or complexity may level off due to relative stability and increased predictability in the life course. A dynamic approach is important to gain a better understanding of when in the life course the complexity of family lives increases and to what level as well as when or whether family lives become stable.

The two other strands of literature shift the focus of family complexity from adults to children. Numerous scholars interested in the impact of the second demographic transition have focused their attention on changes in kinship networks (Kalmijn et al., 2019; Thomson, 2014, 2017). Compared to children residing with both parents, children whose parents separate and re-partner create more complex kinship networks, which may affect the quality of the relationship. Processes such as multi-partner fertility and non-marital childbirth (e.g., Guzzo, 2014; Thomson, 2014), separation and divorce as well as repartnering and remarriage (e.g., Cherlin, 2009; van Houdt, 2021) create larger and more intricate webs of family relationships with less institutionalized and clearly defined roles (Thomson, 2017), such as step-parent, half-sibling, and non-resident parent. For example, contact between children and non-resident separated fathers is lower across the life course than contact between children and resident fathers, especially if a stepfather is also present (van den Berg et al., 2021).

A third strand of literature on family complexity and its impact on children shifts the focus from kinship networks to instability within the household and its potential negative effects on children's wellbeing (Cavanagh & Fomby, 2019). The family instability perspective has emerged as one of the dominant theoretical approaches to the consequences of family transitions for children (Raley & Sweeney, 2020). The approach argues that it is not family structure that has a negative impact on children's life chances, but family transitions. Moreover, the effects tend to be cumulative: more family transitions incur greater consequences. Family transitions are thought to be linked not only with changes in household economic wellbeing and residential moves, but also with stress caused by a disruption of children's sense of security, ambiguity in household rules and relationships, and parental expectations.

There is a tension in the family demographic and family sociological literature between family complexity and the family life course complexity. As discussed above, we conceptualize the complexity of family life courses to be a dynamic process of differentiation as individuals grow older incorporating both the number of family transitions, such as marriage and divorce, as well as the extent of unpredictability. However, the complexity of family relationships and life course family complexity are strongly linked. More complex and intricate family relationships are generated by more complex family life courses. In fact, one of the central pathways through which family complexity has a negative impact on children is by means of family life course instability inducing stress and conflict (Cavanagh & Fomby, 2019). In this study, we concentrate on family life course complexity. Specifically, we apply a dynamic life course approach and sequence-based techniques to estimate the extent that parents and their children are exposed to life course complexity. We therefore follow Cavanagh and Fomby's (2019) call and develop a broader and more dynamic measure for the complexity of children's family life.

10.3 Theoretical Background

10.3.1 Family Complexity Across Birth Cohorts

A number of theoretical narratives have been applied when studying the complexity of family events and transitions within individual life courses (see Van Winkle, 2018). The Second Demographic Transition (SDT) thesis is an ideational account, which associates more complex family life courses with a shift from materialist to post-materialist values (Lesthaeghe, 2014). An increase in family life course complexity has also been connected with increasing economic uncertainty following globalization and deindustrialization (Mills & Blossfeld, 2013). The gender competition approach links both economic and ideational shifts, specifically increased women's labour market participation and gender egalitarian attitudes, to family demographic change by means of greater competition within couples (Schoen, 2010; Schoen & Hargens, 2020). Cohabitation, in contrast to marriage, gives the partner with greater resources – usually men – more leverage in the relationship by enabling them to withhold their support or end the relationship. Similarly, non-marital fertility can be a strategy to shift the costs of childrearing from men to women. Other scholars, such as life course sociologists and welfare state scholars, argue that labor market and family policies are related to the complexity of family lives (Mayer, 2009; Van Winkle, 2019). An emerging biodemographic theoretical perspective on family life course complexity (Van Winkle & Conley, 2021) explores genetic factors that influence the components of family life course complexity and the extent that lower normative barriers to family demographic behaviour and increasing levels of inequality may lead to a greater expression of genetic predispositions for complex family lives.

Regardless of the theoretical approach, early family formation has shifted from a relatively simple, contracted and early pattern to a complex, protracted and late pattern (Billari & Liefbroer, 2010; Buchmann & Kriesi, 2011). We therefore expect that *the level and the growth of family life course complexity has increased across birth cohorts (hypothesis 1)*. With *level of family life course complexity*, we refer to the overall highest achieved extent of complexity independent of age. With *growth of life course family complexity*, we refer to the speed with which family life course complexity increases in young adulthood and the age range when family lives stabilize.

10.3.2 Differences by Gender and Parenthood Status

Few studies on the complexity of family life courses concentrate on gender differences, although many demonstrate that women tend to have more complex family life courses compared to men (e.g. Van Winkle, 2018; Van Winkle & Fasang, 2021). Although men are more likely to live independently before entering marriage or cohabitation, women are more likely than men to form cohabiting or marital unions and more likely to repartner or remarry following the dissolution of a cohabiting or marital union (Cherlin, 2010, 2017; Di Nallo, 2019). Possible explanations range from gendered norms surrounding the role of women in family and employment life and their roles as kinkeepers (Kalmijn et al., 2019; Kaufman, 2000). However, despite advances in women's and mothers' employment, labour market disadvantages by means of discrimination and human capital differences often make women economically more dependent on having a partner in the household (e.g., Charles & Grusky, 2004; Florian, 2018; Ludwig & Brüderl, 2018; Mari, 2019). Thus, in summary, *life course family complexity is larger for women compared to men across birth cohorts (hypothesis 2).*

Furthermore, we expect the level and growth of family complexity to differ between parents and childless individuals. It could be expected that, *the level and growth of family life course complexity is largest for childless women and childless men followed by mothers and fathers across birth cohorts (hypothesis 3a).* Couples without children were shown to drive the divorce revolution (Kalmijn & Leopold, 2021) and therefore might experience more complex family lives. More generally, the lack of children may endow individuals with more freedom and time to choose and change partners more frequently compared to parents. For parents, the responsibility for children as well as the limited time for one's own intimate life could serve as obstacles to repartner frequently (Di Nallo, 2019). In societies where stable marriage and parenthood is the norm, such as in the UK, individuals might select into parenthood and have stable family lives (Liefbroer & Billari, 2010). This norm-based selection into parenthood and childlessness might additionally drive the gap in family complexity between childless individuals and parents.

On the other hand, childlessness may result from remaining single or never entering a stable union (Jalovaara & Fasang, 2017; Mynarska et al., 2015; Raab & Struffolino, 2019). In this case, parents would represent a selective group with active partnerships before having children, which would lead to a steep growth and high levels of family complexity. It would follow that *the level and growth of family life course complexity is largest for mothers and fathers followed by childless women and men across birth cohorts (hypothesis 3b).*

10.3.3 Differences Between Adults and Children

To date, no research has assessed family life course complexity from a child's point of view. However, this is essential to know whether and to what extent cohort changes in the complexity of adults' family life courses actually translate to an increased exposure of children to family complexity. As we argue that the family life courses of parents might be more complex than those of childless adults, and family complexity has increased across cohorts, it is likely that *the level and the growth of family life course complexity for children has increased across birth cohorts (hypothesis 4a).* On the other hand, it is possible that the complexity of to-be parents' family life courses stops increasing in complexity once children are born across all cohorts, for example if parents tend not to divorce and remarry. Therefore, we could also expect that *the level and the growth of family life course complexity for children has remained constant across birth cohorts (hypothesis 4b).*

10.4 Data and Methods

10.4.1 Study Sample

We used harmonized data from Understanding Society,[1] which combines longitudinal data from the UK Household Longitudinal Study (UKHLS) and its predecessor, the British Household Panel Survey (BHPS), covering households in the UK since 1991. For the partnership history we used data from the marital and cohabitation histories, which provides spell data about partnership histories from all UKHLS and BHPS samples and waves up to wave 9 (Nandi et al., 2020) and matched it with cross-wave information on sex as well as year and month of birth (University of Essex, Institute for Social and Economic Research, 2021).

Our adults sample consisted of all respondents covered in the marital and cohabitation histories and without missing information on the socio-demographics of interests. We excluded individuals with missing information on start and end dates for all partnership spells (n = 178 respondents) as well as respondents with partnership sequences containing missing spells (n = 33).

Adults who reported ever having a social or biological child were defined as parents.[2] Mothers and fathers were identified based on their reported sex. Adults were defined as childless if they have not reported to have ever had a social or biological child and were age 40 or older.[3] After harmonising the UKHLS and BHPS childbirth histories, we retained an analysis sample of 77,323 adult individuals.

The data for children was derived from retrospective data on childbirths and prospective data on children living in the household. Children with missing birth dates were excluded from the analysis. We matched each child to the partnership spells of each of their linkable parent from the UKHLS and BHPS sample and created two separate datasets. The first one contained children linked to their *mothers'* partnership history (n = 65,854 children) and the second one matched children to their *fathers'* partnership history (n = 51,061 children).

10.4.2 Sequence Definition

The raw partnership data contains spells on cohabitation, marriage, and civil partnership. Combining this with information on union dissolution and the order of

[1]Understanding Society is an initiative funded by the Economic and Social Research Council and various Government Departments, with scientific leadership by the Institute for Social and Economic Research, University of Essex, and survey delivery by NatCen Social Research and Kantar Public. The research data are distributed by the UK Data Service.

[2]The term 'social child' includes step and adopted children.

[3]This means for all analyses which include parenthood status as dimension (Figs. 10.3 and 10.4), we excluded childless adults observed last before age 40.

Table 10.1 Overview and definition of sequence states

Partnership status	Start of spell	End of spell
Single	Age 16, if no partnership reported yet	Start of first partnership spell or last observed date
Union	Start of marriage, civil partnership or cohabitation spell	End of marriage, civil partnership or cohabitation or last observed date
Divorced	End of marriage or civil partnership spell through divorce or separation	Start of any subsequent partnership spell or last observed date
Widowed	End of marriage or civil partnership spell through widowhood	Start of any subsequent partnership spell or last observed date
Separated	End of cohabitation spell through break-up	Start of any subsequent partnership spell or last observed date
Missing	Start of a spell with missing start or end date or period between partnership spells with unknown union dissolution	Start of any subsequent partnership spell or last observed date

spells we defined five new spell states, resulting in six distinct partnership spells (see Table 10.1). *'Singlehood'* was defined as partnership category before any first partnership spell. We summarized cohabitation, marriage, and civil partnership as one state, namely *'union'*. We did not use cohabitation and marriage as separate states, since we assume, following Hiekel and Vidal (2020), that the transition from cohabitation to marriage does not add complexity to family lives. Periods between the dissolution of cohabitating unions reported as break-up and the start of a new partnership spells or the last observed date were defined as *'separated'*.[4] Similarly, we defined periods between the end of marriage through dissolution (divorce or separation) or widowhood and the start of the subsequent partnership spell or the last observed date as *'divorced'* or *'widowed'*, respectively.[5] Periods with any missing start or end date as well as periods between partnership spells where the type of union dissolution of the previous partnership is not defined were labelled as *'missing'* spells. For the analysis, partnership sequences with any missing spells were excluded to prevent skewing the family complexity of such cases. Thus, the sequence alphabet used for our analysis comprised the first five states shown in Table 10.1.

Overlapping partnership spells were dealt with based on a hierarchy of partnership spells and union dissolutions that prevented concealing any partnership spells. For example, if a union was dissolved but the individual entered a new union in the same month, we included one month for the dissolution spell and started the new

[4]For cohabitation spells we only have information on whether the relationship ended with a break-up or marriage. We do not have information whether the union ended because the partner died (in contrast to marriage spells) and cannot reconstruct this because the partner ID for most of the respondents is missing and cannot be matched to a potential date of death.

[5]27% of the marriage that ended in dissolution are reported to be separated.

union one month later. We did this to prevent the underestimation of life course complexity. However, if the subsequent union spell lasted for only one month, we prioritized the one-month union spell, and did not include a one-month dissolution spell. One limitation of our monthly data was that we cannot observe other multiple transitions within a single month, for example if someone changed their partnership status and returned to their previous status within the same month. Despite this shortcoming, the result was a rich dataset containing the complete partnership history of respondents as distinct partnership spells in the correct order and without any gaps.

For adults, the sequences started with age 16. For children, the matched partnership lives of their parents were analysed for the period between each child's birth and age 16. Based on these partnership histories we calculated the family complexity for each respondent and their children over the life course.

10.4.3 Measuring Family Complexity

We used a composite measure developed in sequence analysis to assess the complexity of sequences of categorical states: the sequence complexity index. This index measured variability within sequences as the geometric mean of normalized sequence transitions and normalized longitudinal sequence entropy (Gabadinho et al., 2010, 2011). The complexity index provides a more nuanced indicator of life course differentiation compared with just the number of transitions or distinct states because the degree of uncertainty within life courses is incorporated through sequence entropy. In addition, multiple transitions between different states are captured, not just the number of a specific transition.

Formally, the complexity, C, of a sequence, x, is defined as follows:

$$C(x) = 100 * \sqrt{\frac{q(x)}{q_{max}} * \frac{h(x)}{h_{max}}}, \tag{10.1}$$

where the number of transitions within a sequence, q(x), is divided by the theoretical maximum number of transitions possible, q_{max}; the longitudinal entropy of a sequence, h(x), is divided by the theoretical maximum, h_{max}. Thus, the complexity index consists of two components: the relative number of transitions *and* the entropy of the sequence. The term *q(x)* in the complexity index equation considers the number of transitions happening within a sequence in reference to the maximal possible number of transitions. The term *h(x)* considers the entropy measured as the share of single states in the whole sequence.

Longitudinal sequence entropy is

$$h(x) = -\sum_{i}^{s} \pi_i \log \pi_i, \tag{10.1a}$$

where π is the proportion of time spent in a given state, i, of the sequence alphabet, s, of sequence x. The sequence alphabet is comprised of the potential family life course states (see Table 10.1). Note that only states that occur within a given sequence are incorporated into the calculation of that sequence's entropy to avoid indeterminate products, i.e. the logarithm of zero.[6] Sequence entropy does not focus on transitions, but measures how (un)equally partnership states are distributed over the whole sequence, focussing on the shares of the single partnership spells. For example, π for the state "single" would be 0.2 in a sequence where 20% of the entire life course is spent never in a cohabiting or marital union. Entropy within sequences is zero when only one state occurs in a sequence and is maximal when each state occurs an equal number of times. Stated otherwise, longitudinal entropy reflects uncertainty in family life courses by means of state (un)predictability. If only one status, e.g. never married, occurs in the sequence, then it is relatively easy to predict that status at any given time in the sequence. In contrast, when a sequence is composed of numerous statuses, it becomes increasingly difficult and less likely to predict the status of an individual at any given time.

Theoretically, complexity can vary between 0 and 1, although we multiply complexity by 100 to allow it to range between 0 and 100. Complexity is 0 when longitudinal entropy minimal, i.e. only one status experienced through the life course ($h(x)$ in Eq. 10.1), and the number of transitions is minimal, i.e. no life course transitions are experienced ($q(x)$ in Eq. 10.1). This will be the case for an individual who does not experience any partnership events, e.g. a person who never forms a cohabiting or marital union. In contrast, complexity is maximal for a sequence with the maximum number of transitions, which for a sequence with monthly states between 16 and 40 would be 287 transitions, and where every status appears in the sequence an equal number of times. This is a theoretical situation, which did not occur in our data. First, it is extremely unlikely for someone to transition between partnership states once a month. Second, it is also not possible for all status to be equally present in sequences, because that would require making invalid transitions, such as transitioning from divorced to single or from divorced to widowed. Empirically, complexity in our sample ranged from a minimum of 0 to a maximum of 39.1, with a mean of 3.55 for mothers and of 1.13 for children in our study (see Tables 10.A1 and 10.A2). These were relatively comparable levels of complexity for adults compared to previous applications (Pelletier et al., 2020; Van Winkle, 2018).

We followed an approach proposed by Pelletier et al. (2020) and calculated sequence complexity dynamically for each year of age. This means the complexity value for age 17 was based on the short family sequences of individuals starting at age 16 up until age 17, i.e. the first twelve months of each sequence. Complexity for age 18 was then calculated on family sequences 24 months in length from age 16 to

[6] Note that eliminating rarer states, such as widowhood, from the analyses are unlikely to affect our results. While removing a state will change maximum entropy (h_{max} in Eq. 10.1) it will not change the entropy of single sequences ($h(x)$ in Eq. 10.1) without those states. Therefore, although absolute complexity values may change when rare states are removed from the sequence alphabet, relative differences and conclusions drawn from those results are unlikely to change substantially.

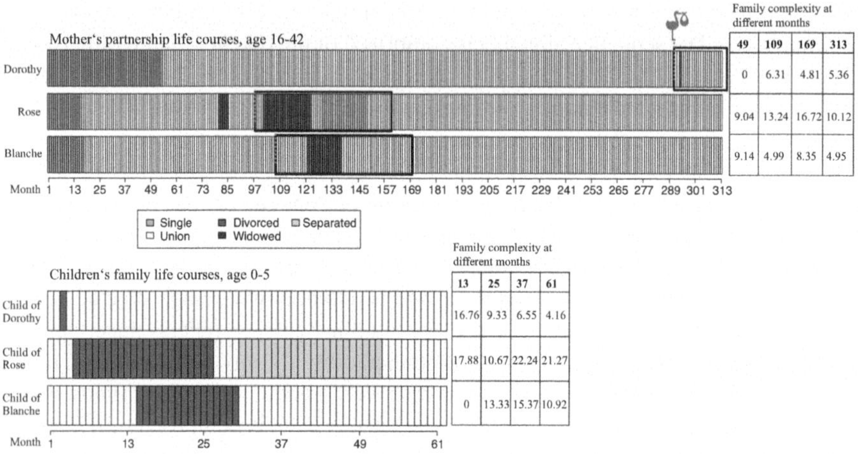

Fig. 10.1 Exemplary family trajectories of mothers, their children, and the complexity at different life course stages

age 18. For adults, we continued this up until age 67 or until we no longer observed family behaviour. For children we calculated complexity in a similar way, starting with twelve-month sequences from age zero to one, followed by 24-month sequences from age zero to two, and so forth up to age 16.

Figure 10.1 depicts three examples of family trajectories for mothers as observed in our data. The Sequence Index Plot (see Fig. 10.1) reveals the family state of each mother per month from age 16 to age 42. The table next to the Sequence Index Plots gives the family complexity at different time points, revealing how family complexity evolves over time. For example, Dorothy had a long and stable period of singlehood at an early age, which is why her family complexity was maximally stable or minimally complex (0 at month 49). However, it increased to 6.31 in month 109 due to her transition to a union and a slight decrease in predictability. In month 169, complexity decreased because she did not experience another transition. Stated otherwise – her family life stabilised. Later in her life course, she experienced two more transitions (from a union to divorce and back into a union) which led to an increase in family complexity. Dorothy's family complexity was highest around month 109 despite experiencing further transitions later in life, because she experienced a high level of unpredictability (reflected by the entropy component) as a result of equal durations in singlehood and in a union.

Similarly, Rose's family complexity increased over time as she experienced a number of family transitions before eventually decreasing after entering into a long-term union. Of the three examples, her family life reached highest levels of complexity as she experienced the most transitions between family states as well as many periods of similar length.

The lower part of Fig. 10.1 depicts the early life courses of the children of Dorothy, Rose, and Blanche – their month of birth is marked with the grey dotted lines (and the stork for Dorothy's life course) in their mother's life courses. As described above and visible in the figure, children's family life courses were based on their mothers' family lives. The section of the family life data that was transposed in our example is marked with a box in the mothers' life course. As can be seen in the example, mothers' family complexity was not necessarily mirrored in their children's complexity values. Instead, children's family complexity was characterised by different levels and dynamics compared to their mothers. This was because we observed adults' family lives over a longer period and at different time points. First, adults' family lives began before the birth of their child and continued past their 16th birthday. Secondly, the crucial factor is *when* family lives were complex: partnership lives of adults might have been volatile before they have children, but stabilized after becoming parents. The relevant question is: How complex are family lives of parents *during* the childhood of their children?

10.4.4 Analytical Strategy

We used interactions in OLS linear regressions to estimate the age trends in family complexity by birth cohort, gender and parenthood status for adults. For children we estimated the age trends in family complexity twice: once based on mothers' family sequences and once based on fathers' family sequences. Adults birth cohorts spanned from 1910 to 2000 and from 1946 to 2018 for children.

10.5 Results

10.5.1 Adults' Family Complexity

Adults' family complexity across the life course is displayed in Fig. 10.2 by birth cohort. In line with our first hypothesis, the family complexity of the oldest cohort, those born in the years 1910–1945, was lowest across the life course both in terms of level and growth. For the baby boomer cohort (1946–64), average complexity was similar to the level of the youngest cohort (1965–2000) approximately until age 25, after which it began to diverge. While the increase in complexity continued for the youngest cohort, it decreased for baby boomers and family lives slowly stabilized from age 30, which resulted in a lower level of family complexity.

Additionally, the age at which family complexity peaked in the life course increased across cohorts. While the highest level of complexity was reached in the early 30s for the oldest cohort, family complexity was highest in the mid-30s for those born 1946–64 and highest in the late mid-30s for the youngest cohort. In line with this, the complexity of family lives stabilized at older ages across cohorts. Whereas the average cumulative complexity declined for the oldest cohort from the early 30s on, for the youngest cohort complexity only declined after age 37 and at a slower rate.

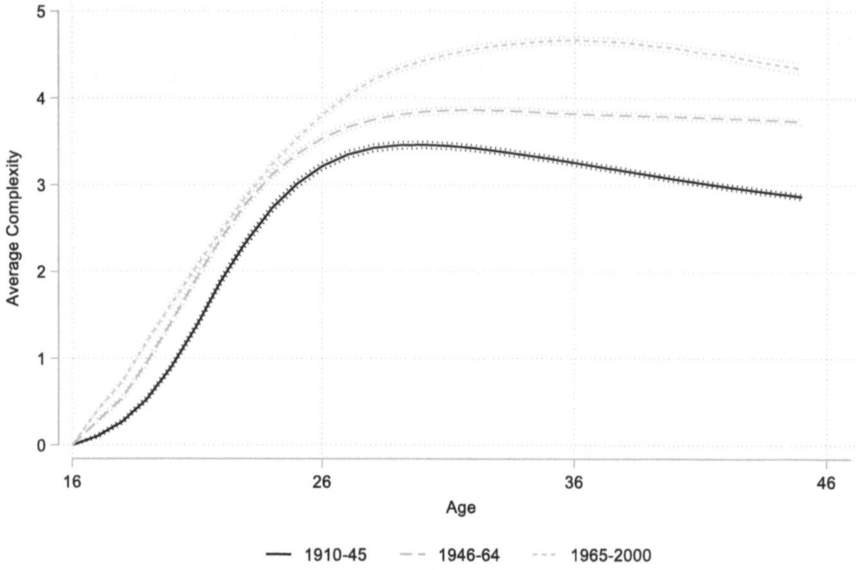

Fig. 10.2 Adults' family complexity across the life course by birth cohort. (OLS linear regressions based on authors' analysis sample from the UKHLS & BHPS)

Family complexity across the life courses of childless men and women as well as mothers and fathers is displayed in Fig. 10.3. We found that regardless of parenthood status, women had higher family life complexity at almost all ages over the life course compared to their male peers (hypothesis 2). In line with our hypothesis 3b, mothers and fathers exhibited higher levels of family complexity followed by childless women and childless men respectively, although there was some variation across the life course. For mothers, family complexity increased dramatically early in the life course. Before approximately age 22, childless women had somewhat more complex family lives compared to fathers and childless men due to a relatively steep increase early in life. However, father's family complexity continued to increase after the early 20s, while the family complexity of childless women began to stabilize and decrease. Family complexity for childless men was lowest across the life course.

Figure 10.4 demonstrates that differences in family complexity by parenthood status decreased considerably across birth cohorts, while gender differences increased. Variation by parenthood status was most pronounced amongst our oldest birth cohort, followed by the baby boomer cohort. For both cohorts, the complexity of family lives was highest and grew fastest among mothers and fathers followed by childless women and childless men. The decrease in these differences across cohorts was due to the much stronger rise of family complexity for childless women and men compared to parents. For parents, the stabilisation of family life course complexity after the peak of complexity was less pronounced, i.e. complexity decreased at lower rates, across cohorts.

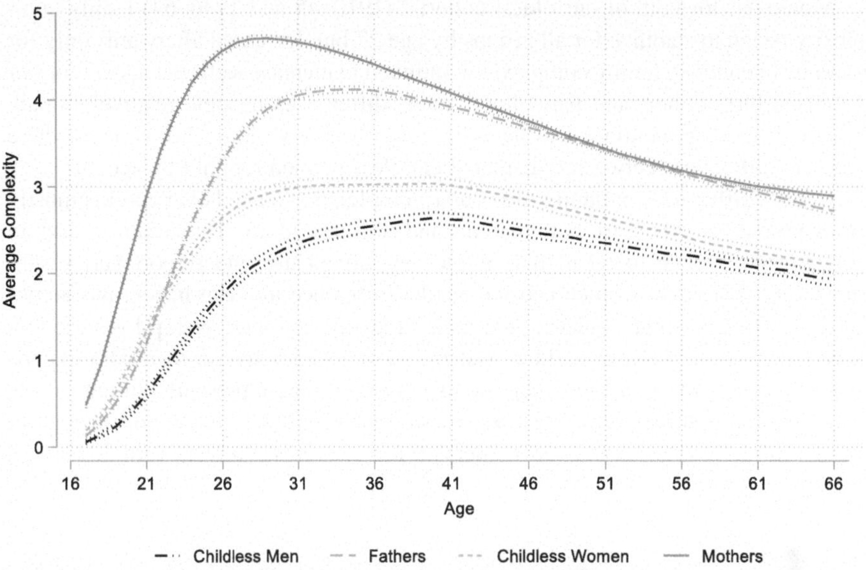

Fig. 10.3 Adults' family complexity across the life course by gender and parenthood status. (OLS linear regressions based on authors' analysis sample from the UKHLS & BHPS)

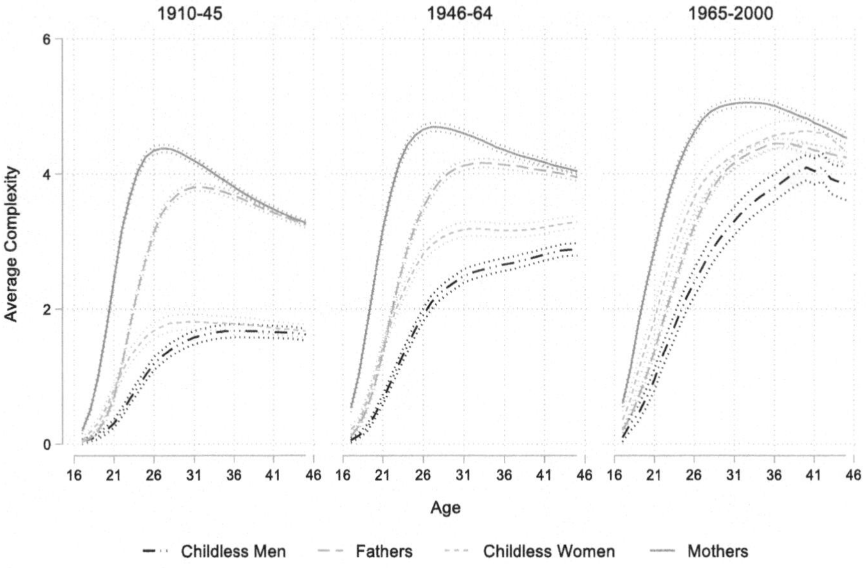

Fig. 10.4 Adults' family complexity across the life course by gender, parenthood status, and birth cohort. (OLS linear regressions based on authors' analysis sample from the UKHLS & BHPS)

Moreover, for both of our oldest cohorts' (1910–45 and 1946–64) family complexity began to stabilize for all groups by age 27 but decreased afterwards only for parents. In contrast, family complexity continued to increase well past age 27 for our youngest birth cohort and parenthood status differences become relatively small. Although mothers continued to have the most complex family life courses, there were no differences between fathers and childless women roughly by age 30.

Gender differences in family life course complexity widened over cohorts mostly from around age 30 on, for both, parents and childless adults. This finding could, in part, be attributable to recall bias if men systematically underreport partnership transitions more than women and the gender difference in recall bias grows across cohorts. There is some evidence that men's retrospective partnership lives are less accurately reported (Kreyenfeld & Bastin, 2016). Alternatively, men who experienced many family transitions may be increasingly underrepresented in the survey over cohorts or survey waves. However, we find it unlikely that cohort change in gender differential recall bias of partnership life or representativeness in the survey drives our results.

10.5.2 Children's Family Complexity

Figure 10.5a depicts the evolution of family complexity from children's perspective based on their mothers' family life courses across cohorts. Figure 10.5b shows complexity trends from children's point of view based on their fathers' family life.

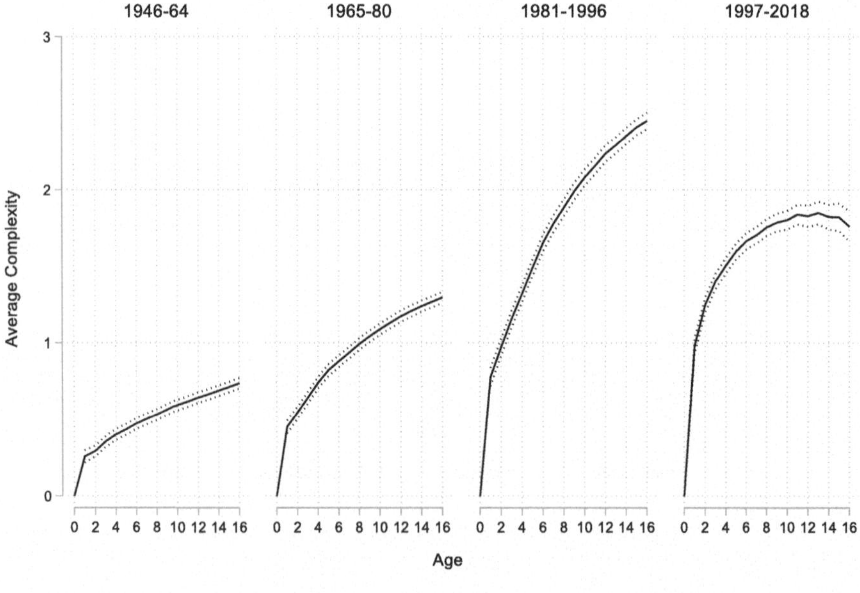

Fig. 10.5a Children's family complexity across the life course by birth cohort (Mothers). (OLS linear regressions based on authors' analysis sample from the UKHLS and the BHPS sample)

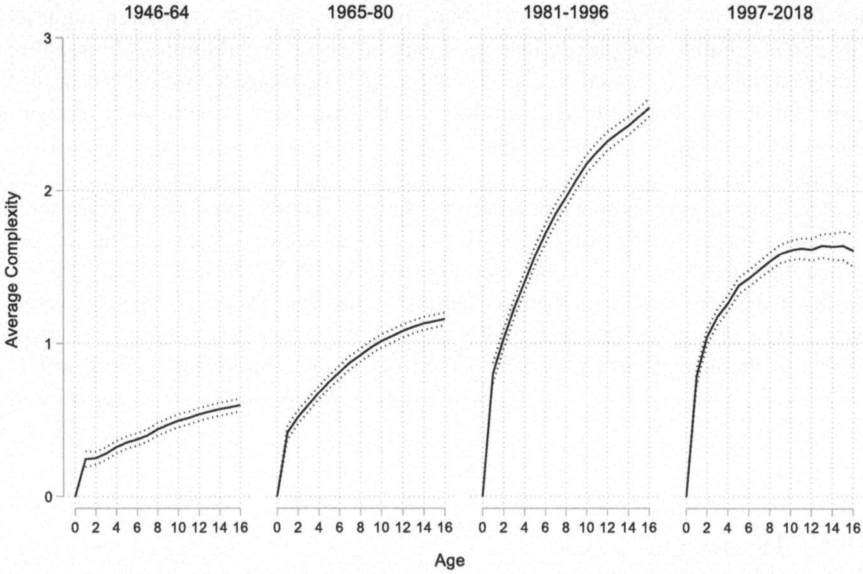

Fig. 10.5b Children's family complexity across the life course by birth cohort (Fathers). (OLS linear regressions based on authors' analysis sample from the UKHLS and the BHPS sample)

We found that family complexity increased over the life course not just for adults, but also for children. Moreover, and in line with hypothesis 4a, our results showed that family complexity for children increased considerably across birth cohorts. For our oldest birth cohort of children, the baby boomers (1946–1964), family complexity remained relatively low. This corresponds with the notion that the complexity of mothers' and fathers' family life courses stabilized when they enter parenthood. However, we observed a large increase across birth cohorts, especially for the cohort of children born between 1981 and 1996 (the millennial cohort): millennials experienced on average the steepest growth of family complexity based on their mothers' (and their fathers', see Fig. 10.5b) family lives. For all cohorts, the growth of mothers' family life course complexity decreased somewhat after age two of their children. But the stabilisation was strongest for the oldest cohort and shrinked over cohorts until the millennial cohort. This steady increase led to millennials average family complexity reaching levels about three times as high as those experienced by children in the baby boomer cohort.

For the youngest cohort (1997–2018) we observed a stronger stabilisation of family lives during late childhood compared to the millennials, leading to a lower level of family complexity at age 16. One reason for this moderate stabilisation may be the recent decrease in divorce rates among adults ages under the age of 45 (ONS, 2022). At the same time, however, the family complexity of children of the youngest cohorts increased more dramatically up until age 6, indicating that these children experienced the highest number of family transitions and unpredictability at very young ages. Given that we only observed a modest rise in complexity for mothers and father across cohorts (Fig. 10.4), changing the perspective to children suggests that parents' family complexity increased particularly after childbirth. Additionally, family complexity increased at a faster rate for the two youngest birth cohorts during early childhood. For example, children of the youngest cohorts were already exposed to a level of family complexity at age one which was never reached for the oldest cohort.

We found a very similar pattern using fathers' family lives to calculate their children's family complexity (Fig. 10.5b). For all child cohorts except for the millennials, their mothers' family life course complexity reached slightly higher levels at age 16 compared to their fathers'. This was in line with our overall observation of a higher average family complexity for women compared to men. However, the increase in complexity between the baby boomer and the millennials cohort was more extreme for children when considering their fathers' partnership lives.

10.6 Discussion

In this study, we assessed how family complexity evolved over the life course of adults in the United Kingdom, how it varied by birth cohort, gender, and parenthood status, and most importantly, how family complexity differed across the early life courses of children by birth cohort. We used rich retrospective data on partnership histories from the UK Household Longitudinal Study (UKHLS) and the British Household Panel Survey (BHPS) to reconstruct adults' family life courses and calculate their complexity for men and women born across the twentieth century. We then transposed parents' family sequences to reflect what their children experienced in their first 16 years of life.

As would be expected by various theoretical accounts of family life course change, we found that the level and the growth of adults' life course family complexity increased across birth cohorts (hypothesis 1). In addition, we found that the level and growth of life course family complexity was largest for women compared to men (hypothesis 2) and for mothers and fathers followed by childless women and men (hypothesis 3b). Differences in family complexity over the life course by parenthood converged over cohorts due to the sharp rise in family complexity for childless adults. On the other hand, differences by gender increased across cohorts, with mothers and childless women experiencing more complex family lives compared to their male peers, especially from age 30 on. However, most importantly, we demonstrated for the first time that the level and the growth of life course family complexity for children increased dramatically across birth cohorts (hypothesis 4a). Parents' family lives became particularly more complex and unpredictable across cohorts during their children's early childhood.

Our descriptive findings highlight at least two paths for future research. First, in this study we were unable to identify the family states and transitions behind increasing family complexity, especially in the earliest years of childhood. While previous research relates low family complexity of childless adults to the lack of partners (Jalovaara & Fasang, 2017; Mynarska et al., 2015; Raab & Struffolino, 2019), our results hint that childless adults experience more active partnership life later in the life course compared to parents. Thus, the group of parents may be becoming less selective across cohorts when it comes to union formation. The increased exposure of children to family complexity, especially at very young ages, is likely attributable to increasing numbers of union dissolutions but possibly the formation of unions. For both adults and children, it remains relevant for future research to reveal and quantify the drivers for such dynamics across cohorts, for example by decomposing the complexity index (Westerman et al., 2021).

Secondly, future research may take advantage of the dynamic and holistic measure of family complexity developed in this study to estimate the consequences of family instability for adults and their children. Recent evidence suggests that family complexity might result from structural disadvantage and a lack of socio-economic opportunities (Mills & Blossfeld, 2013). McLanahan (2004) highlighted a polarization of low family complexity among economically resourceful families compared with increasing family complexity among economically deprived families in the United States and several European countries (McLanahan & Jacobsen, 2015). Family complexity may be negatively related to children's wellbeing solely due to negative socioeconomic selection.

However, the numerous transitions and heightened unpredictability of complex family lives that younger birth cohorts of children experience may induce stress with negative effects on socioemotional behaviour, cognitive ability, and school performance (Cavanagh & Fomby, 2019). This may depend on the complexity of the custodial parent's family life, but also on the availability of grandparents or siblings who may help buffer the negative effects of volatility across the lives of children. Similar to other studies (e.g. Hiekel & Vidal, 2020), we focused on family complexity based on partnership histories. However, our measure is also capable to incorporate complexities related to fertility, e.g. step- or half-siblings, the presence of extended kin in the household as well as geographical moves and school changes.

In future work, it will be important to assess the impact of children's family complexity on school grades and attitudes along their educational trajectories. This will contribute to recent research on inequality in educational performance as well as inequality in opportunities. Thus, our methodological approach presents the first steps in pairing techniques developed in sequence analysis with longitudinal regression-based analyses for estimating the association between life course family complexity and children's wellbeing.

Acknowledgements We would like to thank the participants of the social demography reading group at the Department of Sociology and Nuffield College, especially Christiaan Monden, and Robert Schoen for their valuable feedback at various stages of the manuscript. The study was supported by the John Fell OUP project "The Consequences of Family Complexity for Adults and Children".

Appendix

Table 10.A1 Summary statistics: Family complexity for adults by gender and parenthood status

	Childless Men	Fathers	Childless Women	Mothers
Minimum	0.00	0.00	0.00	0.00
Maximum	26.73	38.98	33.34	33.64
Mean	1.92	3.00	2.39	3.55
25th percentile	0.00	0.00	0.00	0.00
Median	0.00	2.98	1.45	3.40
75th percentile	3.48	4.57	4.13	5.23
90th percentile	5.47	6.53	6.40	7.36

Note: Own calculations based on authors' analysis sample from the UKHLS and the BHPS sample. Unit: person-year spells

Table 10.A2 Summary statistics: Family complexity for children

	Mothers life course	Fathers life course
Minimum	0.00	0.00
Maximum	39.10	37.62
Mean	1.13	1.12
25th percentile	0.00	0.00
Median	0.00	0.00
75th percentile	0.00	0.00
90th percentile	5.35	5.27

Note: Own calculations based on authors' analysis sample from the UKHLS and the BHPS sample. Unit: person-year spells

References

Biemann, T., Fasang, A. E., & Grunow, D. (2011). Do economic globalization and industry growth destabilize careers? An analysis of career complexity and career patterns over time. *Organization Studies, 32*(12), 1639–1663. https://doi.org/10.1177/0170840611421246

Billari, F. C., & Liefbroer, A. C. (2010). Towards a new pattern of transition to adulthood? *Advances in Life Course Research, 15*(2–3), 59–75. https://doi.org/10.1016/j.alcr.2010.10.003

Brückner, H., & Mayer, K. U. (2005). The De-standardization of the life course: What it might mean and if it means anything whether it actually took place. In R. Macmillan (Ed.), *The structure of the life course. Standardized? Individualized? Differentiated?* (pp. 27–54). Elsevier.

Buchmann, M. C., & Kriesi, I. (2011). Transition to adulthood in Europe. *Annual Review of Sociology, 37*(1), 481–503. https://doi.org/10.1146/annurev-soc-081309-150212

Cavanagh, S. E., & Fomby, P. (2019). Family instability in the lives of American children. *Annual Review of Sociology, 45*(1), 493–513. https://doi.org/10.1146/annurev-soc-073018-022633

Charles, M., & Grusky, D. (2004). *Occupational ghettos: The worldwide segregation of women and men*. Stanford University Press.

Cherlin, A. (2009). *Marriage, divorce, remarriage, Revised and Enlarged Edition*. Harvard University Press.

Cherlin, A. J. (2010). Demographic trends in the United States: A review of research in the 2000s. *Journal of Marriage and Family, 72*(3), 403–419. https://doi.org/10.1111/j.1741-3737.2010.00710.x

Cherlin, A. J. (2017). Introduction to the special collection on separation, divorce, repartnering, and remarriage around the world. *Demographic Research, 37*, 1275–1296.

Ciganda, D. (2015). Unstable work histories and fertility in France: An adaptation of sequence complexity measures to employment trajectories. *Demographic Research, 32*(1), 843–876. https://doi.org/10.4054/DemRes.2015.32.28

Di Nallo, A. (2019). Gender gap in repartnering: The role of parental status and custodial arrangements: Gender gap in repartnering. *Journal of Marriage and Family, 81*(1), 59–78. https://doi.org/10.1111/jomf.12527

Elzinga, C. H., & Liefbroer, A. C. (2007). De-standardization of family-life trajectories of young adults: A Cross-National Comparison Using Sequence Analysis. *European Journal of Population/Revue Européenne de Démographie, 23*(3–4), 225–250. https://doi.org/10.1007/s10680-007-9133-7

Florian, S. M. (2018). Motherhood and employment among whites, hispanics, and blacks: A life course approach: Motherhood and employment across race and age. *Journal of Marriage and Family, 80*(1), 134–149. https://doi.org/10.1111/jomf.12448

Frejka, T., & Sobotka, T. (2008). Overview Chapter 1: Fertility in Europe: Diverse, delayed and below replacement. *Demographic Research, 19*, 15–46. https://doi.org/10.4054/DemRes.2008.19.3

Gabadinho, A., Ritschard, G., Studer, M., & Müller, N. S. (2010). Indice de complexité pour le tri et la comparaison de séquences catégorielles. *Revue Des Nouvelles Technologies de l'information RNTI E-19, September 2015*, 61–66.

Gabadinho, A., Ritschard, G., Müller, N. S., & Studer, M. (2011). Analyzing and visualizing state sequences in R with TraMineR. *Journal of Statistical Software, 40*(4), 1–37.

Guzzo, K. B. (2014). New partners, more kids: Multiple-partner fertility in the United States. *The Annals of the American Academy of Political and Social Science, 654*(1), 66–86. https://doi.org/10.1177/0002716214525571

Härkönen, J., Bernardi, F., & Boertien, D. (2017). Family dynamics and child outcomes: An overview of research and open questions. *European Journal of Population, 33*(2), 163–184. https://doi.org/10.1007/s10680-017-9424-6

Hiekel, N., & Vidal, S. (2020). Childhood family structure and complexity in partnership life courses. *Social Science Research, 87*, 102400. https://doi.org/10.1016/j.ssresearch.2019.102400

Jalovaara, M., & Fasang, A. E. (2017). From never partnered to serial cohabitors: Union trajectories to childlessness. *Demographic Research, 36*(55), 1703–1720. https://doi.org/10.4054/DemRes.2017.36.55

Kalmijn, M., de Leeuw, S. G., Hornstra, M., Ivanova, K., van Gaalen, R., & van Houdt, K. (2019). Family complexity into adulthood: The central role of mothers in shaping intergenerational ties. *American Sociological Review, 84*(5), 876–904. https://doi.org/10.1177/0003122419871959

Kalmijn, M., & Leopold, T. (2021). A new look at the separation surge in Europe: Contrasting adult and child perspectives. *American Sociological Review, 86*(1), 1–34. https://doi.org/10.1177/0003122420973982

Kaufman, G. (2000). Do gender role attitudes matter?: Family formation and dissolution among traditional and egalitarian men and women. *Journal of Family Issues*. https://journals.sagepub.com/doi/abs/10.1177/019251300021001006?casa_token=Ae-kelRNB6MAAAAA:HqIk0K0yTKWHA6n0VMYGLb1wPOGTd08TE-ow1VKV_4b97jUx_Su2XWjZgWMitHI0f7GWVdjeERsa, *21*, 128–144.

Kreyenfeld, M., & Bastin, S. (2016). Reliability of union histories in social science surveys: Blurred memory, deliberate misreporting, or true tales? *Advances in Life Course Research, 27*, 30–42. https://doi.org/10.1016/j.alcr.2015.11.001

Lesthaeghe, R. (2014). The second demographic transition: A concise overview of its development: Table 1. *Proceedings of the National Academy of Sciences, 111*(51), 18112–18115. https://doi.org/10.1073/pnas.1420441111

Liefbroer, A. C., & Billari, F. C. (2010). Bringing norms back in: A theoretical and empirical discussion of their importance for understanding demographic behaviour. *Population, Space and Place, 16*(4), 287–305. https://doi.org/10.1002/psp.552

Ludwig, V., & Brüderl, J. (2018). Is there a male marital wage premium? New evidence from the United States. *American Sociological Review, 83*(4), 744–770. https://doi.org/10.1177/0003122418784909

Mari, G. (2019). Is there a fatherhood wage premium? A reassessment in societies with strong male-breadwinner legacies. *Journal of Marriage and Family, 81*(5), 1033–1052. https://doi.org/10.1111/jomf.12600

Mayer, K. U. (2009). New directions in life course research. *Annual Review of Sociology, 35*(1), 413–433. https://doi.org/10.1146/annurev.soc.34.040507.134619

McLanahan, S. (2004). Diverging destinies: How children are faring under the second demographic transition. *Demography, 41*(4), 607–627. https://doi.org/10.1353/dem.2004.0033

McLanahan, S., & Jacobsen, W. (2015). Diverging destinies revisited. In P. R. Amato, A. Booth, S. M. McHale, & J. Van Hook (Eds.), *Families in an era of increasing inequality: Diverging destinies* (pp. 3–23). Springer. https://doi.org/10.1007/978-3-319-08308-7_1

McLanahan, S., & Percheski, C. (2008). Family structure and the reproduction of inequalities. *Annual Review of Sociology, 34*(1), 257–276. https://doi.org/10.1146/annurev.soc.34.040507.134549

Mills, M., & Blossfeld, H.-P. (2013). The second demographic transition meets globalization: A comprehensive theory to understand changes in family formation in an era of rising uncertainty. In A. Evans & J. Baxter (Eds.), *Negotiating the life course: Stability and change in life pathways* (pp. 9–33). Springer. https://doi.org/10.1007/978-90-481-8912-0_2

Mynarska, M., Matysiak, A., Rybińska, A., Tocchioni, V., & Vignoli, D. (2015). Diverse paths into childlessness over the life course. *Advances in Life Course Research, 25*, 35–48. https://doi.org/10.1016/j.alcr.2015.05.003

Nandi, A., Menon, S., & Smith, R. (2020). Understanding society: Marital and cohabitation histories, 1991–2018 [Data collection]. In *UK Data Service* (2nd ed.). UK Data Service. https://doi.org/10.5255/UKDA-SN-8473-2

ONS. (2022). *Divorces in England and Wales: 2021* (Statistical Bulletin) (pp. 1–10). Office for National Statistics. https://www.ons.gov.uk/peoplepopulationandcommunity/birthsdeathsandmarriages/divorce/bulletins/divorcesinenglandandwales/latest

Pelletier, D., Bignami-Van Assche, S., & Simard-Gendron, A. (2020). Measuring life course complexity with dynamic sequence analysis. *Social Indicators Research, 152*(3), 1127–1151. https://doi.org/10.1007/s11205-020-02464-y

Raab, M., & Struffolino, E. (2019). The heterogeneity of partnership trajectories to childlessness in Germany. *European Journal of Population, 36*, 1–18.

Raley, R. K., & Sweeney, M. M. (2020). Divorce, repartnering, and stepfamilies: A decade in review. *Journal of Marriage and Family, 82*(1), 81–99. https://doi.org/10.1111/jomf.12651

Riekhoff, A.-J. (2018). Extended working lives and late-career destabilisation: A longitudinal study of Finnish register data. *Advances in Life Course Research, 35*(June 2017), 114–125. https://doi.org/10.1016/j.alcr.2018.01.007

Schoen, R. (2010). Gender competition and family change. *Genus, 66*(3), 27.

Schoen, R., & Hargens, L. (2020). Social capital, gender competition, and the resurgence of childlessness. In R. Schoen (Ed.), *Analyzing contemporary fertility* (pp. 9–24). Springer. https://doi.org/10.1007/978-3-030-48519-1_2

Thomson, E. (2014). Family complexity in Europe. *The Annals of the American Academy of Political and Social Science, 654*(1), 245–258. https://doi.org/10.1177/0002716214531384

Thomson, E. (2017). *Family complexity and kinship*. Wiley. http://urn.kb.se/resolve?urn=urn:nbn:se:su:diva-165555

University of Essex, Institute for Social and Economic Research. (2021). Understanding Society: Waves 1–9, 2009–2021 and Harmonised BHPS: Waves 1–18, 1991–2009: Special Licence Access. [data collection] (16th ed.). UK Data Service. SN: 6931. https://doi.org/10.5255/UKDA-SN-6931-15

van den Berg, L., Kalmijn, M., & Leopold, T. (2021). Stepfamily effects on early home-leaving: The role of conflict and closeness. *Journal of Marriage and Family, 83*(2), 305–321. https://doi.org/10.1111/jomf.12700

van Houdt, K. (2021). Adult (step) parent-child relationships in complex families: A latent profile analysis. *Journal of Family Studies, 0*(0), 1–23. https://doi.org/10.1080/13229400.2021.1962730

Van Winkle, Z. (2018). Family trajectories across time and space: Increasing complexity in family life courses in Europe? *Demography, 55*(1), 135–164. https://doi.org/10.1007/s13524-017-0628-5

Van Winkle, Z. (2019). Family polices and family life course complexity across 20th century Europe. *Journal of European Social Policy, 0*(0), 1–19. https://doi.org/10.1177/0958928719880508

Van Winkle, Z., & Conley, D. (2021). Genome-wide heritability estimates of family life course complexity. *Demography, 58*, 1575–1602.

Van Winkle, Z., & Fasang, A. (2017). Complexity in employment life courses in Europe in the twentieth century—Large cross-national differences but little change across birth cohorts. *Social Forces, 96*(1), 1–30. https://doi.org/10.1093/sf/sox032

Van Winkle, Z., & Fasang, A. (2021). The complexity of employment & family life courses across 20th century Europe: An update. *Demographic Research, 44*, 775–810.

Waldfogel, J., Craigie, T.-A., & Brooks-Gunn, J. (2010). Fragile families and child wellbeing. *The Future of Children/Center for the Future of Children, the David and Lucile Packard Foundation, 20*(2), 87–112.

Westerman, J., Witteveen, D., Bihagen, E., & Shahbazian, R. (2021). *Career complexity no longer on the rise: Comparing early- and mid-career complexity across the 1930s thru 1980s birth cohorts in Sweden* [Preprint]. SocArXiv. https://doi.org/10.31235/osf.io/md4t3

Chapter 11
Union Experience and Stability of Parental Unions in Sweden and Norway

Elizabeth Thomson and Jennifer A. Holland

11.1 Introduction

Over the past 50 years, a large number of European and other wealthy countries have witnessed an unprecedented decrease in the stability of intimate unions. Even when couples have children, their chances of separating before the child's 15th birthday has reached 25–30% in several countries (Andersson et al., 2017). What seems somewhat paradoxical is the fact that young adults' opportunities to find a partner and establish a stable relationship have increased, i.e., the period between leaving home or completing education and the transition to parenthood is longer than in the recent past (Billari & Liefbroer, 2010). Furthermore, young adults have acquired new opportunities to thoroughly test a relationship before becoming parents, i.e., to cohabit without children. Relationships that pass the test usually result in marriage, sometimes after a birth but often before.

Many scholars have viewed delayed childbearing, cohabitation and union instability as part of a package. One argument is that all three changes arise from a process of secularization and individuation (Lesthaeghe, 2010). Young adults place greater importance on economic achievements and personal development than on intimate relationships, or at least place greater demands on intimate relationships and are more willing than in the past to dissolve a union that does not meet those demands. Other theorists argue that shifts in gender arrangements and ideology are of greatest importance (Esping-Andersen & Billari, 2015; Goldscheider et al., 2015;

E. Thomson (✉)
Department of Sociology, Stockholm University, Stockholm, Sweden

Department of Sociology, University of Wisconsin-Madison, Madison, WI, USA
e-mail: Elizabeth.thomson@sociology.su.se

J. A. Holland
Erasmus University Rotterdam, Rotterdam, The Netherlands

R. Schoen (ed.), *The Demography of Transforming Families*, The Springer Series on Demographic Methods and Population Analysis 56,
https://doi.org/10.1007/978-3-031-29666-6_11

Schoen, 2010). Whether or not all of the changes observed arise from broader changes in individuation or gender, they have an internal logic that is not always consistent with a theory of parallel change. It remains a puzzle, for example, that taking more time and testing relationships before having children does not appear to have increased union stability in the long run, i.e., after becoming a parent (Kalmijn & Leopold, 2021).[1]

In this chapter, we ask whether increases in parental separation might not have been greater had not the accompanying shifts in parental age and union experience occurred. We investigate the question in two contexts where marriage and childbearing were dramatically delayed, while at the same time young people continued to leave home and enter partnerships at relatively young ages, i.e., Sweden and Norway (Billari & Liefbroer, 2010). We use union and birth histories from the Generations and Gender Surveys (conducted in 2012–2013 and 2007–2008, respectively) to estimate separation risks for parents who had their first child between 1960 and 10 years before the interview. We decompose those risks in terms of the parents' union experiences prior to first birth, to identify those that contributed to or suppressed increases over time in parental separation. We conclude that the increasing differentiation of parents' union experience contributed to increases in parental separation. Pure compositional effects did not, though they likely compensated each other, some generating increased likelihood, others a decreased likelihood of parental separation.

11.2 Postponed Parenthood and Shifts in Union Experience

In most of Western Europe and in many other affluent countries, the age at which young people become parents has dramatically increased. Starting in about 1975, women's average age at first birth shifted upward by three to five years, from the middle 20s to the late 20s (Frejka & Sobotka, 2008; Neels et al., 2017). This shift was also reflected in an increase in the median age at first birth across birth cohorts (Billari & Liefbroer, 2010).[2]

Delays in parenthood were for the most part accompanied by parallel delays in marriage (Beaujouan & Ní Bhrolcháin, 2011; Billari & Liefbroer, 2010; Bumpass et al., 1991; Kamp Dush et al., 2018; Manning et al., 2014; Prioux & Mandelbaum, 2003; Sobotka & Toulemon, 2008; Sobotka et al., 2003; Wright, 2016). Both marriage and parenthood constitute a threshold of commitment to a particular relationship for the foreseeable future. Marriage and parenthood establish a set of

[1] Goldscheider and colleagues do not see cohabitation and delayed childbearing as problematic or driven by the gender revolution, rather focusing on explanations for declining fertility and union stability.

[2] Parallel shifts are observed in the formerly socialist countries of east and central Europe, but not until 1990 when the Soviet Union dissolved (Frejka & Sobotka, 2008; Neels et al., 2017).

extended kin relationships and are recognized by the wider community as clear markers of adulthood.

Young adults did not, however, simply stay at home and wait until their late 20s to find partners and plan families. In some contexts, home-leaving and partnership were postponed, but not to the same extent as marriage and parenthood. In most countries, young adults left home and began living with intimate partners at about the same or even younger ages as in the past (Billari & Liefbroer, 2010; Bumpass et al., 1991; Ermisch & Francesconi, 2002; Katus et al., 2007; Manning et al., 2014; Prioux & Mandelbaum, 2003; Toulemon, 1996; Wright, 2016). Thus, in almost all affluent countries young adults experienced an extended period of adult living before they made the commitment of marriage or parenthood (Billari & Liefbroer, 2010).

During this period, described as "emerging adulthood", Arnett (2000) claims that "explorations in love . . . tend to involve a deeper level of intimacy" with a focus on individual identity and "what kind of person do I wish to have as a partner though life?" The explorations may occur while young adults continue to live at home, or live independently. Where economic resources, including employment and housing, as well as cultural norms allow (Nazio & Blossfeld, 2003), the alternative to relatively early marriage and parenthood became non-marital cohabitation (Billari & Liefbroer, 2010; Hoem et al., 2009; Katus et al., 2007; Kiernan, 2001; Nazio & Blossfeld, 2003; Sobotka & Toulemon, 2008).[3]

This exploration of intimate partnerships produces, quite by design, the high likelihood of separation from a first cohabitation, generally within a relatively short period of time (Bumpass & Sweet, 1989; Jalovaara, 2013; Jalovaara & Kulu, 2018; Schnor, 2015). The inherent nature and purpose of cohabitation therefore underlies its greater instability in comparison to marriage (Andersson & Philipov, 2002; Andersson et al., 2017; Bumpass & Sweet, 1989; Eickmeyer, 2019; Jalovaara, 2013; Jalovaara & Kulu, 2018; Liefbroer & Dourleijn, 2006; Raley & Bumpass, 2003; Teachman et al., 1991; Žilinčíková, 2017). This means that many young adults enter more than one cohabitation before "settling down" with a life partner and having children. The likelihood of experiencing more than one cohabiting union has increased across cohorts (Bukodi, 2012; Dommermuth & Wiik, 2014; Eickmeyer & Manning, 2018; Lichter & Qian, 2008; Lichter et al., 2010; Sobotka et al., 2003; Vespa, 2014). On the other hand, if a first cohabitation proves satisfactory, postponing parenthood means that couples live together much longer before becoming parents than did the generations before them. In the U.S. Lamidi et al. (2019) found that cohabitations formed around 2010 lasted longer, about 18 months, than those formed in the mid-1980s (about 12 months), due mostly to delayed marriage. Because the study did not censor at first birth, we don't know whether couples have also had more time together before becoming parents.

Cohabitation has also increased as a context for parenthood. Dramatic increases in non-marital births (Klüsener, 2015; Sobotka & Toulemon, 2008) are comprised

[3] References to a large number of country-specific increases in cohabitation can be found in Thomson (2022).

entirely of increases in births to cohabiting couples (Bumpass & Lu, 2000; Ermisch, 2001; Kennedy & Bumpass, 2008; Kiernan, 2001; Laplante & Fostik, 2015; Le Bourdais & Lapierre-Adamcyk, 2004; Perelli-Harris et al., 2012; Raley, 2001; Thomson & Eriksson, 2013; Wright, 2019). Though many couples marry after having a first child together (Holland, 2013, 2017), they begin their parental experience in cohabitation. Finally, increasing rates of parental separation have generated an increased pool of parents among potential partners. Thus, an increasing proportion of "first" births will occur in stepfamilies. As discussed further below, the state of the couple's relationship at first birth, as well as their earlier "explorations in love" have varying implications for subsequent family stability.

11.3 Implications of Union Experience for Family Stability

At the same time that parenthood was dramatically postponed, rates of parental separation were increasing (Andersson & Philipov, 2002; Andersson et al., 2017; Beaujouan, 2016; Kalmijn & Leopold, 2021; Kennedy & Thomson, 2010; Musick & Michelmore, 2015; Thomson & Eriksson, 2013). These parallel trends have been explained in terms of increasing secularization and individualism (Lesthaeghe, 2010) or changing gender arrangements and ideology (Esping-Andersen & Billari, 2015; Goldscheider et al., 2015; Schoen, 2010). Secularization and individualism were purported to increase acceptance of less and later childbearing as well as more fluid sexual relationships. Increasing gender equality made early motherhood more costly and commitment to a lifetime partner for economic support less necessary.

On the other hand, the internal life course dynamics of these changes could have generated a different trend in parental separation. Older parents are more emotionally and cognitively mature. They have acquired more human capital, and have often established wide, stable social networks. They may also have developed clearer ideas about the gender arrangements they seek as partners and parents. These conditions bode well for relationship quality and stability. Indeed, age at first birth is strongly associated with a lower risk of parental separation (Berrington & Diamond, 1999; Kennedy & Thomson, 2010; Lichter et al., 2016; Manning et al., 2004; Pelletier, 2016; Schnor, 2014; Wu & Musick, 2008).

The option to cohabit rather than marry also provided prospective parents with the opportunity to better assess their relationship for the long-term commitment of parenthood. Most couples cohabit with such a test explicitly in mind (Huang et al., 2011; Perelli-Harris & Bernardi, 2015; Perelli-Harris et al., 2014). The theoretical implications of cohabitation for parental separation depend on when cohabitation and parenthood occur in the couple's relationship. Cohabiting couples who marry before having children might be expected to have more relationship experience and be better prepared for parenthood than couples who marry directly.

Most studies find, contrary to expectations, that premarital cohabitation is associated with higher divorce risks (see Thomson, 2022 for an extensive list of such studies). Analyses with more extensive controls or that incorporate unobserved differences between cohabiters and those who marry directly have shown that selection mechanisms accounted entirely for the higher divorce rates of those who cohabited (ibid.). In addition, the relationship may vary across time and place (Kiernan, 2001; Manning & Cohen, 2012; Reinhold, 2010; Svarer, 2004). Higher divorce rates for premarital cohabiters appear to occur when cohabitation is rare or almost universal, i.e., when those who cohabit or marry directly comprise a small minority (Liefbroer & Dourleijn, 2006; Wagner & Weiss, 2006). Some studies have found the expected negative effect of cohabitation on divorce – consistent with the relationship testing mechanism – once observed and unobserved differences between cohabiters and non-cohabiters were controlled (Brüderl et al., 1997; Kulu & Boyle, 2010; Reinhold, 2010; Svarer, 2004). In these studies, parenthood was included as a time-varying covariate, suggesting that parenthood is selective of the most committed marriages. The models do not, however, enable us to determine how premarital cohabitation is associated with divorce *among* those who had children.

While couples are cohabiting, time itself has the potential for improving the quality of the relationship and its subsequent stability. Time together is, in fact, one of the arguments for the hypothesized lower divorce rates among couples who cohabited prior to marriage. Couples are able to develop the practical and emotional dimensions of their relationship so that it better suits them both. Over time, the relationship may also benefit from being more extensively embedded in a network of friendships and kin. These strengths should remain when the couple becomes parents.

As for premarital cohabitation, almost all research on how a couple's relationship develops over time does not distinguish separation or divorce among parents from the separations of childless couples. Union stability is positively associated with the length of time a couple dated prior to marriage (Brüderl & Kalter, 2001; Murphy, 1985) or cohabitation (Schnor, 2015). On the other hand, evidence is completely contradictory for the association between duration of premarital cohabitation and divorce (see Thomson, 2022 for a review). The few studies that have investigated the association between union duration and separation after a child's birth generally find a negligible or no association (Kennedy & Thomson, 2010; Musick & Michelmore, 2015, 2018).

Some evidence for time together prior to parenthood is in relation to pregnancy. Separation risks are higher for cohabitations and marriages occurring during pregnancy (Berrington & Diamond, 1999; Bracher et al., 1993; Gibson-Davis et al., 2016; Lichter et al., 2016; Murphy, 1985; Rackin & Gibson-Davis, 2012; Teachman & Polonko, 1990; but see Teachman et al., 1991). Pregnancy may interrupt the normal process of selection out of lower quality relationships, keeping couples together who might otherwise have separated. In addition, however, it may not be the shorter time together, but the stress of an unplanned pregnancy that generates higher separation risks (Guzzo & Hayford, 2012; Manning et al., 2004).

The idea of cohabitation as a testing ground for relationships suggests that even those who end a first cohabitation may have acquired insights and skills for choosing a more suitable partner and/or developing a high-quality relationship (Young et al., 2011). Opportunities to try out different relationships might therefore be positively associated with the stability of the relationship in which one eventually has children. On the other hand, having experienced a failed coresidential relationship may be an indicator of poor relationship skills, or may generate social and emotional damage that is carried over to new relationships (Young et al., 2011). It is also possible that most dissolved cohabitations were never viewed as potential long-term relationships or as practice for future relationships, but simply as practical arrangements for a stable sexual, social and economic life (Huang et al., 2011; Nazio & Blossfeld, 2003). In that case, prior cohabitations would have no implications for the stability of a first-birth union.

Again, almost all of the evidence on separation rates in second- or higher-order unions does not distinguish unions with and without children. Studies in the U.K. and U.S. report higher separation rates and lower marriage intentions or marriage rates for those in a second- or higher-order cohabitation (Berrington & Diamond, 1999; Bukodi, 2012; Cohen & Manning, 2010; Lichter & Qian, 2008; Vespa, 2014). A pooled analysis of 18 countries also found higher separation rates in second or higher-order unions (Žilinčíková, 2017). On the other hand, no differences were found in Germany (Hiekel & Fulda, 2018), though Schnor (2015) reported a higher separation rate when couples had dated for 7–24 months prior to cohabitation or marriage. Using models that control for the underlying propensity to form a second cohabiting union, separation risks were found to be the same for first and second cohabiting unions in the U.K. (Steele et al., 2006) and Norway (Poortman & Lyngstad, 2007). Marriages that follow a first cohabitation were also less stable in the U.K. and U.S. (Steele et al., 2006; Teachman & Polonko, 1990). But in Norway, where almost all couples cohabit prior to marriage, those who married after a previous cohabitation were less likely to divorce than those who married their first partner, either directly or after cohabiting (Poortman & Lyngstad, 2007).

The few studies of prior unions and parental separation produce quite mixed findings. Studies in the U.S. and Sweden based on children's risk of their parent's separation found a higher risk if their parent had a prior union (Kennedy & Thomson, 2010; Manning et al., 2004). Similarly, Musick and Michelmore (2015) reported an increased risk for U.S. parents having a first child in the 1990s, but not in the 2000s. Wu and Musick (2008) found no differences among U.S. parents, and no differences were found for several other countries (Musick & Michelmore, 2018). Differences in model specification may underlie the conflicting findings.

When cohabiting couples do not marry before having a child together, the evidence is quite clear that they are at higher risk for eventual separation (Andersson & Philipov, 2002; Andersson et al., 2017; Heuveline et al., 2003; Kiernan, 1999, 2001; Manning et al., 2004; Musick & Michelmore, 2018; Schnor, 2014; Wu & Musick, 2008; Žilinčíková, 2017). As for the association between premarital cohabitation and divorce, the difference is smaller where cohabiting parenthood is more common (Andersson et al., 2017; Clarke & Jensen, 2004; Le Bourdais &

Lapierre-Adamcyk, 2004; Pelletier, 2016; Schnor, 2014; but see Jensen & Clausen, 2003; Kennedy & Bumpass, 2008).[4]

As a result of increases in parental separation, the pool of single persons increasingly includes those who have children. Consequently, the chances that one partner's first birth occurs in the context of a stepfamily has increased (Andersson & Philipov, 2002; Andersson et al., 2017; Guzzo, 2017). Stepfamily couples face complexities in household and family arrangements that may decrease relationship quality and increase the likelihood of separation (Beaujouan, 2016; Booth & Edwards, 1992; Cherlin, 1978; Henz & Thomson, 2005; White & Booth, 1985).

11.4 Parallel Life Experiences Prior to Parenthood

The increasing gap between home-leaving and first-time parenthood has, of course, been filled with experiences other than intimate partnerships. The primary shifts are in tertiary education and women's careers. Theoretically, most of the pathways through which education may influence union stability would predict *decreases* in parental separation, contrary to what has been observed. Possible mechanisms are educational effects on the partnership experiences prior to first birth outlined above, as well as potential direct effects on the quality of relationships and/or ideas about separation and divorce.

The evidence is clear that educational enrollment inhibits childbearing (see review in Neels et al., 2017). Increases in tertiary educational enrollment are estimated to account for at least half of increases in age at first birth (Neels & De Wachter, 2010; Neels et al., 2017; Ní Bhrolcháin & Beaujouan, 2012). Accumulation of career resources, measured by employment and occupational experience, has also been associated with delayed childbearing (Blossfeld & Huinink, 1991).

Although in some contexts the higher educated were pioneers in cohabitation, the educational gradient is uniformly negative with respect to cohabiting births (Gibson-Davis & Rackin, 2014; Kennedy & Thomson, 2010; Jalovaara & Andersson, 2018; Mikolai et al., 2018; Perelli-Harris et al., 2010b; Schnor & Jalovaara, 2019; Trimarchi & van Bavel, 2018). Very little evidence exists for educational differentials in multiple unions or longer unions prior to parenthood, the direction of these associations is mixed, and distinctions are not clearly made between unions prior to or after first birth (Dommermuth & Wiik, 2014; Hiekel & Fulda, 2018; Lamidi et al., 2019; Lichter & Qian, 2008).

Net of union experience, increases in education ought to provide greater resources for union stability, including material conditions and interpersonal skills (Härkönen

[4]Many studies find that couples who marry after a first birth have similar divorce rates to those who married before (Kiernan, 1999; Manning et al., 2004; Musick & Michelmore, 2015, 2018; Wu & Musick, 2008). In some countries and for some population groups, however, post-birth marriages were less stable than pre-birth marriages (Manning et al., 2004; Musick & Michelmore, 2018; Kiernan, 2001; Žilinčíková, 2017).

& Dronkers, 2006). Especially in recent decades, education is associated with gender egalitarian view and family arrangements, which in turn appear to increase union stability (Kaufman, 2000; Oláh & Gähler, 2014; Sigle-Rushton, 2010). On the other hand, education may foster secular and individualistic beliefs that reduce barriers to union dissolution (Aassve et al., 2013; Fučík, 2020; Liefbroer & Billari, 2010). Their relative economic independence may further reduce barriers to separation among highly educated couples (Grow et al., 2017; Henz & Jonsson, 2003; Schwartz & Han, 2014; South, 2001). It appears that the forces for stability are stronger as higher-educated parents are less likely to separate (Jalovaara & Andersson, 2018; Kalmijn & Leopold, 2021; Kennedy & Thomson, 2010). Kalmijn and Leopold (2021) showed, furthermore, that increases in separation have been much greater for low- versus high-educated parents and that in some contexts separation rates have been stable over a 50-year period for high-educated parents.

11.5 Identifying Contributions of Changes in Young Adult Experience to Parental Separation

A few studies have investigated the contributions of changes in partnership experience and higher education to increases in parental separation at the aggregate level. Härkönen (2017) used Swedish register data to show that parental separation increased from the 1970 to the 1990 first-birth cohorts, then slightly decreased. Comparing coefficients from successive models of the separation risk, he showed that increases in age at first birth and educational attainment suppressed what would have otherwise been a greater increase in separation. On the other hand, increases in cohabiting first births accounted for a small portion of the increase in parental separation.

Musick and Michelmore (2015) analyzed increases in parental separation from the 1990s to the 2000s in the United States. For each decade, they estimated the risk of parental separation after the birth of any child within 10 years of the interview, then generated predicted probabilities of separation within 5 years of the child's birth. The analysis focused on parental separation by union status, with time-varying indicators for the couple's marriage at or after the birth. Despite considerable change in union status, predicted probabilities of parental separation were essentially the same in each decade. When union status indicators for the 1990s were substituted using coefficients for the 2000s, the predicted probability of parental separation was only slightly decreased.

Thomson et al. (2019) conducted a microsimulation of women's life courses in Italy, the United Kingdom, and Scandinavia (combining Sweden and Norway), focusing on cohabitation at first births to women born from the 1940s to the

1970s.[5] They estimated a considerable contribution of cohabiting parenthood to parental separation for cohorts in which cohabiting parenthood had "taken off", i.e., reached levels of acceptability. For the youngest Scandinavian cohorts, of whom more than half had a first birth in cohabitation, the lower rate of separation (divorce) among married parents was counterbalanced by a higher separation rate for cohabiting parents, so that overall children's experience of parental separation was about the same as for earlier cohorts. Increasing age at first birth contributed only marginally to offset increases in parental separation associated with cohabitation at birth (Thomson et al., 2017).

Taken together, the studies provide some evidence that cohabitation at birth contributed to increases rather than decreases in parental separation, opposite predictions based on relationship testing, while education and age at first birth offset those contributions to some degree. While the study by Musick and Michelmore (2015) suggests more modest contributions, the periods they observed are those when parental separation was leveling off in the U.S. and may not reflect contributions of union experience to changes for earlier periods and cohorts. None of the studies estimated contributions of the full complement of partnership and educational shifts that are the focus of this study.

11.6 Union Experience, Education, and Parental Separation in Norway and Sweden

Norway and Sweden were among the countries in northern and western Europe that experienced dramatic increases in age at first birth, beginning in 1970 and almost linear through the early 2000s (Frejka & Sobotka, 2008; Neels et al., 2017; Sobotka & Toulemon, 2008). As in other Nordic and some Western European countries, Swedes and Norwegians have a long history of relatively early home-leaving, and across cohorts form first unions in their very early 20 s (Billari & Liefbroer, 2010). Both countries have, however, been leaders in the postponement of marriage, increases in cohabitation, and in particular cohabitation as a context for childbearing (Sobotka & Toulemon, 2008; Klüsener, 2015; Andersson et al., 2017). Trend data on the other union experiences that might influence parental separation are limited; Dommermuth and Wiik (2014) reported cohort increases in the number of unions Norwegian women and men have entered by age 35. Norway and Sweden were also in the vanguard of increases in divorce (Sobotka & Toulemon, 2008) and parental separation (Andersson & Philipov, 2002; Andersson et al., 2017; Thomson & Eriksson, 2013). Because both countries have experienced changes in union formation, childbearing, and union dissolution over several decades, they provide a

[5] Although the models include prior union experiences, the decompositions did not investigate their contribution to increasing rates of parental separation.

context in which it is possible to investigate how shifts in union experience prior to first birth may contribute to the stability of parental unions.

Despite high levels of economic equality, the Nordic countries also remain a reasonable laboratory for identifying the role of increasing educational attainment on parental separation across cohorts. Tertiary education expanded quite rapidly in both countries, especially in the late 1980s and 1990s (OECD, 2011), and as in other countries is associated with postponement of marriage (Sobotka & Toulemon, 2008) and childbearing (Neels et al., 2017), and with having a first birth in cohabitation (Kennedy & Thomson, 2010; Perelli-Harris et al., 2010b; Trimarchi & van Bavel, 2018). A negative educational gradient is also observed for separation or divorce (Kennedy & Thomson, 2010; Lyngstad, 2004).

As noted above, previous studies have identified positive contributions of cohabiting first birth and negative contributions of increasing education and age at first birth to increase in parental separation. Those that cover cohorts where family changes were most dramatic include a limited set of union experiences, while the U.S. study with a broader set of experiences covers only a short period of family change. Our analyses bring together the longer period of observation and wider union experience.

11.7 Data and Methods

The Swedish and Norwegian Generations and Gender Surveys provide union and birth histories required to construct indicators of union experience prior to first birth and estimates of separation after a first birth in a union. Each survey is based on a random selection of the population between 18 and 79 years of age, stratified by sex, age (under 50, 50+) and large cities vs. other places of residence. The Swedish survey was conducted in 2012–2013 with a response rate of 54%, the Norwegian survey in 2007–2008 with a response rate of 60%. For our analysis, we used versions of data files available in the Harmonized Histories (Perelli-Harris et al., 2010a).

Our analysis is limited to respondents with a first birth in a cohabiting or marital union between 1960 and up to 10 years before the interview, 1997 for Norway and 2003 for Sweden. The cutoff prior to interview enables us to observe separations up to the first child's 10th birthday. Samples sizes were further reduced by exclusions of inconsistent or missing data from union and birth histories, leaving analytic samples of 6343 (Norway) and 4541 (Sweden).

Birth and union histories were combined to produce the indicators of union experience: first birth cohort (1960s, 1970s, 1980s, 1990s); age at first birth (<20, 20–24, 25–29, 30–34, 35+); first birth in cohabitation versus marriage; number of unions prior to the first birth union (0, 1, 2+); length of union prior to first birth (months: 0–7, 8–12, 13–24, 25–36, 37–48, 49–60, 60+); and whether the partner had prior children (stepfamily).[6] Educational attainment was measured on the ISCED scale and categorized as less than secondary, secondary, post-secondary. We also included indicators of the parent's childhood experiences that might underlie young adult union experiences, educational attainment, and/or union stability: respondent's sex and immigrant status (Härkönen, 2017), and whether parents had separated prior to the respondent's 15th birthday (see review and results in Härkönen et al., 2021). We observe separation from the first birth union within the subsequent 10 years (yes/no).

Models of separation after first birth were estimated with discrete-time logistic regression from the first child's birth to the child's 10th birthday, parents' separation or the end of our observation window, whichever came first. Duration dependence was specified in categories of months: 0–7, 8–12, 13–24, 25–36, 37–48, 60+. Separate models were generated for each first-birth cohort in each country.

To estimate contributions of partnership experience and/or education to increasing parental separation, we first used the average marginal effects and mean values of each covariate to generate predicted probabilities of parental separation for each cohort and country. We then generated predicted probabilities using the average marginal effects for a given cohort and the mean values of covariates for each other cohort. Comparing predicted probabilities of parental separation with different mean values or different average marginal effects shows how cohort changes in life course experiences and/or their effects on parental separation contributed to cohort change in parental separation.

11.8 Results

Table 11.1 presents changes across first-birth cohorts in union and other experiences, separately for Norway and Sweden. The first row shows the steady increase in parental separation from first births in the 1960s to those in the 1990s. In Norway, almost 15% and in Sweden 16% had separated by the child's 10th birthday. The next two rows show that those who became parents in the 1960s and the 1990s formed their first unions at about the same age. To the contrary, age at first birth increased dramatically. As a result, the gap between first union and first birth also increased, by 3.5 years in Norway, almost 4 years in Sweden. The fourth row shows that average union duration at first birth also increased over these years, from 20 or fewer months in the 1960s to above 40 months in the 1990s. Across first-birth cohorts, the gap between first union and first birth was filled for the most part by time spent in the union that would produce the first birth, but among younger cohorts, there was an increase in time out of union or in a union that did not produce a first birth.

[6] Top or bottom categories were combined for cohorts where the category had insufficient observations for valid estimates.

Table 11.1 Cohort change in union characteristics, education, family background, and parental separation

	Norway				Sweden				
First Child's Birth Cohort:	1960s	1970s	1980s	1990s	1960s	1970s	1980s	1990s	2000s
	Percent of parents								
Separated 10 years > 1st birth	6.2	9.7	12.5	14.7	9.0	12.7	13.1	16.1	9.3
	Mean (years)								
Age at 1st union	23.2	23.1	23.3	23.2	22.2	22.6	22.7	22.9	23.6
Age at 1st birth	24.4	25.1	26.7	27.8	23.9	25.8	27.4	28.5	30.2
	Mean (months)								
Union duration at birth	16.0	23.8	35.8	41.8	20.2	34.9	44.3	46.4	49.9
	Percent of parents								
Union < 1st birth union	0.4	1.9	6.8	18.9	1.4	8.0	18.4	27.7	35.3
Cohabiting at birth	3.0	10.3	32.1	53.8	11.8	38.5	55.4	60.7	61.6
Stepchild at union	1.7	4.1	6.2	8.7	4.1	8.5	8.8	9.0	9.5
Tertiary education	21.9	32.1	35.6	39.7	26.0	32.0	36.4	37.2	46.7
Foreign born	3.2	3.4	5.7	7.5	9.1	9.7	11.0	12.4	13.9
Parents separated < age 15	4.2	3.4	6.2	8.5	6.5	9.7	12.7	17.8	21.8

Data: Harmonized Histories (www.ggp-i.org; downloaded 2016-02-22)

The next set of rows shows changes in other aspects of union experience. Compared to first-time parents in the 1960s, those making the transition to parenthood in the 1990s were much more likely to have had two or more partners, to be cohabiting rather than married at first birth, and to have a first birth with someone who was already a parent.

In both countries (bottom three rows), increases were observed across cohorts in those with a tertiary education (with a corresponding decrease in compulsory education, not shown). Small increases were also found in the percent foreign-born. The percent of first-time parents whose own parents had separated or divorced increased substantially across first-birth cohorts.

Tables 11.2a and 11.2b provide marginal effects from the logistic regressions within country and first birth cohort. In both countries, age at first birth – but not age at first union (analyses available on request) – was inversely associated with separation within 10 years of the birth. In Sweden, differentiation increased for the 1980s cohort, while in Norway differences were especially pronounced for the 1990s cohort. Separation was less likely for those who had lived together longer, in both countries appearing predominantly in the 1990s cohort. Those who cohabited, had a prior union, or had a stepchild at first birth had higher separation risks, with the

Table 11.2a Multivariate models of parental separation by birth cohort, Sweden

	Birth cohort											
	1960s			1970s			1980s			1990s		
	dy/dx	(SE)		dy/dx	(SE)		dy/dx	(SE)		dy/dx	(SE)	
Female	−0.01	(0.02)		−0.01	(0.02)		0.01	(0.02)		−0.01	(0.02)	
Cohabiting at 1st birth	0.04	(0.03)		0.09	(0.02)	***	0.03	(0.02)		0.08	(0.02)	***
Age at 1st birth (ref 10–19 years)												
20–24 years	−0.14	(0.06)	*	−0.15	(0.07)	*	−0.22	(0.10)	*	−0.12	(0.08)	+
25–29 years	−0.20	(0.06)	**	−0.23	(0.07)	***	−0.31	(0.10)	***	−0.18	(0.08)	*
30–34 years[a]	−0.21	(0.07)	**	−0.24	(0.07)	***	−0.35	(0.10)	***	−0.20	(0.08)	**
35+ years	–			−0.28	(0.07)	***	−0.39	(0.10)	***	−0.19	(0.08)	*
Stepchild at 1st birth	0.04	(0.06)		0.16	(0.04)	***	0.03	(0.04)		0.06	(0.04)	
Union duration 1st birth (ref 0–7)												
8–12 months	−0.05	(0.03)	+	0.05	(0.04)		−0.05	(0.05)		−0.06	(0.07)	
13–24 months	−0.02	(0.03)		−0.01	(0.03)		0.02	(0.04)		−0.12	(0.06)	*
25–36 months	−0.05	(0.03)		−0.02	(0.04)		−0.05	(0.04)		−0.18	(0.06)	**
37–48 months	0.03	(0.06)		−0.06	(0.04)		−0.05	(0.04)		−0.21	(0.06)	***
49–60 months[b]	−0.07	(0.04)	+	−0.08	(0.04)	*	−0.08	(0.05)	+	−0.23	(0.06)	***
>60 months	–			−0.06	(0.04)		−0.12	(0.04)	**	−0.27	(0.06)	***
Prior unions (none)												
1[c]	0.15	(0.14)		−0.04	(0.03)		0.05	(0.03)	+	0.01	(0.03)	
2+	–			0.40	(0.20)	*	0.19	(0.10)	+	0.05	(0.05)	
Parents separated <15	0.09	(0.05)	+	−0.01	(0.03)		0.08	(0.03)	*	0.12	(0.03)	***

(continued)

Table 11.2a (continued)

	Birth cohort											
	1960s			1970s			1980s			1990s		
	dy/dx	(SE)		dy/dx	(SE)		dy/dx	(SE)		dy/dx	(SE)	
Education (ref: compulsory)												
Secondary	0.01	(0.02)		0.06	(0.02)	*	0.03	(0.03)		0.02	(0.04)	
Tertiary	0.01	(0.03)		0.07	(0.03)	*	0.02	(0.03)		−0.03	(0.04)	
Foreign-born	0.08	(0.04)	+	0.02	(0.03)		0.03	(0.03)		0.05	(0.04)	
N	704			1077			1129			1149		

Note: + $p < 0.1$ * $p < 0.05$ ** $p < 0.01$ *** $p < 0.001$

Data: Harmonized Histories (www.ggp-i.org; downloaded 2016-02-22)

[a]1960s cohort category is 30+ years

[b]1960s cohort category is >48 months

[c]1960s cohort category is 1+

Table 11.2b Multivariate models of parental separation by birth cohort, Norway

	Birth cohort											
	1960s			1970s			1980s			1990s		
	dy/dx	(SE)		dy/dx	(SE)		dy/dx	(SE)		dy/dx	(SE)	
Female	0.04	(0.01)	**	0.00	(0.01)		−0.02	(0.02)		0.01	(0.02)	
Cohabiting at 1st birth	0.03	(0.04)		0.12	(0.03)	***	0.09	(0.02)	***	0.10	(0.02)	***
Age at 1st birth (ref: 10–19 years)												
20–24 years	−0.03	(0.03)		−0.08	(0.04)	+	−0.04	(0.05)		−0.38	(0.11)	***
25–29 years	−0.06	(0.03)	+	−0.13	(0.04)	**	−0.11	(0.05)	*	−0.47	(0.11)	***
30–34 years[a]	−0.05	(0.04)		−0.16	(0.04)	***	−0.13	(0.05)	*	−0.46	(0.11)	***
35+ years	–			−0.17	(0.05)	***	−0.12	(0.06)	*	−0.42	(0.12)	***
Stepchild at 1st birth	−0.05	(0.05)		0.08	(0.04)	+	0.11	(0.04)	**	0.09	(0.03)	**
Union duration 1st birth (ref: 0–7)												
8–12 months	0.07	(0.06)		0.02	(0.02)		−0.01	(0.03)		−0.08	(0.04)	+
13–24 months	−0.02	(0.02)		0.03	(0.02)		−0.02	(0.03)		−0.06	(0.04)	
25–36 months	0.03	(0.02)		0.01	(0.02)		0.01	(0.03)		−0.06	(0.04)	
37–48 months	0.00	(0.03)		0.02	(0.03)		−0.04	(0.03)		−0.03	(0.04)	
49–60 months[b]	−0.02	(0.03)		0.04	(0.05)		−0.01	(0.04)		−0.11	(0.04)	**
>60 months	–			−0.03	(0.03)		−0.09	(0.03)	**	−0.15	(0.04)	***
Prior unions (none)												
1[c]	−0.02	(0.03)		0.02	(0.05)		−0.01	(0.03)		0.01	(0.02)	
2+	–			–						0.11	(0.07)	
Parents separated <15	0.09	(0.05)	+	0.07	(0.05)		0.09	(0.04)	**	0.07	(0.03)	*

(continued)

Table 11.2b (continued)

		Birth cohort											
		1960s			1970s			1980s			1990s		
		dy/dx	(SE)		dy/dx	(SE)		dy/dx	(SE)		dy/dx	(SE)	
Education (ref: compulsory)													
Secondary		−0.02	(0.02)		0.02	(0.02)		−0.02	(0.02)		−0.02	(0.02)	
Tertiary		0.01	(0.02)		0.03	(0.02)		−0.03	(0.02)		−0.02	(0.03)	
Foreign-born		0.02	(0.05)		0.10	(0.05)		0.10	(0.04)	*	0.02	(0.04)	
N		1208			1712			1761			1662		

Note: + $p < 0.1$ * $p < 0.05$ ** $p < 0.01$ *** $p < 0.001$

Data: Harmonized Histories (www.ggp-i.org; downloaded 2016-02-22)

[a]1960s cohort category is 30+ years

[b]1960s cohort category is >48 months

[c]1960s, 1970s, 1980s cohort category is 1+

Table 11.3 Decomposition of Cohort change in parental separation

Composition	Coefficient	Predicted proportion separated	
First birth cohort		Norway	Sweden
1960s	1960s	0.05	0.05
1990s	1960s	0.05	0.07
1960s	1990s	0.12	0.13
1990s	1990s	0.10	0.15

difference fluctuating across cohorts but not showing an increasing or decreasing trend. In both countries, experiencing the separation or divorce of one's own parents was positively associated with the risk for oneself, again with fluctuations but no clear increase or decrease across cohorts. Educational differences and those between native- and foreign-born individuals were modest and also did not show clear patterns across cohorts.

Table 11.3 presents results of the decomposition for change between first-birth cohorts of the 1960s and 1990s. The top and bottom rows are predicted probabilities from the 1960s and 1990s equations, respectively. Predicted probabilities of separation within 10 years of the first child's birth are slightly lower than observed, but it is the relative size of the predicted values under different models and characteristics that shows how union and other experiences generated change in parental separation.

The second row includes predicted separation probabilities from the 1960s model, assuming the experiences of first-time parents in the 1960s are the same as those having a first birth in the 1990s. No changes are found in Norway, a slight increase in Sweden. The third row presents estimates using the 1990s model, but assuming experiences of first-time parents in the 1960s. In both Norway and Sweden, parental separation would have been much higher – at levels observed for later cohorts of first-time parents – even with the composition of experiences for the 1960s. This result suggests that it is not the changing composition in terms of union experiences of new parents that mattered, but the increased differentiation arising from those changes.

On the other hand, the differentials presented in Tables 11.2a and 11.2b show that while compositional changes did occur, they could have been completely offsetting in their implications for the risk of separation after first birth. Cohabitation, prior unions, stepchildren, and having separated parents all increased and all were positively associated with separation. At the same time, age at first birth and time living together before a first birth also increased and were negatively associated with separation. This cancelling out is why the compositional shifts did not produce shifts in parental separation.

The fact that the population became increasingly differentiated in experiences relevant for union stability seems to have contributed more to the overall increase in parental separation. This is particularly true for age at first birth and time living together as a childless couple. While increasing proportions delayed parenthood but not cohabitation, some continued to have children at earlier ages and shorter union durations. By the 1990s, this increased differentiation appears to have produced considerable differentiation in the risk of separation. One could think of the underlying change as compositional change that produces the shift in differentiation.

11.9 Conclusions and Discussion

Our analysis focused on the contribution of cohort change in union experiences prior to first birth to changes in the likelihood of parental separation. We posited that increases in age at first birth, opportunities to fully test intimate relationships before having a child, and the economic resources provided by increased education should have generated lower rather than the observed higher rates of parental separation. We found, indeed, that age at first birth and longer periods of coresidence (almost all of it in cohabitation) had increased across cohorts and were associated with lower likelihood of separation after a first birth. Increasing proportions of first-time parents had prior cohabiting or marital partners, but that experience was *positively* associated with separation, suggesting that those with previous unsuccessful partnerships had not acquired experience that might lead to a more stable subsequent partnership. Swedish and Norwegian parents were also increasingly likely to remain unmarried at the birth of their first child, to have experienced their own parents' separation, and to have a stepchild at first birth; as many studies have shown, both experiences were strongly positively associated with the likelihood of separation after first birth. Educational and immigrant experiences had also changed but had little association with parental separation.

Increases in parental separation were not, however, accounted for simply by compositional changes in experiences of first-time parents. Assigning the 1960s parents to have the same experiences as the 1990s parents did not substantially change their predicted separation. As noted above, the result could be due to completely compensating compositional changes. That is, the stabilizing effect of older ages or longer periods of coresidence prior to first birth could be completely offset by what appear to be indicators of lower relationship quality or commitment – having one or more previous partners and choosing not to marry before having a child. Had it not been for the increases in stabilizing experience, increases in parental separation might have been much larger; had it not been for increases in destabilizing experiences, parental separation rates might have been lower in the 1990s.

On the other hand, the *differentiation* of first-time parents in these experiences also shifted over time and did account for a considerable amount of the increased probability of separation. Had the same differentiation been observed for earlier cohorts, parental separation would have been more common in the 1960s. Of course, increasing differentiation arises from the fact that the "ceilings" have moved up while the "floors" have not. Many couples are still quite young at first birth and have children after only a short time living together. The vast majority of couples still have a first child in the first union, and neither has prior children. These couples are increasingly differentiated from couples with other experiences that, on balance, increase their propensity to separate.

The fact that dramatic increases in educational attainment did not also exert a stabilizing effect on parental unions suggests that education serves primarily to delay first births and prolong unions prior to birth, both of which reduce parental separation. As first births increasingly occur well after completing education and with the intervening periods of employment and career building, education per se may have a less direct effect on relationship quality or commitment. We note, however, that we could not directly observe the employment or income associated with education that might have produced different risks of parental separation. Neither did we have data on the couple's gender ideology or practice that might contribute to the stability of parental unions (Esping-Andersen & Billari, 2015; Goldscheider et al., 2015; Schoen, 2010).

As forerunners in family change, Sweden and Norway provided an appropriate context for investigating long-term change in union experience and parental separation. On the other hand, they share two key features that might limit the generalization of our findings to other contexts. Both countries are marked by a strong welfare state that provides economic supports to all families with children, regardless of the parents' marital status or coresidence. Minimal distinctions are made in law between the rights and responsibilities of cohabiting and married couples who have children together (Sánchez Gassen & Perelli-Harris, 2015). Legal barriers to separation are not that much different, again reducing a potential theoretical reason for differences in separation rates. Because the marriage/cohabitation differential in separation is smaller in Norway and Sweden than in most other wealthy countries (Andersson et al., 2017), we might expect increases in cohabiting parenthood to have greater implications for parental separation in other contexts.

Another contextual factor is gender equality; both countries are among those with the highest levels of gender equality – not only in the public but also in the private sphere. Among western countries, they led the increase in female labor force participation during the last half of the twentieth century (Organisation for Economic Co-operation and Development, 2022). Gender egalitarian ideals are widely held, much more so than in other countries (Aassve et al., 2014; Baxter, 1997; Breen & Cooke, 2005). Gender-neutral systems of parental leave have made it possible in theory for couples to more equally distribute the time-intensive work of early childhood, so that increases in paternal care of children were observed earlier in Sweden and Norway than elsewhere (Altintas & Sullivan, 2017; Neilsson & Stanfors, 2014; Stanfors & Goldscheider, 2017). The societal gender context may underlie the minimal educational differences observed in parental separation. In less gender egalitarian contexts, we might expect a stronger difference between highly educated (and gender egalitarian) couples compared to low educated (and gender traditional) couples. This would be true only if the influence of education on parental separation goes beyond educational effects on age at first birth.

In contexts with substantial legal or economic barriers to parental separation, especially for married parents, or with traditional gender arrangements in the family and public life, increasing differentiation in union experience prior to first birth may not contribute in the same way to parental separation, or the balance of different experiences may not be the same. In the past decade, couples in many other contexts have experienced the changes that characterized Sweden and Norway during the latter part of the twentieth century. It remains to be seen how social and economic context may condition the influences of individual experience on parental separation.

Acknowledgments We are grateful for support from the Swedish Research Council through the Linnaeus Center for Social Policy and Family Dynamics in Europe (Grant 349-2007-8701) and Project Grant 421-2014-1668.

References

Aassve, A., Sironi, M., & Bassi, V. (2013). Explaining attitudes towards demographic behaviour. *European Sociological Review, 29*, 316–333.

Aassve, A., Fuochi, G., & Mencarini, L. (2014). Desperate housework: Relative resources, time availability, economic dependency and gender ideology across Europe. *Journal of Family Issues, 35*(8), 1000–1022.

Altintas, E., & Sullivan, O. (2017). Trends in fathers' contribution to housework and childcare under different welfare policy regimes. *Social Politics, 24*, 81–108.

Andersson, G., & Philipov, D. (2002). Life-table representations of family dynamics in Sweden, Hungary, and 14 other FFS countries. *Demographic Research, 7*, 67–144.

Andersson, G., Thomson, E., & Duntava, A. (2017). Life-table representations of family synamics in the 21st century. *Demographic Research, 37*, 1081–1230.

Arnett, J. J. (2000). Emerging adulthood: A theory of development from the late teens through the twenties. *American Psychologist, 55*(5), 469–480.

Baxter, J. (1997). Gender equality and participation in housework: A cross-national perspective. *Journal of Comparative Family Studies, 28*, 220–247.

Beaujouan, É. (2016). Second unions now more stable than first? A comparison of separation risks by union order in France. *European Journal of Population, 32*, 293–321.

Beaujouan, É., & Ní Bhrolcháin, M. (2011). Cohabitation and marriage in Britain since the 1970s. *Population Trends, 145*, 35–59.

Berrington, A., & Diamond, I. (1999). Marital dissolution among the 1958 British birth cohort: The role of cohabitation. *Population Studies, 53*(1), 19–38.

Billari, F. C., & Liefbroer, A. C. (2010). Towards a new pattern of transition to adulthood? *Advances in Life Course Research, 15*(2–3), 59–75.

Blossfeld, H. P., & Huinink, J. (1991). Human-capital investments or norms of role transition – How women's schooling and career affect the process of family formation. *American Journal of Sociology, 97*(1), 143–168.

Booth, A., & Edwards, J. N. (1992). Starting over – Why remarriages are more unstable. *Journal of Family Issues, 13*(2), 179–194.

Bracher, M., Santow, G., Morgan, S. P., & Trussell, J. (1993). Marriage dissolution in Australia: Models and explanations. *Population Studies, 47*(3), 403–425.

Breen, R., & Cooke, L. (2005). The persistence of the gendered division of labor. *European Sociological Review, 21*(1), 43–57.

Brüderl, J., & Kalter, F. (2001). The dissolution of marriages: The role of information and marital-specific capital. *Journal of Mathematical Sociology, 25*, 403–421.

Brüderl, J., Diekmann, A., & Engelhardt, H. (1997). Premarital cohabitation and marital stability in West Germany. *Kölner Zeitschrift für Soziologie und Sozialpsychologie, 49*, 205–222.

Bukodi, E. (2012). Serial cohabitation among men in Britain: Does work history matter? *European Journal of Population, 28*(4), 441–466.

Bumpass, L., & Lu, H.-H. (2000). Trends in cohabitation and implications for children's family contexts in the United States. *Population Studies, 54*(1), 29–41.

Bumpass, L. L., & Sweet, J. A. (1989). National estimates of cohabitation. *Demography, 26*, 615–625.

Bumpass, L. L., Sweet, J. A., & Cherlin, A. (1991). The role of cohabitation in declining rates of marriage. *Journal of Marriage and the Family, 53*, 913–927.

Cherlin, A. (1978). Remarriage as an incomplete institution. *American Journal of Sociology, 84*(3), 634–650.

Clarke, L., & Jensen, A.-M. (2004). Children's risk of parental break-up: Norway and England/ Wales compared. *Acta Sociologica, 47*, 51–69.

Cohen, J., & Manning, W. D. (2010). The relationship context of premarital serial cohabitation. *Social Science Research, 395*, 766–776.

Dommermuth, L., & Wiik, K. A. (2014). First, second or third time around? The number of co-residential relationships among young Norwegians. *Young, 22*(4), 323–343.

Eickmeyer, K. J. (2019). Cohort trends in union dissolution during young adulthood. *Journal of Marriage and Family, 81*(June), 760–770.

Eickmeyer, K. J., & Manning, W. D. (2018). Serial cohabitation in young adulthood: Baby Boomers to Millennials. *Journal of Marriage and Family, 80*(August), 826–840.

Ermisch, J. (2001). Cohabitation and childbearing outside marriage in Britain. In L. Wu & B. Wolfe (Eds.), *Out of wedlock: Causes and consequences of non-marital fertility* (pp. 109–139). Russell Sage Foundation.

Ermisch, J., & Francesconi, M. (2002). Cohabitation in Great Britain: Not for long, but here to stay. *Journal of the Royal Statistical Society: Series A Statistics in Society, 163*, 153–171.

Esping-Andersen, G., & Billari, F. C. (2015). Re-theorizing family demographics. *Population and Development Review, 41*(1), 1–31.015.

Frejka, T., & Sobotka, T. (2008). Fertility in Europe: Diverse, delayed and below replacement. *Demographic Research, 19*, 15–45.

Fučík, P. (2020). Trends in divorce acceptance and its correlates across European countries. *Czech Sociological Review, 56*(6), 863–895.

Gibson-Davis, C., & Rackin, H. (2014). Marriage or carriage? Trends in union context and birth type by education. *Journal of Marriage and Family, 76*(3), 506–519.

Gibson-Davis, C. M., Ananat, E., & Gassman-Pines, A. (2016). Midpregnancy marriage and divorce: Why the death of shotgun marriage has been greatly exaggerated. *Demography, 53*, 1693–1715.

Goldscheider, F., Bernhardt, E., & Lappegård, T. (2015). The gender revolution: A theoretical framework for understanding changing family and demographic behavior. *Population and Development Review, 41*(2), 207–239.

Grow, A., Schnor, C., & Van Bavel, J. (2017). The reversal of the gender gap in education and relative divorce risks: A matter of alternatives in partner choice? *Population Studies, 71*(sup1), 15–34.

Guzzo, K. B. (2017). Shifts in higher-order unions and stepfamilies among currently cohabiting and married women of childbearing age. *Journal of Family Issues, 38*(12), 1775–1799.

Guzzo, K. B., & Hayford, S. R. (2012). Unintended fertility and the stability of coresidential relationships. *Social Science Research, 41*, 1138–1151.

Härkönen, J. (2017). *Cohort trends in divorce and family dissolution in Sweden, 1970–2005*. Paper presented at the GENDERBALL meeting, Leuven, Belgium.

Härkönen, J., & Dronkers, J. (2006). Stability and change in the educational gradient of divorce: A comparison of seventeen countries. *European Sociological Review, 22*(5), 501–517.

Härkönen, J., Brons, M. D., & Dronkers, J. (2021). Family forerunners? Parental separation and partnership formation in 16 countries. *Journal of Marriage and Family, 83*(1), 119–136.

Henz, U., & Jonsson, J. O. (2003). Union disruption in Sweden: Does economic dependency inhibit separation? *International Journal of Sociology, 33*(1), 3–39.

Henz, U., & Thomson, E. (2005). Union stability and stepfamily fertility in Austria, Finland, France & West Germany. *European Journal of Population, 21*(1), 3–29.

Heuveline, P., Timberlake, J. M., & Furstenberg, F. F., Jr. (2003). Shifting childrearing to single mothers: Results from 17 Western countries. *Population and Development Review, 29*, 47–71.
Hiekel, N., & Fulda, B. E. (2018). Love. Break up. Repeat: The prevalence and stability of serial cohabitation among West German women and men born in the early 1970s. *Demographic Research, 39*, 855–870.
Hoem, J. M., Kostova, D., Jasilioniene, A., & Muresan, C. (2009). Traces of the second demographic transition in central and Eastern Europe: Union formation as a demographic manifestation. *European Journal of Population, 25*, 239–255.
Holland, J. A. (2013). Love, marriage, then the baby carriage? Marriage timing and childbearing in Sweden. *Demographic Research, 29*, 275–306.
Holland, J. A. (2017). The timing of marriage vis-à-vis coresidence and childbearing in Europe and the United States. *Demographic Research, 36*, 610–626.
Huang, P. M., Smock, P. J., Manning, W. D., & Bergstrom-Lynch, C. A. (2011). He says, she says: Gender and cohabitation. *Journal of Family Issues, 32*, 876–905.
Jalovaara, M. (2013). Socioeconomic resources and the dissolution of cohabitations and marriages. *European Journal of Population, 29*(2), 167–193.
Jalovaara, M., & Andersson, G. (2018). Disparities in children's family experiences by mother's socioeconomic status: The case of Finland. *Population Research and Policy Review, 37*(5), 751–768.
Jalovaara, M., & Kulu, H. (2018). Separation risk over union duration: An immediate itch? *European Sociological Review, 34*, 486–500.
Jensen, A.-M., & Clausen, S.-E. (2003). Children and family dissolution in Norway: The impact of consensual unions. *Childhood, 10*(1), 65–81.
Kalmijn, M., & Leopold, T. (2021). A new look at the separation surge in Europe: Contrasting adult and child perspectives. *American Sociological Review, 86*(1), 1–34.
Kamp Dush, C. M., Jang, B., & Snyder, A. R. (2018). A cohort comparison of predictors of young adult union formation and dissolution in the US. *Advances in Life Course Research, 38*, 37–49.
Katus, K., Puur, A., Põldma, A., & Sakkeus, L. (2007). First union formation in Estonia, Latvia and Lithuania: Patterns across countries and gender. *Demographic Research, 17*, 247–300.
Kaufman, G. (2000). Do gender role attitudes matter? Family formation and dissolution among traditional and egalitarian men and women. *Journal of Family Issues, 21*, 128128–128144.
Kennedy, S., & Bumpass, L. L. (2008). Cohabitation and children's living arrangements: New estimates from the United States. *Demographic Research, 19*, 1663–1692.
Kennedy, S., & Thomson, E. (2010). Children's experiences of family disruption in Sweden: Differentials by parent education over three decades. *Demographic Research, 23*, 479–508.
Kiernan, K. (1999). Childbearing outside marriage in Western Europe. *Population Trends, 98*, 11–20.
Kiernan, K. (2001). The rise of cohabitation and childbearing outside marriage in Western Europe. *International Journal of Law, Policy and the Family, 15*, 1–21.
Klüsener, S. (2015). Spatial variation in non-marital fertility across Europe in the twentieth and twenty-first centuries: Recent trends, persistence of the past, and potential future pathways. *The History of the Family, 20*(4), 593–628.
Kulu, H., & Boyle, P. (2010). Premarital cohabitation and divorce: Support for the 'trial marriage' theory? *Demographic Research, 23*, 879–904.
Lamidi, E. O., Manning, W. D., & Brown, S. L. (2019). Change in the stability of first premarital cohabitation among women in the United States, 1983–2013. *Demography, 56*, 427–450.
Laplante, B., & Fostik, A. L. (2015). Disentangling the Quebec fertility paradox: The recent evolution of fertility within marriage and consensual union in Quebec and Ontario. *Canadian Studies in Population, 42*(1–2), 81–101.
Le Bourdais, C., & Lapierre-Adamcyk, É. (2004). Changes in conjugal life in Canada: Is cohabitation progressively replacing marriage? *Journal of Marriage and Family, 66*(4), 929–942.
Lesthaeghe, R. (2010). The unfolding story of the second demographic transition. *Population and Development Review, 36*(2), 211–251.

Lichter, D. T., & Qian, Z. (2008). Serial cohabitation and the marital life course. *Journal of Marriage and Family, 70*, 861–878.

Lichter, D. T., Turner, R. N., & Sassler, S. (2010). National estimates of the rise in serial cohabitation. *Social Science Research, 39*, 754–765.

Lichter, D. T., Michelmore, K., Turner, R. N., & Sassler, S. (2016). Pathways to a stable union? Pregnancy and childbearing among cohabiting and married couples. *Population Research and Policy Review, 35*(3), 377–399.

Liefbroer, A. C., & Dourleijn, E. (2006). Unmarried cohabitation and union stability: Testing the role of diffusion using data from 16 European countries. *Demography, 43*(2), 203–221.

Liefbroer, A. C., & Billari, F. C. (2010). Bringing norms back. A theoretical and empirical discussion of their importance for understanding demographic behavior. *Population, Space and Place, 16*(4), 287–305.

Lyngstad, T. H. (2004). The impact of parents' and spouses' education on divorce rates in Norway. *Demographic Research, 10*, 121–142.

Manning, W. D., & Cohen, J. A. (2012). Premarital cohabitation and marital dissolution: An examination of recent marriages. *Journal of Marriage and Family, 74*, 377–387.

Manning, W. D., Smock, P. J., & Majumdar, D. (2004). The relative stability of cohabiting and marital unions for children. *Population Research and Policy Review, 23*, 135–159.

Manning, W. D., Brown, S. L., & Payne, K. K. (2014). Two decades of stability and change in age at first union formation. *Journal of Marriage and Family, 76*(2), 247–260.

Mikolai, J., Berrington, A., & Perelli-Harris, B. (2018). The role of education in the intersection of partnership transitions and motherhood in Europe and the United States. *Demographic Research, 39*, 753–794.

Murphy, M. J. (1985). Demographic and socio-economic influences on recent British marital breakdown patterns. *Population Studies, 39*(3), 441–460.

Musick, K., & Michelmore, K. (2015). Change in the stability of marital and cohabiting unions following the birth of a child. *Demography, 52*, 1463–1485.

Musick, K., & Michelmore, K. (2018). Cross-national comparisons of union stability in cohabiting and married families with children. *Demography, 55*, 1389–1421.

Nazio, T., & Blossfeld, H.-P. (2003). The diffusion of cohabitation among young women in West Germany, East Germany and Italy. *European Journal of Population, 19*, 47–82.

Neels, K., & De Wachter, D. (2010). Postponement and recuperation of Belgian fertility: How are they related to rising female educational attainment? *Vienna Yearbook of Population Research, 8*, 77–106.

Neels, K., Murphy, M., Ní Bhrolcháin, M., & Beaujouan, É. (2017). Rising educational participation and the trend to later childbearing. *Population and Development Review, 43*(4), 667–693.

Neilsson, J., & Stanfors, M. (2014). It's about time! Gender, parenthood, and household divisions of labor under different welfare regimes. *Journal of Family Issues, 35*(8), 1066–1088.

Ní Bhrolcháin, M., & Beaujouan, É. (2012). Fertility postponement is largely due to rising educational enrolment. *Population Studies, 66*(3), 311–327.

Oláh, L. S., & Gähler, M. (2014). Gender equality perceptions, division of paid and unpaid work, and partnership dissolution in Sweden. *Social Forces, 93*(2), 571–594.

Organisation for Economic Co-operation and Development. (2011). Editorial. In *Education at a glance* (pp. 13–20).

Organisation for Economic Co-operation and Development. (2022). https://ourworldindata.org/grapher/female-labor-force-participation-oecd

Pelletier, D. (2016). The diffusion of cohabitation and children's risks of family dissolution in Canada. *Demographic Research, 35*, 1317–1342.

Perelli-Harris, B., & Bernardi, L. (2015). Exploring social norms around cohabitation: The life course, individualization, and culture. Introduction to special collection: Focus on partnerships: Discourses on cohabitation and marriage throughout Europe and Australia. *Demographic Research, 33*, 701–732.

Perelli-Harris, B., Kreyenfeld, M., & Kubisch, K. (2010a). *Harmonised histories manual for the preparation of comparative fertility and union histories* (MPIDR Working Paper 2010-011). Max Planck Institute for Demographic Research.
Perelli-Harris, B., Sigle-Rushton, W., Kreyenfeld, M., Lappegård, T., Keizer, R., & Berghammer, C. (2010b). The educational gradient of childbearing within cohabitation in Europe. *Population and Development Review, 36*(4), 775–801.
Perelli-Harris, B., Kreyenfeld, M., Sigle-Rushton, W., Keizer, R., Lappegård, T., Jasilioniene, A., Berghammer, C., & Di Giulio, P. (2012). Changes in union status during the transition to parenthood in eleven European countries, 1970s to early 2000s. *Population Studies, 66*(2), 167–182.
Perelli-Harris, B., Mynarska, M., Berrington, A., Evans, A., Berghammer, C., Isupova, O., Keizer, R., Klaerner, A., Lappegård, T., & Vignoli, D. (2014). Towards a deeper understanding of cohabitation: Insights from focus group research across Europe and Australia. *Demographic Research, 34*, 1043–1078.
Poortman, A.-R., & Lyngstad, T. H. (2007). Dissolution risks in first and higher order marital and cohabiting unions. *Social Science Research, 36*(4), 1431–1446.
Prioux, F., & Mandelbaum, J. (2003). Age at first union in France: A two-stage process of change. *Population, English Edition, 58*(4/5), 559–578.
Rackin, H., & Gibson-Davis, C. M. (2012). The role of pre-and postconception relationships for first-time parents. *Journal of Marriage and Family, 74*(3), 526–539.
Raley, R. K. (2001). Increasing fertility in cohabitating unions: Evidence for the second demographic transition in the United States? *Demography, 38*(1), 59–66.
Raley, R. K., & Bumpass, L. (2003). The topography of the divorce plateau: Levels and trends in union stability in the United States after 1980. *Demographic Research, 8*, 246–260.
Reinhold, S. (2010). Reassessing the link between premarital cohabitation and marital instability. *Demography, 47*, 719–733.
Sánchez Gassen, N., & Perelli-Harris, B. (2015). The increase in cohabitation and the role of union status in family policies: A comparison of 12 European countries. *Journal of European Social Policy, 25*(4), 431–449.
Schnor, C. (2014). The effect of union status at first childbirth on union stability: Evidence from Eastern and Western Germany. *European Journal of Population, 30*(2), 129–160.
Schnor, C. (2015). Does waiting pay off for couples? Partnership duration prior to household formation and union stability. *Demographic Research, 33*, 611–652.
Schnor, C., & Jalovaara, M. (2019). The spread of non-marital childbearing and its link to educational expansion. *Acta Sociologica, 63*(4), 400–421.
Schoen, R. (2010). Gender competition and family change. *Genus, 66*(3), 95–120.
Schwartz, C. R., & Han, H. (2014). The reversal of the gender gap in education and trends in marital dissolution. *American Sociological Review, 79*(4), 605–629.
Sigle-Rushton, W. (2010). Men's unpaid work and divorce: Reassessing specialization and trade. *Feminist Economics, 16*(2), 1–26.
Sobotka, T., & Toulemon, L. (2008). Overview Chapter 4: Changing family and partnership behavior: Common trends and persistent diversity across Europe. *Demographic Research, 19*, 85–138.
Sobotka, T., Zeman, K., & Kantorova, V. (2003). Demographic shifts in the Czech Republic after 1989: A second demographic transition view. *European Journal of Population, 19*, 249–277.
South, S. J. (2001). Time-dependent effects of wives' employment on marital dissolution. *American Sociological Review, 66*(2), 226–245.
Stanfors, M., & Goldscheider, F. (2017). The forest and the trees: Industrialization, demographic change, and the ongoing gender revolution in the United States and Sweden, 1870–2010. *Demographic Research, 36*, 173–226.
Steele, F., Kallis, C., & Joshi, H. (2006). The formation and outcomes of cohabiting and marital partnerships in early adulthood: The role of previous partnership experience. *Journal of the Royal Statistical Society A, 169*(4), 757–779.

Svarer, M. (2004). Is your love in vain? Another look at premarital cohabitation and divorce. *Journal of Human Resources, 39*(2), 523–535.

Teachman, J. D., & Polonko, K. A. (1990). Cohabitation and marital stability in the United States. *Social Forces, 69*(1), 207–220.

Teachman, J. D., Thomas, J., & Paasch, K. (1991). Legal status and the instability of coresidential unions. *Demography, 28*(4), 207–220.

Thomson, E. (2022). Chapter 17: Cohabitation through the life course. In M. Daly, N. Gilbert, B. Pfau-Effinger, & D. Besharov (Eds.), *International handbook on family policy: A life course perspective*. Oxford University Press.

Thomson, E., & Eriksson, H. (2013). Register-based estimates of parental separation in Sweden. *Demographic Research, 29*, 1153–1186.

Thomson, E., Winkler-Dworak, M., & Beaujoaun, È. (2017). *Contributions of cohabitation to parental separation: Microsimulations for Italy, Great Britain, and Norway*. Paper presented at the international population conference (International Union for the Scientific Study of Population), Cape Town, South Africa, October 29–December 4.

Thomson, E., Winkler-Dworak, M., & Beaujoaun, É. (2019). Contribution of the rise in cohabiting parenthood to family instability: Cohort change in Italy, Great Britain, and Scandinavia. *Demography, 56*(6), 2063–2082.

Toulemon, L. (1996). Cohabitation is here to stay. *Population: An English Selection, 9*, 11–46.

Trimarchi, A., & van Bavel, J. (2018). Pathways to marital and non-marital first birth: The role of his and her education. *Vienna Yearbook of Population Research, 15*, 143–179.

Vespa, J. (2014). Historical trends in the marital intentions of one-time and serial cohabitors. *Journal of Marriage and Family, 76*, 207–217.

Wagner, M., & Weiss, B. (2006). On the variation of divorce risks in Europe: Findings from a meta-analysis of European longitudinal studies. *European Sociological Review, 22*(5), 483–500.

White, L. K., & Booth, A. (1985). The quality and stability of remarriages – The role of stepchildren. *American Sociological Review, 50*(5), 689–698.

Wright, L. (2016). Type and timing of first union formation in Québec and the rest of Canada: Continuity and change across the 1930–79 birth cohorts. *Canadian Studies in Population, 43*(3–4), 234–248.

Wright, L. (2019). Union transitions and fertility within first premarital cohabitations in Canada: Diverging patterns by education? *Demography, 56*(1), 151–167.

Wu, L. L., & Musick, K. (2008). Stability of marital and cohabiting unions following a first birth. *Population Research and Policy Review, 27*(6), 713–727.

Young, B. J., Furman, W., & Laursen, B. (2011). Models of change and continuity in romantic experiences. In F. D. Fincham & M. Chui (Eds.), *Romantic relationships in emerging adulthood* (pp. 44–66). Cambridge University Press.

Žilinčíková, Z. (2017). Do children matter for the stability of cohabitation? A cross-national comparison. *Population-E, 72*(4), 649–670.

Part IV
Deviance and the Family

Chapter 12
Criminal Offending Trajectories During the Transition to Adulthood and Subsequent Fertility

Brittany Ganser and Karen Benjamin Guzzo

From a life course perspective, fertility is part of a larger set of linked behaviors in different domains, such as employment, health, and family. Activities in these domains ebb and flow as people pass through different life course stages, but adolescence and the transition to adulthood are considered particularly important because they can influence long-term life trajectories. For instance, early entrance into some domains and roles, even socially acceptable ones such as employment, is linked to an earlier transition to parenthood (Rauscher, 2011). Unsurprisingly, activities that are less socially acceptable, such as criminal behavior, that occur during adolescence and the transition to adulthood also have long-term – and negative – impacts on other domains, such as health and well-being (Baćak & Karim, 2019). Yet the influence of criminal behavior on fertility has largely remained unexplored even though such activities are not uncommon. The age-crime curve generally shows that most offending occurs in adolescence and that involvement usually fades in early adulthood (Hirschi & Gottfredson, 1983); early adulthood, in turn, is when individuals start engaging in family formation behaviors, such as becoming a parent, more commonly. In the United States context, the age-crime curve means that there are time periods when criminal behavior, though not encouraged, may be more socially acceptable (Massoglia & Uggen, 2010). Those who continue to offend past relatively normative ages or who have a delayed onset of criminal behavior may experience a range of issues throughout the prime childbearing years that ultimately impact their family behaviors.

B. Ganser
Bowling Green State University, Bowling Green, OH, USA

K. B. Guzzo (✉)
Department of Sociology, and Carolina Population Center, University of North Carolina, Chapel Hill, NC, USA
e-mail: Karen.Guzzo@unc.edu

R. Schoen (ed.), *The Demography of Transforming Families*, The Springer Series on Demographic Methods and Population Analysis 56,
https://doi.org/10.1007/978-3-031-29666-6_12

There are reasons to suspect that engaging in offending could be associated with childbearing behaviors, including the number of children men and women have. For instance, sustained offending could lead to fewer children if it makes individuals less attractive to potential partners and thus less likely to form and maintain relationships in which to have children. Alternatively, persistent or delayed offending may signify impulsivity and risky behaviors, which could be linked to higher fertility if such behaviors include sexual risk-taking. Thus, although patterns of criminal offending in adolescence and adulthood may impact adult fertility in the long run, the direction of the link is unclear. Further, any link may differ by gender. Though criminal behavior is not encouraged for any group, it is more common among men, especially in adolescence. Given that women are a minority of those incarcerated and arrested and are less likely to be violent offenders, women who exhibit high levels of criminal involvement may be viewed more negatively by potential partners than men with similar levels of involvement (Greenfeld & Snell, 1999). Conversely, among men – for whom some criminal involvement may be, if not normative, less uncommon – perhaps desirability is less impacted by these behaviors than for women.

In this study, we use several waves of the National Study of Adolescent to Adult Health (Add Health) to assess the impact of the timing and duration of criminal behavior during adolescence and young adulthood on the number of children among individuals in the early mid-adult years (late 30 s and early 40 s) and account for factors that may affect any linkage, such as sexual risk-taking, union formation, and incarceration experiences. Add Health's longitudinal design and long time period permit analyses not available with many other datasets, and we also take advantage of Add Health's rich sociodemographic information to account for possible selection factors associated with both criminal activity and fertility. For both men and women, we find that offending is linked to fewer children. Compared to those with no history of offending, men who began offending in young adulthood and women who offended in both adolescence and young adulthood have significantly fewer children even after accounting for potentially confounding factors. Offending in young adulthood appears to indicate unique processes that depress fertility among both men and women.

12.1 Offending Trajectories

Research on offending trajectories reveals a variety of patterns. Moffitt (1993) finds two main pathways to criminal involvement. One, adolescent-limited individuals follow a relatively normative pattern, offending throughout adolescence but desisting by the time they reach adulthood. This limited engagement is largely the result of the increased social rewards of deviance in adolescence compared to other periods of the life course. Two, life course-persistent individuals engage in a variety of deviant behaviors throughout the life course, beginning in childhood and extending into adulthood. Conversely, Sampson and Laub (2003) find other patterns but note that all offending groups seem to desist with age, though the shape and level of offending may differ. However, risk factors and individual characteristics do little to explain what trajectory group an individual falls into. Other studies examine specific offending populations and types, such as mafia members (Campedelli et al., 2019), sex offenders (Lussier et al., 2010), and white collar offenders (van Onna et al., 2014). These studies indicate a variety of different category types but differ as to whether group membership is stable or whether it is difficult to predict. Overall, though, trajectory groups differ in onset, persistence, and level of offending over time.

12.2 Literature on Offending

There is a voluminous literature on offending, with much of it focused on the effects of delinquency. Delinquency by age 16, for example, reduces the odds of completing high school (Tanner et al., 1999; Ward & Williams, 2015). Offending in adolescence is linked to detrimental effects on future occupational outcomes (Tanner et al., 1999). While many adolescents offend as a way to gain status, offending after adolescence is less acceptable and relatively rare (Moffitt, 1997). Those who do not offend at all or who desist after adolescence are unlikely to experience long-term impacts of criminal behavior later in the life course, whereas individuals following other patterns – such as late-onset offending (not engaging in criminal acts in adolescence but doing so in young adulthood) and persistent offending – may have very different experiences. For instance, Reising et al. (2019) find that depression and anxiety are highest for those who started offending in adulthood. Persistent offending might be particularly problematic. Persistent offenders have significantly lower odds of employment in adulthood and higher odds of lifetime mental illness (Drury et al., 2020). Offending, of course, also carries the risk of criminal justice contact, especially after the adolescent years; criminal justice intervention, in turn, also impacts multiple life domains and key events in the transition to adulthood, such as home-leaving (Warner & Remster, 2021). Incarceration is also linked to poorer health and a higher risk of depression (Esposito et al., 2017).

These differences in health and socioeconomic outcomes based on the timing and persistence of offending category suggest that family behaviors are another domain that could be impacted. There is relatively little research directly connecting criminal behavior and subsequent fertility, though. Instead, much of the work on offending, crime, and fertility focuses on the role of parenthood in affecting desistance (e.g., Abell, 2018; Kreager et al., 2010; Ziegler et al., 2017). What evidence is available, though, does indeed suggest a link between criminal behavior and at least certain aspects of fertility. For instance, a macro-level study in Taiwan found that crime had a positive, moderate, significant effect on fertility (Huang Jr. et al., 2015). Landeis et al. (2020) discovered that both men and women who experienced arrest transitioned to parenthood earlier than those who had not been arrested.

However, these studies do not consider how offending might ultimately be linked to the number of children men and women have, yet there are several possible reasons there would be an association. One, criminal offending is often socially stigmatized and may be a red flag for potential partners. Moreover, criminal behavior that occurs past the more socially acceptable adolescent stage may reflect individual personality or social problems. As such, late-onset and persistent offenders may be less attractive to potential partners and thus less likely to form the kinds of unions that are conducive to childbearing. Two, even if they form serious romantic relationships, men and women who engage in criminal behavior may be evaluated by partners as unfit to parent or unlikely to stick around for the long term. As such, fertility would be lower because partners and would-be partners could be reluctant to have children with individuals who engage in persistent offending or delayed-onset offending. Three, the higher risk of incarceration among those who offend in young adulthood could potentially remove these men and women for periods of their childbearing years. In this sense, offending would reduce fertility in a largely mechanical way, by limiting exposure to births.

Conversely, it is also possible that fertility would be higher among offenders. If individuals with criminal involvement are also sexual risk-takers – perhaps engaging in sex at an early age or having multiple partners – it is possible that they could have more children than their counterparts with no criminal activity. In particular, those with persistent offending – those whose criminal activity extends past adolescence – may be especially like to engage in sexual risk-taking, as opportunities for sexual activity tend to increase during the transition to adulthood. Lansford et al. (2014), for example, find that delinquency at age 16 has a significant and positive direct effect on risky sexual behavior through age 27. Moreover, to the extent that extended criminal behavior may make it difficult to maintain relationships, patterns of frequent repartnering may also increase fertility.

12.3 Gender, Offending, and Fertility

It is well established that criminal trajectories differ by gender (Bradshaw et al., 2010; Ferrante, 2013). For instance, while both boys and girls exhibit adolescent-limited and persistent offending trajectories, typically only boys exhibit late-onset offending (Ashcraft, 2009). Similarly, women exhibit different childbearing behavior than their male counterparts, with an earlier age at first birth and lower levels of childlessness by age 40 (Martinez et al., 2018).[1] More interesting, though, is the possibility that criminal behavior may have different consequences for young men and women, particularly in adolescence and young adulthood, that are linked to childbearing. To some extent, risk-taking behavior is associated with popularity for young men – but not women (Rebellon et al., 2019); if this association extends into

[1] Some of these differences may be due to issues with the accuracy of male childbearing data in surveys (Joyner et al., 2012; Monte & Fields, 2020), with evidence that some births to men are missing, particularly among disadvantaged men.

adulthood, it implies that men who engage in some criminal behavior may actually be more attractive to potential partners, leading to more children. Similarly, Closson (2009) finds that popular boys were likely to be described as deviant/risk-takers, while this was not the case for popular girls. However, Mayeux et al. (2008) find that adolescent popularity is related to increased alcohol use and sexual activity for both boys and girls, which may indicate a lack of gender differences. In this paper, we assess gender differences in the relationship between risky behavior and fertility by disaggregating analyses by gender.

12.4 Current Research

We address one key research question: How do offending patterns across adolescence and young adulthood affect achieved fertility for men and women who are approaching the end of their childbearing years? We test competing hypotheses:

Hypothesis 1a: Compared to those with no criminal behavior in adolescence and young adulthood, those who have any criminal behavior will have fewer children, especially among those with persistent offending and late-onset offending.

Hypothesis 1b: Compared to those with no offending in adolescence and young adulthood, those who have any offending will have more children, especially among those with persistent offending and late-onset offending.

In general, we expect that Hypothesis 1a is more likely to be supported, but we cannot dismiss Hypothesis 1b. We run all models separately by gender.

We account for two sets of potentially confounding factors: partnership experiences (number of marriages and cohabiting unions) and incarceration experiences. Both of these essentially represent exposure to childbearing. Despite the rise of nonmarital fertility, most childbearing occurs within coresidential unions. Fewer unions, or more unstable unions, are linked to higher levels of childlessness and fewer children (Hayford, 2013; Thomson et al., 2012). Incarceration experiences represent periods of non-exposure to potentially procreative sex and thus childbearing. If a negative relationship exists between criminal behavior and fertility but occurs largely due to the fact that those who offend more have less exposure to childbearing because they have fewer or more unstable unions and are more often incarcerated, accounting for these factors should attenuate the link. We also control for selection by including sexual risk-taking (age at first sex and number of sexual partners). A positive link may exist if people who engage in criminal behavior are also engaging in sexual risk-taking, with an earlier sexual debut and more sexual partners. Again, accounting for this should attenuate any positive association. All analyses also control for characteristics linked to both fertility and offending. For instance, as noted above, those with histories of delinquency often have lower socioeconomic status as adults; socioeconomic status, in turn, is linked to fertility. Less advantaged adults, often proxied by educational attainment, have more children than their more educated counterparts (Martinez et al., 2018).

It is worth noting that some have argued that the causal link between fertility and offending could run in the opposite direction. For instance, Augustyn and Jackson (2020) highlight that socioeconomic status and other factors can influence the impact of precocious exits (early entry into adult statuses, such as parenthood) on criminal activity. In this project, we restrict analyses to those who have yet to have any children prior to the first round of data collection to better establish causal links between offending and subsequent fertility.

12.5 Data

Data come from the National Longitudinal Study of Adolescent to Adult Health (Add Health), a nationally representative longitudinal survey of adolescent boys and girls in grades 7–12 (ages 12–19) in the 1994–95 school year. The original sampling frame included 80 high schools and their feeder middle schools, stratified by region, urbanicity, sector, race, and size. From school rosters, adolescents were selected to complete in-home interviews at Wave I (1995); some of these were oversamples of key groups (certain minority groups, sibling pairs, disabled youth, and adopted youth). Youth still in school one year later (grades 8–12) were re-interviewed at Wave II (1996). The original Wave I respondents were re-interviewed three more times: 2001–02, ages 18–24; 2008, ages 26–31; 2016–18, 35–40.[2] Our measures of criminal involvement in adolescence and young adulthood are taken from Waves I and III; the smaller sampling frame of Wave II (enrolled students only) and the shorter time period between waves (roughly a year later) precluded the inclusion of that wave. The focus on criminal behavior during adolescence and young adulthood precluded the use of Wave IV, and Wave V did not include the same set of offending questions. The dependent variable – number of children – is taken from Wave V. There are 12,300 respondents in Wave V of Add Health, of whom 10,220 were interviewed at Waves I and III. Of those, 213 were part of the oversamples, without sample weights, and were excluded from the analyses. To better establish causality, we drop respondents who reported a pregnancy at Wave I (n = 366). At this point, we have a possible sample size of 9641 respondents, but missing or inconsistent data on the dependent variable or key independent variables led to further excluded cases, discussed below. Our final sample size is 8909.

[2] At Wave IV, the full age range is 24–34, but 93% of the sample was between 26–31. At Wave V, the full age range is 33–44, but 91% of the sample was 35–40.

12.5.1 Dependent Variable

The dependent variable is number of live births (parity) at Wave V. This is missing for 12 cases.

12.5.2 Focal Independent Variable

We used several questions to assess criminal behavior in adolescence and young adulthood, taken from Waves I and III, using the same measures as others using Add Health to study criminal behavior during these life course stages (Demuth & Brown, 2004; Dennison & Swisher, 2019; Haynie et al., 2005; McGloin, 2009). At both waves, respondents were asked about a variety of criminal activities in the past year: (1) deliberately damage property that didn't belong to you, (2) steal something worth more than $50, (3) hurt someone badly enough to need bandages or care from a doctor or nurse, (4) go into a house or building to steal something, (5) sell marijuana or other drugs, (6) steal something worth less than $50, (7) take part in a fight where a group of your friends was against another group, and (8) use or threaten to use a weapon to get something from someone. Respondents who were missing on any of these measures at either wave were dropped from the analysis ($n = 301$). From these measures, we constructed a measure of any offending, which is a dichotomous measure of whether the respondent reporting engaging in any criminal acts. Next, we combined the information from the two waves to indicate both onset and duration of offending. This produced our focal independent variable, with four categories: (1) engaged at neither wave, (2) engaged at Wave I, but not Wave III (desistance), (3) engaged at Wave III, but not Wave I (late-onset), and (4) involved in offending at both waves (persistence).

12.5.3 Control Variables

Analyses include several Wave V socioeconomic and demographic controls linked to fertility (race-ethnicity, educational attainment, household income, and religiosity) as well as family background characteristics taken from Wave I (family structure and family socioeconomic status). Race categories include non-Hispanic white, non-Hispanic black, Hispanic, and Asian/other. Educational attainment has the following categories: (1) less than high school, (2) high school degree or GED, (3) some college or vocational training, (4) college degree or completed vocational training, (5) some graduate school, and (6) graduate school degree. Household income is a categorical variable (13 income groupings), entered in the models as a linear variable. Religiosity includes four categories about the importance of religion: (1) not important, (2) somewhat important, (3) very important, and (4) more important than anything else. From Wave I, household family structure includes two-parent, single parent, stepparent, and other, and household family socioeconomic status uses using Bearman and Moody's (2004) operationalization, which combines information on occupation and education for both mothers and fathers to create an index for each parent ranging from 1–10 and then uses the higher of the two scores.

The measures of risky sexual behavior are age at first sex (with an opposite-sex partner) and number of opposite sex partners, both taken at Wave V. Age at first sex is based on respondents' Wave V reports of age at first sex, originally a linear variable and recoded into three categories to better capture the nonlinearity in the relationship between sexual debut and fertility: 15 or less, 16–18, or 19 and older. The number of opposite sex partners is also categorical, with the categories as originally specified in the questionnaire: 1–4, 5–9, 11–20, 21–30, and more than 30. Originally, to incorporate those who had not yet had sex by Wave V (n = 419), we created categories of "never had sex" for both age at first sex and number of sexual partners. However, since these two variables have complete overlap in that category, the category was dropped for one of the variables when models were run, muddying the interpretation of the risky sexual behavior variables. Further, although those who had never had intercourse with a member of the opposite sex were significantly less likely to have any children, about a third of this group did have children. This suggests either a data problem for these individuals or fairly unusual situations that neither our hypotheses nor our analyses are able to capture. As such, we chose to exclude these individuals.[3] Union status is measured as two linear variables indicating the number of marriages and the number of cohabiting unions by Wave V. Finally, we have a categorical measure of the number of incarcerations as of Wave V: no incarcerations, one incarceration, and two or more incarcerations. Analytical sample characteristics are shown in Table 12.1.

All analyses are weighted using Stata's *svy* commands to account for Add Health's sampling design, and *mi* commands were used to impute missing data for all but the fertility and offending variables. Missing data occurred for less than 30 respondents for most measures, with the exception of household income, which was missing for 104 respondents in the analytical sample. Multicollinearity tests showed that the vast majority of the variance inflation factors (VIFs) did not exceed 2 (Allison, 1991), with the exception of religiosity for women (2.11) and education for men (2.01) (Allison, 1991). The mean VIF was 1.35 for women and 1.36 for men. Therefore, we conclude that multicollinearity is not affecting our results significantly.

[3]Supplementary models in which we included these individuals did not yield substantively different results for our main variables of interest. Exploratory work showed that the vast majority of the individuals who reported never having sex but who had at least one child were men (85%) and identified as heterosexual (96%). For these individuals, it is unclear whether the information on sexual activity was incorrect, the data on fertility was incorrect, or some other process was occurring, such as pursuing assisted reproductive technologies (which is unfortunately not available in Add Health).

Table 12.1 Weighted percentage or mean (Std. Error) descriptive statistics, N = 8909

	WomenN = 5142	MenN = 3767
Any offending		
Engaged at neither wave	58.0%	32.5%
Engaged at wave I, but not wave III	27.6%	29.9%
Engaged at wave III, but not wave I	6.5%	12.0%
Engaged at both waves	8.0%	25.5%
Wave V parity	1.70 (0.024)	1.54 (0.037)
Socioeconomic & Demographic Characteristics		
Age	37.6 years (0.122)	37.9 years (0.126)
Race-ethnicity		
Non-Hispanic white	69.6%	69.6%
Non-Hispanic black	13.7%	11.6%
Hispanic	9.7%	10.3%
Asian/other	7.0%	8.6%
Education		
Less than HS	3.5%	5.5%
HS degree/GED	11.2%	18.7%
Some college	23.5%	26.3%
AA/vocational degree	17.6%	14.9%
College degree	21.8%	20.6%
Some graduate school	4.1%	3.1%
Graduate degree	18.3%	11.0%
Household income		
Less than $5000	4.2%	3.8%
$5000–$9999	3.3%	2.3%
$10,000–$14,999	3.0%	3.0%
$15,000–$19,999	2.7%	1.6%
$20,000–$24,999	4.1%	2.9%
$25,000–$29,999	4.0%	2.9%
$30,000–$39,999	7.6%	5.9%
$40,000–$49,999	7.0%	8.0%
$50,000–$74,999	17.2%	17.4%
$75,000–$99,999	15.0%	16.8%
$100,000–$149,999	17.0%	19.5%
$150,000–$199,999	7.8%	8.7%
$200,000 or more	7.0%	7.3%
Religiosity		
Not important	18.1%	28.3%
Somewhat important	28.5%	29.8%
Very important	38.6%	30.9%
More important than anything Else	14.8%	11.0%
Family structure at wave I		
Single parent	21.0%	18.8%

(continued)

Table 12.1 (continued)

	WomenN = 5142	MenN = 3767
Stepparent	15.2%	14.5%
Two-parent	60.1%	61.1%
Other	3.8%	5.6%
Family SES at wave I (range 1–10)	5.60 (0.12)	5.82 (0.11)
Sexual risk-taking		
Age at first sex		
15 or less	31.0%	29.6%
16–18	46.8%	46.1%
19 or older	22.2%	24.3%
Lifetime number of sex partners		
1–4	33.1%	24.2%
5–10	38.3%	31.2%
11–20	17.2%	20.9%
21–30	6.2%	8.2%
30 or more	5.2%	15.5%
Union experiences		
Times married	0.92 (0.02)	0.85 (0.02)
Times cohabited	1.01 (0.03)	1.10 (0.04)
Incarceration experience		
Lifetime number of incarcerations		
Never incarcerated	94.0%	78.1%
Incarcerated once	3.8%	9.8%
Incarcerated more than once	2.2%	12.1%

12.5.4 Analytical Approach

We begin by showing the weighted descriptive statistics of the analytical sample. All descriptive statistics and models are separated by gender. We then show the mean number of children in early mid-adulthood across the four patterns of criminal involvement timing and duration. Then, we move on to multivariate models. Because of the skewed nature of the number of children, we use Poisson regression to predict parity; overdispersion was present for men but not women, but negative binomial models (not shown) yielded nearly identical results for men as the Poisson regression. Though we use multiple waves of longitudinal data, these are not multilevel analyses since the dependent variable is taken from only the last wave. We present four models. Model 1 includes the focal offending measure and socio-economic and demographic variables. Model 2 adds sexual risk-taking. Model 3 adds relationship experiences to Model 2, and Model 4 adds incarceration experiences to Model 3.

12.6 Results

The top of Table 12.1 shows the offending patterns for the analytical sample. For any offending, the most common scenario for women was one in which the respondent did not engage in any criminal activities at either Wave I or Wave III (58.0%), whereas only a third of men did not engage in any criminal activities at either wave. Just under one in three respondents (27.6% for women, 29.9% for men) reported engaging in at least one criminal behavior in adolescence but not did not report doing so in early young adulthood, indicative of a pattern of desistance. Late-onset offending (offending only at Wave III) was twice as high among men (12%) than women (6.5%), and persistent offending (offending at both waves) was more than three times as high for men (25.5%) than women (8%).

Table 12.2 shows mean parity at Wave V, when respondents had an average age of 38. The overall number of children (shown in Table 12.1) was 1.70 for women and 1.54 for men, but the number is lowest among those with persistent offending and highest among those desisted. For men and women in the any offending category, the differences in parity are significant between offending groups. Among women, both those who never engaged and those who desisted have a similar average number of children, at 1.75 and 1.74, while late-onset individuals and those who were persistent offenders had significantly different parities at 1.43 and 1.40.

12.6.1 Multivariate Results

Table 12.3 shows the Poisson regression results predicting the number of children in early mid-adulthood by the measure of any offending during adolescence and young adulthood. We present four models, beginning with a model with the offending measure and the socioeconomic and demographic controls, then adding sexual

Table 12.2 Mean parity by offending pattern, N = 8909

	Women		Men	
	Mean	Linearized SE	Mean	Linearized SE
Any offending				
Engaged at neither wave	$1.75^{c,d}$	0.03	$1.57^{b,c}$	0.05
Engaged at Wave I, but not Wave III	$1.74^{c,d}$	0.06	$1.73^{a,c,d}$	0.07
Engaged at Wave III, but not Wave I	$1.43^{a,b}$	0.10	$1.20^{a,b,d}$	0.09
Engaged at both waves	$1.40^{a,b}$	0.08	$1.44^{b,c}$	0.06

Superscripts indicate significant differences across categories at $p \leq .05$

[a]different from engaged at neither wave

[b]different from engaged at Wave I, but not Wave III

[c]different from engaged at Wave III, but not Wave I

[d]different from engaged at both waves

Table 12.3 Poisson regression of Wave V fertility on any offending for women, N = 5142

	Model 1		Model 2		Model 3		Model 4	
	b	Linearized SE	b	Linearized SE	b	Linearized SE	b	Linearized SE
Any offending (neither wave)								
Wave I, but not Wave III	−0.001	0.036	−0.009	0.036	−0.002	0.036	−0.004	0.036
Wave III, but not Wave I	−0.159	0.075*	−0.134	0.075	−0.104	0.074	−0.107	0.074
Both waves	−0.188	0.060**	−0.162	0.062*	−0.117	0.061	−0.136	0.063*
Socioeconomic & Demographic Characteristics								
Age	0.024	0.006***	0.028	0.006***	0.021	0.006***	0.019	0.006**
Race (non-Hispanic white)								
Non-Hispanic black	−0.037	0.038	−0.041	0.040	0.070	0.042	0.077	0.041
Hispanic	−0.094	0.046*	−0.069	0.046	−0.046	0.046	−0.046	0.046
Asian/other	−0.118	0.055*	−0.115	0.052*	−0.091	0.055	−0.083	0.053
Education (BA)								
Less than HS	0.345	0.079***	0.275	0.078**	0.258	0.081**	0.240	0.079**
HS/GED	0.248	0.047***	0.202	0.048***	0.168	0.047**	0.161	0.047**
Some college	0.237	0.041***	0.215	0.041***	0.182	0.038***	0.175	0.038***
AA/vocational degree	0.145	0.048**	0.126	0.048*	0.082	0.047	0.078	0.046
Some graduate school	0.089	0.070	0.104	0.068	0.074	0.067	0.077	0.066
Graduate degree	−0.027	0.043	−0.012	0.042	−0.029	0.042	−0.032	0.041
Household income	0.005	0.006	0.000	0.005	−0.010	0.005	−0.008	0.005
Religiosity (not at all important)								
Somewhat important	0.173	0.052**	0.167	0.050**	0.168	0.050**	0.165	0.049**
Very important	0.247	0.056***	0.233	0.053***	0.194	0.053***	0.189	0.053***
More important than anything else	0.436	0.059***	0.423	0.059***	0.364	0.057***	0.362	0.057***
Wave I family structure (two parent)								
Single parent	0.024	0.041	0.023	0.042	0.030	0.041	0.026	0.041
Stepparents	0.068	0.036	0.050	0.038	0.035	0.036	0.031	0.036

Other	0.083	0.068	0.063	0.072	0.061	0.070	0.060	0.071
Wave I family SES	−0.007	0.006	0.000	0.006	0.003	0.006	0.003	0.006
Sexual risk-taking								
Age at first sex (16–18)								
15 or less			0.144	0.032***	0.125	0.031***	0.124	0.031***
19 or older			−0.254	0.034***	−0.235	0.035***	−0.234	0.035***
Number of sex partners (1–4)								
5–10			−0.163	0.032***	−0.176	0.031***	−0.180	0.031***
11–20			−0.203	0.041***	−0.207	0.041***	0.213	0.041***
21–30			−0.433	0.088***	−0.454	0.090***	−0.471	0.087***
30+			−0.321	0.077***	−0.301	0.079***	−0.319	0.079***
Union experiences								
Times married					0.235	0.021***	0.236	0.021***
Times cohabited					−0.009	0.012	−0.015	0.012
Incarceration experiences								
Number of Incarcerations (0)								
1							0.187	0.065**
> 1							0.262	0.102*
Intercept	−0.683	0.242**	−0.688	0.232**	−0.541	0.224*	−0.490	0.224*
F	13.42***	16.24***		20.52***			19.99***	

* $p \leq 0.05$ ** $p \leq 0.01$ *** $p \leq 0.001$

experiences, relationship experiences, and incarceration in the following models. In the interest of brevity, we focus this discussion on the any offending measure and the possible selection and confounding factors added in Models 2–4. In Model 1 for women, compared to individuals with no offending in either adolescence or young adulthood, late-onset offenders and persistent offenders had significantly fewer children at ages 35–40 (b = −0.159 and b = −0.188, respectively). Adding in related selection experiences (number of sex partners and age at first sex) in Model 2, the difference between late-onset offenders and those who never offended is no longer significant, but those who persistently offended continue to have significantly fewer children (b = −0.162). This is true despite the links between sexual risk-taking and fertility – the later women first had sex (ages 19 or older), the fewer children they had by Wave V (b = −0.254) compared to those who first had sex at ages 16–18. Fewer sexual partners translated into more children: compared to women with 1–4 partners, women with more partners had significantly fewer children. Model 3 adds in union experiences, which attenuate the association between persistent offending in adolescence and young adulthood and the number of children in late mid-adulthood. Not surprisingly, union experiences are important, with the number of marriages – but not cohabitations – increasing the number of children (b = 0.235). Finally, Model 4 adds in incarceration experiences. Interestingly, offending again becomes important when both incarceration and union experiences are included – persistent offending remains significantly and negatively associated with parity (b = −0.136). Incarceration experiences themselves are significant, with those who have been incarcerated once and more than once having more children than those who were never incarcerated (b = 0.187 and b = 0.262, respectively). In sum, among women, persistent offenders have fewer children by their late 30 s and early 40 s regardless of controls.

The same models are shown in Table 12.4 for men. Here, we see that only late-onset offending is associated with the number of children – men who did not engage in offending in adolescence but did as young adults have significantly fewer children than their peers who did not engage in offending at all (b = −0.229) when controlling for socioeconomic and demographic characteristics (Model 1). This remains true after for accounting for sexual risk-taking in Model 2, though slightly attenuated (b = −0.194). Sexual behaviors are related to fertility in a similar fashion as women – a later age at first sex (age 19 or older) decreases the number of children in early to mid-adulthood (b = −0.234) relative to those who have sex aged 16–18 whereas an earlier sexual debut is associated with more children (b = 0.178). Having more than 1–4 partners is associated with fewer children. Model 3 adds union experiences, and the negative link between late-onset offending and parity persists (b = −0.166). As with women, the number of marriages is positively associated with the number of children at Wave V (b = 0.390), but the number of cohabitations is not. Finally, incarceration experiences are included in Model 4. Although incarceration matters – men who have been incarcerated two or more times have more children than those never incarcerated (b = 0.205) – late-onset offending continues to be associated with fewer children (b = −0.175). Thus, as with women, there is a persistent link between offending in young adulthood and the number of children.

Table 12.4 Poisson regression of Wave V fertility on any offending for men, N = 3767

	Model 1		Model 2		Model 3		Model 4	
	b	Linearized SE	b	Linearized SE	b	Linearized SE	b	Linearized SE
Any offending (neither wave)								
Wave I, but not Wave III	0.075	0.046	0.064	0.045	0.051	0.045	0.040	0.045
Wave III, but not Wave I	−0.229	0.084**	−0.194	0.086*	−0.166	0.078*	−0.175	0.077*
Both waves	−0.052	0.051	−0.055	0.054	−0.024	0.054	−0.044	0.054
Socioeconomic & Demographic Characteristics								
Age	0.037	0.011**	0.040	0.011***	0.023	0.011	0.021	0.011
Race (non-Hispanic white)								
Non-Hispanic black	0.039	0.081	0.036	0.083	0.121	0.071	0.130	0.071
Hispanic	0.128	0.082	0.138	0.080	0.164	0.072*	0.166	0.074*
Asian/other	0.035	0.074	0.051	0.069	0.115	0.069	0.106	0.070
Education (BA)								
Less than HS	0.563	0.102***	0.473	0.101***	0.440	0.103***	0.428	0.104***
HS/GED	0.229	0.073**	0.161	0.072*	0.079	0.070	0.055	0.070
Some college	0.171	0.066*	0.134	0.065*	0.073	0.063	0.071	0.064
AA/vocational degree	0.118	0.074	0.084	0.073	0.030	0.072	0.030	0.071
Some graduate school	0.220	0.103*	0.190	0.108	0.164	0.103	0.166	0.104
Graduate degree	0.112	0.075	0.127	0.077	0.119	0.076	0.120	0.076
Household income	0.039	0.009***	0.033	0.009***	0.016	0.008	0.020	0.008*
Religiosity (not at all important)								
Somewhat important	0.093	0.057	0.069	0.058	0.066	0.056	0.060	0.056
Very important	0.253	0.054***	0.230	0.052***	0.164	0.052**	0.163	0.052**
More important than anything else	0.340	0.075***	0.311	0.076***	0.202	0.074**	0.190	0.072*
Wave I family structure (two parent)								
Single parent	−0.024	0.064	−0.038	0.063	−0.023	0.060	−0.022	0.060

(continued)

Table 12.4 (continued)

	Model 1		Model 2		Model 3		Model 4	
	b	Linearized SE	b	Linearized SE	b	Linearized SE	b	Linearized SE
Stepparents	0.110	0.049*	0.100	0.048*	0.088	0.045	0.080	0.044
Other	0.173	0.080*	0.127	0.081	0.097	0.085	0.110	0.087
Wave I family SES	−0.008	0.010	−0.003	0.010	−0.004	0.010	−0.003	0.010
Sexual risk-taking								
Age at first sex (16–18)								
15 or less			0.178	0.054**	0.181	0.052**	0.167	0.052**
19 or older			−0.234	0.049***	−0.228	0.046***	−0.224	0.046***
Number of sex partners (1–4)								
5–9			−0.174	0.048***	−0.221	0.048***	−0.227	0.046***
11–20			−0.209	0.064**	−0.217	0.062**	−0.228	0.062***
21–30			−0.201	0.082*	−0.250	0.087**	−0.257	0.087**
30+			−0.320	0.075***	−0.352	0.075***	−0.369	0.076***
Union experiences								
Times married					0.390	0.035***	0.393	0.036***
Times cohabited					0.002	0.017	−0.007	0.017
Incarceration experiences								
Number of Incarcerations (0)								
1							0.034	0.069
> 1							0.205	0.070**
Intercept	−1.619	0.453***	−1.511	0.443**	−0.970	0.456*	−0.949	0.455*
F	7.40***		9.55***		12.16***		11.35***	

* $p \leq 0.05$ ** $p \leq 0.01$ *** $p \leq 0.001$

12.6.2 Supplementary Models

We also explored two alternate specifications of offending: serious offending (violence or threat of violence) and intense offending (three or more crimes). Fewer men and women engaged in either serious or intense offending, but the distributions across gender followed a similar pattern to any offending. At the bivariate level, the patterns were similar to what was observed for any offending (Appendix A), but at the multivariate level, we did not find any link between serious or intense offending in the transition to adulthood and the number of children in the late 30 s and early 40 s in the presence of the full set of coveriates (Appendix B). We also examined each offense independently, as shown in Appendices C (women) and D (men). For women, we find two of the more minor offenses being important: persistently engaging in property damage was associated with lower fertility ($b = -0.438$), and stealing something worth less than $50 at Wave III but not Wave I (late-onset) was also associated with lower fertility ($b = -0.204$). For men, late-onset property damage offending was linked to lower fertility ($b = -0.147$).

12.7 Discussion

In this paper, we examined how patterns of offending in adolescence and young adulthood influenced the number of children ever born among a cohort of adults approaching the end of their childbearing years. While the criminology literature has considered how parenthood affects criminal behavior (Giordano et al., 2011; Ziegler et al., 2017), there is considerably less research linking criminal behavior to later childbearing. Criminal behavior could disrupt the process of forming relationships that ultimately produce children (perhaps by making individuals less attractive to partners or, at the extreme, limiting exposure to childbearing via incarceration). Alternatively, it could increase fertility to the extent that criminal behavior is associated with risk-taking more generally, including sexual risk-taking, which may lead to more births. It is also possible that criminal behavior may reduce relationship stability, creating exposure to more births through repartnering. On balance, we expected those engaging in criminal activity – especially in young adulthood – would have fewer children (Hypothesis 1a).

In general, Hypothesis 1a was supported, with slightly different results across gender. Although women with persistent offending had significantly fewer children, for men, it was those with late-onset offending who had the lowest fertility. These results persist when we account for the number of sexual partners and age at first sex, the number of cohabiting and marital unions, and the number of incarceration experiences. Perhaps most interesting is that incarceration itself is associated with a *higher* parity in early to mid-adulthood. This suggests that something unique about childbearing processes is captured by adolescent and young adult offending behaviors. Further, supplementary models indicated that this was true for any offending but not for more violent or intense patterns of offending; in fact, it seems that the associations we found are driven by quite minor offenses (property damage and stealing something worth less than $50). These types of offenses may capture social and psychological issues, such as anger or compulsion, that may be particularly impactful for the processes leading to childbearing. Individuals with such issues may avoid childbearing for their own reasons (such as not wanting children or not thinking they would be good parents) or may be viewed by would-be co-parents as unfit for parenthood.

While offending in young adulthood is associated with lower fertility for both men and women, there are slight differences in the pattern of offending that was relevant for men and women – persistent offending was unrelated for men, while late-onset was unrelated for women. Why might this be the case? These results may be a product of small numbers of late-onset female offenders, reducing statistical power. There is also the possibility that the phenomenon found by Rebellon et al. (2019) persists throughout the life course. If young men's criminal behaviors are associated with increased popularity not just in adolescence but throughout adulthood, those involved in such behaviors could potentially be more attractive to potential partners and thus more likely to have children. Conversely, women who offend persistently could be a particularly select group, experiencing a unique gender penalty in social interactions and social status. Thus, they may not have any gains in popularity and could even lose popularity; further, given the rarity of offending among young women, those who persistently offend may have personality or other mental health disorders, which would impede relationship formation. It is also possible that criminal activity may be more stigmatizing among women in ways that impact their social interactions. Moore and Tangey (Moore & Tangney, 2017) note that, among incarcerated individuals, those who anticipate high stigma post-release are more likely to retreat from broader society. Perhaps this withdrawal also applies to romantic relationships among women, thus limiting their opportunities to have children.

For both men and women, though, we found the incarceration itself was linked to higher parity, even when controlling for factors such as age at first sex and number of partners. The mechanisms driving this are unclear, as we cannot identify whether these births happened before or after incarceration. It may be possible that incarceration leads individuals to become more family-oriented and make a conscious choice to have more children. Alternatively, and probably more likely, incarceration experiences are tapping into some other factor that would be linked to fertility, such as extreme social and economic disadvantage. Other than educational attainment and religiosity, we found few links between our sociodemographic and psychosocial characteristics and the number of children. For instance, childhood family structure was unrelated to the number of children respondents had at Wave V. It may be the case that family structure's impact on fertility works primarily through union formation and the context in which children are born (such as age at entry into parenthood and marital status at birth), rather than the number of children.

12.7.1 Limitations

There are several limitations to this project. As a school-based longitudinal sample, Add Health's respondents are a select group. Those with high engagement in criminal activity are less likely to be in the initial sampling frame and more likely to attrit from the sample over time. Individuals also under-report sensitive information like criminal behavior. We also lack information on contraceptive inconsistency, another aspect of sexual risk-taking. In general, we could not identify specific pathways or mechanisms, such as stigmatization or partners limiting their fertility with individuals engaged in offending. Additionally, Add Health lacks prospective measures of intended childbearing early in the life course, so it is not possible to know whether these groups differed in their desire to have children, and the analyses did not consider whether offending patterns were linked to unintended vs intended childbearing.

12.7.2 Conclusion

What does this piece add to the existing literature? Though some work exists regarding fertility and later criminal involvement, little research examines multiple trajectories of criminal offending in relation to fertility patterns. Men and women who engage in criminal acts in their late teens and early twenties have lower fertility than their peers who never engaged in offending. This pattern is not related to their union experiences, their sexual experiences, or their incarceration experiences, suggesting that offending – and particularly rather minor types of offending – in young adulthood entails unique processes related to childbearing that should be explored in future work. Future research should also investigate different aspects of fertility, such as the timing, union context, and planning status of births. Our research is also unique in examining gendered impacts of criminal offending on fertility. This can and should be expanded upon; datasets with larger numbers of persistent female offenders or qualitative research with the ability to delve into gender differences and their explanations is key. In general, taking a broader approach to consider the myriad factors that may influence fertility – and how these factors may differ not only by gender but other avenues of marginalization and inequality, such as race/ethnicity, nativity, and sexual orientation – is warranted.

Acknowledgements This research was supported in part by center grants to Bowling Green State University's Center for Family and Demographic Research (P2C-HD050959) and the University of North Carolina at Chapel Hill's Carolina Population Center (P2C HD050924). A prior version was presented at the 2021 annual meeting of the Population Association of America. This project uses data from the National Longitudinal Study of Adolescent to Adult Health (Add Health). Add Health is directed by Robert A. Hummer and funded by the National Institute on Aging cooperative agreements U01 AG071448 (Hummer) and U01 AG071450 (Aiello and Hummer) at the University of North Carolina at Chapel Hill. Waves I-V data are from the Add Health Program Project, grant P01 HD31921 (Harris) from *Eunice Kennedy Shriver* National Institute of Child Health and Human Development (NICHD), with cooperative funding from 23 other federal agencies and foundations. Add Health was designed by J. Richard Udry, Peter S. Bearman, and Kathleen Mullan Harris at the University of North Carolina at Chapel Hill. Information on obtaining Add Health data is available on the project website (http://www.cpc.unc.edu/addhealth).

Appendix A: Mean Parity by Serious and Intense Offending, N = 8909

	Women		Men	
	Mean	Linearized SE	Mean	Linearized SE
Serious offending				
Engaged at neither wave	1.69	0.03	1.47[b,c,d]	0.04
Engaged at wave I, but not wave III	1.74	0.06	1.74[a,c]	0.08
Engaged at wave III, but not wave I	1.69	0.15	1.25[a,b,d]	0.10
Engaged at both waves	1.82	0.19	1.70 [a,c]	0.11
Intense offending				
Engaged at neither wave	1.70	0.03	1.52	0.04
Engaged at wave I, but not wave III	1.74	0.11	1.71[c]	0.10
Engaged at wave III, but not wave I	1.60	0.26	1.34[b]	0.12
Engaged at both waves	1.16	0.35	1.57	0.18

Superscripts indicate significant differences across categories at $p \leq .05$
[a] different from engaged at neither wave
[b] different from engaged at Wave I, but not Wave III
[c] different from engaged at Wave III, but not Wave I
[d] different from engaged at both waves

Appendix B: Full Models of Poisson Regression of Serious and Intense Offending, Women and Men

	Women, Serious Offending		Women, Intense Offending		Men, Serious Offending		Men, Intense Offending	
	b	SE	b	SE	b	SE	b	SE
Serious offending (neither wave)[a]								
Wave I, but not wave III	−0.006	0.035			0.082	0.045		
Wave III, but not wave I	0.037	0.096			−0.097	0.082		
Both waves	0.043	0.101			0.105	0.063		
Intense offending (neither wave)[b]								
Wave I, but not wave III			0.012	0.057			0.049	0.056
Wave III, but not Wave I			0.008	0.141			−0.029	0.083
Both waves			−0.294	0.272			0.093	0.124

* $p \leq 0.05$ ** $p \leq 0.01$ *** $p \leq 0.001$. Models control for full set of covariates, analogous to Models 4 in Tables 12.3 and 12.4
[a] Serious offending is composed of the following questions: (1) hurt someone badly enough to need bandages or care from a doctor or nurse, (2) take part in a fight where a group of your friends was against another group, and (3) use or threaten to use a weapon to get something from someone
[b] Intense offending consists of the same offending measures used in any offending. Intense offending is indicated when a respondent has reported engaged in three or more of the offending behaviors per wave

Appendix C: Poisson Regression of Wave V Fertility on Specific Offenses,spiepr146 Women

	Property Offenses							
	Deliberately damage property that didn't belong to you		Steal something worth more than $50		Go into a house or building to steal something		Steal something worth less than $50	
	b	SE	b	SE	b	SE	b	SE
Any offending (neither wave)								
Wave I, but not Wave III	–0.005	0.049	–0.059	0.087	0.083	0.085	0.025	0.048
Wave III, but not Wave I	–0.152	0.117	–0.097	0.139	–0.209	0.219	–0.204	0.092*
Both waves	–0.438	0.160**	0.160	0.243	0.100	0.272	–0.050	0.146

	Drug and violent offenses							
	Sell marijuana or other drugs		Hurt someone badly enough to need bandages or care[a]		Take part in a fight[b]		Use or threaten to use a weapon to get something	
	b	SE	b	SE	b	SE	b	SE
Any offending (neither wave)								
Wave I, but not wave III	0.011	0.099	0.056	0.044	–0.008	0.040	–0.028	0.072
Wave III, but not wave I	–0.058	0.088	0.063	0.153	0.177	0.097	0.006	0.150
Both waves	–0.091	0.198	–0.043	0.196	–0.084	0.156	n/a	n/a

* $p \leq 0.05$ ** $p \leq 0.01$ *** $p \leq 0.001$ Models control for full set of covariates, analogous to Models 4 in Tables 12.3 and 12.4

[a] Full question: hurt someone badly enough to need bandages or care from a doctor or nurse

[b] Full question: take part in a fight where a group of your friends was against another group

Appendix D: Poisson Regression of Wave V Fertility on Specific Offenses, Men

	Property Offenses							
	Deliberately damage property that didn't belong to you		Steal something worth more than $50		Go into a house or building to steal something		Steal something worth less than $50	
	b	SE	b	SE	b	SE	b	SE
Any offending (neither wave)								
Wave I, but not Wave III	0.046	0.048	–0.015	0.075	0.071	0.075	–0.070	0.053
Wave III, but not Wave I	–0.147	0.073*	–0.069	0.096	0.199	0.105	–0.039	0.077
Both waves	–0.115	0.091	–0.049	0.206	–0.388	0.335	–0.022	0.101

	Drug and violent offenses							
	Sell marijuana or other drugs		Hurt someone badly enough to need bandages or care[a]		Take part in a fight[b]		Use or threaten to use a weapon to get something	
	b	SE	b	SE	b	SE	b	SE
Any offending (neither wave)								
Wave I, but not Wave III	–0.027	0.069	0.080	0.045	0.108	0.060	0.112	0.079
Wave III, but not Wave I	–0.129	0.074	–0.017	0.089	0.034	0.073	0.095	0.135
Both waves	0.072	0.104	0.050	0.116	0.102	0.076	0.096	0.113

* $p \leq 0.05$ ** $p \leq 0.01$ *** $p \leq 0.001$ Models control for full set of covariates, analogous to Models 4 in Tables 12.3 and 12.4

[a] Full question: hurt someone badly enough to need bandages or care from a doctor or nurse

[b] Full question: take part in a fight where a group of your friends was against another group

References

Abell, L. (2018). Exploring the transition to parenthood as a pathway to desistance. *Journal of Developmental and Life-Course Criminology, 4*(4), 395–426.

Allison, P. D. (1991). *Logistic regression using the SAS system: Theory and application*. SAS Institute.

Ashcraft, R. (2009). *The Association of Adolescent Criminal Trajectories with social support, gender, and ethnicity*. [Unpublished dissertation]. Alliant International University.

Augustyn, M. B., & Jackson, D. B. (2020). An intersectional look at the "rush to adulthood": Considering the role of gender, race and SES in the link between precocious transitions and adult antisocial behavior. *Youth & Society, 52*(1), 3–26.

Baćak, V., & Karim, M. E. (2019). The effect of serious offending on health: A marginal structural model. *Society and Mental Health, 9*(1), 18–32.

Bearman, P. S., & Moody, J. (2004). Suicide and friendships among American adolescents. *American Journal of Public Health, 94*(1), 89–95.

Bradshaw, C. P., Schaeffer, C. M., Petras, H., & Ialongo, N. (2010). Predicting negative life outcomes from early aggressive-disruptive behavior trajectories: Gender differences in maladaptation across life domains. *Journal of Youth and Adolescence, 39*, 953–966.

Campedelli, G. M., Calderoni, F., Comunale, T., & Meneghini, C. (2019). Life course trajectories of mafia members. *Crime and Delinquency, 67*(1), 1–31.

Closson, L. M. (2009). Status and gender differences in early adolescents' descriptions of popularity. *Social Development, 18*(2), 412–426.

Demuth, S., & Brown, S. L. (2004). Family structure, family processes, and adolescent delinquency: The significance of parental absence versus parental gender. *Journal of Research in Crime and Delinquency, 41*(1), 58–81.

Dennison, C. R., & Swisher, R. R. (2019). Postsecondary education, neighborhood disadvantage, and crime; an examination of life course relative deprivation. *Crime & Delinquency, 65*(2), 215–238.

Drury, A. J., DeLisi, M., & Elbert, M. J. (2020). What becomes of chronic juvenile delinquents? Multifinality at midlife. *Youth Violence and Juvenile Justice, 18*(2), 119–134.

Esposito, M. H., Lee, H., Hicken, M. T., Porter, L. C., & Herting, J. R. (2017). The consequences of contact with the criminal justice system for health in the transition to adulthood. *Longitudinal and Life Course Studies, 8*(1), 57–74.

Ferrante, A. M. (2013). Assessing gender and ethnic differences in developmental trajectories of offending. *Australian and New Zealand Journal of Criminology, 46*(3), 379–402.

Giordano, P. C., Seffrin, P. M., Manning, W. D., & Longmore, M. A. (2011). Parenthood and crime: The role of wantedness, relationships with partners, and SES. *Journal of Criminal Justice, 39*(5), 405–416.

Greenfeld, L. A., & Snell, T. L. (1999). Bureau of Justice Statistics. In *Women Offenders*. (Publication No. 175688). Retrieved from https://www.ojp.gov/ncjrs/virtual-library/abstracts/women-offenders-0

Hayford, S. R. (2013). Marriage (still) matters: The contribution of demographic change to trends in childlessness in the United States. *Demography, 50*(5), 1641–1661.

Haynie, D. L., Giordano, P. C., Manning, W. D., & Longmore, M. A. (2005). Adolescent romantic relationships and delinquency involvement. *Criminology, 43*(1), 177–210.

Hirschi, T., & Gottfredson, M. (1983). Age and the explanation of crime. *The American Journal of Sociology, 89*(3), 552–584.

Huang, T., Jr., Chiang, T.-F. F., & Pan, J.-N. J. N. (2015). Fertility and crime: Evidence from spatial analysis of Taiwan. *Journal of Family and Economic Issues, 36*(3), 319–327.

Joyner, K., Peters, H. E., Hynes, K., Sikora, A., Taber, J. R., & Rendall, M. S. (2012). The quality of male fertility data in major U.S. Surveys. *Demography, 49*, 101–124.

Kreager, D. A., Matsueda, R. L., & Erosheva, E. A. (2010). Motherhood and criminal desistance in disadvantaged neighborhoods. *Criminology, 48*(1), 221–258.

Landeis, M., Manning, W. D., Longmore, M. A., Giordano, P. C., & Joyner, K. (2020). The relationship context of early transitions to parenthood: The influence of arrest. *Population Research and Policy Review, 40*, 723–746.

Lansford, J. E., Dodge, K. A., Fontaine, R. G., Bates, J. E., & Pettit, G. S. (2014). Peer rejection, affiliation with deviant peers, delinquency, and risky sexual behavior. *Journal of Youth and Adolescence, 43*(10), 1742–1751.

Lussier, P., Tzoumakis, S., Cale, J., & Amirault, J. (2010). Criminal trajectories of adult sex offenders and the age effect: Examining the dynamic aspect of offending in adulthood. *International Criminal Justice Review, 20*(2), 147–168.

Martinez, Gladys M., Daniels, Kimberly, and Isaedmarie Febo-Vazquez. (2018). *Fertility of Men and Women Aged 15–44 in the United States: National Survey of Family Growth, 2011–2015.* (Publication No. 113). Department of Health and Human Services. Retrieved from https://pubmed.ncbi.nlm.nih.gov/30248009/

Massoglia, M., & Uggen, C. (2010). Settling down and aging out: Toward an interactionist theory of desistance and the transition to adulthood. *American Journal of Sociology, 116*(2), 543–582.

Mayeux, L., Sandstrom, M. J., & Cillessen, A. H. N. (2008). Is being popular a risky proposition? *Journal of Research on Adolescence, 18*(1), 49–74.

McGloin, J. M. (2009). Delinquency balance: Revisiting peer influence. *Criminology, 47*(2), 439–477.

Moffitt, T. (1993). Adolescence-limited and life-course-persistent offending: A developmental taxonomy. *Psychological Review, 100*(4), 674–701.

Moffitt, T. (1997). Adolescence-limited and life-course-persistent offending: A complementary pair of developmental theories. In T. P. Thornberry (Ed.), *Developmental theories of crime and delinquency* (1st ed., pp. 11–54). Routledge.

Monte, L. M., & Fields, J. M. (2020). Where's daddy? Challenges in the measurement of Men's fertility. In R. Schoen (Ed.), *Analyzing contemporary fertility* (1st ed., pp. 257–284). Springer.

Moore, K. E., & Tangney, J. P. (2017). Managing the concealable stigma of criminal justice system involvement: A longitudinal examination of anticipated stigma, social withdrawal, and post-release adjustment. *Journal of Social Issues, 73*(2), 322–340.

Rauscher, E. (2011). Producing adulthood: Adolescent employment, fertility, and the life course. *Social Science Research, 40*(2), 552–571.

Rebellon, C. J., Trinkner, R., Gundy, V., Karen, T., & Cohn, E. S. (2019). No guts, no glory: The influence of risk-taking on adolescent popularity. *Deviant Behavior, 40*(12), 1464–1479.

Reising, K., Ttofi, M. M., Farrington, D. P., & Piquero, A. R. (2019). The impact of longitudinal offending trajectories on mental health: Lifetime consequences and intergenerational transfer. *Journal of Criminal Justice, 62*, 16–22.

Sampson, R. J., & Laub, J. H. (2003). Life-course Desisters? Trajectories of crime among delinquent boys followed to age 70. *Criminology, 41*(3), 555–592.

Tanner, J., Davies, S., & O'Grady, B. (1999). Whatever happened to Yesterday's rebels? Longitudinal effects of youth delinquency on education and employment. *Social Problems, 46*(2), 250–274.

Thomson, E., Winkler-Dworak, M., Spielauer, M., & Prskawetz, A. (2012). Union instability as an engine of fertility? *A Microsimulation Model for France. Demography, 49*(1), 175–195.

van Onna, J. H. R., van der Geest, V. R., Huisman, W., & Denkers, A. J. M. (2014). Criminal trajectories of white-collar offenders. *Journal of Research in Crime and Delinquency, 51*(6), 759–784.

Ward, S., & Williams, J. (2015). Does juvenile delinquency reduce educational attainment? *Journal of Empirical Legal Studies, 12*(4), 716–756.

Warner, C., & Remster, B. (2021). Criminal justice contact, residential Independence, and returns to the parental home. *Journal of Marriage and Family, 83*(2), 322–339.

Ziegler, J. A., Kuhl, D. C., Swisher, R. R., & Chavez, J. M. (2017). Parenthood residency status and criminal desistance across neighborhood contexts. *Deviant Behavior, 38*(1), 17–33.

Chapter 13
The Influence of Intimate Partner Violence on Early and Unintended Parenthood

Marissa Landeis, Karen Benjamin Guzzo, Wendy D. Manning, Monica A. Longmore, and Peggy C. Giordano

13.1 The Influence of Intimate Partner Violence on Early and Unintended Parenthood

Compared to other industrialized countries, the United States has a high rate of unintended childbearing – that is, births occurring early in the life course or occurring to women who do not intend to get pregnant. Just under half of all pregnancies are reported as unintended (Finer & Zolna, 2016). Unintended childbearing is associated negatively with maternal and child health, although the causal linkages are debated (Abajobir et al., 2017; Chowdhury et al., 2020; Claridge, 2021; Everett et al., 2016; Gharaee & Baradaran, 2020; Guzzo & Hayford, 2014; Su, 2017; Yeatman & Smith-Greenaway, 2021). Unintended childbearing occurs disproportionately among young women, socioeconomically disadvantaged populations, and racial/ethnic minority women (Finer & Zolna, 2014, 2016). Although researchers have demonstrated negative associations between unintended childbearing and a range of well-being indicators, there are gaps in the explanations of the processes by which unintended parenthood affects well-being.

Like unintended childbearing, intimate partner violence (IPV) is linked to adverse outcomes for families and children (Black, 2011; Fong et al., 2019; Samankasikorn et al., 2019). Moreover, there is a body of work demonstrating associations between intimate partner violence and unintended childbearing. Scholars have documented

M. Landeis · W. D. Manning · M. A. Longmore · P. C. Giordano
Department of Sociology, and Center for Family and Demographic Research, Bowling Green State University, Bowling Green, OH, USA

K. B. Guzzo (✉)
Department of Sociology, and Carolina Population Center, University of North Carolina, Chapel Hill, NC, USA
e-mail: Karen.Guzzo@unc.edu

R. Schoen (ed.), *The Demography of Transforming Families*, The Springer Series on Demographic Methods and Population Analysis 56,
https://doi.org/10.1007/978-3-031-29666-6_13

two different associations between intimate partner violence and unintended childbearing. First, intimate partner violence may be a significant predictor of unintended childbearing by limiting women's abilities to manage their own sexual and contraceptive behavior (Grace et al., 2022; Sarkar, 2008). Specifically, women who have experienced violence may feel that they are unable to choose when and whether to have sex and whether to use contraception, thus increasing the risk of an unintended birth. Conversely, unintended childbearing could lead to intimate partner violence if the stress of an off-time or unwanted pregnancy increased conflict as some evidence has suggested that early pregnancy often is a period of heightened volatility (Macy et al., 2007; Wang et al., 2017). Although both views have received substantial analytical attention, yet more for the first argument, issues of causality and selection remain unaddressed. For instance, rates of intimate partner violence are highest in young adulthood compared with other stages in the life course (Hardesty & Ogolsky, 2020; Johnson et al., 2015), and births that occur in early adulthood are disproportionately characterized as unintended (Ahrens et al., 2018; Cronley et al., 2020; Finer & Zolna, 2016). To the extent that intimate partner violence corresponds with the stage in the life course associated with higher odds of unintended parenthood, the direct causal link may be overstated. In this chapter, we considered whether experiences of intimate partner violence have a causal impact on unintended parenthood using prospective survey data.

Drawing on a population-based cohort sample, the Toledo Adolescent Relationships Study (TARS), and using event history techniques, we investigated whether prior experiences with physical relationship violence were associated with (1) early parenthood (a birth by age 25), and (2) reported intendedness of the first birth. The TARS longitudinal data contained a rich set of correlates potentially associated with both intimate partner violence and unintended parenthood to establish temporal links between prior violence experiences and first births, including whether such births were unintended. Additionally, we incorporated the perspective and experiences of young men, who have received considerably less attention in both intimate partner violence as well as childbearing/parenthood research. The findings make an important contribution to the intimate partner violence and birth intendedness literatures by examining the causal relationship that prior intimate partner violence has, or does not have, with unintended parenthood for young adult men and women.

13.1.1 Intimate Partner Violence and Birth Intendedness

Nationally, roughly one in four women and one in ten men are victims of severe physical violence, and one in three women and one in three men have been pushed, slapped, or shoved by an intimate partner (Smith et al., 2017). Although much research has focused on male-to-female violence, in survey research mutual or reciprocal violence is the most common form of violence reported (Cunradi et al., 2020; Fernández-Montalvo et al., 2020; Giordano et al., 2016).

Intimate partner violence perpetration and victimization are, in general, more common among the disadvantaged (Breiding et al., 2014; Schumacher et al., 2001), as is early and unintended childbearing.

Prior research has demonstrated that women who have experienced intimate partner violence have an increased risk of an early pregnancy (Barber et al., 2018) and an unintended pregnancy (Miller & Silverman, 2010; Samankasikorn et al., 2019). One recent study showed that young women in violent relationships were more than twice as likely to desire a pregnancy than those in non-violent relationships (Barber et al., 2019). One explanation is that intimate partner violence and sexual intimacy are strongly linked, with couples in such volatile relationships often enmeshed and experiencing heightened emotionality (Corbett et al., 2009; Giordano et al., 2010; Kaestle & Halpern, 2005; Powers & Kaukinen, 2022). For example, early research showed that husbands' violence was associated with greater frequency of sexual activity in marriage (DeMaris, 1997). The potential emotionality and passion of these volatile relationships may increase pregnancy desires as a strategy to demonstrate devotion or in an attempt to stabilize the relationship. Some partners also explicitly try to convince a partner to have a baby (Barber et al., 2018), and women often adjust their pregnancy desires to correspond with their partners' desires (Barber et al., 2018; Miller et al., 2017).

Even if young adults who have experienced intimate partner violence, as victims, perpetrators, or both, do not actively desire to have a child, relationship as well as partner characteristics may increase the risk of an early or unintended birth. Issues of reproductive coercion in which partners control women's independent reproductive decisions certainly affect the risk of childbearing (Samankasikorn et al., 2019). Further, some scholars have argued that violent or controlling men want to impregnate their partners as a means of exerting dominance and demonstrating masculinity (Corbett et al., 2009; Grace & Anderson, 2018). Conversely, some young men are worried that partners may try to trap them into a relationship by becoming pregnant (Alexander et al., 2021; Silverman et al., 2007). For example, partners may deliberately sabotage contraceptive methods or exert pressure to have sex without contraception (Barber et al., 2018; Miller & Silverman, 2010).

Even when overt efforts to limit contraceptive use are not present, it seems that intimate partner violence may affect sexual risk-taking. For instance, teens and young adults who have experienced intimate partner violence, even in a past relationship, have reported high levels of risky sexual behaviors, such as greater number of sexual partners and greater frequency of unprotected sex (Alleyne-Green et al., 2012; Kusunoki et al., 2018; Peasant et al., 2018). As such, young adults who have experienced IPV potentially would have an elevated risk of early births, although accounting for contraceptive efficacy – degree of certainty about using contraception in sexual encounters (Longmore et al., 2003) – may attenuate the risk between past intimate partner violence experiences and early births.

Yet, much prior research omits the intentionality of births. There does, however, appear to be a link between intimate partner violence and unintended childbearing (e.g., Miller & Silverman, 2010; Samankasikorn et al., 2019). The relationship appears to work through reproductive coercion (Miller et al., 2014), but more generally, intimate partner violence may increase the risk of an unintended birth through its effects on contraceptive use. Young adult daters who have experienced relationship violence have also reported less consistent condom use (Braham et al., 2019; Gibbs et al., 2014; Peasant et al., 2018). Women who have experienced physical or emotional abuse were less likely to use their preferred method of contraception relative to women who did not experience relationship abuse (Bergmann & Stockman, 2015; Paul & Mondal, 2021; Williams et al., 2008). If women are unable to control their own reproductive behaviors, then they are more likely to have an unintended birth. The causal ordering of these associations, however, is unclear because (a) pregnancy may lead to IPV, especially an unintended pregnancy that introduces stressors and strains and (b) the standard measurement of unintended itself may be unable to account for ambivalence and risk-taking.

Research on unintended childbearing has increasingly recognized that for many parents, their feelings about a particular birth cannot be neatly categorized (Aiken et al., 2016; Gomez et al., 2018). Thus, looking at both overall risks of a birth and types of births by intendedness provides important nuance to the conversation about intimate partner violence and childbearing.

In sum, although there appear to be ways that intimate partner violence may increase the risk of an unintended or ambivalent birth, it is not clear whether this is always the case, especially given the limitations of prior research. First, past research has relied on cross-sectional data so drawing causal conclusions is not possible (e.g., Miller & Silverman, 2010). Longitudinal data are necessary to analyze the timing of intimate partner violence experiences and parenthood. Second, many studies have only considered women's victimization (e.g., Yakubovich et al., 2018), yet mutual or reciprocal violence is the most common type of violence (Cunradi et al., 2020; Fernández-Montalvo et al., 2020; Giordano et al., 2016) and is also the type of violence in which women are more likely to experience serious physical harm (Smith et al., 2018). As noted above, most studies on intimate partner violence have focused primarily on women's experiences, and most studies of childbearing have focused on women as well; thus, whether intimate partner violence is associated with men's early and unintended parenthood remains unclear. Fourth, the bulk of prior studies have used dichotomous or narrowly defined measures of unintended childbearing (e.g., Yakubovich et al., 2018), ignoring the possibility that intimate partner violence may lead to a sense of ambivalence about childbearing. Finally, most prior research has been restricted to those with a birth, that is, studying the IPV experiences before, during, and after a pregnancy. In doing so, prior studies have not considered how intimate partner violence may be linked to the risk of a birth at all and so are, quite possibly, selecting on the dependent variable.

Perhaps the most critical shortcoming of much prior work is that it has not accounted for key factors that are associated with both intimate partner violence and early and unintended childbearing. For instance, the majority of births to young adults are unintended (Ahrens et al., 2018; Finer & Zolna, 2016), and rates of intimate partner violence are highest during young adulthood relative to other stages in the life course (Hardesty & Ogolsky, 2020; Johnson et al., 2015). Similarly, relationship violence during pregnancy is concentrated among younger, poorer women, especially those not living with their partners (Daoud et al., 2012). As such, there is reason to expect that the association between intimate partner violence and unintended childbearing is weaker than prior work has suggested. For example, many prior studies are based on samples of only those with intimate partner violence experience, while others have looked only among those with a pregnancy; in both cases, selection on the dependent or key independent variable meant analyses were unable to account for other life course, relational, and reproductive characteristics associated with either intimate partner violence or unintended parenthood. Even those studies that have included socioeconomic and demographic factors, such as age, family background, and race/ethnicity often have not included union and family planning characteristics. For instance, union status is associated with both unintended childbearing and intimate partner violence (Capaldi et al., 2012; Finer & Zolna, 2016; Manning et al., 2018; Masho et al., 2018). Attitudes about contraception, and beliefs in being able to use contraception consistently and effectively, are associated with intimate partner violence and unintended childbearing (Gibbs, 2013; Guzzo & Hayford, 2018; Manning et al., 2012). Other behavioral factors, such as delinquency or poor school performance, might also influence intimate partner violence or unintended childbearing if they reflect risk-taking or difficulty adhering to contraception (Driscoll et al., 2005).

13.1.2 Current Study

In this study, we build on prior research to consider whether intimate partner violence is predictive of early parenthood as well as intendedness among men and women. Although prior research has suggested that intimate partner violence experiences increase the risk of an unintended birth, there is also reason to suspect that the association may be due to an elevated risk of early parenthood given that both intimate partner violence and unintended childbearing occur disproportionately during young adulthood. To account for this, we explicitly focus on the young adult years, up to age 25 (the mean age at first birth in the United States for women in 2012, the final year of data used in the current project, was 25.8 (Martin et al., 2019), with men's ages 2–3 years higher on average (Schweizer, 2019)). Moreover, the risk factors for both intimate partner violence and unintended childbearing suggest that accounting for other proximate factors, such as union type or contraceptive use, as well as indicators of disadvantage, such as involvement in criminal activity and substance use, may explain any established linkage.

We capitalized on longitudinal data that are uniquely suited to overcome many of the challenges identified above, including measures of both perpetration and victimization, nuanced categories of birth intendedness, and a rich set of background and union characteristics to better establish causal connections.

13.2 Data and Methods

13.2.1 Data

We analyzed longitudinal data from the Toledo Adolescent Relationships Study (TARS). TARS is a school-based sample based in Lucas County, Ohio. The 1321 respondents were selected in 2000 from publicly available records of students in the seventh, ninth, and 11th grade. The sampling frame, developed by the National Opinion Research Center, comprised 15,188 eligible students stratified by race/ethnicity (non-Hispanic White, non-Hispanic Black, and Hispanic), gender, and grade into 18 strata. Through random subsamples, 2273 students were selected from each stratum. Black and Hispanic students were oversampled. Of the 2273 students, we contacted 1625 and had 304 refusals, leaving 81.3% or 1321 students. At the time of the first interview to maintain privacy, each respondent had an in-home interview with a questionnaire in the form of the computer-assisted personal interview (CAPI). A parent or caregiver was interviewed separately at the first interview.

There are five waves of data included in this study. Interviews for wave 1 began in 2001, wave 2 was conducted in 2002/2003, wave 3 in 2004/2005, wave 4 in 2006/2007, and wave 5 in 2011/2012. In wave 1 respondents' ages ranged from 12–19 and at wave 5 respondents' ages ranged from 25–32. Respondents had to complete at least one interview beyond the first one to be included in the analyses. We began by excluding those who had a first birth before wave 1 or prior to age 13, resulting in 1283 respondents. Due to small cell sizes, we limited the sample to respondents who reported their race or ethnicity as White, Black, or Hispanic (n = 1257). Respondents who had missing data on the dependent or independent variables were omitted, resulting in 1239 respondents. Finally, we restricted the analysis of first births to those women and men whom we could observe to age 25 (n = 811). Of these respondents, 374 had their first birth by age 25.

13.2.2 Dependent Variable

Respondents reported on the exact dates of live births, and as noted above, those who had already had their first birth by the first wave were excluded from the analyses. At each interview, respondents were asked whether they had ever had any births or fathered any births, and if so, the date of each birth; we focused on live births because pregnancies that end in miscarriage or abortion are underreported in survey data (Lindberg et al., 2020).

The indicator of *intentions* is based on the following question. "At the time your found out you were pregnant [your partner was pregnant], would you say you: (1) Wanted to become pregnant [get your partner pregnant]; (2) Didn't want to become pregnant [get your partner pregnant]; (3) Hadn't thought about whether you wanted to get pregnant [get your partner pregnant]; and (4) Didn't care one way or another." We created three variables including (1) a dichotomous indicator of a live birth; (2) a three-category variable of intendedness using the traditional categories in which ambivalence and not caring were grouped with unwanted (no birth, intended/wanted birth, unintended birth); and (3) a categorical measure that disaggregated unintended births (no birth, intended/wanted birth, unwanted birth, ambivalent birth, and a 'didn't care' birth).

13.2.3 Independent Variables

Intimate Partner Violence included items from the Revised Conflict Tactics Scale (Straus, 2013; Straus & Gelles, 1990) assessing mutual violence. Respondents were asked how often their current or most recent partner has "(1) thrown something at you; (2) pushed, shoved, or grabbed you; (3) slapped you in the face or head with an open hand; and (4) hit you." The responses ranged from "never" to "very often." To increase validity, consistent with a recommendation by Straus (2013) the items were not examined separately. Respondents were also asked the frequency of which they committed these violent behaviors towards their current or most recent partner. For both measures, we created dichotomous indicators of any violence. We considered perpetration and victimization separately; however, the results were similar, so we relied on the ever experience IPV indicator (not shown). This time-varying variable is used to assess the respondents' *prior IPV experience* at the last interview prior to conception (based on date of birth minus eight months). Note that this measure does not necessarily capture, for those who had children, the relationship with child's biological parent. We return to this in the limitations.

We included a number of sociodemographic variables in the models. *Age* and its squared term (in months) were time-varying. *Gender,* a binary variable, specified if the respondent was female. *Race/Ethnicity* (measured at the first interview) was classified into three binary variables: (1) White, (2) Black, and (3) Hispanic with White as the reference category. *Family structure,* from the first interview, was operationalized as two biological parent households versus every other family structure (e.g., stepfamilies, single parent families, living alone, etc.). *Relationship status,* which varies and is indexed to the prior wave, was coded into four categories: (1) single, (2) dating, (3) cohabiting, and (4) married. These were then constructed into four dichotomous variables that indicated relationship status at the month prior to risk. The reference category in models was married union status.

Additional variables included psychosocial factors linked to both IPV and childbearing. *Contraceptive efficacy* is measured by asking at each wave, "If you were to become intimate with someone, how sure are you that you could plan ahead to have some form of birth control available" (Longmore et al., 2003). Response categories included (1) "I never want to use birth control, (2) I never want to become intimate with someone before marriage, (3) very unsure (4) moderately unsure, (5) neither sure nor unsure, (6) moderately sure, and (7) very sure." We created a four-category variable with (1) never use (response 1), (2) no intimacy before marriage (response 2), (3) unsure (response categories 3, 4, and 5), and (4) sure (response categories 6 and 7). Similar to IPV experience, this variable is time-varying, indexed to the last interview prior to the month at risk.

How far in school is a measure that asked respondents at wave 1 how far they think they will go in school. The variable is coded as (1) drop out before graduating from high school, (2) graduate from high school, (3) go to a business, technical school, or junior college after high school, (4) graduate from a four-year college, and (5) go to a graduate or professional school. *Grades,* self-reported at the first interview, were coded so that higher numbers reflected higher grades. *Delinquency*, an eight-item mean scale, asked respondents "In the last two years (or 24 months), how often have you: (1) stolen (or tried to steal) things worth $5 or less; (2) damaged or destroyed property on purpose; (3) carried a hidden weapon other than a plain pocket knife; (4) stolen (or tried to steal) something worth more than $50; (5) attacked someone with the idea of seriously hurting him/her; (6) sold drugs; (7) broken into a building or vehicle (or tried to break in) to steal something or just to look around; and (8) used drugs to get high (not because they were sick)" (Elliott and Ageton Elliot & Ageton, 1980). Responses ranged from (0) "never" to (8) "more than once a day," with a mean scale resulting in a range from 0 to 8 (the α ranged from 0.74 to 0.87 across waves). Although part of the original scale, "Been drunk in a public place" was excluded because we included a separate indicator of substance abuse. Respondents were asked these questions regarding their delinquency at each interview, and for each wave we created a mean scale. This variable is also time-varying, indexed to the last interview prior to the month at risk. *Substance abuse* prior to the birth of the child was operationalized as a 7-item mean scale in which respondents were asked "How often in the past 12 months have you experienced these things because of your drinking/using drugs:" (1) "Not felt so good the next day," (2) "Felt unable to do your best job at work or school," (3) "Hit one of your family members," (4) "Gotten into fights with others," (5) "Had problems with your friends," (6) "Had problems with someone you were dating," and (7) "Gotten into a sexual situation that you later regretted." Responses ranged from (1) never to (8) almost daily (the α ranged from 0.89 to 0.92 across waves).

13.2.4 Analytic Strategy

As noted, we used age 25 to define 'early' parenthood to be consistent with prior work (e.g., Hofferth & Goldscheider, 2010; Hynes et al., 2008; Joyner et al., 2012; Landeis et al., 2021). We excluded respondents who became parents before the first interview to account for the temporal ordering of events. To analyze how IPV experience is associated with expedited entry into parenthood (dichotomous) and the intendedness of this first birth (categorical), independent of related covariates, we estimated competing risk discrete-time logistic and multinomial logistic regression models using person-months (Allison, 2010), presenting the odds ratios (ORs) and relative risk ratios (RRRs), respectively. Beginning with the first interview, we converted data to a person-month file in which respondents contributed monthly observations of pregnancy risk until they either report a pregnancy (date of birth with 8 months subtracted) or reached age 25 with no pregnancy. After accounting for their 25th birthday being the end of the risk period, we had 139,563 observations in the analyses.

Descriptive statistics are presented before proceeding to three multivariable models. We first examined whether prior IPV experience predicts having a first birth. Then we moved to two models that account for birth intentions. The first of these used the more common measure of intended, unintended, and no birth, and the second disaggregated the unintended category to create separate categories for unwanted: "had not thought about it" (risk-taking), and "did not care either way" (ambivalence). In the models, the prior IPV measure is the combined measure of having either perpetrated or been the victim of physical IPV because this scale measures mutual violence, the most common form of partner violence. We then discussed, but do not show, the results from sensitivity tests where we disaggregate victimization and perpetration.

13.2.5 Descriptive Results

Table 13.1 provided descriptive statistics for the overall sample and by parenthood status. We make two key observations: Parents reported significantly higher levels of any IPV compared to respondents without children and the overall sample. Parents in this sample also reported lower levels of contraceptive efficacy than respondents without children.

13.2.6 Regression Results

Table 13.2 showed the odds ratios for the results from the competing risk discrete-time logistic regression model predicting the probability of entering parenthood and also included relative risk ratios for the multinomial model predicting birth intendedness. Model 1 indicated that prior IPV experience was not associated with an increased risk of having a first birth. In bivariate analyses not shown there was a significant association between IPV experience and probability of entering parenthood, consistent with the descriptive results. Further analyses showed that once the respondents' grades were added to the model the significant association between IPV and entering parenthood was attenuated. With regard to demographic indicators, women compared to men in the sample were significantly more likely to enter parenthood by age 25. Single respondents, respondents who reported higher grades at wave 1, and those who reported living with their biological parents at wave 1 (adolescence) were also significantly less likely to enter parenthood by age

Table 13.1 Descriptive statistics measured at the final month of observation

	All respondents		Parents		Childless	
Variables	M or %	SD	M or %	SD	M or %	SD
Prior IPV experience	39%		43%		35%	
Controls						
Age	20.70	2.84	19.99	2.25	21.30	3.14
Gender						
Female	52%		62%		43%	
Male	48%		38%		57%	
Contraceptive efficacy (time-varying)						
Sure	67%		66%		68%	
Never use	4%		5%		3%	
Not before marriage	7%		5%		8%	
Unsure	22%		24%		21%	
Relationship status (time-varying)						
Single	33%		23%		42%	
Dating	49%		58%		41%	
Cohabiting	6%		10%		3%	
Married	12%		8%		14%	
Behavioral indicators (time-varying)						
Delinquency	30%	0.71	30%	0.62	31%	0.77
Substance abuse	21%	0.59	23%	0.64	19%	0.55
School performance						
Grades (wave 1)	5.92	2.02	5.44	2.07	6.33	1.89
How far in school	3.84	0.98	3.73	1.03	3.93	0.93
Race/ethnicity						
White	61%		52%		66%	
Black	28%		32%		24%	
Hispanic	13%		16%		10%	
Family structure at wave 1						
Two biological parents	45%		36%		52%	
Not two biological parents	55%		64%		48%	
Neighborhood poverty wave 1	−0.77	4.73	0.19	4.82	−1.60	4.50
N	811		374		437	

Source: Toledo Adolescent Relationships Study
Note: Contrast categories are in parentheses. Risk period excludes monthly observations after the 25th birthday
Person Months = 139,563

25 than their counterparts with different characteristics. Hispanic respondents and those who lived in neighborhoods with higher levels of neighborhood poverty were more likely to enter parenthood by age 25.

The next set of results reported the multinomial regression results for birth intendedness with each column representing a different contrast. First, we predicted how IPV influenced reporting an intended first birth, compared to not having a birth

Table 13.2 Odds ratios of having A birth and relative risk ratios of birth intentions from competing risk discrete-time logistic and multinomial logistic regression models, respectively

	Model 1: Any birth				Model 2: Traditional intendedness			
Variables	Birth vs. No birth		Intended vs. No birth		Unintended vs. No birth		Intended vs. Unintended	
Prior IPV experience	1.10		1.17		1.11		0.98	
Demographics								
Age	1.34	***	1.21	***	1.42	***	0.85	*
Age^2	1.00	***	1.00	***	1.00	***	1.00	**
Female	2.01	***	1.92	**	2.19	***	0.84	
Contraceptive efficacy								
Sure	–		–	–	–		–	
Never use	1.42		2.50	*	1.07		1.51	
Not before marriage	0.66	†	0.78		0.67		1.06	
Unsure	1.14		1.29		1.14		0.94	
Respondent relationship status								
Single	0.46	**	0.22	*	0.62	†	0.43	†
Dating	0.85		0.56		1.05	†	0.71	
Cohabiting	1.28		1.34		1.17		1.94	
Married	–		–		–		–	
Behavioral indicators								
Delinquency	0.84		1.05		0.82		1.24	
Substance use	1.15		0.51	†	1.42	**	0.51	†
School performance								
Grades (wave 1)	0.82	***	0.81	***	0.84	***	0.94	
How far in school	0.93		0.91		0.93		1.02	
Race/ethnicity								
White	–		–		–		–	

(continued)

Table 13.2 (continued)

	Model 1: Any birth				Model 2: Traditional intendedness			
Variables	Birth vs. No birth		Intended vs. No birth		Unintended vs. No birth		Intended vs. Unintended	
Black	1.09		0.75		1.29		0.66	
Hispanic	1.56	**	1.15		1.73	**	0.77	
Two biological parents at wave 1	0.67	***	0.66	†	0.68	**	0.88	
Neighborhood poverty (wave 1)	1.07	***	1.06	*	1.07	***	0.99	

Source: Toledo Adolescent Relationships Study
† $p < .10$, *$p < .05$, **$p < .01$, ***$p < .001$
Person Months = 139,625

by age 25. The results indicated that there was no association between IPV and reporting an intended first birth relative to no birth. The next column showed that IPV was not significantly associated with having an unintended first birth as compared to not having a child by age 25. The final column showed the contrast between an intended versus unintended birth. Prior IPV experience was not associated with the intention status of the birth. The same pattern of results existed at the bivariate level (results not shown).

Age was associated with the odds of having an intended child with younger women reporting lower odds than older women (last column). Women were more likely to report both an intended or an unintended birth compared to no birth relative to men, but gender was not associated with the intention status of the birth (last column). Respondents who reported never using birth control were significantly more likely to have an intended first birth than no birth, but contraceptive use was not associated with having an unintended birth relative to no birth. Single respondents were likely to have a child and less likely to have an intended birth rather than an unintended birth than married respondents. Those who reported higher levels of substance use in the month prior to their month at risk were significantly more likely to have an unintended first birth than no birth. Individuals who reported higher grades were less likely to have a child before age 25 but shared similar odds of having an intended versus unintended birth (last column). Respondents who reported living with their biological parents at wave 1 (adolescence) were significantly less likely to have a child (unintended or intended) and had similar odds of having an intended rather than unintended child (last column). Hispanic respondents were more likely to report having an unintended birth compared to having no child relative to their non-Hispanic White counterparts. Young men and women living in areas with higher levels of neighborhood poverty at wave 1 were significantly more likely to have a first birth, but neighborhood poverty did not differentiate between having an unintended versus intended child (last column).

The results in the prior table showed no association between IPV and the probability of entering parenthood, as well as the likelihood of such births being characterized as intended. In the final set of models presented in Table 13.3, we consider whether traditional categories of intended versus unintended and ignore how IPV could be related to risk-taking or ambivalence. However, as can be seen in the first row of Table 13.3, there was again no association between IPV and the risk of a birth regardless of how respondents categorized such a birth. All of these were compared to not entering parenthood. Specifically, IPV was not associated with having a wanted first birth, an unwanted first birth, a birth characterized by risk-taking (hadn't thought about it), or a birth characterized by ambivalence (didn't care).

In terms of the remaining covariates, women were significantly more likely to have had a first birth across all four categories compared to men. Respondents who were single or dating in the month prior to their month at risk were significantly less likely to have a wanted first birth than no birth relative to married respondents, but union status was not related to the other indicators. Individuals who never used contraception were twice as likely to have an unwanted first birth than no birth. Also,

Table 13.3 Relative risk ratios of nuanced birth intentions from competing risk discrete-time multinomial logistic regression models

	Model 3: Nuanced birth intendedness vs. No birth							
Variables	Wanted vs. No birth		Didn't want vs. No birth		Hadn't thought vs. No birth		Didn't care vs. No birth	
Prior IPV experience	1.06		1.02		1.32		1.06	
Demographics								
Age	1.24	***	1.50	***	1.50	***	1.28	***
Age^2	1.00	***	1.00	***	1.00	***	1.00	***
Female	1.72	*	2.67	***	1.74	*	2.08	**
Contraceptive efficacy								
Sure								
Never use	1.43		2.09	*	0.94		1.13	
Not before marriage	0.76		0.68		0.50		0.74	
Unsure	0.95		1.49	†	0.66		1.73	†
Respondent relationship status								
Single	0.22	***	0.83		0.62		0.45	
Dating	0.47	*	1.28		1.26		0.97	
Cohabiting	0.87		1.78		0.43		2.56	†
Married	–		–		–		–	
Behavioral indicators								
Delinquency	0.86		0.91		0.79		0.91	
Substance abuse	0.50	†	1.55	**	1.19		0.87	
School performance								
Grades (wave 1)	0.80	***	0.83	**	0.86	*	0.81	**
How far in school	0.99		0.92		0.85		0.90	
Race/ethnicity								
White	–		–		–		–	
Black	0.87		1.13		0.97		1.60	
Hispanic	1.85	*	1.31		1.34		1.93	†
Two biological parents at wave 1	0.63	*	0.68	†	0.51	**	1.13	
Neighborhood poverty (wave 1)	1.03		1.08	***	1.08	**	1.07	*

Source: Toledo Adolescent Relationships Study
†$p < .10$, *$p < .0$, **$p < .01$, ***$p < .001$
Person Months = 139,563

respondents who reported higher levels of substance use had higher odds of having an unwanted birth than no birth. Further, respondents who reported higher grades were less likely to have a first birth across all categorizations. Compared to non-Hispanic White individuals, Hispanic individuals had a higher probability of reporting a wanted first birth and more often reported ambivalence (didn't care) than no birth. Respondents living with their biological parents at wave 1 less often reported having a wanted birth than no birth and less often reported a birth categorized as risk-taking (hadn't thought) than no birth. Respondents who grew up in a neighborhood characterized by higher levels of poverty were more likely to report having an unwanted birth and more often characterized their first birth as ambivalent (didn't care) or risk-taking (hadn't thought).

13.2.7 Supplemental Analyses

While the results refute some prior literature, one argument may be perhaps the lack of significance is due to the IPV measure combining both perpetration and victimization. The justification for combining them is that in national surveys, about half of intimate partner violence victims are also perpetrators of aggression against partners (Anderson, 2013). In sensitivity analyses we explored how the results may differ once IPV experience is divided into whether respondents were a perpetrator or a victim. Like the analyses for any IPV, however, we did not find any statistically significant associations for perpetration alone or victimization alone (not shown but available upon request). This was true for all three dependent variables – any birth, the three-category measure of intendedness, and the five-category measure of intendedness.

13.2.8 Discussion

Compared to other westernized countries, the United States has high levels of unintended fertility. Intimate partner violence is also a concern in the United States, affecting men and women alike (Giordano et al. forthcoming, Giordano et al., 2016). We assessed whether there was an association between intimate partner violence and entry into early parenthood as well as having an unintended first birth. Based on prior work on women, we expected that IPV experience would be associated with early entry into parenthood and greater odds of classifying first births as unintended (Barber et al., 2018). The primary rationale rests on contraceptive use challenges for individuals who have experienced relationship violence. Moreover, many of the same factors, including risky behaviors (substance use, criminal behavior, poor school performance) and economic disadvantage, that are associated with elevated experiences with IPV are also linked to early parenthood and unintended parenthood. Given these shared risk profiles and that IPV and unintended fertility peak in the teenage and early adult years, the links could be largely correlational and not causal.

The results indicate that at the bivariate level respondents who experienced IPV in a given survey wave did have a higher probability of entering early parenthood by the next wave compared to those who did not experience IPV. However, this association was explained with the inclusion of adolescent performance in school.

Thus, it appears that the link between IPV and early entry into parenthood is explained by adolescent indicators that are often excluded from analyses. Teens with better grades might have more to lose by entering into more serious relationships during young adulthood, thus limiting the risk of both IPV and fertility (Longmore et al., 2009, 2013). They may have more resources and knowledge to identify unhealthy relationships and to protect themselves against the risk of pregnancy. Grades during adolescence may also be an indicator of planful competence and purposive efforts (Clausen & Jones, 1998), which may be a protective factor against both IPV and early and unintended fertility. Finally, good grades in adolescence may tap into parental support, peer support, school connectedness) and other background resources (Bradley et al., 2021; Kaufman-Parks et al., 2021) that may help youths avoid, or disengage from, relationships with higher risk of IPV or unintended fertility. The contraceptive use indicators did not explain the association between IPV and early entry into parenthood. These results held for both IPV overall and when disaggregated by perpetration and victimization.

The analysis of birth intentions indicates that young men and women who experienced IPV had similar odds of having an unintended birth as their counterparts who had no prior IPV experiences. These findings exist at both the bivariate and multivariate levels. Similar results were obtained when we relied on a more nuanced indicator of intendedness that included ambivalence and risk-taking. In contrast to prior work, then, the findings suggest that there is no strong association between IPV and unintended fertility, at least among young adults; put differently, these findings suggest that the link found in prior literature may not be causal.

While this study provides new insights into IPV and unintended fertility, there are a few limitations. First and foremost, the reports of IPV experience are not necessarily from the same relationship as the pregnancy. The experience of IPV on fertility may be a result of IPV experienced in a specific relationship; future work would ideally link IPV to specific relationships and the risk of fertility within that relationship. Second, we have no direct measure of reproductive coercion, which may influence how individuals are reporting the intention of their first birth. Future work should consider how reproductive coercion influences the odds of parenthood and the intentions of births. Further, TARS is not a nationally representative dataset, and these results may not reflect the general patterns of IPV and birth intendedness. We also only analyzed respondents' first birth in early parenthood; results may not be generalizable to all births.

Additionally, our operationalization of intimate partner violence used the revised conflict tactics scale. The scale was designed to measure violence used during family conflicts. Specifically, it assesses whether both men and women have perpetrated a range of aggressive tactics or have been victims of aggression at the hands of intimate partners (Straus et al. 1996). The theoretical perspective underlying the revised conflict tactics is the family violence perspective. An assumption of this perspective is that conflict per se is not problematic because conflict is a part of all relationships. However, destructive, violent approaches to conflict resolution are problematic. The family violence perspective emphasizes assessing violence in community or population-based samples as opposed to known groups, such as women in shelters seeking protection from violent partners, individuals seeking medical attention for injuries, or those who have come to the attention of law enforcement due to intimate partner violence. In national and community surveys a controversial but common finding that has emerged using the conflict tactics scale as well as supported by extensive reviews of the literature (e.g., Ali et al., 2016; Bates & Graham-Kevan, 2016; Hardesty & Ogolsky, 2020) is that rates of women's perpetration of violence are similar to or exceed the levels reported by men (e.g., Cooper et al., 2021; Giordano et al., 2021; Hardesty & Ogolsky, 2020; Nowinski & Bowen, 2012). This gender symmetry finding, however, is not consistent with some findings drawn from other sources of data that are not based on community surveys. Johnson (1995, Kelly & Johnson, 2008) attempted to address the controversial gender symmetry finding by distinguishing between different types of intimate partner violence. For example, situational couple violence is a form of intimate partner violence that includes mutual or reciprocal violence and is most often documented in community surveys. Conversely, intimate terrorism is one-sided violence (primarily men's violence against women) based on coercive control, and is most often found in known group samples such as women's shelters, social service agencies, and criminal justice settings. Consequently, it is possible that findings would be different if we examined women who experienced intimate terrorism.

13.3 Conclusions

Despite these limitations, this study adds to the literature on how IPV and the timing of parenthood, as well as birth intendedness, may be related. The results highlight that rather than a causal relationship between IPV and the entrance to parenthood, IPV and unintended fertility are linked because both are concentrated among young adults. That is, there does not appear to be a causal relationship where IPV directly influences birth intendedness. This is especially true given the results suggest the importance of early adolescent academic achievement – this is an interesting finding that merits additional work to determine what, exactly, it is about academic achievement during adolescence that seems to be protective against early fertility in the context of IPV. These results also give insight to potential policy implications. One in particular would be to simultaneously address IPV and early childbearing in programs geared toward adolescents and young adults (rather than separate programs for each). Further, there is a continued need for better sexual education for teens and young adults, along with greater access to family planning services. These policy improvements could contribute to a decline in the number of young individuals experiencing IPV and unintended fertility.

Acknowledgements This research was supported by grants from The Eunice Kennedy Shriver National Institute of Child Health and Human Development (HD036223 and HD044206), the Department of Health and Human Services (5APRPA006009), the National Institute of Justice, Office of Justice Programs, U. S. Department of Justice (Award Nos. 2009-IJ-CX-0503 and

2010-MU-MU-0031), and in part by the Center for Family and Demographic Research, Bowling Green State University, which has core funding from The Eunice Kennedy Shriver National Institute of Child Health and Human Development (P2CHD050959). The opinions, findings, and conclusions or recommendations expressed in this publication are those of the authors and do not necessarily reflect the official views of the National Institutes of Health, Department of Health and Human Services, or Department of Justice.

References

Abajobir, A. A., Kisely, S., & Najman, J. M. (2017). A systematic review of unintended pregnancy in cross-cultural settings: Does it have adverse consequences for children? *Ethiopian Journal of Health Development, 31*(3), 138–154.

Ahrens, K. A., Thoma, M. E., Copen, C. E., Frederiksen, B. N., Decker, E. J., & Moskosky, S. (2018). Unintended pregnancy and interpregnancy interval by maternal age, National Survey of Family Growth. *Contraception, 98*(1), 52–55.

Aiken, A. R. A., Borrero, S., Callegari, L. S., & Dehlendorf, C. (2016). Rethinking the pregnancy planning paradigm: Unintended conceptions or unrepresentative concepts? *Perspectives on Sexual & Reproductive Health, 48*(3), 147–151. https://doi.org/10.1363/48e10316

Alexander, K. A., Arrington Sanders, R., Grace, K. T., Thorpe, R. J., Doro, E., & Bowleg, L. (2021). "Having a child meant I had a real life": Reproductive coercion and childbearing motivations among young black men living in Baltimore. *Journal of Interpersonal Violence, 36*(17–18), NP9197-NP9225. https://doi.org/10.1177/0886260519853400

Ali, P. A., Dhingra, K., & McGarry, J. (2016). A literature review of intimate partner violence and its classifications. *Aggression and Violent Behavior, 31*, 16–25.

Alleyne-Green, B., Coleman-Cowger, V. H., & Henry, D. B. (2012). Dating violence perpetration and/or victimization and associated sexual risk behaviors among a sample of inner-city African American and Hispanic adolescent females. *Journal of Interpersonal Violence, 27*(8), 1457–1473. https://doi.org/10.1177/0886260511425788

Allison, P. D. (2010). Survival analysis. In G. R. Hancock & R. O. Mueller (Eds.), *The Reviewer's guide to quantitative methods in the social sciences* (pp. 413–425). Routledge.

Anderson, K. L. (2013). Why do we fail to ask "Why" about gender and intimate partner violence?. *Journal of Marriage and Family, 75*(2), 314–318.

Barber, J. S., Kusunoki, Y., Gatny, H. H., & Budnick, J. (2018). The dynamics of intimate partner violence and the risk of pregnancy during the transition to adulthood. *American Sociological Review, 83*(5), 1020–1047. https://doi.org/10.1177/0003122418795856

Barber, J. S., Miller, W., Kusunoki, Y., Hayford, S. R., & Guzzo, K. B. (2019). Intimate relationship dynamics and changing desire for pregnancy among young women. *Perspectives on Sexual & Reproductive Health, 51*(3), 143–152. https://doi.org/10.1363/psrh.12119

Bates, E. A., & Graham-Kevan, N. (2016). Is the presence of control related to help-seeking behavior? A test of Johnson's assumptions regarding sex differences and the role of control in intimate partner violence. *Partner Abuse, 7*(1), 3–25.

Bergmann, J. N., & Stockman, J. K. (2015). How does intimate partner violence affect condom and oral contraceptive use in the United States: A systematic review of the literature. *Contraception, 91*(6), 438–455. https://doi.org/10.1016/j.contraception.2015.02.009

Black, M. C. (2011). Intimate partner violence and adverse health consequences: Implications for clinicians. *American Journal of Lifestyle Medicine, 5*(5), 428–439.

Bradley, G. L., Ferguson, S., & Zimmer-Gembeck, M. J. (2021). Parental support, peer support and school connectedness as foundations for student engagement and academic achievement in Australian youth. In *Handbook of positive youth development: Advancing research, policy, and practice in global contexts* (pp. 219–236). Springer.

Braham, J., Skakoon-Sparling, S., Kilimnik, C., & Milhausen, R. (2019). Intimate partner violence history and its association with condom use negotiation. *Personality and Individual Differences, 147*, 256–260. https://doi.org/10.1016/j.paid.2019.04.004
Breiding, M. J., Chen, J., & Black, M. C. (2014). *Intimate partner violence in the United States — 2010*. National Center for Injury Prevention and Control, Centers for Disease Control and Prevention.
Capaldi, D. M., Knoble, N. B., Wu Shortt, J., & Hyoun, K. K. (2012). A systematic review of risk factors for intimate partner violence. *Partner Abuse, 3*, 321–280.
Chowdhury, P., Garg, M. K., & Sk, M. I. K. (2020). Does mother's pregnancy intention affect child healthcare and growth in India? Evidence from a longitudinal survey. In *medRxiv*.
Claridge, A. M. (2021). Pregnancy intentions of first-time mothers and their children's outcomes: Unraveling reciprocal pathways. *Journal of Marriage & Family, 83*(4), 942–960.
Clausen, J. A., & Jones, C. J. (1998). Predicting personality stability across the life span: The role of competence and work and family commitments. *Journal of Adult Development, 5*(2), 73–83.
Cooper, L. M., Longmore, M. A., Manning, W. D., & Giordano, P. C. (2021). The influence of demographic, relational, and risk asymmetries on the frequency of intimate partner violence in young adulthood. *Journal of Family Issues, 42*(1), 136–155.
Corbett, A. M., Dickson-Gómez, J., Hilario, H., & Weeks, M. R. (2009). A little thing called love: Condom use in high-risk primary heterosexual relationships. *Perspectives on Sexual & Reproductive Health, 41*(4), 218–224.
Cronley, C., Nahar, S., & Hohn, K. (2020). "There's like no support system": The life course stories of women with children about growing up, becoming mothers, and becoming homeless. *Journal of Social Distress and Homelessness, 29*(2), 127–136.
Cunradi, C. B., Dellor, E., Alter, H. J., Caetano, R., & Mair, C. (2020). Problem drinking and marijuana use as risks for unidirectional and bidirectional partner violence. *Partner Abuse, 11*(1), 57–75.
Daoud, N., Urquia, M. L., O'Campo, P., Heaman, M., Janssen, P. A., Smylie, J., & Thiessen, K. (2012). Prevalence of abuse and violence before, during, and after pregnancy in a national sample of Canadian women. *American Journal of Public Health, 102*(10), 1893–1901. https://doi.org/10.2105/AJPH.2012.300843
DeMaris, A. (1997). Elevated sexual activity in violent marriages: Hypersexuality or sexual extortion? *Journal of Sex Research, 34*(4), 361–373. https://doi.org/10.1080/00224499709551904
Driscoll, A. K., Sugland, B. W., Manlove, J., & Papillo, A. R. (2005). Community opportunity, perceptions of opportunity, and the odds of an adolescent birth. *Youth & Society, 37*(1), 33–61.
Elliot, D. S., & Ageton, S. S. (1980). Reconciling race and class difference in self-reported and official estimates of delinquency. *American Sociological Association, 2*, 95–110.
Everett, B. G., McCabe, K. F., & Hughes, T. L. (2016). Unintended pregnancy, depression, and hazardous drinking in a community-based sample of sexual minority women. *Journal of Women's Health, 25*(9), 904–911.
Fernández-Montalvo, J., López-Goñi, J. J., Arteaga, A., & Haro, B. (2020). Gender differences in unidirectional and bidirectional intimate partner violence in addictions. *The American Journal of Drug and Alcohol Abuse, 46*(2), 194–202.
Finer, L. B., & Zolna, M. R. (2014). Shifts in intended and unintended pregnancies in the United States, 2001-2008. *American Journal of Public Health, 104*, S43–S48.
Finer, L. B., & Zolna, M. R. (2016). Declines in unintended pregnancy in the United States, 2008-2011. *The New England Journal of Medicine, 375*, 843–852.
Fong, V. C., Hawes, D., & Allen, J. L. (2019). A systematic review of risk and protective factors for externalizing problems in children exposed to intimate partner violence. *Trauma, Violence, & Abuse, 20*(2), 149–167.
Gharaee, M., & Baradaran, H. R. (2020). Consequences of unintended pregnancy on mother and fetus and newborn in north-east of Iran. *The Journal of Maternal-Fetal & Neonatal Medicine, 33*(5), 876–879.

Gibbs, L. (2013). Gender, relationship type, and contraceptive use at first intercourse. *Contraception, 87*, 906–812.

Gibbs, L., Manning, W. D., Longmore, M. A., & Giordano, P. C. (2014). Qualities of romantic relationships and consistent condom use among dating young adults. In L. Bourgois & S. Cauchois (Eds.), *Contraceptives: Predictors of use, role of cultural attitudes & practices and levels of effectiveness* (pp. 157–182). Nova Science Publishers.

Giordano, P. C., Soto, D. A., Manning, W. D., & Longmore, M. A. (2010). The characteristics of romantic relationships associated with teen dating violence. *Social Science Research, 39*(6), 863–874. https://doi.org/10.1016/j.ssresearch.2010.03.009

Giordano, P. C., Copp, J. E., Longmore, M. A., & Manning, W. D. (2016). Anger, control, and intimate partner violence in young adulthood. *Journal of Family Violence, 31*(1), 1–13.

Giordano, P. C., Copp, J. E., Manning, W. D., & Longmore, M. A. (2021). Relationship dynamics associated with dating violence among adolescents and young adults: A feminist post-structural analysis. *Feminist Criminology, 16*(3), 320–336.

Gomez, A. M., Arteaga, S., Ingraham, N., Arcara, J., & Villaseñor, E. (2018). It's not planned, but is it okay? The acceptability of unplanned pregnancy among young people. *Women's Health Issues, 28*(5), 408–414. https://doi.org/10.1016/j.whi.2018.07.001

Grace, K. T., & Anderson, J. C. (2018). Reproductive coercion: A systematic review. *Trauma, Violence, & Abuse, 19*(4), 371–390. https://doi.org/10.1177/1524838016663935

Grace, K. T., Decker, M. R., Alexander, K. A., Campbell, J., Miller, E., Perrin, N., & Glass, N. (2022). Reproductive coercion, intimate partner violence, and unintended pregnancy among Latina women. *Journal of Interpersonal Violence, 37*(3–4), 1604–1636.

Guzzo, K. B., & Hayford, S. R. (2014). Revisiting retrospective reporting of first-birth intendedness. *Maternal & Child Health Journal, 18*, 2141–2147. https://doi.org/10.1007/s10995-014-1462-7

Guzzo, K. B., & Hayford, S. (2018). Adolescent reproductive and contraceptive knowledge and attitudes and adult contraceptive behavior. *Maternal & Child Health, 22*, 32–40.

Hardesty, J. L., & Ogolsky, B. G. (2020). A sociological perspective on intimate partner violence research: A decade in review. *Journal of Marriage & Family, 82*(1), 454–477. https://doi.org/10.1111/jomf.12652

Hofferth, S. L., & Goldscheider, F. (2010). Family structure and the transition to early parenthood. *Demography, 47*(2), 415–437.

Hynes, K., Joyner, K., Peters, H. E., & DeLeone, F. Y. (2008). The transition to early fatherhood: National estimates based on multiple surveys. *Demographic Research, 18*(12), 337–376.

Johnson, M. P. (1995). Patriarchal terrorism and common couple violence: Two forms of violence against women. *Journal of Marriage and the Family, 57*, 283–294.

Johnson, W. L., Giordano, P. C., Manning, W. D., & Longmore, M. A. (2015). The IPV-age curve: Changes in intimate partner violence perpetration during adolescence and young adulthood. *Journal of Youth & Adolescence, 44*, 708–726.

Joyner, K., Peters, H. E., Hynes, K., Sikora, A., Taber, J. R., & Rendall, M. S. (2012). The quality of male fertility data in major U.S. surveys. *Demography, 49*(1), 101–124.

Kaufman-Parks, A. M., Longmore, M. A., Manning, W. D., & Giordano, P. C. (2021). The long reach of peer influence on emerging adults' sexual activity. *Sexuality in Emerging Adulthood*, 295.

Kaestle, C. E., & Halpern, C. T. (2005). Sexual intercourse precedes partner violence in adolescent romantic relationships. *Journal of Adolescent Health, 36*(5), 386–392. https://doi.org/10.1016/j.jadohealth.2004.02.030

Kelly, J. B., & Johnson, M. P. (2008). Differentiation among types of intimate partner violence: Research update and implications for interventions. *Family Court Review, 46*(3), 476–499.

Kusunoki, Y., Barber, J. S., Gatny, H. H., & Melendez, R. (2018). Physical intimate partner violence and contraceptive behaviors among young women. *Journal of Women's Health, 27*(8), 1016–1025. https://doi.org/10.1089/jwh.2016.6246

Landeis, M., Manning, W. D., Longmore, M. A., Giordano, P. C., & Joyner, K. (2021). The relationship context of early transitions to parenthood: The influence of arrest. *Population Research and Policy Review, 40*(4), 723–746.

Lindberg, L., Kost, K., Maddow-Zimet, I., Desai, S., & Zolna, M. (2020). Abortion reporting in the United States: An assessment of three national fertility surveys. *Demography, 57*(3), 899–925. https://doi.org/10.1007/s13524-020-00886-4

Longmore, M. A., Manning, W. D., Giordano, P. C., & Rudolph, J. L. (2003). Contraceptive self-efficacy: Does it influence adolescents' contraceptive use? *Journal of Health & Social Behavior, 44*(1), 45–90. https://doi.org/10.2307/1519815

Longmore, M. A., Eng, A. L., Giordano, P. C., & Manning, W. D. (2009). Parenting and adolescents' sexual initiation. *Journal of Marriage and Family, 71*(4), 969–982.

Longmore, M. A., Johnson, W. L., Manning, W. D., & Giordano, P. C. (2013). HIV testing among heterosexual young adults: The influence of partners' risk behaviors and relationship dynamics. *Journal of Sex Research, 50*(5), 489–501.

Macy, R. J., Martin, S. L., Kupper, L. L., Casanueva, C., & Guo, S. (2007). Partner violence among women before, during, and after pregnancy: Multiple opportunities for intervention. *Women's Health Issues, 17*(5), 290–299. https://doi.org/10.1016/j.whi.2007.03.006

Manning, W. D., Giordano, P. C., Longmore, M. A., & Flanigan, C. M. (2012). Young adult dating relationships and management of sexual risk. *Population Research & Policy Review, 31*, 165–185.

Manning, W. D., Longmore, M. A., & Giordano, P. C. (2018). Cohabitation and intimate partner violence during emerging adulthood: High constraints and low commitment. *Journal of Family Issues, 39*(4), 1030–1055.

Martin, J. A., Hamilton, B. E., Osterman, M. J. K., & Driscoll, A. K. (2019). Births: Final data for 2018. *National Vital Statistics Reports, 68*(13). National Center for Health Statistics.

Masho, S. W., Rozario, S., Walker, D. W., & Cha, S. (2018). Racial differences and the role of marital status in the association between intimate partner violence and unintended pregnancy. *Journal of Interpersonal Violence, 33*(20), 3162–3185.

Miller, E., & Silverman, J. C. (2010). Reproductive coercion and partner violence: Implications for clinical assessment of unintended pregnancy. *Expert Review of Obstetrics & Gynecology, 5*, 511–515.

Miller, E., McCauley, H. L., Tancredi, D. J., Decker, M. R., Anderson, H., & Silverman, J. G. (2014). Recent reproductive coercion and unintended pregnancy among female family planning clients. *Contraception, 89*(2), 122–128. https://doi.org/10.1016/j.contraception.2013.10.011

Miller, W. B., Barber, J. S., & Schultz, P. (2017). Do perceptions of their partners' childbearing desires affect young women's pregnancy risk? Further study of ambivalence. *Population Studies: A Journal of Demography, 71*(1), 101–116. https://doi.org/10.1080/00324728.2016.1253858

Nowinski, S. N., & Bowen, E. (2012). Partner violence against heterosexual and gay men: Prevalence and correlates. *Aggression and Violent Behavior, 17*(1), 36–52.

Paul, P., & Mondal, D. (2021). Association between intimate partner violence and contraceptive use in India: Exploring the moderating role of husband's controlling behaviors. *Journal of Interpersonal Violence, 08862605211015212*, NP15405–NP15433. https://doi.org/10.1177/08862605211015212

Peasant, C., Sullivan, T. P., Ritchwood, T. D., Parra, G. R., Weiss, N. H., Meyer, J. P., & Murphy, J. G. (2018). Words can hurt: The effects of physical and psychological partner violence on condom negotiation and condom use among young women. *Women & Health, 58*(5), 483–497. https://doi.org/10.1080/03630242.2017.1316345

Powers, R. A., & Kaukinen, C. E. (2022). Gender differences in the relationship between sexual activity and dating violence: The role of satisfaction, jealousy, and self-control. *Journal of Interpersonal Violence*. https://doi.org/10.1177/0886260520983274

Samankasikorn, W., Alhusen, J., Yan, G., Schminkey, D. L., & Bullock, L. (2019). Relationships of reproductive coercion and intimate partner violence to unintended pregnancy. *Journal of Obstetric, Gynecologic & Neonatal Nursing, 48*(1), 50–58.

Sarkar, N. N. (2008). The impact of intimate partner violence on women's reproductive health and pregnancy outcome. *Journal of Obstetrics & Gynecology, 28*(3), 266–271.

Schumacher, J. A., Feld-bau-Kohn, S., Smith Slep, A. M., & Heyman, R. E. (2001). Risk factors for male-to-female partner physical abuse. *Aggression & Violence Behavior, 6*, 281–352.

Schweizer, V. J. (2019). Thirty years of change in men's entry into fatherhood, 1987–2017. In *Family profiles*, FP-19-28. National Center for Family & Marriage Research. https://doi.org/10.25035/ncfmr/fp-19-28

Silverman, J. G., Gupta, J., Decker, M. R., Kapur, N., & Raj, A. (2007). Intimate partner violence and unwanted pregnancy, miscarriage, induced abortion, and stillbirth among a national sample of Bangladeshi women. *BJOG: An International Journal of Obstetrics & Gynecology, 114*(10), 1246–1252.

Smith, S. G., Chen, J., Basile, K. C., Gilbert, L. K., Merrick, M. T., Patel, N., Walling, M., & Jain, A. (2017). *The National Intimate Partner and sexual violence survey (NISVS): 2010–2012 state report*. National Center for Injury Prevention and Control, Centers for Disease Control and Prevention.

Smith, S. G., Zhang, X., Basile, K. C., Merrick, M. T., Wang, J., Kresnow, M., & Chen, J. (2018). *The National Intimate Partner and sexual violence survey (NISVS): 2015 data brief – Updated release*. National Center for Injury Prevention and Control, Centers for Disease Control and Prevention.

Straus, M. A. (2013). Conflict tactics scales. In *Handbook of measurements for marriage and family therapy* (pp. 159–163). Routledge.

Straus, M. A., & Gelles, R. J. (1990). *Behind closed doors: Violence in the American family*. Anchor/Doubleday Press.

Straus, M. A., Hamby, S. L., Boney-McCoy, S. U. E., & Sugarman, D. B. (1996). The revised conflict tactics scales (CTS2) development and preliminary psychometric data. *Journal of Family Issues, 17*(3), 283–316.

Su, J. H. (2017). Unintended birth and children's long-term mental health. *Journal of Health & Social Behavior, 58*(3), 357–370.

Wang, T., Liu, Y., Li, Z., Liu, K., Xu, Y., Shi, W., & Chen, L. (2017). Prevalence of intimate partner violence (IPV) during pregnancy in China: A systematic review and meta-analysis. *PLoS One, 12*(10), e0175108. https://doi.org/10.1371/journal.pone.0175108

Williams, C. M., Larsen, U., & McCloskey, L. A. (2008). Intimate partner violence and women's contraceptive use. *Violence Against Women, 14*(12), 1382–1396. https://doi.org/10.1177/1077801208325187

Yakubovich, A. R., Stockl, H., Murray, J., Melendez-Torres, G. J., Steinert, J. I., Galvin, E. Y., & Humphreys, D. K. (2018). Risk and protective factors for intimate partner violence against women: Systematic review and meta-analyses of prospective-longitudinal studies. *American Journal of Public Health, 108*, 1–1.

Yeatman, S., & Smith-Greenaway, E. (2021). Women's health decline following (some) unintended births. *Demographic Research, 45*, 547–576.

The manufacturer's authorised representative in the EU is Springer Nature Customer Service Centre GmbH, Europaplatz 3, 69115 Heidelberg, Germany. If you have any concerns regarding our products, please contact ProductSafety@springernature.com

Printed and bound by CPI Group (UK) Ltd, Croydon, CR0 4YY
01/10/2026
02225865-0011